A UNION OF MANY TRADES

The History of USDAW

Price £5.75

A UNION OF MANY TRADES

The History of USDAW

BY
SIR WILLIAM RICHARDSON

Published by the
UNION OF SHOP, DISTRIBUTIVE AND ALLIED WORKERS
"Oakley", 188 Wilmslow Road, Manchester M14 6LJ

Printed and made in Great Britain at the Printing Works
of the Co-operative Press Limited, Newcastle upon Tyne.

CONTENTS

LIST OF ILLUSTRATIONS

AUTHOR'S NOTE

THIS book owes much to men and women who are active in the Union of Shop, Distributive and Allied Workers, and to others who have retired but are rich in memories of the days when they served the Union. It also owes a great deal to some who died many years ago but whose work is enshrined in the records at "Oakley".

You cannot, of course, learn to know a person or an organisation solely through print. But you can learn a great deal if you follow an individual year by year through reported speeches, through articles, pamphlets, interviews, the tributes of contemporaries. I have come to know those personalities of the past from the columns of *Gleanings for Members*, *The Co-operative Employee*, *The AUCE Journal*, *New Dawn* (the successive publications of the Union, now embodied in *Dawn*), from the large pamphlet literature which was a feature of the AUCE, from the printed reports of Annual Delegate Meetings and from the recollections of colleagues. Many of those stalwarts of the past appear in the following pages. I thank the memory of all of them for help in understanding and recording the forces and controversies which in an earlier generation laid the foundations of the large and diversified Union of today.

I thank also those of the present generation who have done much to make this book possible. From present and retired officials and members help and advice have readily been given, both on facts and on the accuracy of chapters or paragraphs dealing with particular events in the Union's history. I have been greatly indebted to Lord Allen, particularly in writing of the complexities of wages relationships between Governments and Trades Unions in recent years, J. D. Hiscock and John Phillips, successively retired from the role of Assistant General Secretary, and John Flood, recently appointed under the new designation of Deputy General Secretary; all of whom have helped me in dealing with the Union's breakthrough into the multiple shop trades, and other developments of recent years.

W. H. P. Whatley, the General Secretary newly elected as this book is completed, has advised on recruitment and other problems of the years since the second World War. National Officer W. Cowan, provided information for the brief history of the Insurance Section (formerly the CIS National Branch), of which he acts as Secretary; and additional information came from F. F. Cullen, editor of the agents' journal. Other National Officers have been ever-ready to help: as have the Administration Officer, H. L. Booth, the Central Treasurer and Executive Officer, A. W. Hilton, P. Rosenfeld (Education), A. C. Heywood (Legal), Diana Jeuda (Research) and members of her staff.

Time and distance did not permit of interviews with all members of the Executive Council nor with all the eight Divisional Officers. From the Executive members I was able to meet I received much useful guidance on past and present problems of the Union. With Divisional Officers, I had informative conversations with A. Forman (Scottish Division), T. P. Callinan (Eastern), R. A. Hammond (Southern) and J. Toogood (Midlands). Retired Divisional Officer, W. A. Hutchinson, one of the few survivors of those who experienced living-in conditions, shared with me his memories of that iniquitous system and I had the opportunity to read some written recollections of another retired officer, Cecil Mortimer, of events following the 1921 merger of AUCE and the National Warehouse and General Workers' Union. W. John Jones, Divisional Officer, South Wales and Western Division, checked the references to the Union in Chapter 34, as did D. Wylie, Area Officer, Northern Ireland. Miss Esther Quinn, Scottish Divisional Council, contributed valuable research material to the same Chapter.

With the President of the Union, S. Tierney, I had a long conversation, as with the four former Presidents now living in retirement — Walter Padley, Rodney Hanes, R. B. Seabrook and J. Hughes. All of them gave freely of their time in discussing past and future problems of the Union and/or checking my research on particular events. Two retired senior officials, Lord Hamnett and H. G. Pridmore, were equally helpful; and the latter also prepared the Index.

The closest working association during research and writing was with the Publicity and Public Relations Department under P. H. Jones. To him and his staff, Ken Edwards, Mrs. Sylvia Bertenshaw and Mrs. Bessa Head I owe much for their guidance to sources of information and on the general administrative structure of the Union. To their names I add that of Mrs. Sheila Walker, who has typed every word of this book. The accuracy of her typescripts has been a tribute to her skill in interpreting the variable quality of my handwriting. I am indebted also to A. Rathbone and his staff in the Printing Department at "Oakley" for the rapid duplication of chapters.

The Union's own library at "Oakley" has been the principal source of research material, running to many hundred pages of notes. But I also thanks Roy Garratt and his staff at the Co-operative Union library in Manchester for research facilities into the days when Co-operative "servants" were first turning to Trades Unionism, and to the staff of the TUC library at Congress House, London. For general historical background extensive use was also made of the British Newspaper Library at Colindale, London, the Stockport Reference Library and the files of the *Co-operative News* and *Scottish Co-operator*.

I am grateful to the management and staff of the Co-operative Press printing works at Newcastle upon Tyne and the Sales Department in Manchester who carried out promptly and efficiently the operations involved in the production of this book.

Finally, an overall "thank you" to the many I have not been able to name, and in particular to the efficient USDAW staff at Central Office, who never failed to produce verbal or documentary answers to my many questions.

FOREWORD

by Lord Allen of Fallowfield, C.B.E.

IT has been my privilege to hold the position of Principal Officer of the Union of Shop, Distributive and Allied Workers for the past 17 years, until my retirement from the full-time service of the Union, and throughout that period to have also been deeply involved, through the General Council of the Trade Union Congress, in the wider problems of the nation and the Trades Union Movement. They have been years of spectacular change in the size and scope of USDAW and in the influence that Trades Unionism generally now exerts on the affairs of the United Kingdom.

In not much more than two decades we have also seen fundamental alterations in industry and commerce. Nuclear power, the computer, plastics, entry into outer space and now microelectronics are a new industrial revolution in themselves. To these could be added the revolution in retailing. The pace of change has been so rapid that we scarcely realise its extent. For that reason, and also because there are lessons for today that new members and old can draw from the past, the Executive Council decided, following a recommendation made to them some two years ago, that this was a good time to tell the Union's story from the closing years of Queen Victoria's reign to the new age we are entering today.

When, as a young employee of Bristol Co-operative Society

in 1930, I was learning the rudiments of Trade Unionism in the then National Union of Distributive and Allied Workers (NUDAW) by far the greater number of the Union's members were Co-operative employees. We, together with colleagues in the then National Amalgamated Union of Shop Assistants, Warehousemen and Clerks (NAUSA) had been actively recruiting in the private trade sector for many years but had made only marginal impact on the national and transnational multiples, the department stores and chains, food manufacture and processing (outside the then two Co-operative Wholesale Societies) or the many specialist trades and services that are now organised by USDAW.

Neither the Co-operative Movement nor NUDAW itself was greatly different, except in size, from the structure that had been familiar to early Co-operators and to the pioneers who founded the Manchester District Co-operative Employees' Association in 1891. Had any of our progenitors in the Union paid a brief return visit to the scene of their terrestrial activities, he or she would have found much that had changed in scale but little that had altered in substance.

They would have had no difficulty in recognising both the Union and the Co-ops of 1930. Retailing practice was much as they had known it. The familiar 'divi' checks or tokens were still part of every purchase. In the Union's Annual Report they would still see the familiar names of branches that went back to the pioneer days of the nineties.

A return visit today, however, would astonish our pioneers with a scene of almost total change, not only in the Union they had helped to build, but in the nation as a whole. Not, however, I am pleased to say, change in essentials. There has been no change in the democratic base of the Union nor in its primary purpose of striving to improve the material and social standards of working people and the quality of their life. These have remained constant.

In retailing practice, however, in comparatively a few years — most certainly in my active service within the Union — we have leapt from counter service and small shops, in which our imaginary pioneers would probably have spent their working lives, to self-service and self-selection, supermarkets, hypermarkets, discount houses, shopping precincts in which almost the entire range of human needs is gathered under one roof as a gigantic palace of the consumer.

But it is in our own Union, in USDAW (a merger in 1947 of NUDAW and NAUSA), that they would see the most striking evidence of change. Co-operative members are still a large, active and loyal section of the Union but in my term as General Secretary, our base of recruitment has shifted massively towards those fields of private trade employment that our predecessors strove so long to organise.

Also, as readers will see in one chapter of this book, the proportion of women workers in Union membership, which in the thirties hovered around 28 per cent of the total, has now risen to more than 60 per cent. The greatest change, however, has been in the Union's relationship with the national and multinational retailers and department stores.

This history shows that it was a long, hard struggle and even a few years ago it would have taken an act of faith to believe that by 1979 the Union would have substantive agreements with most of these giants of the retail scene which today are household names. Mainly, the agreements cover both their shop and store employees, in addition to those in manufacturing and warehousing.

It is pleasing to record that there are now few sections of the retail and associated trades in which USDAW is not established and many in which it has a closed shop or is the sole representative of organised workers.

None of this success has easily been achieved. Which brings me to one conclusion that can be drawn from this history — the hard core of the Union today, as in so many yesterdays, is still the activists in the branches, Divisional Councils and the Executive Council, and in the ranks of the national, divisional and area officers and other officials who have directed, planned, encouraged and given a fine example of how to administer the great march forward of the past few years. The pioneers who in 1891 went out to recruit for their infant Association can be matched by their many successors today; now, however, with women colleagues by their side and with the expertise and experience of skilled departmental staff and the back-up resources they provide.

For most of its history, USDAW has been affiliated to the

TUC and the Labour Party. Two of the four General Secretaries of the Union, of whom I am proud and privileged to be one, have presided over the TUC Congress, the other being Sir Joseph Hallsworth. Sir Alan Birch, who I succeeded in 1962, and I each presided over the Economic Committee of the General Council of the TUC. Three of the Union's MPs, Ellen Wilkinson, Wilfrid Burke and Walter Padley, have been Chairmen of the Labour Party's Annual Conference.

As I know from experience as Chairman of the Economic Committee for the past four years, the role of the TUC has become much more important since both Conservative and Labour Governments began to intervene as third parties in wage negotiations and industrial relations, and even Conservative Administrations have had to at least profess interest in national economic planning.

From the early fifties, Government guidelines on, or direct imposition of, the rate of wage increases have been the biggest single issue before the General Council and its relevant committees. For the whole of the 19th century and a large part of the 20th, national economic policy was determined by Government and employers. Today the Trades Union Movement is an essential third partner. It is a role which imposes heavy new burdens and responsibilities and offers new opportunties to lead the nation out of its present malaise. Several chapters record how USDAW has faced these new problems, particularly on wages and industrial relations.

Another strand in the Union's long history will be noted. Ours has always been a grass roots democracy. The power of decision runs direct from the branch to the Annual Delegate Meeting. Specialist trade conferences play an increasing part in the Union and are themselves derivative from the basic democratic principle. But the final decision on all matters of policy lies with the ADM, and each branch from the smallest to the largest has the right of representation. Long may it continue to be so.

Almost every major event in the Union's history features in one way or another in the pages that follow. Veteran members will be reminded of struggles and triumphs in which they took part. New members will, I hope, draw inspiration and encouragement when they see how rights and standards which we take for granted in the Union of today were once, and not so long ago in some cases, seen as almost impossible of attainment. There are, however, still victories to be won, wrongs to be righted, none greater than the continuing scandal of low pay. In my lifetime, USDAW has substantially raised the real standards of the majority of its members, but there are still too many in or near the poverty trap. Distributive workers have not yet attained the status that is commensurate with their essential role in society. They are technicians in their own field but this is not yet reflected in career structures and training.

Even greater efforts will be necessary to win equality of opportunity for women members.

The principal employers with whom we deal now accept and respect the Union. But respect is earned by strength and our strength can only derive from unceasing vigilance in recruitment, in the scope of service we provide for members and in an efficient administration soundly based financially.

Yes, there is plenty to challenge the younger generation. There are those in the media and in politics who at times appear to be puzzled by the influence which Unions such as USDAW exert over their members. The answer, which is perhaps too simple for them to understand, is implicit in this book. It is that many generations of working people have learnt from experience that their only strength lies collectively in unity and that only through unity can they protect and improve their standards of living. Never was this more true than in the age we are now entering, when new technologies can wreak havoc in jobs and conditions unless their introduction is controlled and planned and when transnational companies can shift their operations round the world in search of cheaper and more docile labour.

It is trite, but nevertheless true, that in unity is strength and in the years ahead it will be needed more than at any time since the first industrial revolution.

PART 1

ORGANISING THE UNORGANISABLE—THE FIRST TWENTY-FOUR YEARS

1 "LIFE IN THE SHOP" — a tale of hardship and tyranny

THE Union of Shop, Distributive and Allied Workers is the sixth largest British Trade Union and it is third in size among the general Unions. Its membership spreads over workers in traditional food shops, modern supermarkets and hypermarkets, department stores, dairies, bakeries, breweries, laundries, food manufacturing and processing factories, dental and optical technicians, research and laboratory assistants and dozens of other manufacturing or service operations. But historically USDAW began as a Union of Co-operative employees and it was not until the end of the first World War that it expanded into a wide-ranging general Union of distributive, productive and service workers.

The story begins in the period between Queen Victoria's two Jubilees of 1887 and 1897. The Industrial Revolution had run its course of good and evil. Britain was one of the richest nations and the greatest colonial power in the world. True, increasingly severe competition from the industries of Germany and the United States was beginning to alarm a people accustomed to thinking of their country as the workshop of the world, and Socialism, after flickering faintly for many years, was again beginning to cast a red glow on the political arena. But on the whole, all seemed well for those at the top and middle of the social scale.

In his *English Social History* G. M. Trevelyan thus sums up the mood of the decade: "The Queen's Jubilees of 1887 and 1897 were celebrated by all classes with real pride and thankfulness ... for the 'hungry forties' were still remembered. Manners were gentler, streets were safer, life was more humane, sanitation was improving fast, working-class housing, though still bad, was less bad than ever before. Conditions of labour had been improved, real wages had risen, hours had shortened. But unemployment, sickness and old age, not yet regularly provided for by the State, still held terrors for the workman."

"But" is the significant word in Trevelyan's paragraph. And while no doubt all classes cheered the parades and other events of each Royal occasion, the middle and upper classes had much more to cheer about than the great majority of working people. The euphoria of the two Jubilees concealed poverty and insecurity for most of those who lived by their labour, and whose share in the wealth created during Victoria's reign was either minute or non-existent. Approximately one in five manual workers had fought their way through Trades Union action to a reasonable level. But behind this elite of the working class was a great army of the unorganised and the underpaid. In 1891, when USDAW began (although under another name) there were 1,502,000 agricultural workers whose lot in terms of income and social status was possibly worse than that of their peasant ancestors of the Middle Ages. Domestic servants, including catering and hairdressing but excluding coachmen, grooms and gardeners, numbered 2,329,000, for most of whom hours were excessively long and earnings miserably low.

Distributive workers, whose story is the subject of the first part of this book, were estimated to number between 700,000 and 750,000, and were mostly employed in shops. In wages, hours and working conditions they were one of the most exploited sections of the employed population. They had greatly increased in number during the nineteenth century. The newly affluent middle-class had developed more sophisticated tastes and shops expanded to supply them. Industry and importation multiplied the quantity and variety of goods. The development of the department store, particularly in London and the larger cities, required scores and sometimes hundreds of workers to be gathered under one roof. The traditional pattern of binding one or two apprentices to a grocer or draper was declining. Shop work in most cases did not require long training or special skill, and attracted an ever-growing number of younger people.

The fact that the rewards were poor did not deter recruits. A job was a job, whatever the wage, and if you did not have the protection of a powerful Trade Union you had to take what you could get, starve or seek the death-in-life of the Poor Law. Trades Unionism was non-existent in distribution. In the shops worker competed with worker for jobs, for individual wage-rates, for the slight chance of promotion, for commission rates, for "spiffs" (the premium given for selling more or less unsaleable goods, or special lines).

In this chapter we shall look at the hours, wages and general conditions of distributive workers at the end of the last century; firstly, from the standpoint of the greater number who were employed by private firms, secondly from that of Co-operative employees, who formed a rapidly growing section of distributive employment, and were the founders of what has since become the Union of Shop, Distributive and Allied Workers.

Socially, the status of the male shop worker was low. In Victorian literature he was the "counter-jumper", lacking the "manly" qualities of the industrial worker. Hours of work were long in all industries, but in distribution they were brutally so. And in most of the drapery stores work was carried on in conditions which medical men warned were dangerous to health, particularly for women, and inevitably shortened the expectancy of life.

To sit when not serving a customer was forbidden in many stores by the house rules which governed and also terrorised the assistants. For most of the working day they had to stand — or run, if brought back from a brief meal break to serve an exigent customer. A vivid picture of "Life in the Shop" was drawn in 1898 in a series of articles published by the *Daily Chronicle* (many years later to become part of the now defunct *News Chronicle*). The articles were a first-class example of what nowadays would be called investigative journalism. Although written by a member of the paper's staff they were basically the work of a quiet little woman employed in the drapery trade who moved from job to job, noting in minute detail the conditions in which the assistants worked and lived. She was Margaret Bondfield, who carried out her under-cover assignment at the request of the Women's Industrial Council. Later she was assistant secretary of the Shop Assistants' Union, became a Labour MP, and was the first woman Cabinet Minister. Since little of her data was controverted in subsequent official enquiries, we shall draw on her research for much of the first part of this chapter.

In one of two of the "better-class" West-end shops the *Chronicle* articles reported that the average hours actually worked were about 67¾ in the winter months, 69 to 70 in the summer. In the other case the hours were: August to March 61½, March to June 63, July summer sale (first week) 68, February (winter sale) 64. In suburban shops carrying on miscellaneous trades it was reported that " . . . the drapers and grocers are the hardest worked. The hours are anything from 75 per week up to 85 and in some districts 90 or more".

Nor could the exhausted worker, at the end of the day, take his tired body to a home or a room of his own. He, and more than 400,000 of his colleagues, male and female, lived on the job. "Living in" prevailed in hundreds of stores, large and small. It was a method of paying wages in kind through the provision of accommodation and meals that were often abominable and rarely provided more than a bleak minimum of comfort. A Committee of Enquiry into the operation of the Truck Acts (which did not apply to shops) was set up in 1906, and was told that an estimated 400,000 to 450,000 shop assistants thus worked, ate, lived and slept at the will of their employers.

Men and women could be packed half-a-dozen to a score in a room, sometimes two in a bed. In a great many cases there was minimal provision of sanitary and washing facilities. They were subject to capricious fines and deductions. One large store had 198 rules with fines attached. A common penalty was sixpence for "unnecessary talking and noise in bedrooms". (One wonders whether this applied to the harsh cough of the many who contracted tuberculosis under those unhealthy conditions). Instant dismissal from a well-known West-end store was the penalty for "any assistant allowing a customer to go away unserved without first appealing to the buyer or a superintendent". Presumably, the counterman or woman was expected to forcibly detain an impatient customer while frantically beckoning for a buyer or superintendent. A more "merciful" version of the rule in other stores substituted a 6d fine for allowing a customer to escape. Not uncommon was a catch-all rule which a bullying shop-walker could interpret as he wished — a sixpenny fine "for unbusinesslike conduct".

The employers who drafted these rules (and frequently charged their workers 6d for a copy) were not necessarily callous men. Many of them had come up through the same system and, like most "self-made men" considered that if they had succeeded under these conditions, others could do the same. But if they were not consciously cruel they were incredibly insensitive in stamping out any touch of domesticity in the lives of their assistants. In some of the rules it was an offence "to put flowers in water-glasses or bottles". One firm, acknowledged for being among the best in London in the provision it made for living-in, still ruled "No needlework to be done in bedrooms". In many cases no pictures or photographs, nothing to remind of home and family, could be allowed "to disfigure the walls of bedrooms". And while no employer dared formally to forbid assistants to marry, it was generally known that to do so meant the sack.

Against such a background it is not surprising that the only common factor about wages was that invariably they were low. "Each makes his own terms" said the *Daily Chronicle* writer and in conditions where each worker must bargain for himself, secrecy about individual earnings was the general practice, encouraged by the employers. P. C. Hoffman, who became a Labour MP but was for many years an officer of the Shop Assistants' Union (now merged with USDAW), recounts how William Whiteley, in personally engaging staff for his great store in Westbourne Grove, London, always ended with the question "What is the lowest possible salary you will take?" But Margaret Bondfield did succeed in unearthing some startling examples of beggarly payment. In one firm assistants were expected to work for a period in return for board and lodgings only. In another they would be engaged on a salary of, say £30, but at the end of two months this would be reduced by £10 and a commission of 1½ per cent given. A "well-known and very high-class West-end draper" paid only £20 starting salary to men, whatever their experience. In a store with twenty-eight women assistants, twenty-four were paid between £10 and £25, plus premiums which ranged from £8 - £18.

Finally, there was The Terror — the threat of instant dismissal. Many workers at that period were subject to dismissal at a minute's notice. But only shop assistants living-in could find themselves in a single minute without a job or a roof over their heads. At any hour of any day, they could be ordered to pack and get off the premises. A great many London assistants came from Wales and the West of England. For them there was the terrifying possibility of finding themselves homeless on the streets of London, perhaps on a winter's day, and without even the fare to carry them back to their native place.

Most of the nineteenth century shop workers, particularly in drapery, endured these conditions and, frequently died young or left the trade at an early age. Charles Booth, in his survey of *Life and Labour of the People in London* (carried out between 1887 and 1892), when analysing the Census returns, noted that "While 49 per cent of the men returned as drapers are under 25 years of age, no less than 65 per cent of the women are below that age".

A few assistants clawed their way upwards to become shopwalkers or buyers (and were themselves then vulnerable to hungry competitors treading on their heels). Even fewer would become the Lords of All, one of the shop owners who determined wages, exercised the power of dismissal and drew up the rules that governed the waking and sleeping hours of their staffs.

It is hard today to realise that within living memory these conditions were a way of life for tens of thousands of ordinary people. They were not without sympathisers and some employers were opposed to living-in. Among public figures, George Bernard Shaw, Mary MacArthur, Ramsay Macdonald, H. W. Massingham (the reforming editor of *The Nation*), H. G. Wells (who had been apprenticed to a draper and after two years of living-in ran home to his mother. He tells the story in his novel *Kipps*), prominent clergymen, medical men, progressive store owners who had abandoned the system: all denounced the serfdom of the shops. But in the end it was only when the shop workers belatedly turned to Trade Union action, principally through the National Union of Shop Assistants, that the walls of tyranny began to crumble.

So much for the private sector of distribution. We now turn to those workers whose story is in part the special purpose of this book — the employees of the Co-operative Movement. The living-in system scarcely existed in the Co-ops. Co-operative societies in general, with some bad exceptions, were better employers than the average and by the early eighteen-nineties a few societies in Northumberland and Durham were introducing the 48-hour week. But many societies fell short of the standards which should have been observed by a Movement which itself had been founded as a challenge to capitalist exploitation of working people. The consumer dividends of the retail societies, particularly in the North, were then very high, and in some cases had become almost the sole preoccupation of managers and committees. Management Committees insisted that they must follow the level of shop hours and wages prevailing in their localities, however bad, and some side-stepped their principles with the argument that where wages in local employment generally were low, they could not be any better in the Co-op.

By the eighteen-nineties the Movement was firmly established, based on the principles successfully launched in 1844 by the Rochdale Society of Equitable Pioneers. It was still growing, not only in total membership but in the number of societies. In 1890 123 new societies were registered under the Industrial and Provident Societies Acts. Of them, about one third, judging from their titles, were probably consumer retail societies (the balance included many building and land societies and such oddities as the South Shields and District Hire Purchase Society, the Bull's Head Inn Permanent Money Lending Society and the Joint Stock Trust Society). But while more than 1,400 consumer societies were listed in Co-operative Union statistics for 1890, many were very small.

In the Midland Section of the Union 119 out of 194 societies had fewer than 250 members. Only four had more than 5,000 — Leicester, Dudley, Derby and Lincoln. In the Northern Section (mainly Northumberland and Durham) 39 societies out of 130 were under 250 in membership. But the Section also included 40 with 1,000 members or more, of which Newcastle upon Tyne was one of the Co-operative giants of its day with 10,089 members. Bishop Auckland came close with 8,541. The North-Western Section (which then included much of Yorkshire, now in the North-Eastern Section) had 164 societies out of 436 in the under 250 category. But the Section towered above all others in the number of societies with over 1,000 members (97), and it could boast seven of the giants — Barnsley British (12,228), Bradford (10,336), Leeds (26,846 — biggest membership in the Movement), Bolton (15,080), Manchester Equitable (11,936), Oldham Industrial (10,566) and Rochdale Pioneers (11,352).

Huddersfield, Bury and Pendleton were all within a few dozen
of the ten thousand. Only two other societies (apart from
Newcastle upon Tyne, already mentioned) had passed the
10,000 — Aberdeen Northern (11,169) and Plymouth (16,902).

Like Topsy, the Movement had "just growed", and in growing
it had given no systematic attention to clarifying its relations
with those it employed. Employees could be members of their
societies (although in most cases they were denied the right to
vote or seek election to the management or other committees)
and the theory was that they could not be exploited by a body
of which they were part. But a general theory can have particular
applications, and no attempt had been made to recognise in
national or sectional scales of wages and hours that employees
were members with a special relationship to their societies.

The man behind the counter or in the warehouse rarely
appears in Co-operative Congress reports until the eighteen-
nineties. Between 1870 and 1888, scores of discussion papers
were presented at the annual Co-operative Congresses and,
whether actually read or not, were printed in the report of the
Congress proceedings. They covered almost every subject
affecting the Movement — except the position and role of
shop employees. Not, however, that the Co-operative worker
was entirely ignored in the Congress debates; if anything, the
role of one minority group absorbed too much attention. Long,
and sometimes impassioned, debates were staged on the esoteric
issue of "bonus on wages" (ie, a share in the profits), mainly
for Co-operative workers in the productive factories of the
CWS, the Scottish CWS and, to a lesser extent, of retail
societies. This issue was kept before the Movement by the
Christian Socialists, a group of clergymen and lawyers who
repudiated what they regarded as the un-Christian basis of the
factory system established by the Industrial Revolution. In
its place they urged the establishment of self-governing Co-
operative workshops, in which workers would share in the
control and profits. The group included the Rev. Charles
Kingsley (author of *Westward Ho!* and *Hereward the Wake*),
Thomas Hughes (author of *Tom Brown's Schooldays*), Edward
Vansittart Neale, first secretary of the Co-operative Union,
J. M. Ludlow, who became Registrar of Friendly Societies, and
the Rev. F. D. Maurice, who was the inspiration and leader of

the group. Many of these "productive societies", as they were called, were established and a few, although in a modified form, are still in existence. James Dyson, the first president of the Co-operative Employees' Association which developed into the present USDAW, was for many years manager of a productive society, the Working Hatters' Co-operative Association.

The Christian Socialists exercised great influence over Co-operative opinion, and they had earned it. They had been largely responsible for securing the passage of the Industrial and Provident Societies Act of 1852, which gave a legal identity and protection to registered societies, and for the Act of 1862, which permitted one society to invest in another and thus made possible the formation of the Co-operative Wholesale Society. They were always on call when the Movement required help in Parliament or along what are now called the corridors of power. But battle was joined when the CWS began to open its own factories and contended that the profits rightly belonged to the consumer and should be returned to him (more usually, her) through the CWS dividend.

The argument raged for years. While it centred mainly around productive workers, there was a somewhat lukewarm acceptance that distributive workers, too, should not be denied their share, and the principle was adopted by some retail societies. In too many cases, however, it degenerated into an excuse for failing to pay a decent basic wage. Eventually, the issue died of its own accord, as experience proved that the two Co-operative Wholesale Societies were by far the most successful means of carrying out Co-operative production on a national scale, and the productive workers of retail societies — bakers, tailors, clogmakers, etc. — found Trade Union action a more effective means of improving their earnings.

The Christian Socialists were a grand body of dedicated and unselfish men. But it must be admitted that their particular doctrine absorbed so much Co-operative energy for so long a period that it probably postponed by many years the attention which the Movement should have been giving to the main body of its employees — the men and women in the shops.

We saw earlier that many Co-operators serving on the committees of retail societies genuinely believed that there

could be no need for a Trade Union among Co-operative
workers. That view was shared by not a few of the men who
founded on 18th March, 1891, the Manchester District Co-
operative Employees' Association, the progenitor of the
present USDAW. They knew that there was increasing dissatisfaction among "Co-operative servants" (as the term then
was) over wages, hours and conditions. But as they saw it, all
that was necessary was to go to societies with a reasonable and
documented case in harmony with Co-operative principles and
their grievances would be remedied. They were not wrong in
the long term. But to breathe life and general acceptance into
a principle can often take much hard negotiating, in which
muscle as well as principle is required. In future chapters we
shall see how the gradual realisation of these facts influenced
the policies that led the MDCEA into wider and rougher
fields than had been foreseen by the founders.

2 THE BEGINNING OF REVOLT

WE have now looked at the position of distributive employment in private trade and in the Co-operative Movement.
In the first case the picture was dark with hardship and
exploitation. In the second, it was very far from what it should
have been. In both cases the traditional remedy of the worker
was Trades Unionism, and by the last two decades of the
nineteenth century the Union Movement was strongly established in an important, though still limited, area of the economy.
But it was no longer the fiery crusade of an earlier period, and
showed little interest in the plight of shop assistants and other
unorganised workers.

By the eighteen eighties the Movement was concentrated
mainly in the metal working, mining and cotton textile trades,
plus a large variety of small Unions of men engaged in specialist
crafts (eg, Liverpool Mast and Block Makers' Association —
120 members, Granite Workers' Protection Union, Aberdeen —
380 members, Scissor Grinders' Society, Sheffield — 200
members). Sidney and Beatrice Webb in their *History of Trade
Unionism* calculated that of approximately 1,500,000 Union
members in the United Kingdom in 1892, half were employed
in cotton, coal mining and engineering, and only about one
manual worker in five was organised.

Trades Unionists and other reformers had almost despaired
of many large bodies of workers, distributive workers in
particular, ever organising to improve their lot. The only
reference at any length to distributive workers that this writer
could find in TUC reports of the period occurs in the presidential address of R. D. B. Ritchie at the Dundee Congress of
1889, and even he appeared to consider shop assistants incapable of Trade Union action. "How, apart from legislation",
he asked, "can the case of the shop assistants be met? . . . .
Hitherto shopkeepers' assistants have been exempted from
participation in the beneficent legislation which has been

extracted from Parliament in behalf of other classes of workers.
Future legislation must, however, be more comprehensive,
embracing as nearly as can be all classes of wage-earners".

His remedy for long hours was the shift system. He was
" ... not prepared to say that shops shall only remain open
for eight hours each day ... A reduction of the hours of labour
must be effected by other means than that. A wider adaptation
of the shift system to suit the exigencies of the various trades
seems to be a simple and effective method of overcoming
objections".

No clarion call there to exploited workers to unite and seek
salvation through their own exertions! Socialists of the period
seemed equally despondent of shop workers ever acting
collectively, as witness this extract from a Fabian Society
pamphlet of 1898 on *Shop Life and its reform*, which declared
" ... no other class of workers have shown themselves so
careless of their responsibilities towards themselves as shop
assistants ...".

So — outside Trades Union ranks remained the great army
of the unorganised (many said the unorganisable). Our concern
is with the shop workers, but the wilderness was crowded with
other trades where conditions ranged from the abominable to
the barely tolerable. General labourers, home workers, most
agricultural workers, dock and riverside workers, many clerks,
employees of the numerous "small masters" who existed in
scores of trades, many railway workers, women workers,
domestic servants; they were joined in a common tragedy of
low wages, long hours, absence of job security, and with
charity and the Poor Law as the only "social services" available
to them.

Nor, for many years, did the leaders of the long established
Unions appear to be concerned that so great an army of the
working people was outside Trades Union ranks. The "Front
Bench", as the Webbs called the leaders of the TUC, was
composed of able and sincere men. Most of them had spent the
greater part of their lives in building up craft or occupational
Unions. They had fought many battles, and won great victories,
for Trades Union rights in their earlier days.

At the beginning of the century, from 1799 to 1824, the
Combination Acts had legally prohibited any collective action

to raise wages or reduce hours. Even to talk about action was an offence and many workers went to prison for daring to preach organisation, or had to submit to the humiliation of pleading with their employers to withdraw prosecutions begun under the Acts. By the end of the century, however, Trades Unionism had come out from under the shadow of the law, and for the skilled workers had won many improvements in wages and conditions. The "Front Bench" of the Movement was proud of the legal and respected place that had been secured in society. But respectability often breeds complacency, and complacency was the prevailing mood. Leaders of the TUC just did not want to know that for at least four-fifths of the working class Trades Unionism meant nothing and had done nothing.

It took the "New Unionism" of the eighteen-eighties and nineties, and the work of such social investigators as Charles Booth — mentioned in the previous chapter — and Seebohm Rowntree (*Poverty: A Study of Town Life*, published in 1899) to galvanise the Movement into the energy and policies more appropriate to its purpose and traditions. The "New Unionists" were led (and sometimes divided) by a number of middle and working-class Socialists which included H. M. Hyndman, Marx, Ben Tillett, Tom Mann, William Morris, Annie Besant, John Burns, Keir Hardie, the Webbs, Will Thorne. Those of the group who were active Trades Unionists as well as Socialist politicians sought to put more muscle into the TUC and to direct it into wider fields; both through international links abroad, political action and more energetic industrial policies at home. Congresses of the late eighties became a battleground between the "Front Bench" and the new militants. They preached Socialism and also practised Trades Unionism by going to the reputedly unorganisable masses, organising them, and leading them to victories that echoed round the country.

Nowhere would the news of these victories be followed more attentively than among the underpaid and the overworked (except perhaps among those members of the middle-class who saw the spectre of Red Revolution peering through the window). News of the East London girls employed in the unhealthy occupation of making lucifer matches; girls who probably never previously had organised anything more ambitious than a tea party, but who came out in 1888 against intolerable conditions and under the leadership of Annie Besant won their strike in two weeks. Even more resounding news from the London docks where in 1889 thousands of casual workers, led by Ben Tillett and some of his Socialist allies, closed the Port of London for four weeks and won the "dockers' tanner" as an hourly rate. Equally remarkable, in the same year, news that without having to strike, the newly formed Gas Workers' and General Labourers' Union, led by Will Thorne, had brought about a reduction in the working day from twelve hours to eight, and had won a slight increase in wages.

Shop workers played no part in these great events. But the industrial drama of the eighties must deeply have influenced thoughtful men in both the private and the Co-operative sectors of distribution. Here was clear evidence that no body of workers, however apparently fragmented and demoralised, was outside the scope of successful collective action. The message would be pondered and discussed — probably in whispers — in many a living-in dormitory and more openly in Co-operative stores. Within three years of the London dock strike the Manchester District Co-operative Employees' Association was formed on 18th March, 1891 — and eleven days later the National Union of Shop Assistants, Warehousemen and Clerks (as it eventually became known) came into existence at a Birmingham meeting on March 29th and 30th.

The two Unions existed side by side for more than half a century. There were periods of conflict between them, particularly over the organisation of Co-operative workers, and at other times they co-operated on issues common to all their members. Eventually, in 1947, they merged to form the present Union of Shop, Distributive and Alled Workers. But we have to pass through two world wars and a host of other problems and achievements before we reach that happy event. This chapter ends in March, 1891, when shop workers at long last have their feet on a road that their brothers in many other industries had travelled since early in the century.

3 FROM MDCEA TO AUCE

IN the last chapter the Manchester District Co-operative Employees' Association was brought onto the stage. We must now back-track a little in time to study the events that led up to the historic decision of 18th March, 1891. There is still available a fairly full documentation from which, with a little imagination, one can trace the cautious movement of "Co-operative servants" from isolation into collective action. The New Unionism was the catalyst. But it worked on discontents that had been simmering over a long period of time. The feeling that committees of management took their "servants" too much for granted, that hours were too long, wages too low, and resentment that both were arbitrarily determined by committees. The feeling that societies were becoming so obsessed with dividend that in thus seeking to return to the consumer the margin between wholesale and retail prices they were ignoring the essential role and legitimate interests of their employees.

No doubt these grievances were often locally expressed when employees of neighbouring societies met each other on business or at social or sporting events. They surfaced nationally in the pages of *The Co-operative News*, which published a weekly Employees' Column (actually, a page) consisting of news and letters. A few excerpts will show the way the wind was blowing.

In the *News* issue of 20th June, 1885, a letter from "A.C.B." asked for information on times of opening and closing of Co-operative stores in the North; also if a weekly half holiday was given or "only from four or five o'clock one day in the week" (a question which indicates that when some societies claimed they gave a half holiday, it wasn't quite what most people would understand the words to mean). In subsequent issues during July and August information on hours came from several sources, of which one will be quoted. From "one of the largest societies in Northumberland" a correspondent wrote

c

that they opened every morning at 8.00 a.m. except Wednesday,
when the time was 7.00 a.m. They closed Monday, Tuesday
and Saturday at 6.00 p.m., Wednesday 11.00 a.m. (the half
holiday), Thursday 7.00 p.m. and Friday 9.00 p.m. Which
makes 58 hours, with 13 hours on the Friday.

"A.C.B.", in a further letter, found that on these hours
Northumberland employees were "singularly favoured" compared with fellow workers on the "monotonous round" from
7.30 a.m. to 7.30 p.m. and 10.15 on Saturdays, which assuming
him to be writing about his own conditions, gave him a working
week of 62¾ hours, with no half holiday. And, as we shall see
later in this chapter, 62¾ hours was far from being the limit.

A correspondence on hours soon broadens out to include
wages and *News* readers were quick to raise that topic. "Practical", in the paper's issue of 22nd August, 1885, cited "a large
society in the Midlands" which paid managers from 18/–
to 30/– a week, "most of them having less than 20/–". A writer
over the initial "F" suggested that "a union of storekeepers . . .
would not only result in their material benefit but also [be] to
the benefit of all interested in the Co-operative Movement".
This brought an offer from "Unionist" to co-operate with any
store managers "who would undertake to carry out the formation of a society". J. Goldsmith, of Hampton, Middlesex,
wrote approving of the idea and declared that "A Co-operative
employees' union would show directors that their servants
are not slaves of the stores, but that the well-being of the one
is bound up with the other". W. Rayner, of Hammersmith,
recommended " . . . more storekeepers' conferences and a
closer union between them and committees". He added "It is
painful to witness the domineering way in which committeemen
talk to employees".

In Yorkshire, it was reported, there were societies which paid
wages by a method not unlike the "butty" system that operated
in some industries and coalmines, in which a ganger contracted
for so much work and was responsible for hiring labour and
paying wages. In these societies branch managers were paid a
commission ranging from 4d to 6d in the £, leaving them to
hire and fire at will. This system continued well into the
twentieth century, although before it disappeared AUCE had
in some cases established that the Union rate must be paid to

shopmen.

For year after year wages, hours, conditions and status were the principal subject of the Employees' Page. But letters to *The Co-operative News* would only be the tip of the iceberg. They appeared with such regularity over so many years that they must have measured a growing volume of discontent expressed whenever employees discussed their jobs and conditions. Sick and benefit clubs were then common in societies and they may frequently have become a forum for ventilating wider grievances. There were false starts on the road to united action. A. Hewitt (first secretary of the MDCEA and of its successor, the Amalgamated Union of Co-operative Employees), in describing the establishment of the Association, refers to "experimental associations" which were still-born or died an early death. Moreover, in spite of the harsh words that have been used about committeemen, in many boardrooms there were members who sympathised with employee aspirations and were willing to help in efforts to harmonise relations between committees and "servants".

One such development, reported in *The Co-operative News* of 6th April, 1889, was a conference of the Manchester District Co-operative Association — one of the area groupings into which the Co-operative Union divided its society members — jointly attended by representatives of committees and employees, at which the subject was "The Co-operative Employee: his position and influence in the Movement". The speaker, J. Thompson, secretary of the Ashton-under-Lyne Society, accepted that as buyers and sellers of labour, committees and employees were opposed to each other, but in the Co-operative world this should be subordinate to the relation of " . . . fellow labourers in a great and noble effort to improve the conditions of the people". But employees " . . . are in many cases not looked upon as very important factors in the Co-operative world but treated more as divi-making machines". Strong stuff — but qualified by the speaker deploring that few employees " . . . take any real interest in the principles of the Movement or know or even care to know anything of the nature or working of those principles". He suggested that committees should form classes for teaching the history of Co-operation, not only to their employees but (a sharp barb, this) to *themselves*.

The chairman of the conference was a Mr. Hollingworth, Manager of the Pendleton Society, who probably undid whatever good had been done by the speaker by remarking that he " . . . did not know that Co-operative employees had much to complain about . . . the chief thing for employees to do was to study their employer's interests, keep the shops tidy and make the most profit. It was all very well to talk about the glory of the cause, but to him the glory of the cause was to make as much profit as he could, sell as low as he could, and do a large trade". One can imagine a few mutterings as those words rolled around the conference room.

This ferment of complaints, ideas and discussion was soon to lead to action. But the first moves did not, as is widely assumed, come in the Manchester district. A. Hewitt states in a brief history of the MDCEA that the idea of an association of employees with members in many — and, ideally, all — societies originated in London in 1889, and this is confirmed by a letter in *The Co-operative News* of 30th November of that year. Signed by C. Cooper, it reports that a total of 150 employees from St. Mary Cray, Gravesend, Cambridge, Ashford, Grays, New Brampton, Brixton, Brighton, Bromley, Hastings Societies, the CWS and the Co-operative Printing Society had agreed to join a Co-operative Employees' Association. But London, too, could be challenged for the position of first in the field. In 1887 a Northumberland Co-operative Employees' Mutual Protection and Aid Association had been formed "Based on Trade Union principles" and with the purpose of securing "adequate remuneration, protection in case of oppression and to help members who are thrown out of employment". It was registered as a Trade Union in 1888, but thereafter disappears from the records. An employees' Trade Union had also been established in Bolton Society by branch managers and second shopmen in 1892. It was not registered, and was to merge with MDCEA when that organisation was converted into a registered Union. It is not uncommon, however, to find that an organisation which has given its name to a movement or a social tendency was not actually first in the field. The Co-operative priority of the Rochdale Pioneers has been questioned in both England and Scotland. What matters is: which local or regional group or association went on to become truly national, and on that score we can safely date Trades Unionism among Co-operative employees from the formation of the MDCEA.

A series of conferences led up to the establishment of the Association. The first was held in the Co-operative Hall, Failsworth, on 21st October, 1890, and was sponsored by the Manchester District Association of the Co-operative Union. Committmen of societies as well as employees attended and to that extent Trades Unionism in the Co-operative Movement was born under the joint auspices of employers and workers. But it was a committee of employees that carried the project to fruition. They decided on an independent association for the Manchester area on the grounds that it " . . . will have a better chance of success than the formation of a branch of the London Association". After much debate, definite proposals were put to a meeting on CWS premises, Manchester, on 18th March, 1891, attended by thirty delegates representing employees' and societies' committees. The name "Manchester District Co-operative Employees' Association" was formally adopted, together with a code of rules. It was announced that upwards of 150 employees had signified their willingness to join.

Officers elected were: President, J. Dyson (Manchester Equitable), treasurer T. Fowe (Manchester Equitable), joint secretaries A. Hewitt (Co-operative Newspaper Society) and J. Thompson (Ashton-under-Lyne). The latter gave up his position for personal reasons in October, 1891, and thereafter A. Hewitt was sole secretary. Although the membership of the committee changed rapidly in the early years, the pioneer members are given here for the record — J. T. Watson (Droylsden), J. Bills (Eccles), J. T. Wrigley (Failsworth), A. H. Booth (Hyde), A. Winkle (Pendleton), J. Hibbert (Prestwich), W. Raw (Ringley and Kearsley), A. Morrell (Mosley).

Thus did Trade Unionism come to a Movement where many employees themselves had considered that it was unnecessary. But the first rules contained little hint of what the future was to bring. Unlike the Bolton Employees' Union, MDCEA did not immediately set its sights on the improvement of wages, hours and conditions. These problems were not mentioned, except insofar as an ambiguous reference might be read into clause (c) below. The objects of the Association were given as " . . . to

promote the social and intellectual welfare of its members by
(a) periodical discussions and meetings for the interchange of
ideas on practical and theoretical subjects affecting the well-
being of Co-operative employees and the Movement (b) com-
piling and keeping a register of all members out of employment
or desirous of a change of situation, and recommending such to
societies when requested (c) the advancement of the Co-operative
cause generally and of the interests of employees in particular,
by any means which may appear to the members judicious".
Twelve miles from Manchester was to be the area of operation
but if members were recruited outside that limit, sections could
be formed and were soon to exist in the Airedale area of Yorkshire and the Northumberland/Durham area. Subscriptions
were to be not less than 6d a quarter, and if there was any
surplus after paying expenses it was to go into a fund for the
relief of distress among members.

The first committee meeting was held on 21st April, 1891, at
the Downing Street premises of the Manchester Equitable
Society. Thereafter, meetings were mainly at Co-operative
Union offices, City Buildings, Corporation Street, Manchester,
until that organisation and the (by then) Amalgamated Union
of Co-operative Employees both moved in 1901 to newly built
premises of the Co-operative Newspaper Society in Long
Millgate.

The early days of a new organisation, particularly one with
a crusading purpose, are often dangerous and sometimes fatal.
The energy and enthusiasm expended in getting it off the ground
can, when the organisation is ready to walk, deteriorate into
inertia and occasionally differences of opinion. Not so with the
committee of MDCEA. Its members were dedicated men. To
them what had gone before was the preliminary, the real
challenge had only begun. Most of them worked very long
hours but they devoted many hours more to committee
meetings, followed by forays in and around Manchester to
address meetings of employees. Eighty societies were circularised in the first few months, and in many cases meetings were
arranged.

The jobs registry was established in November, 1891, (with
A. Hewitt in charge) and by the time of the first annual meeting
in July, 1892, there were 117 names on record, 217 had been

supplied to 66 societies and 19 had received appointments. A fee of 1/- was charged to societies that applied for names, and the London Association also took part in the scheme. Wages, whether or not they were included in the objects rule, soon reached the committee's agenda. The meeting on 1st September, 1891, resolved "That this committee take steps to obtain all the information possible relating to the wages paid by Co-operative societies". Repeatedly, in the years ahead this issue was to come up as MDCEA and, later, the Amalgamated Union of Co-operative Employees, sought to obtain a clearer picture of the infinitely varying wages and hours that then prevailed in Co-operative service.

The first of the discussion conferences provided for in the rules was held at Belle Vue Gardens, Manchester, on 8th July, 1891, and dealt with a question which frequently complicated the Association's affairs — the day of the weekly half holiday, on which most meetings must necessarily be held. Societies in one part of Manchester closed on a Tuesday, in the other part, on a Wednesday. The conference came down unanimously for Wednesday, and many societies conformed when approached. But not all, and for long dual meetings had to be held for "Tuesday closers" and "Wednesday closers".

The Belle Vue meeting ended with the company dispersing " . . . to seek an evening's rational enjoyment among the diversified attractions of the gardens" (to quote *The Co-operative News*). There was a sequel, slightly comic to us today but a more serious matter in the nineties, when there was a large and powerful total abstinence movement. J. Tyldesley, of Roe Green, suspected that the demon drink might have been an irrational contributor to the "rational enjoyment". He had a son who was a member of the Association, and in a letter to the *News* he deplored that his time of recreation should be " . . . spent at a pub, whether there be a monkey house added or not" (for readers unfamiliar with Manchester's still flourishing Belle Vue, the zoo was for long a popular feature). A. Hewitt pointed out in reply that "While there are on the premises licensed refreshment rooms for those who require them, the extent and completeness of the arrangements for the accommodation of abstainers and tea drinkers, apart from the places where intoxicants are sold, are unrivalled".

The first annual meeting of the Association was held at
Belle Vue on 20th July, 1892, for "Wednesday closers", with a
second meeting for "Tuesday closers" on 2nd August. Modest
progress was reported. There were 738 members in 47 societies
(but the committee reminded the meeting that there were an
estimated 30,000 employees of retail societies). Apart from the
Belle Vue event, conferences had been held at Eccles, Oldham,
Heywood and the CWS. The President and other members of
the committee had addressed meetings at Bury, Radcliffe,
Pendleton, Crewe, Hebden Bridge, Shipley (Yorkshire) and
Preston. At the four last named, branches had been formed.
A scheme for sickness and unemployment benefit was being
considered, and the meeting authorised the committee to
prepare detailed proposals.

Sound organisation is the only permanent basis for a successful Trade Union or any other concern. But a little luck helps.
In 1893 help from an unforeseen quarter gave the Association
added strength and impetus in its relations with employees and
the committees of retail societies. At the Co-operative Congress
of that year, held at Bristol, a paper by William Maxwell, the
President of the Scottish CWS, broke the "conspiracy of
indifference" which had hitherto marked the attitude of the
Congress to the Movement's shop employees. His basic theme
was expressed in one sentence — " . . . if we take the greak bulk
of [Co-operative] retail distributive employees . . . it will be
found that they do not consider it any part of their business to
interest themselves in a cause which many of them think exists
only for the enrichment of purchasers and which up to now
has done very little to improve the position of their class as a
whole".

He gave a table of hours showing 1,096 societies where shops
were open for more than 60 hours weekly, 509 of them open
more than 66 hours and 163 with hours ranging from 70 to 85.
And for good — or, rather, bad — measure he added that
closing the shop did not mean the end of the working day.
Up to four hours a week more could be added on preparatory
work for the next day. With the exception of managers and
head shopmen, he considered that wages were also too low.
He made many suggestions for improvement, one being that
the MDCEA could become the centre of a national organisation

of employees.

There was little dissent from his conclusions in the Congress debate and on the motion of W. Campbell (Harrington and Skipton Society) a resolution was adopted declaring that " . . . the long hours of labour and the small remuneration paid to employees in a large number of Co-operative stores is descreditable to the Movement and opposed to the principles and aims of Co-operation; and the Central Board are requested to take immediate action with a view to bringing the subject prominently before the different sections of the [Co-operative] Union". Seconding the resolution G. Scott (CWS Newcastle) accurately described it as the "explosion of a bombshell".

Co-operative Congress resolutions are not mandatory and many a resounding declaration has been acclaimed at Congress and ignored in local boardrooms. But after Maxwell's speech things could never be quite the same again, particularly with what was soon to be a vigorous Trade Union of Co-operative employees to drive home the message to hundreds of committees.

The logic of Maxwell's paper and the Congress resolution must have impressed itself on many employees. True, the resolution called only upon the Co-operative Union to take specific action. But implicitly it advised employees to support that action by their own exertions. And a century of industrial history had demonstrated that only by collective action through a Trade Union could the individual worker exert any influence on his wages and conditions.

So far as the MDCEA was concerned, other developments were impelling the Association towards the same conclusion. The first annual meeting had authorised the committee to prepare a contributory scheme of sickness, unemployment and other benefits, and almost every committee meeting of 1893 had spent much time on this far from simple project (the first draft scheme was rejected after discussion at conferences and in branches). There had been several contacts with the Trade Union of the Bolton Co-operative Employees which was also preparing a benefits scheme and these led to proposals for amalgamation.

To give legal protection to the funds of MDCEA in whatever form it operated it was desirable to register under an appropriate statute. The Association could have registered under the Friendly Societies or the Industrial and Provident Societies Acts and undoubtedly one or other of these would have been preferred by some of its members. But provision for out-of-work payments was a basic part of the benefits scheme and this was precluded to bodies registered under these two Statutes. Another reason was that registration as a Union would facilitate amalgamation with Bolton. All of which led to one conclusion — that the Association should become the Union.

It is unlikely that all members of the Committee were wholeheartedly in favour of the change and there is evidence that the chairman, J. Dyson, and the secretary, A. Hewitt, held different views; the former against and the latter in favour. But both were realists: if disagreement existed it was probably more philosophical than practical and negotiations for amalgamation, on the benefits scale and for registration as a Trade Union continued throughout 1893 and 1894. One problem was the insistence by Bolton that all members of the new Union should compulsorily subscribe to the benefits scheme. A vote of MDCEA members on this point showed that at least 500 preferred an optional provision (mainly because so many of them were already contributing to local benefit clubs). This difficulty was overcome by providing that membership should comprise associates who would pay 6d a quarter and members who paid according to their choice of a varying scale of benefits.

Eventually, rules for the new body were agreed, and sent out to branches of the MDCEA for discussion and decision. At the committee meeting of 20th November, 1894, the secretary reported that there was "an overwhelming majority in favour of the new rules." As a title for the new organisations the committee itself had preferred Co-operative Employees' Association, or, as a second choice, Federation of Co-operative Employees. But wisely the members voted to give the Union a title which spelt out precisely what it was — the amalgamated Union of Co-operative Employees. "Amalgamated" was included in the title partly to cover the impending adhesion of Bolton but also in the hope of future amalgamation with London and Scotland.

The final step was registration, which was carried out immediately, the temporary registered address being the secretary's home in Romiley, near Stockport. The AUCE then came formally into being on 28th January, 1895. The next step was to complete the amalgamation with Bolton and on 16th April, 1895, a form of agreement to that end was signed by J. Dyson, J. Lees and K. H. Whitehead for the MDCEA and for Bolton by J. Wallbank, C. Wood, A. Sheppard and E. Tunstall. The benefits scheme which had taken so long to agree was:

Scale	Weekly Subscriptions	*A* Weekly payments when out of employment			*B* Permanent Disablement Fund	*C* Weekly payments when sick or temporarily disabled			Funeral Allowance
		First 4 weeks	Second 4 weeks	Third 4 weeks		First 6 weeks	Second 6 weeks	Third 6 weeks	
I	4d	15/-	10/-	5/-	£5	9/-	4/6	2/-	£4
II	3d	10/-	6/6	3/-	£3	6/-	3/-	1/6	£3
III	2d	5/-	3/-	1/6	£2	4/-	2/-	1/-	£2

While "upon the funds" members had to pay full contributions. It was not necessary to take the entire range of any scale, e.g. a member could opt for sick, temporary disablement and funeral benefit only, at a reduced contribution. Superannuation, based on a special fund, was also optional. As was common in benefit schemes, members drawing sick benefit were subject to close supervision. They were not to be out of the house after specified hours (unless with the consent of the branch visitor whose duty it was to call upon sick members once a week).

The preamble to the AUCE objects rule was broadly similar to that of the MDCEA, plus provision for the benefits scheme, legal aid and affiliation to local Trades Councils. The detailed rules provided that District Councils of the Union were " . . . at all times to be subject . . . to the control of the Central Executive Council".

The benefits scheme was based on a principle which was strongly evident in long-established Trades Unions, although by the end of the century it was being challenged. It was a century which revered the principle of self-help (and for long abused it as an excuse to deny social legislation). The benefit provisions of Friendly Societies and Trade Unions were then

the only form of self-protection against the hazards of unemployment, sickness, disablement and old age. Many of the
New Unionists, however, repudiated the whole concept of
benefit scales, arguing that concentration on benefit funds
weakened the will of Trades Unions to fight for better immediate
conditions and for State provision for the unemployed and the
physically helpless. But MDCEA of those years was very
much a product of the Co-operative Movement, itself strongly
imbued with belief in thrift and self-help, and to this day the
Union (as the Union of Shop, Distributive and Allied Workers)
provides unemployment, sickness and death benefits on a
generous scale.

We have now brought Co-operative employees along a slow,
cautious road to fully pledged Trade Unionism. We shall soon
see that within a surprisingly short period of time their Union
was to develop a militancy that would have been inconceivable
to some of its founders.

4 LAYING THE FOUNDATIONS

In the last chapter we described the higher strategy, so to speak, of MDCEA/AUCE in the four years and a few days between the formation of the Association in March, 1891, and its transformation into a national Trade Union in 1895. But the days between those two dates were filled by much more than issues of high policy, and in this chapter we shall look at some of the activities through which MDCEA and the Association Movement generally became established as a permenent part of the Co-operative scene. What, for instance, was happening in other parts of the country beyond the immediate neighbourhood of Manchester?

London had been first in the field and for a time the Association Movement seemed to flourish in and around the capital. In 1893 there was even a proposal to establish a branch so far north as Newcastle upon Tyne, where MDCEA was itself trying to recruit and where there were moves on Tyneside by the employees of the Walker Society to form a separate Northern Association. London, however, never really got off the ground as the base for a national organisation. There was some talk of amalgamation with Manchester. But the rot had already set in and at the MDCEA committee meeting of 19th March, 1895, a letter was read from W. Openshaw announcing the demise of the once promising London Association.

The separatist moves on Tyneside died out. A conference of northern employees at Newcastle upon Tyne in December, 1893, made the decision to join Manchester, and in due course a Northern District Council was formed. The report of MDCEA for the year ended 30th June, 1894, records the existence of 27 branches in Northumberland and Durham, linked under the Northern Council, with 948 members, almost half the total of the Association's then membership of 2,151.

What of Scotland? A Glasgow Association was formed in the Autumn of 1889 and as late as 1893 was reported by

MDCEA as "making great strides among the servants over the border". Many branches were formed, but they vanished into the mists. The diary of an AUCE organiser who campaigned in Scotland in 1907 has survived, and he records many cases of recruiting from zero in societies that were reported to have Association branches in 1893. The Movement continued to exist but did not develop the strong national organisation that was growing south of the border. There was a tenuous "Co-operative Employees' National Association", with which AUCE unsuccessfully sought amalgamation. When this failed, the Union began in 1907 to recruit and open branches in Scotland, today one of the strongest of USDAW's Divisions.

Branches which faded out were not a problem peculiar to Scotland. There must have been many bitter disappointments at MDCEA committee meetings when, as too often happened, the secretary had to announce that promising branches had withered away. The committee's second annual report, while happy that recruitment had been particularly successful in the West Riding of Yorkshire, stated that elsewhere some branches had failed to renew their subscriptions and some had been dissolved. The report blamed a "materialistic turn of mind" among members who expected immediate results in cash or hours, and if they were not forthcoming, lapsed their membership — a problem not unknown to many other movements of reform.

But the committee never gave up. The word used in the minutes to report the collapse of a branch was "secession" and invariably it was followed by plans for "resuscitation", based on retaining contact with local enthusiasts in readiness for a new start. The fourth annual report, in welcoming a large influx of new branches, was particularly proud that several prodigal branches which "had become inert" were active again, "Ashington, Crewe, Manchester and Pendleton being particularly promising among this class".

Since both idealism and materialism are qualities of human nature it was to be expected that many employees would judge the Association by the material benefits it gained for them. So what did the MDCEA actually achieve in its early years?

On wages, it would have been impossible to make an immediate breakthrough. There were well over a thousand separate retail societies when the Association was formed and there were certainly scores, and possibly hundreds, of bases on which pay was determined. Almost the only common factor was that decisions were made arbitrarily and without any negotiation with employees as an organised group. We saw earlier that one of the first tasks of MDCEA was to seek information on rates that were actually being paid. The committee, or the Executive Council when AUCE was formed, was repeatedly frustrated in its efforts to get a comprehensive picture. It was six years before there was sufficient data on which to adopt a minimum wage policy. But that was in 1897, and belongs to the next chapter. In the earlier years it is probable that little advance was made on the wages front.

It was a more hopeful story with hours. There had long been a national movement for the earlier closing of shops. In many Co-operatives the weekly half holiday was already operating (it became general through the Shops' Act of 1912). From 1892 onwards many retail societies were persuaded to reduce the total number of hours worked. The Association reported in 1893 that about 90 societies were known to have granted reductions of from one to eight (eight!) hours per week. "Of these, ten at least reduced their working week to 48 hours . . ." The total of 90 corresponds closely to lists published weekly in *The Co-operative News* during 1892 and 1893. The pioneering ten on 48 hours were all in Northumberland and Durham, where Co-operative Societies must have been the first employers in the country to reduce shop hours to what was then a Utopian level.

The 1893 report voiced a complaint which Co-operative and other shop workers have echoed many a time since. Writing of those customers who persistently arrive just on closing time, the committee commented: "Among the greatest offenders are members living nearest to the shops, and people who have nothing to prevent them coming earlier. Some of these make it a rule to be the 'last customer' no matter at what hours the shops close and those who were last before earlier closing was adopted still maintain their position". As they say in the North, "There's nowt as queer as folk".

Most of the reductions in hours resulted from applications made by the employees, and many of these based their case on information supplied by the Association. On hours at least it could be claimed that a large number of Co-operative workers had benefitted from their subscription of 6d. a quarter — not to mention those who had not joined the Association but none the less enjoyed the benefits of the shorter hours.

The Association continued to seek close links with the official organisations of the Co-operative Movement. From its first year it had sought and obtained representation at conferences of the Manchester District Association of the Co-operative Union. It sought the help of other District or Sectional Boards of the Union in organising joint conferences to introduce the Association to employees and management committees. At its 16th August meeting of 1892 the committee instructed the President and Secretary to seek an interview with J. C. Gray, the General Secretary of the Co-operative Union " . . . with respect to a scheme for obtaining reliable returns as to rates of wages and hours of labour; also as to the eligibility of the Association to become a member of the Co-operative Union and thus secure the right of representation at Congress".

On the first subject they were advised to seek the information direct from societies. On the second, the minutes are silent. A formal application for membership was, however, made in 1897, by which date the Association had become the Amalgamated Union of Co-operative Employees. It was rejected on the grounds that in the opinion of the Co-operative Union's legal advisers AUCE did not conform to the rules of the Union nor to the statutory provisions — the Industrial and Provident Societies Acts — under which the latter operated. Accepting this situation, the Executive asked for the privilege of fraternal representation at the Co-operative Congress. But by then the AUCE had affiliated to the TUC and it was pointed out that the annual fraternal delegation from the TUC to the Co-operative Congress represented all affiliated Trades Unions. The Co-operative Union did, however, urge societies, especially the large ones, to include at least one employee in their delegations to Congress, and AUCE had some success in securing that this became a practice. Other means were also adopted to bring the Union to the attention of what Co-operators called their Parliament (although they frequently ignored its "legislation"). An employees' day, participation in the Congress exhibition of

Co-operative trades, and a window-dressing competition were long used to put over the message that "we, too, are part of the Co-operative Movement".

These experiences underline a quality which makes AUCE probably unique amongst British Trades Unions. Most Unions had to establish themselves against the opposition of employers who denied, or, at any rate, grudged their right to exist. Co-operative employees began Trade Unionism with a considerable measure of goodwill, and frequently of help, from their employers. True, there could be discord when goodwill had to be translated into wages and hours and, as we shall see, there were to be occasions of open conflict between the Union and individual societies or group of societies. But over the greater part of a century the Union's relationship with the Co-operatives has developed as one of mutual respect, and free from the tradition of hostility which to this day embitters employee-worker relations in some British industries.

Model branch rules were drafted in 1893. This book is completed in 1979, in a decade when, more than once, USDAW has discussed the possibility of specialising its branch and national structure on the basis of individual trades. It is interesting to note that 86 years earlier the first rules for branches provided that they should comprise "Delegates [elected] from the grocery, butchering, drapery, boot & shoe and other departments . . ." The rules also provided for interests somewhat beyond those now common in USDAW or other Trade Unions. The duties of a branch included arrangements " . . . of a more social character, such as . . . say, social parties, singing and elocution classes, or debating classes for mutual subjects during the winter months; and picnics and rambles in the summer". There were to be separate meetings of head shopmen and employees " . . . namely, grocers, butchers, drapers, shoe and clog . . . to discuss and exchange ideas on the work of their departments".

One of the rambles similar to those visualised in the rules was reported in *The Co-operative News* and was probably typical of many. On an Autumn Wednesday of 1891, 153 employees, of both sexes, gathered for a ramble along the Manchester Ship Canal (then being excavated) from Salford to Barton, on to "a 9d tea" in Eccles Society's hall, followed by

D

inspection of the Society's bakery and other premises, then a meeting at which the Association President, J. Dyson, read a progress report, followed by a concert and ending in a dance. It is not recorded at what time the party ended or how they made their way back home. But there must have been some tired feet in the shops next morning to face a long working day.

It all sounds rather quaintly old fashioned today. But in the eighteen-nineties people had largely to make their own entertainment, and leisure was a scarce commodity for most workers. They knew, perhaps better than we do now, how to make the most of it — and it was not all spent at the "pub with the monkey house" that so concerned J. Tyldsley of the previous chapter.

5 BEGINS WITH A MINIMUM WAGE, ENDS WITH A STRIKE FUND

IN the last chapter we went on a ramble. In this chapter, with AUCE now registered on the roll of British Trades Unions, we must return to more serious subjects, of which the first was wages, hours and conditions. The Executive Council was well aware that this was the make-or-break issue for the Union. If AUCE was to grow in membership and influence it must demonstrate to employees that only by acting collectively could they raise the wages and reduce the hours against which they complained individually.

The first task was to get the facts on record, to obtain an overall picture. With hours that was not too difficult, for they were publicly known. But with wages it was at first impossible. The variations between neighbouring societies, between workers in individual societies, between North and South, were too wide. Even an apparently adequate rate of, say 24/- for males at age 21 could in some societies conceal an unacceptable practice of employing large numbers of low-wage juniors and sacking them when they came of age. Alternatively, they could be kept on but their number used to justify an appallingly low adult rate.

The problem was further complicated by the inability or reluctance of many branches of the Union to supply accurate information. Possibly the secrecy over individual wages that was common in private trade was not unknown in Co-operative service. Yet, so tangled was the web that some societies went to the opposite extreme — they published individual wages of employees in their reports to members.

All that AUCE could establish in the early years, and all that can be given here, was a tendency built up from numerous indicators. Thus, the first annual report in 1892 gave some figures on wages, based on information supplied by branches at twelve societies in the neighbourhood of Manchester. They were:

	Wages per Week
General Manager	24/- to 95/-
Departmental Managers	21/- to 60/-
Branch Managers or head countermen	18/- to 40/-
Other countermen	7/- to 25/-
Warehousemen, porters, etc.....	6/- to 30/-
Boys	2/- to 13/-

The report stated that there was probably some confusion in the three last items — boys in some cases having been included with porters or countermen. As the figures were for the Movement's heartland in and around Manchester, they would include some long established and — for the period — large societies. Unfortunately, no indication is given of the *numbers* at each end of the scale. But most would be countermen and, even allowing for the confusion over the last three items, there must have been many men in the shops on or below wages of 20/- a week at the age of 21 and over.

These figures are partly substantiated by information for the late 1890s from two large North-Western societies, Oldham Industrial and Bolton, both by then strongly established and prosperous. L. Lumley, soon to become the Union's first full-time organiser, listed actual individual wages for 26 employees in six trade groups at Oldham Industrial in April, 1898. The following examples are the highest rates given:—

Branch Managers,	21 years' service	— 36/-
,, ,,	15 ,, ,,	— 30/-
Drapery Managers,	13 ,, ,,	— 32/-
,, ,,	12 ,, ,,	— 34/-
Second Counterman,	29 years of age	— 28/-
Third ,,	22 ,, ,, ,,	— 18/-
Drapery Assistant	22 ,, ,, ,,	— 21/-
Butcher	31 ,, ,, ,,	— 32/-
Youths	18 ,, ,, ,,	— 12/-

Note that these figures are for *individuals* and do not reflect an age/wages scale. Thus, behind the 31 years old butcher on 32/- was a 33 years old colleague on 28/-, the draper of 22 years on 21/- had two colleagues of 18 and 19 years respectively who were on 14/- and one of 18 years on 12/-: the drapery manager with the longest service (13 years) was 2/- a week below his colleague with 12 years' service. The Society did have a list which was supposed to be a guide to payment at each age, ranging from 6/– at 14 to 24/– at 22. But A. W. Burrows, who, in 1943, made an analysis of Lumley's data, said that it was found in practice to vary "from 6/– less to 3/– more". Chance, favouritism and possibly in some cases outstanding ability determined what an employee was paid.

Bolton also had a scale, ranging from 5/– at 13 to 24/– at 21, branch managers from 30/– to 38/–, butchers from 19/– to 33/– and shoe managers from 28/– to 33/–. It is not known, however, whether every employee received no less than these amounts.

Both these societies, by the standards of the day, ranked as good employers. Among a great many others, particularly in the South and Midlands, wages and conditions were very much worse. The variations in pay for the same jobs were frequently breathtaking. A. W. Burrows, in another article, quotes these figures from a table given in 1910 by a Mr. Anderson, Secretary of the Ayrshire Co-operative Conference Association:

ADULT ASSISTANTS—

			Highest	Lowest
Grocery	—	Males	30/–	15/–
		Females	17/–	10/–
Drapery	—	Males	35/–	20/–
		Females	20/–	10/–
Butchery	—	Males	30/–	14/–
		Females	14/–	14/–

Against this background it is apparent that wages depended on the degree of social — or Co-operative — conscience prevalent in any individual society's Committee, on the Union's ability to stir the membership to protest against excessively low pay, or, as Burrows put it, " . . . if you were one of the 'white-haired' boys, you might, if you went to the same chapel as the President, get one shilling a week merit increase — but under a solemn pledge not to reveal this to anyone".

As late as 1908 the Union was frequently informed of cases of men being paid 17/– for a net working week of anything from 54 to 60 hours. The Women's Co-operative Guild, which developed close links with AUCE on the issue of wages, discovered that in the North considerably more than one-third, and in the South, South-west and Yorkshire, rather more than

one-half, of the women working in societies were paid under
13/– a week. One example will personalise a situation that
was far from being uncommon. Ted Skinner, now a life
member of USDAW, recalls joining the grocery department of a
Suffolk Society at the age of 13, on a wage of 3/– for a 60 hour
week, with 10 p.m. closing on Saturday.

As data slowly accumulated the Executive Council and the
District Councils obtained a clearer view of the challenge they
had to meet. But they were also aware that they must tread
carefully. The Union was still a delicate plant (there were only
2,151 members when AUCE was formed, with cash in hand and
in the bank of £98.3.2). Among Co-operative employees there
was no tradition of collective action on which to build. There
were members who still had reservations about the need for a
Union at all. In other cases, employees hesitated to join (or
kept quiet about their membership) for a very human reason —
wind-up. They feared a black mark from manager or committee.
A. Hewitt, writing in 1909, recalled that " . . . their enthusiasm
was damped . . . by an oblique glance directed by a manager or
committeeman against the Union", or they panicked at the
thought of the word "strike". "Many of the employees were
timid as hares and the least hint by a speaker of the possibility
of trade disputes was sufficient to send them flying back to
their burrows of individualism", wrote Hewitt in the same
article.

But the Union had two advantages, one human, the other
moral, in the campaign to raise standards which must begin if
AUCE was to justify its existence. It was led nationally by men
of strong and resilient character, not easily rebuffed and moti-
vated by idealism and convictions that had been formed and
hardened by their experience in life. In most retail societies
there was a nucleus of employees who shared these qualities
and were to become the pioneers and leaders of local branches.

The moral asset was in the nature of the Co-operative
Movement. Not even the most reactionary committee could
deny that in Co-operative principle, fair treatment of the worker
ranked with a fair deal for the consumer. Joseph Hallsworth
made telling use of this argument in an article in *The Co-operative Employee* (more about this journal later), when he quoted
from the then basic textbooks of the Movement, *Working Men*

Co-operators (by Ben Jones and A. H. D. Acland, MP) and *Industrial Co-operation* (edited by Catherine Webb). He pointed out that in the latter, and most up-to-date of the two, the purpose of the Movement was defined as " . . . including among its root principles the payment of fair wages to, and the just treatment of, employees". For good measure he also drew on the printed notes for correspondence courses on Co-operation issued by the Co-operative Union, which included among the Movement's leading principles "workers to have (a) good conditions, (b) fair wages, (c) fair hours".

Unfortunately, too many committeemen did not read the Movement's textbooks. But many did, and the Union frequently had allies in the seats of power who realised that the dichotomy between principle and practice could not permanently be tolerated.

The more active branches began to argue the case for a minimum wage policy almost as soon as the Union had been formed, and from then on the subject was rarely missing from the agenda of the annual delegate meeting. In 1896 the West Pelton (Durham) branch proposed that the Union should adopt a uniform scale of wages. The Executive Council did not need to be pushed — it was already engaged in tabulating data on wages and hours received from 35 branches, to be circulated to District Councils and branches, discussed at conferences and, finally, put before the annual meeting of 1897. At this meeting the first step was taken to establish a national scale, with local or regional variations. A resolution proposed by the Executive Council and adopted by an almost unanimous vote declared Union policy to be " . . . a minimum wage of 24/– per week for all employees over 21 years of age, each district and branch to be empowered to adopt a higher scale if practicable." A proposal by West Pelton calling for a 48-hour week and pay at the rate of 7½d an hour was heavily defeated. The minimum wage clause was also incorporated in the rules.

But the decision left unanswered one short interrogative word: how? The dread word "strike" was not mentioned, although it must have been in the minds of many of those present at the annual meeting. Action was to be through persuasion of societies' committees, and by appeal to Co-operative principle. Nor was this reticence necessarily an evidence of timidity. Apart from the lukewarm attitude of some members towards full scale Trade Union action, AUCE still in 1897 had only 3,186 members and associates. Although 126 branches were claimed, only four numbered more than one hundred members (Oldham Industrial, Pendleton, Annfield Plain and Bolton), and in many cases single members were listed as a branch. The general fund stood at only £873.19.2½. After all, David made sure he had a sizeable stone ready before he took on Goliath!

But the 24/- minimum had now been nailed to the mast and it was for branches to carry it into action, aided and advised when necessary by the Executive Council or, more usually, the appropriate District Council. The first year's experience (if one reads correctly between the lines of the annual report) was not particularly good. The best the Executive could say in the 1898 report was that "Many branches have taken steps to secure the observation of the minimum wage clause with varying success, while some societies have voluntarily adopted a minimum far above the modest sum our rules suggest" (Sunderland and Jarrow were specially mentioned as leaders in this respect).

It had been a slow start, but the campaign began to gather momentum, strengthened by two national developments. Early in 1896 the Executive Council had considered the publication of a journal and after various enquiries decided to recommend an employee edition of the *Wheatsheaf*. This monthly publication was issued by the CWS with a basic content of general magazine reading and publicity for the CWS, plus at front and end local pages which were changed for subscribing retail societies. The original intention was to publish a Union edition of 3,000 copies quarterly, but when publication began in January, 1898, this had been altered to a monthly issue of 2,500 copies carrying four pages of Union material under the title of *Gleanings for Members*. Branches received free copies pro rata to membership and could have extra copies at 3d per dozen. The number of pages was increased to eight in 1900 (sometimes more for special events, such as the annual delegate meeting).

The publication, of which A. Hewitt was appointed editor, helped to energise the wages policy by carrying news of the campaign to all parts of the country. It also helped to create a corporate identity for the Union by encouraging employees isolated in small branches to feel that they were part of a nation-wide movement. The *Gleanings* continued to spread the good seed until 1908, when, in June, the Union began to publish a self-contained monthly journal of its own under the title *The Co-operative Employee.*

The second development also concerned A. Hewitt. The ever-active West Pelton branch had successfully proposed to the 1898 annual meeting that the Union should have a full-time general secretary. By that date there were 4,320 members and an accumulated fund of £1,785. An elaborate benefits scheme, the employment register (with 272 names on the books at June, 1898), contact with 147 branches, a vital wages policy to stimulate and service, editorship of *Gleanings* — these constituted a formidable work load for a part-time secretary who had his living to earn as a proof-reader at the Co-operative Newspaper Society. In due course, at the Executive meeting of 28th February 1899, Augustus Hewitt — to give his full name — was appointed as the first full-time general secretary.

Improved national administration and communication was reinforced by a more flexible organisation. To the three existing District Councils of Manchester (later to be re-titled North-Western), Northern and Yorkshire (formerly known as Airedale), there were added a Midland Council in 1898, Southern in 1901, Western in 1905, a cumberland Sub-District in 1906 and a Scottish Council in 1908. The annual meeting was held on a District basis, the votes of each District being aggregated when decisions had to be made. Also, in 1906, L. Lumley was appointed to the staff and soon became a full-time organiser, the first of a devoted band who have since served the Union in that capacity. The annual meeting of 1908 recommended the appointment of two more organisers, but rejected an amendment from Leith and Cowdenbeath branches that one should be male and one female (at that date the Union had 1,020 women members). W. T. Scott (Sunderland) and E. J. Bull were later appointed.

Supported by more efficient central and district services the campaign for the minimum — plus improvements in hours, holidays and sickness pay — waxed and waned in the earlier

years of the twentieth century. In 1901 branches were reported
to be "doing their utmost to secure recognition of a flat rate".
By 1904 the "deplorable state of the general trade of the country"
led to a slackening of pressure. By 1906 District Councils were
attempting to work out regional scales from junior to branch
manager. In the same year a minimum of 30/– for branch
managers was added to the national scale.

The Union continued to have the support of those societies
that operated the minimum and in some cases had improved it.
Moreover, the long drawn out campaign troubled the conscience
of sincere Co-operators who accepted that conditions in too
many societies were a denial of the Movement's reforming
principles. The Co-operative Congress of 1893 when W. Maxwell
read his historic paper, had been the first to express these
feelings. They surfaced again in the Congresses of 1907, 1908,
1909 and 1910. At the first of the series, held at Preston, a
resolution affirmed that the Movement " . . . should establish
a minimum wage for various classes of workers below which
the societies should pledge themselves not to fall". A sub-
committee was appointed to draw up a scale. From AUCE,
R. J. Wilson and A. Hewitt, together with representatives of
the Women's Guild, assisted the Committee in its work. At
Newport a year later it recommended a minimum wage
" . . . which we hope will not be applied as a maximum", of
24/– for adult males at 21, and for females, 17/– at age 20.
For younger workers the scale proposed was:

BOYS

14	15	16	17	18	19	20	21
6/–	8/–	10/–	12/–	15/–	18/–	21/–	24/–

GIRLS

5/–	7/–	9/–	11/–	13/–	15/–	17/–	—

This scale was remitted for discussion throughout the
Movement and at the Newcastle Congress of 1909 was adopted,
with the recommendation that it should be operated by all
societies.

But for each delegate at Congress there was a varying number
of committeemen at home. Barely a third of the 1,251 societies
which the Co-operative Union urged by circular to implement
the scales had been represented at Newcastle, and there was a
different mood when the circular reached committee room

tables. The Plymouth Congress of 1910 was informed that of the 195 societies which replied to the Union, only 79 were willing to act and 116 declared that they were unable to do so. These dismal figures do not, however, reflect the full results of AUCE's campaign. While the Union does not appear ever to have obtained in those days a complete picture of the wages scene, figures drawn up by Messrs. Hallsworth and Davies and published in their *Working Life of Shop Assistants*, covering Co-operative grocery assistants and shop managers, show the results achieved between 1907 and 1910. The average works out as follows:—

	Shop Managers				Shop Assistants			
Year	Number of Societies	Average of Minimum Rate	Number of Societies	Average of Maximum Rate	Number of Societies	Average of Minimum Rate	Number of Societies	Average of Maximum Rate
1907	167	30/10	162	37/8	179	23/2	179	28/1
1910	195	31/8	176	38/3	210	24/2	186	28/8

Nothing spectacular in these figures. For the first time, however, in Co-operative history minimum scales were being established and what was equally significant, they were being *negotiated* by organised employees. But ... more than a thousand societies were still on the bad old system of arbitrarily determined and frequently beggarly wage rates.

Nevertheless, the Union's continuous campaign, often supported by local Trades Councils and branches of the Women's Guild was slowly pushing recalcitrant societies onto the defensive, and what was to become known as the "Congress Scale" added to the pressure.

It will be noted, too, that the figures so far given applied to shop workers. The so-called unskilled workers — warehouse and flour room men, carters and bread deliverers — were usually worse off on wages and over the limit on hours, particularly the latter two, who could have to come in twice on Sundays to attend to their horses — for 18/- or 20/- a week. In due course, this challenge, too, was taken up by the Union.

But meantime something more was needed. Persuasion and moral pressure had been successful up to a point. What was lacking was the power of enforcement. "Strike" was no longer a dirty word to a new generation of Union members. At the annual meeting of 1908 the Oldham Industrial and Coventry branches proposed the establishment of a strike fund. As adopted by the conference the proposal read "That the desirability of establishing a strike fund, adding new rules to govern strike pay, and making provision for the maintenance of such a fund be . . . referred to District Councils and branches for discussion".

For some members this was still a traumatic issue. They flinched from the last recourse of Trades Unionism and clung to the belief that in the end persuasion and principle would win the day. To judge from the columns of the *Co-operative News* and *The Co-operative Employee* during 1909 it almost seemed that the Union as a whole was reluctant to face the issue. In 71 reports of branch meetings and 89 of social gatherings and excursions published in the *News* there are few references to the strike fund nor, surprisingly, were there many letters on the subject.

In its report for the year the Executive Council acknowledged that "Opinions are divided on the matter", and evidently decided that more must be done to stimulate debate. It proposed that a decision should be deferred until discussion papers on the subject had been prepared and circulated, and this proposal was adopted. The same annual meeting carried another resolution which, in itself, epitomised the Union's dilemma over the strike issue. This resolution set out a plan for inducing more societies to adopt the minimum scales. District Councils were to write to off-scale committees asking them to pay up, followed if necessary by a deputation, followed by a challenge at members' meetings if a committee refused to budge, followed by public demonstrations supported by other Trades Unions. Then, "As a last resource, the Executive Council be empowered to take what steps they deem necessary". All these methods, singly or in combination, had been tried. In some cases they had won results, and were to continue to do so. But when all had been tried and failed, what was to be the "last resource"?

As decided by the 1909 ADM, separate discussion papers were prepared. They were by A. Hewitt and by anonymous authors in the Coventry and Oldham Industrial branches. Each was printed in *The Co-operative Employee* and circulated to branches for discussion. In his paper the General Secretary gave a brief historical description of the strike as an industrial weapon, ending with the words "The perfectly successful and acceptable substitute for the strike has, however, yet to be discovered, and the employees of Co-operative societies appear to have . . . a far better chance of securing their joint demands by the use of the means already at their disposal than most of their contemporary workers have by such means plus the strike". Coventry's case was based on two propositions: that the policy of moderation and conciliation had been treated by some societies as evidence of weakness and this accounted for the failure to win general recognition of the minimum scales. Resolutions would not change the situation without power to enforce them.

Oldham Industrial argued that in the ten years that the minimum had been Union policy "we have done too much requesting . . . we are at present held cheap". It acknowledged that the strike " . . . is a rather clumsy weapon but, . . . better have a clumsy weapon in reserve than none at all".

The debate continued, with the balance of argument swinging towards giving the Executive powers to call a strike, but with opinion divided on the necessity to raise an immediate strike fund. Both points of view were neatly covered in an Executive resolution adopted by the 1910 annual meeting. It provided "That an early opportunity be taken to include in the rules such an amplification of the present provisions as shall provide support for members who may lose their situations through disputes with their employers, whether in the nature of strikes, lockouts or discharges in consequence of action taken by or on behalf of the Union, when approved by the Executive Council". The "early opportunity" was the following year's ADM, and at the 1911 meeting a lengthy resolution set out the powers and procedure of the Executive Council in calling a strike, financing the cost and enlisting the support of non-members.

A strike could be called by the Executive "with the consent of the majority of the members of the branch concerned, and after consulting with the District Council . . .". In such a case all members were simultaneously to tender notice and any member who refused to do so was to be expelled. To provide a strike fund an initial levy of 6d from adult males, and 3d from females and juniors under 21, was to be called for, with further levies

if the special fund fell below £500. Strike benefits were to be
20/- a week for adult males, 10/- for females and juniors, for
"as long as the strike shall last"; with the same benefits in the
case of a lockout. For non-members who supported a strike,
the Executive Council was given power to make weekly allowances not exceeding half of what was paid to members, but
which would not be made in the event of a lockout. A new rule
embodying these proposals was adopted with what the Executive
described as "practical unanimity".

So — in twenty years the wheel had completed the circle.
First, the Manchester District Association of Co-operative
Employees had flinched from the name of Trade Union, then
it had become a Union but without providing for full Trade
Union action. Next it had adopted a wages policy, still hoping
that it could be implemented by persuasion. Now, after much
hard experience and much heart-searching, it had decided that
when all else had failed it would use the last sanction of a free
Trade Union — it would strike.

The strike clause was no paper tiger. The first stoppage was
in 1912 at the CWS Avonmouth flour mill. The Union lost that
dispute when it went before the Joint Committee of Trades
Unionists and Co-operators which, under the auspices of the
TUC and the Co-operative Union, had existed since 1893 to
conciliate or arbitrate on disputes between Co-operative
employees and societies. Moving a year ahead of the time span
of this chapter, there were disputes in 1913 with the Grays
(Essex), Warrington, Lincoln, Leeds and Coalburn (Scotland)
societies. The Executive reported "At the two first named places
a settlement was arrived at and notices withdrawn before they
expired. At Leeds and Lincoln agreements more or less satisfactory to the Union took place within a week of the withdrawal
of labour". At Coalburn, thirty employees were still out. The
dispute began over the dismissal of a Union member on the
unsupported evidence of a customer. It was a bitter battle,
with strike-breakers brought in, violence, and, as the organiser
in charge (W. T. Scott) recalled, several warnings by the police,
that the lives of strike leaders were in danger. The strike continued to the end of 1914, when the Union called it off and
members still out, or who had not obtained other jobs, were
placed on out-of-work benefit. AUCE lost the battle but the

tenacity with which it fought increased its prestige throughout Scotland.

It was said at the beginning of this chapter that it was essential for AUCE in its early years to convince lukewarm Co-operative employees that a Union could win for them better wages, hours and conditions. We have seen the methods adopted to bring this about. How far had they succeeded by 1914, when the world lurched into war. We cannot give an exact figure of the number of societies covered, for so casual were some branches that a society could have been on the 24/– minimum or other scale for some time before the news reached Central Office. But in 1912, the Executive Council reported "So many societies have now come to recognise our minima as a matter of course, that some of our friends have been encouraged to advocate the fixing of higher rates for certain districts".

As this passage indicates, District scales were multiplying. The 1915 report lists such scales for most Districts, plus variations covering groups of societies inside Districts; Oldham and Manchester scales in the North-West, six local scales in Scotland (including the mysteriously named Old Pink Scale and the White Scale). But whatever the variety, all scales started with the Union's minimum and not infrequently went beyond it (eg the Manchester District scale went up to 28/– at 25). Considerable progress was also being made in the number of societies that had reduced the working week to 53 hours or less.

Another measure of success was the ever-increasing membership. In 1896, when discussion on the minimum began, there were 2,179 members, in 1912, 32,741.

A Union which had to spend its early years in " . . . coaxing, persuading, urging and enticing Co-operative employees to join . . . a large percentage of them regarded Trade Unionism as unnecessary in the Co-operative world, and strikes were anathema" had increased its membership fifteenfold since the minimum wage campaign began. We can end on that note. AUCE had passed the test. It had been proved that it could deliver the goods.

6 1912 — COMING OF AGE

IN 1912 AUCE members could sing of their Union "We're twenty-one today". Appropriately, the coming-of-age was celebrated in Manchester. The annual delegate meeting was held there, no longer on a divisional basis, but for the first time as a single national event. A souvenir record of 21 years progress was published and a memorable social gathering was held prior to the meeting, not only for delegates, but for any members who could come into the city for the evening. Among them were pioneers of the original Manchester District Association, many of them retired stalwarts who could tell younger members how they had braved the frowns of committee or manager in forming a branch, and perhaps warn them that there were battles still to be won.

It will be noted that 1912 was the first *national* annual delegate meeting. The Executive Council had been working towards this reform for some time. The increase in the number of District Councils, each holding its own regional version of the ADM (although for decision-making the votes were aggregated), had led to seven meetings by 1909. For 1910 this was reduced to three; one for Lancashire, Yorkshire, Ireland and the North Midlands, one for the South Midlands, South and West of England and South Wales, and the third for Scotland and the North of England.

This was administratively a tidier system. But the case for a single national meeting did not rest on administrative convenience. AUCE must stand or fall as a national Union, seen to be such by employers and other Unions, felt to be such by its members. Regional meetings could encourage regional attitudes, blur the wider vision, and the change was accepted as a means of concentrating and symbolising the national character of the Union. District conferences continued to be held, however, and frequently policy issues were remitted to them — and to branches — for discussion before they reached the annual delegate meeting. Consultation at geographical level and at specialist trade and professional level is still intensive within USDAW. But since 1912 policy decision has been the prerogative of the national "Parliament" of the Union.

Previous chapters have dealt with the highlights of the first twenty-one years, in particular the development from comparative placidity to a fighting policy on wages and conditions. But the Union was also branching out in many other directions. In particular, it was establishing links within the wider working class movement.

The first was with the Trade Union Congress, or the Parliamentary Committee of the TUC, as it was then generally known. A proposal to affiliate was brought before the annual meeting of 1898 by the Executive Council. It was accepted, but with some reluctance. The Yorkshire and Northern meetings voted against, some delegates (according to the report in *Gleanings*) " . . . contending that the Congress was becoming so much of a Party Political organisation as to render inadvisable the close connection with it of Co-operative employees". But Manchester was in favour, and provided an overall majority of twenty for affiliation. A year later the Union was represented for the first time at the Congress of the TUC, held that year at Plymouth.

Political action through membership of the Labour Party was an even more contentious subject. The Union was still strongly influenced by what could be called, without disrespect, and Old Guard of Liberals. They could accept TUC affiliation at a pinch, but in their belief, support for Lib-Lab MPs was as far as Trades Unions ought to go in politics. They successfully resisted early attempts to bring AUCE into the Labour Party. But both the law and the revival of interest in Socialism were turning the tide towards independent working class politics. The law was invoked against Trades Unions in two notorious Court judgments: in the Taff Vale case of 1901, which crippled the right to strike, and the Osborne case of 1909, which had a similar effect on the right to spend money for political purposes. These decisions were overruled by subsequent legislation. But at the time thoughtful workers in AUCE and other Unions saw them as class discrimination which could only be defeated by political action.

The annual meeting of 1905 voted for politics and a year

E

later the rules were altered to authorise membership of the Labour Representation Committee, as the Party was originally named, and expenditure of Union funds for local and Parliamentary purposes. For a period the Union's involvement was limited mainly to representation at the annual Party conference. But in 1908 R. J. Wilson, President of the Northern District Council, was elected to the Labour Party executive and in 1910 the ADM decided to seek Parliamentary representation, the choice of a potential MP to be made by ballot. Fourteen members came forward, five withdrew and the rest went on to the vote, from which R. J. Wilson emerged as the Union's nominee to go on the Labour Party's list of approved Parliamentary candidates. Later, the Union was to be briefly out of the Party, and for a period not quite in and not quite out — but these adventures belong to future chapters.

In chapter 3 we saw that AUCE and the National Amalgamated Union of Shop Assistants were formed within a few days of each other. In 1895 the Shop Assistants' Union invited AUCE to become affiliated, but nothing came of that proposal. By 1912 they were the only two medium-sized Unions in the distributive trades. The Shop Assistants' had members in Co-operative service but by far the greater number of Co-operative employees was in AUCE. From time to time there were discussions on amalgamation, usually direct between the two Unions, on occasion under the auspices of the TUC. But AUCE, while in favour of joint action, did not believe that there would be any virtue in outright amalgamation. It argued that the number of unorganised workers in the private distributive trades was so enormous that to turn two comparatively small Unions into one would not make a worthwhile impact on the problem. It would however, probably dilute and weaken the efforts through which AUCE was winning improved conditions in the Co-operative sector of distribution.

The Shop Assistants' considered that an amalgamated Union should confine itself to distributive workers. AUCE, based as it was on the diversified operations of the Co-operative Movement, took in productive and service workers in the retail societies, the CWS and the Scottish CWS (although, by a decision of 1903, it excluded craft workers for whom there was an appropriate Union unless they continued membership of their craft Union as well as AUCE).

There was also a difference of opinion over benefit funds. AUCE held to the principle that the advance or defence of wages and conditions took precedence over all other purposes, including benefit provision. Basically the Union operated on only two funds, a general fund and one for political purposes (the latter required by law) and, as we shall see later, it did not hesitate to reduce benefit provision in a time of crisis. This policy had a practical base in the substantial degree of stability in Co-operative service. Most members of the Shop Assistants' Union, however, worked in private trade, where employment was much more hazardous. That Union fought some redoubtable battles on behalf of its members, but it also placed a high priority on the separation and safeguarding of its benefit funds, and this factor was a recurring difficulty in amalgamation discussions.

AUCE continued to press for joint action on common purposes, leading to a federal organisation which would include both distributive and service (eg, clerical) workers. A joint action programme with NAUSA was agreed in 1906. It included a provision that organisers of either Union, when canvassing, would not seek to recruit anyone they found to be a member of the other Union. In the same year the agreement was reflected in a Trafalgar Square demonstration to protest against the exclusion of shop assistants from a Workmen's Compensation Bill than before Parliament.

A year later a federal body was formed, adopting a title which used up almost a quarter of the alphabet — National Federation of Trade Unions representing Shop Workers, Warehousemen and Clerks. The basic objects rule was "To combine for trade purposes, to secure unity of action" between the members. The members were AUCE, National Amalgamated Union of Shop Assistants and the National Union of Clerks, shortly to be joined by the Railway Clerks' Association.

The Federation did some useful work in such matters as organising a petition in support of a Shops' Hours Bill (AUCE branches secured about half of the 80,000 signatures), agitating against living-in (yes, that abomination was still in existence), and in mediating in disputes between AUCE and the Shop Assistants' Union over recruitment and other activities, particularly in Scotland. But for one reason or another, relations between the two Unions continued to deteriorate. No doubt there were faults on both sides but it was the Shop Assistants' who brought the issue to open war on a national scale.

A further attempt to amalgamate the two distributive Unions had been made by the TUC in 1913. AUCE stood by the principle that the service (clerical) Unions should also be brought in. Rather than immediate amalgamation, it proposed they should plan for a more active and militant Federation. That was the breaking point for NAUSA, which persisted in pressing for a two-part amalgamation of the distributive Unions (although it must have known that AUCE's annual meeting of 1912 had voted against amalgamation by a large majority). The Shop Workers' National Executive served notice on AUCE that all agreements on canvassing and organising Co-operative workers were ended. All Co-operative societies were informed that the NAUSA was the Union for the distributive trades and must have a voice in any settlement for shop workers. Thereafter, NAUSA left the Federation, which broke up. It was to be open war between the two Unions for some years, plus, as we shall see in the next Chapter, a widening gap between AUCE and the TUC.

Next in influence to wages and conditions was a soundly based benefit scheme. We saw the first scale of benefits and contributions in Chapter 3. The scales were adjusted from time to time during the first two decades and because of lack of support provision for superannuation was dropped in 1907, contributions being returned to members. By 1912 a total of £93,972 had been paid out since benefit provision began in 1896. When the National Insurance Act came into operation on 15th July, 1912, AUCE became an Approved Society for Health Insurance purposes and thereafter the report of the National Insurance Department became a special section of the annual report.

By 1912 women were becoming an increasingly important part of the Union's membership. They were first particularised in the membership figures in 1898, when their number was only 127 — 2 in the Airedale District, 45 in Manchester, 96 in Northern (23 of them in the Annfield Plain branch, which also had the largest total membership — 142 — in the District). By 1912 there were 3,014 women in a total national membership of 32,741. Northern District was still ahead with 754 women members.

There was fear that low-wage women workers would replace men. But, perversely — as it was reported to a Sunderland conference in 1908 — some branches refused to take the obvious course of inviting them into the Union. A letter from Mari Yarworth in a 1908 issue of *The Co-operative Employee* declared "It is not our desire to oust men from positions; our aim is to attain a higher standard of efficiency, to obtain better work and better pay, to obtain equal educational advantages for the making of better saleswomen, clever dressmakers, artistic milliners and capable manageresses".

The AUCE also had close links with the Women's Co-operative Guild which since 1906 had been campaigning for a minimum wage for women in Co-operative service, particularly in the factories of the CWS. There were joint committees with the Guild in AUCE districts and close contact in many branches where the Guild was an ally in working for acceptance of the minimum wage for Co-operative shop workers.

The Legal Department of a Trade Union rarely gets a thought from members — until they need it, when, for a time, it can become a major factor in personal or family affairs. From early days the Executive minutes record payments for legal advice and assistance. Illegal deductions from wages, compensation in cases of accident, shortages of cash or goods, wages in sickness, slander of Union members; on these and other hazards AUCE provided a shield of law in cases where the individual employee would virtually have been helpless against an arbitrary decision of committee or manager. Grocery workers were warned by the legal department against one new hazard of shop life in the annual report for 1909, when it was reported that "A terrible accident resulting in the death of a member should make everyone employed in a grocery department alive to the new peril in shop life caused by the introduction of bacon-cutting machines, and the necessity of fixing them securely on counters or elsewhere".

Throughout the first twenty-one years the Employment Register continued to provide a useful service. During the period there had been 1,822 applications by societies for names of "servants" (the term was still being used in 1912, although "employees" was gradually being substituted). These societies had been supplied with 7,731 names, and 489 appointments had been made. Rank and file employees were not the only ones to use the service. General, departmental and branch managers and secretaries were on the 1912 list.

Many other events of the first twenty-one years can only briefly be mentioned. The Union began the interest in international affairs which continues to this day. The first direct overseas contact was with the German Co-operative Shop Assistants' Union in 1901. AUCE was represented at the Congress of the International Co-operative Alliance held in Manchester in 1902 and for some years subscribed to the funds of the ICA. In 1908 it affiliated to the International Federation of Employees in the Distributive Trades, and in 1910 to the Scottish TUC. In 1903 A. Hewitt was elected to the Board of the Co-operative Newspaper Society now Co-operative Press; a representation which has continued down to the present time. Educational work was continuous in the columns of *The Co-operative Employee*, pamphlets, conferences and association with the Co-operative Union through a seat on its Central Educational Committee and participation at district level. There had been a small beginning in persuading societies to include a fair wages clause in their rules, and rather more success in establishing Trade Union membership as a condition of employment (in the annual report for 1913 60 societies were named as following this practice).

When so many men and women give their time and energy to a cause it is a delicate task to name individuals. But three must be mentioned before this chapter ends. In 1897 J. Dyson failed to secure re-election as General President and was succeeded by T. Howe (Sunderland). And at the Executive meeting of 26th November, 1901, J. (Joseph) Hallsworth, aged 17, member of the Droylsden branch, was appointed to the staff on a wage of 15/- a week. We shall see much more of him in later chapters.

PART 2

THE WAR OF 1914-18 — AND THE ROAD THAT LED TO NUDAW

7 AUCE IN THE FIRST WORLD WAR—1

Break with the TUC: A National Policy:
Open membership

WE now move into an ominous year — 1914. The world was delusively peaceful, or, at least, with no more cause for concern than the habitual bickering among nations. Many people believed that it was no longer possible for the great powers to wage war on each other. Had not Sir Norman Angell demonstrated in *The Great Illusion* (published in 1910 and translated into twenty-five languages) that the consequences for victors and vanquished alike would be so terrible that no nation could contemplate them? His was the illusion. On 1 August, 1914, Germany declared war on Russia. On 4 August Britain declared war on Germany; France, Austria-Hungary, Belgium, Serbia all joined in. The streets of Berlin, Paris, London, Moscow, Vienna, Budapest were filled by crowds cheering the outbreak of war.

Those who cheered no doubt saw it as the great adventure, a new excitement in dull lives, with one's own side to be welcomed home as victors after a few weeks or months of glory. Few realised how long such evenly matched powers could batter each other or on the toll that must be paid in lives before one side was forced to admit defeat. And none of those who cheered in the streets of the great capitals on those sunny August days of 1914 could even dimly have imagined that twenty-five years and one month later their sons and grandsons would be facing a second and even more destructive war. This time, without cheers.

But that is for future chapters. Here, we are concerned with the experience of AUCE between 1914 and the immediate post-war years. For the Union, it was a period of sorrow and of crisis in its own affairs. Sorrow at the loss of hundreds of young members who died in the endless and usually futile offensives on the Western front, on the seas and in other theatres of war. Crisis because AUCE's very right to exist was challenged by other Unions. Yet, paradoxically, but for this challenge AUCE might have remained a comparatively small organisation specialising in distributive employees of the Co-operative Movement. The influential and widespread USDAW of today was, in fact, conceived and born in conflicts of Trades Union policy fought out more than sixty years ago. This turning point in the Union's story is the main subject of the present chapter.

The issue arose largely through the structure of the Trades Union Movement and the trading success of Co-operative Societies. There was no standard basis of organisation for Trades Unions at the turn of the century (nor is there today, for that matter). Craft and skilled Unions operating, or professing to operate, nationally had great influence in the TUC, but the New Unionism had brought in an influx of general Unions with loosely defined (sometimes undefined) fields of recruitment. Long established single-industry Unions such as the Miners' and the Railwaymen, had broadened their base to become industrial Unions, taking in anyone, regardless of craft, who worked in or around the mines or railways. Occupational Unions in the public service had similar all-in objectives.

AUCE was entirely based on the Co-operative Movement and at this stage in its history had no desire to go outside. But the very success of the Movement raised recruitment problems for the Union. Societies, according to enterprise and size, spread out into most of the main consumer trades, including productive operations in bakeries, tailoring, clog making and boot and shoe repairing, and services such as clerical, transport, maintenance. The CWS and the Scottish CWS were even more diversified in their range of employment. Many retail societies were small and might employ only a couple of bakers, a tailor, a clogmaker, a boot repairer, one or two carters, and so on. There were craft and general Unions that claimed to cater for these and other productive or service trades carried on in the Movement. But because of the small numbers involved and the distance from any branch of an appropriate Union, more often than not these other Unions did nothing to organise Co-operative workers except, in some cases, in the large city societies.

There was only one Union on the spot — AUCE. It had 667

branches (many covering more than one society) when this issue first came before the TUC in 1911. It was understandable that many productive workers would seek to join their distributive colleagues in the only local Union available to them, one, moreover, which provided good benefit scales and had proved its ability to look after its members. There is evidence in speeches and writings of the period that some leaders of AUCE, particularly J. Hallsworth, were advocates of industrial Unionism. But the Union did not seek actively to recruit all the workers, productive and distributive, in Co-operative service. There is no evidence that justifies the accusation, later to be made, that AUCE sought deliberately to poach from craft Unions. As we saw in the last chapter, in 1903 the Executive had instructed branches "that piece workers and others engaged in trades which have effective and available Unions of their own, must not be accepted as members unless they are at the same time members of the Unions connected with their respective trades, and willing to continue such membership".

Some of the craft Unions, however, began to cast a jealous eye not only on recruitment of new productive workers but on the membership of those who had been in AUCE for many years. The Shop Assistants' Union, too, was sharpening its axe for open war with AUCE. To some degree, AUCE was to become the scapegoat for wider conflicts over Trades Union organisation. The first clash came at the Newcastle TUC of 1911. AUCE had submitted a resolution calling on Co-operative Societies to be willing to receive deputations of employees on questions affecting employment, and to allow them to be accompanied by their Union representatives. The Amalgamated Society of Tailors proposed as an amendment to add words instructing the Parliamentary Committee " . . . to enquire into the bona-fides of the Co-operative Employees' Union from a Trade Union standpoint". This was, effectively, a separate resolution, but rather than have two debates the AUCE representatives somewhat rashly agreed to it being added to their own resolution, and it was carried.

In due course the enquiry took place, a number of craft and general Unions, together with AUCE, giving evidence to a sub-committee set up by the Parliamentary Committee. The recommendations of the sub-committee were presented to the Newport Congress of 1912. They were: "1. That the Co-operative Employees' Union should refrain from accepting as members workers in skilled trades, for whom separate and well recognised Unions had been established. 2. That where such workers have been admitted to membership the Co-operative Employees' Union should insist that they retain membership of their own craft Union, and see the craft Union card at least once per quarter in accordance with their own rules". J. Hallsworth, for AUCE, accepted this as "satisfactory to our organisation".

This view was endorsed by a special meeting of AUCE on Easter Monday, 1913, which reaffirmed the Executive decision of 1903 by embodying in the Rules a provision that "Applications for membership shall not be entertained from persons employed in productive departments or workshops" where there were "effective Unions of their own". It was, however, a reluctant decision. W. Orchard, member of the Executive Council for the Southern District, probably spoke for the instinctive feelings of many members when he contended that every class of worker employed in the Co-operative Movement should logically be with AUCE. If, he said, the TUC was against the Union on that point, then it would be for the AUCE to go its own way. Nevertheless, the Union had accepted the right of the TUC to carry out the enquiry, its case had been heard, it had accepted the decision announced at Congress and it would have been democratically indefensible to reject the recommendations at so late a stage. The exclusion rule was adopted by 312 votes to 35. More than 600 applications for membership from productive workers which had been held up during the enquiry were returned with the entrance fee and a letter to each applicant suggesting that he should join his craft Union. AUCE had accepted an adverse verdict in the interests of Trades Union unity, and expected that to end the matter. Unfortunately, it did not. But before we reach the next, and critical, stage, a digression is necessary.

The special delegate meeting of 1913 had another purpose, more directly related to the needs of the Union's members. In the Executive Council and many branches there was a feeling that the Union was losing impetus in the drive to improve wages and conditions. A stronger sense of urgency was required and the objectives should be defined more clearly, both in total and in detail. This issue was brought before the special meeting in proposals for action on a broad front, with a national policy that would bring together in one programme demands that had previously been fought for piecemeal.

The programme was to increase pressure for the minimum wage scales of the District Councils not simply through the Districts or individual branches but in a national demand to all the societies in which AUCE had members; to seek a maximum working week of, first, 53 hours, with a phased reduction to 48 and the abolition of excessive overtime; eliminate overwork caused by inadequate staffing, regulate the proportion of junior to adult workers; and for none but Trades Union labour to be employed.

There was to be a timetable which envisaged that the policy should be carried out by 30th September, 1913. It was to be communicated to all societies in which the Union had members with a request that it should be introduced, in its entirety where necessary, or in part where some of the provisions were already observed. In cases where it met with a hostile reception, those branches that were sufficiently organised were, first, to try pressure on the recalcitrant committee through members' meetings and public opinion, and if this failed, to strike.

When strike action was necessary, the General President, T. Howe, emphasised that the Union would not accept the adjudication of the Joint Committee of Trade Unionists and Co-operators, on the grounds that " ... the right to strike claimed so vigorously by the Trade Union Congress and at Labour Party Conferences should not be denied to Co-operative employees". Moreover, said the President, the Joint Committee was based on the principle of compulsory arbitration " ... to which, in common with the great majority of Trades Unionists generally, we are opposed".

Finally, this new forward policy was to be financially under-written by a "war chest" of £10,000 to be raised through levies. Following a long discussion *The Co-operative Employee* reports that "Amidst a scene of great enthusiasm the resolution adopting the policy of the Executive Council, and giving them the mandate and power to carry it out, was unanimously adopted".

It was certainly a bold programme. Some might have said

it was a rash one, for it was inconceivable that it could be realised throughout the Co-operative Movement in the 188 days between Easter Monday (25th March) and 30th September. But the Executive probably had psychological as well as practical targets in its sights. Increasing membership had induced a degree of apathy and some sectionalism in the attitude of Districts towards the national purpose of the Union. A national policy attacking grievances that were common to employees everywhere was a healthy antidote to sectionalism and a stimulant to the apathetic.

The policy would also be intended to shake the nerves of those societies that refused to give wages and conditions consistent with Co-operative principles, a subject on which *The Co-operative News* leader of 29th March, 1913, commented " . . . it is not pleasant to have to repeat that had it not been for Co-operative employees being represented . . . by a Union many of them would not have been in as good a position as they are tobay with regard to wages . . . AUCE must have found out long ago that where Trade Unionists have become Co-operative 'masters', they have in too many cases not been always too ready to grant conditions to employees that they are always seeking for themselves".

We shall "report progress" with the national policy later. Now, we must return to the main issue of this chapter — the Union's relations with the TUC. All seemed well after the agreement to refrain from recruiting productive workers. Unfortunately, some of the craft Unions could not leave well alone. They returned to the attack in 1913 with an appeal to the Parliamentary Committee to rule that its adjudication was intended to be retrospective. There were more hearings, more arguments, and eventually the Parliamentary Committee stated its intention to report to the 1914 TUC that it considered the findings of eighteen months earlier *were* intended to be retropective. Not only was AUCE to be limited mainly to Co-operative shop workers; every baker, tailor, clog maker, boot repairer already in the Union, some with many years of membership, was to be thrown out. And to rub salt in the wound, this was to be done at a time when many of the would-be members rejected under the 1912 findings were still outside any Union; the Executive report for 1913 stating " . . . little or no effort having been made by the respective Unions concerned to enrol them".

It was an intolerable decision, reflecting more the Parliamentary Committee's reluctance to stand up to craft Unions than any respect for equity, or even for commonsense. A Union deputation met the Committee on 14th May, 1914, in an unsuccessful attempt to persuade it to withdraw the retrospective finding. All they gained was a decision to refer the whole issue to the Trade Union Congress due to be held in Portsmouth in September (the Congress was cancelled because of the outbreak of war). Neither the Executive Council nor the membership of AUCE were prepared to remain in limbo between May and September. A special delegate meeting was called for 26th July, 1914, and made two major decisions. One was that "under no circumstances" would AUCE accept the retrospective interpretation of the award of 1912. The other was that if they lost the day at Portsmouth there should be immediate "secession of our Union from the TUC".

We have now reached the end of a long and frustrating trail, marked by the jealousy of some Unions at the growth of AUCE, the timidity of the Parliamentary Committee as it was then constituted and, indeed, by the reluctance of AUCE itself to break with the historic industrial organisation of the Labour Movement. The turning point came at the Leicester ADM held over Easter Sunday and Monday, 1915 (4th/5th April). One decision reaffirmed the resolution of the previous year's special meeting by empowering the Executive Council " . . . to withdraw from the Trade Union Congress immediately they feel our status as a Trade Union will be jeopardised by remaining affiliated". More significant was a resolution from the Manchester Central branch "That all persons engaged in Co-operative employment be eligible to apply for, and, subject to the confirmation of the Executive Council, be admitted to membership of the Union . . .".

J. Hallsworth, in moving, said they already had in membership bakers, painters, flour millers, laundry workers, soap workers, lard and butter makers, fellmongers, shoe makers and repairers, chemists, jewellers, bacon curers, jam workers, tea packers, tailors, carters, vanmen, motormen, printers, shop assistants and all kinds of warehousemen, clerks and

general labourers and even *poets*. (The poets must remain a
fascinating mystery; but how delightful if one could have traced
a group of rhymsters, historically the lowest paid of all, who
had banded together under the banner of AUCE!) He cited
the CWS and some of the larger retail societies as bodies under
single control but with employees either unorganised or divided
over many Unions, some of them "craft Unions with their
miserable little groups peddling away for their own edification
and satisfaction". Their quarrel with the TUC was not on
principle "but rather on the form of organisation" and if they
had to "slip away in grief, they would come back again". The
resolution was carried by an "overwhelming majority".

It is virtually certain that Hallsworth himself, and many of
those who supported him, were well aware of the wider impli-
cations of this historic decision. It would not be by chance that
he catalogued the great variety of trades represented in Co-
operative service. For the logical next question was: Why stop
at the Co-ops? The "open door", as the new policy was
described was still only ajar. Why not open it fully, to organise
and seek to lead in the vast army of private trade distributive,
service, and some productive workers still outside any Union?
That was soon to become the policy of AUCE and we can
properly date the beginning of the present USDAW from the
1915 debate in the Secular Hall, Leicester.

Three months after the ADM the Executive Council exercised
the power given to it and notified the TUC of its withdrawal,
citing first the Union's refusal to accept the retrospective
application of the 1912 findings, and secondly, the Leicester
decision to open the ranks to all Co-operative employees
" ... which makes the aforesaid findings nugatory". A similar
notice of withdrawal was sent to the Scottish TUC.

It was to be only a temporary break. AUCE was too much
part of the mainstream of the British Labour Movement to
remain permanently in the shallows. But the immediate effect
was a challenge to the Union's right to exist, organised and led
by a Federation of Trades Unions, self-styled as "representing
Co-operative employees". The Federation, or at any rate, some
of its members, was almost vulture-like in the avidity with
which it sought to destroy and devour AUCE. It was contended
that AUCE "was not a Trade Union" because it was no longer

in the TUC; an argument which, apart from its basic falsity, ignored the fact that other powerful Unions had at times been outside the Congress over issues of policy. The Miners' and Railwaymen's Unions were already organising all workers, regardless of craft, who were employed in their industries. But they did not suffer the national obloquy that was levelled at the Co-operative Employees' Union. Attempts were made to have the Union expelled from Trades Councils. During the war years there were major strikes within the Co-operative Movement, mainly over war bonuses and wage increases, and some of the Federation Unions were prepared to blackleg the AUCE. The management committees of some societies also sought to influence their employees to leave AUCE for the Shop Assistants or craft Unions.

There is no point, however, in reciting details of these battles long ago, fought against the awesome background of what up to then was the most devastating war in history. AUCE suffered some sore wounds, but its members showed by their loyalty (and the increase in their number) that it truly reflected their interests. In the words of the classical zoological phrase, AUCE proved that "this animal is dangerous, if attacked it defends itself". By the early years of peace the heat was cooling. If it was not loved by its former opponents in the Trades Union Movement, AUCE was accepted, and had to be dealt with sensibly on common issues of Trades Union action and organisation.

More important for the future than this fratricidal conflict was a decision of a special delegate meeting in Leeds on 7th January, 1917. Executive Council and members had recognised that once the door to membership had been opened by the decision of 1915, it could not remain half open and half shut. At Leeds the Executive declared that it should be opened wide and free. The meeting had before it a resolution proposing to amend the constitution by " . . . the opening of a separate section for membership of and to which such persons engaged in commercial employment and as allied workers shall be eligible to apply and be admitted as the Executive Council may determine". Or, to disentangle the verbiage, to accept members from the whole field of distribution and commerce, private as well as Co-operative. A second resolution altered the title of

F

the Union to "Amalgamated Union of Co-operative and Commercial Employees and Allied Workers". But the Executive knew that while the new title might be descriptive, a mouthful like AUCCEAW was not likely to pass into common usage. So it was provided that "the short title shall continue to be 'the AUCE'."

The principal speaker for this revolutionary change in the Union was the General Secretary, J. Hallsworth. He spoke at length of the changes that were likely to follow the end of the war. Many of the thousands of Union members in the Forces would not return to Co-operative service. Were they to be allowed to drift away from the Union? Many of the women who had replaced men and were also in the Union would not "go back to mending socks" but would continue in industry. Were they, too, to be lost? There were an estimated one-and-a-half million shop assistants, clerks, commercial travellers and warehousemen in the distributive trades and only a small proportion had been organised. AUCE should play its part in bringing them under a Trade Union banner.

He visualised that the Union's new role could be the beginning of federal arrangements with other Unions that had employees in Co-operative service, with transfer arrangements so that no distributive or commercial worker who changed his job need be outside the scope of an appropriate Union. His speech, inadequately summarised here, fills six-and-a-half pages of *The Co-operative Employee*. An exhaustive discussion fills another five-and-a-half pages and at the end of the day the first of the two resolutions mentioned earlier was carried on a card vote by 22,929 votes to 4,022, more than the two-thirds majority required for an alteration of rules. The change of name was adopted by a similar majority. The new General Section was formed immediately after the special meeting at Leeds and by the end of 1917 had 1,686 members.

The ordinary meeting at Easter, 1918, carried matters a stage further. It adopted a resolution authorising the Executive to negotiate with other Unions in the Co-operative and private fields to join in drafting a scheme for amalgamation into one industrial Union, alternatively to form a federation for trade and political purposes.

The prime mover in this profound change in Union direction

and policy was undoubtedly J. Hallsworth. Many members believed instinctively that the Union should take in all who worked in Co-operative service. Hallsworth articulated this feeling, expressed it in terms of logical development, extended it to include the amorphous mass of distributive and general workers who were only fractionally involved in Trades Unionism. He looked to horizons which for long it was beyond the Union's resources to reach. But more than sixty years ago he foresaw the widely diversified Union of today, and in all the hardships and anxieties of a bitter war the delegates at Leeds had the courage to join him in his vision.

So after 26 years the AUCE was out in the big wide world. In 1891 it was a small benefit and mutual improvement association. In 1894 it became a Trade Union with moral force as its only sanction. In 1897 it took the first step towards full Trade Union action by adopting a wages policy. In 1911 it became a fighting Union backed by a strike fund. In 1915 it became an occupational Union by opening the door to anyone employed in the Co-operative Movement. In 1917 it now became a general Union, still predominantly based in the Co-operative Movement but with the world of distributive and commercial industry and service as its oyster. In the remainder of this book we shall follow the Union through many crises and triumphs in this wider world.

8 AUCE IN THE FIRST WORLD WAR—2

The lost generation: "Substituted females":
Conciliation: yes, no, maybe in politics

DURING the second World War the censorship of the Press and other media was qualified through confidential briefings of newspaper editors and specialist correspondents given by Ministers and senior officers of the Forces. The writer recalls a meeting of this sort addressed by Ernest Bevin, then Minister of Labour and National Service, on Government plans for increased mobilisation and direction of workers to serve in war industry. The details I have forgotten, but one remark by the Minister remained in my memory.

Describing the problems involved in organising the entire adult population for war purposes, Bevin said that they constantly came up against what had come to be called the "lost generation". The craftsmen, technicians, planners, organisers and managers whose experience and skill should have been at the service of the nation between 1939 and 1945, but who lay buried in tens of thousands of graves in France and Flanders, killed in the first World War, lost to life and the community before they had fully begun to live. Reading the issues of *The Co-operative Employee* (which became *The AUCE Journal* in 1917) from 1914 to the immediate post-war years brought Bevin's "lost generation" poignantly back to memory. In most months a Roll of Honour was published, giving names, age, unit, rank and peacetime Co-operative employment of Union members who had been killed or died of wounds on land or sea, and for whom funeral benefit was paid to relatives. The total was 2,103. And by far the greater number were young men in their middle twenties. Many were aged 18 or 19. Truly a lost generation, not only in Britain, for in every other belligerent country it was the young who died.

In both world wars the distributive and commercial trades

were called upon for a great contribution in manpower. As early as the summer of 1915 a conference of employers and employed in the trades was told by the then Prime Minister, H. H. Asquith, that up to the middle of April 260,000 shop assistants had voluntarily joined the Forces. If clerks, commercial travellers and miscellaneous jobs connected with shops were added, the volunteers numbered 430,000 and there were 360,000 of military age still in civil employment.

AUCE's record of recruitment to the services can have had few equals in other occupational groups. Shop work, particularly in grocery, which was the basic Co-operative trade, was still predominantly a male occupation and when the war began 80 per cent of the male members of the Union were of military age. Of these, and others who reached recruitment age during the war, 60 per cent — 25,297 — joined the Forces. Their sacrifice in lives was given earlier, to which could be added the great but unknown number who suffered wounds which in many cases weakened or shortened their days.

Throughout that war, distribution was repeatedly combed for manpower; for the Army as the generals demanded more men to replace the casualties of each successive and usually unsuccessful "big push", for industry as older shop workers were drafted into war work to release younger men for the Services. When conscription was introduced in 1916 (it was not abolished until 1920) many of the tribunals, set up to adjudicate on pleas by employers for the exemption of key workers, were loth to regard shop work as essential. Moreover, there were cases where tribunals blatantly discriminated against Co-operative societies (this was one of the factors which led the Co-operative Movement to end three quarters of a century of political neutrality, and establish its own political Party in 1917). AUCE joined in Co-operative protests that women could not entirely replace men and in warning that the vital business of civilian food supply would break down if it was denuded of experienced workers. These protests led to an instruction by the Director-General of Recruiting at the Ministry of National Service in the Spring of 1918 that it was "essential that the staffs employed in food distribution should not be so depleted as to cause serious inefficiency" and temporary exemption had to be given " ... to any man who may reasonably be considered ...

essential to such business". But by then the war was nearing its end, and the damage had been done.

Many of the Union's staff volunteered or were called up. Active branch secretaries and District Council members disappeared into uniform. So heavy was the loss that for a time elections to fill Council vacancies could not be held. It was decided that Council members who joined up should be allowed to complete their term on return to Co-operative service and temporary measures only taken to fill the vacancies. Elections were resumed in 1918. As we saw in the last chapter the Union's wartime difficulties were compounded by the controversy with the TUC and the Federation of craft and other Unions claiming to be the true representatives of Co-operative employees. In spite of these problems AUCE was remarkably successful in retaining gains already made for its members and solving the special problems created by the war.

Once the myth popular in 1914 that "The war will be over by Christmas" had died out and it became obvious that great numbers of women would be replacing men in the shops, the Union went all out to organise these potential recruits. It was Union policy that "substituted females" (as they were called) should be paid the same rate, and enjoy the same conditions, as the men they replaced. There could be one month's probationary payment of AUCE female scales for women without experience, but if a woman employee was kept on after this trial, she should receive the male rate. To look after the interests of women members, and particularly to encourage them to play an active part in the work of their branches, Miss Ellen C. Wilkinson was appointed in July, 1915, as the first woman organiser. She was later to become one of the best known of the MPs who have served the Labour Party and the Union in Parliament.

By 1916 it was reported that 70 societies (some very large) were on equal pay. But the Union did not succeed in establishing equal rates generally throughout the Co-operative Movement. The annual report for 1918 stated that while most societies were willing to accept equality of pay for women employees up to the age of 17, they would not carry the principle through to the higher ages.

By the end of the war in 1918 there were 36,422 women

members in a total membership of 87,134. The new recruits soon disproved fears that through lack of will or interest they might weaken the Union's ability to hold onto conditions won in earlier years and at the same time keep pace with a rising cost of living. There were some hard-fought strikes against Co-operative employers during the war years, and the 1916 annual report had this to say of the part played by women members: "To those who say women workers cannot be organised and have not the will to fight, we would point out the magnificent struggles waged by our newly recruited body of women members whose Trade Union spirit reminds us so forcibly of our better-seasoned male members in the struggles of pre-war days".

Another issue of the war years was the national policy adopted in 1913, and so far as wages were concerned this soon merged into campaigns to keep pace with the cost of living. During 1913 and the early part of 1914 the new policy had been backed-up by successful strikes in England and Scotland, in retail societies and in CWS flour mills. When war broke out there was a pause. As the annual report for 1914 put it "A truce was called . . . [and] on the whole it has been honoured, advantages already gained maintained intact, and the peace, thus kept". A table in the report showed that by December, 1914, 274 societies had accepted the national policy on wages, 295 on hours (53 or less per week) and 92 on the employment of Union labour only. Similar tables were published in 1915, 1916 and 1917 and by the latter year 449 societies were "into line" on wages, 458 on hours, and 151 on Union labour only. In 1918 the report stated the tables had been dropped since nearly all advances in wages by then had been "war wage advances bringing the actual remuneration far above the minimum laid down in our national policy".

Most of the wartime scale increases or war bonuses were negotiated peacefully. But there were many cases where increases were settled by a test of strength. For instance, the August, 1917, meeting of the Executive Council noted satis-factory settlements of four disputes, one of an agreed reference to arbitration, and in six cases authorised strike action if necessary. One particularly bitter dispute with the powerful Plymouth Society lasted for eleven weeks in 1916, and the best that could be claimed was that it ended in a draw, which left AUCE in a weakened position in the Society. In this dispute the Union was allied with the Transport Workers' Union and there are references in reports and minutes to "E. Bevan", later more correctly identified as E. Bevin, soon to become nationally known as the architect of the present Transport and General Workers' Union.

We saw in previous chapters that AUCE moved only slowly and reluctantly towards a militant policy. It had certainly proved itself a "bonny fighter" when it felt it must fight or surrender cherished objectives. But the Union did not glory in industrial battle. It was pacific in principle, and basically, the same could be said of the Co-operative Movement. Both stemmed from common working class roots and ideals and from 1914 onwards they began to search for means which would reduce if they could not totally eliminate the risks of conflict between them.

Hours and Wages Boards were being established by retail societies under the auspices of the Co-operative Union. Initially, AUCE was opposed to them on the grounds that they could only be effective if they were jointly representative of employers and employees (this was actually the case in the Northern District). But by the latter years of the war the Union was beginning to accept them as an established part of the Co-operative scene, and, in any case, their purpose was negotiation rather than conciliation. But even for that purpose many societies refused to join the Wages Board machinery, and for them individual negotiations were necessary.

The Union still refused to recognise the authority of the Joint Committee of Trade Unionists and Co-operators. In AUCE's view the Committee's procedures prohibited, or severely restricted the right of Co-operative Workers to strike, and also prescribed compulsory arbitration, both of them provisions which were rejected by Trades Unionists generally. These objections were frequently expressed in resolutions, speeches and print, although, as we shall see later, the Union was to use the Committee's services in the settlement of some post-war disputes.

Immediately, however, we are concerned with moves to replace the Committee with a more satisfactory form of

conciliation. Discussions with the Co-operative Union led in
1915 to the adoption by the Co-operative Congress and the
Union's ADM of a National Conciliation Board of five AUCE
representatives and five from the Co-operative Union, plus
eight District Boards of four from each side. The National
Board had an independent chairman who could arbitrate if
both sides agreed. Any dispute which could not be settled by a
District Board had to go to the National body. It was optional
upon either party to use the machinery or not. The Boards had
some success in the latter years of the war, but by the early
twenties they had ceased to be used.

In a previous chapter we noted that there was one period in
which AUCE was in the Labour Party, another when it was out
and a third when it was neither in nor out. The first stage was
up to early 1914, by which date the Union had been affiliated
to the Party for eight years. A new Trade Union Act in 1913
had imposed complicated conditions for the registration of
rules permitting a Union to spend money for political purposes.
To safeguard the legal position, a ballot in support of or against
political action as an object of the Union, was taken in March,
1914. The result was: 11,130 members for, 11,967 against.The
Union was out of politics by a majority of 837, and, to quote
The Co-operative Employee in commenting on the result
" . . . AUCE thereby earns the questionable distinction of being
the first among the big Trade Unions to shut itself out from the
right to take part in any sort of political action whatever . . .".
The result was a shock to the Executive Council and to the
majority of the activists in the branches, who, probably, were
partly to blame, for there is little evidence that they had done
much to explain the case for independent Labour politics to
their less active colleagues.

The lesson was taken to heart. At the annual meeting of 1915,
R. J. Davies (then manager of the National Insurance Department, later to be the first AUCE MP) moved that there should
be another ballot on Labour Party affiliation but this time
" . . . before the ballot is taken a campaign shall be carried on
among the members explaining to them the provisions of the
Act, the financial obligations . . . and their right to claim
exemption. Officials, organisers and District Councils to
educate members in the principles of Labour representation".

The resolution was carried by a large majority. Following an intensive campaign of discussion throughout the Union, the ballot took place in March, 1916, and the 1914 decision was reversed, voting being: For political action, 13,754, Against, 5,854.

But this time the Labour Party was coy! The Union was still outside the TUC. There was still hostility, and sometimes open conflict, with the anti-AUCE Federation and the Unions in that body were influential in the Labour Party and the TUC. AUCE was told that its status had been referred to the Joint Board of the Labour Party and the TUC. The Board was itself enmeshed in a spider's web of argument over industrial union-ism and craft unionism and could reach no decision. AUC couldn't get in, and it wasn't quite out. The situation became farcical at the General Election of December, 1918. In addition to the existing potential candidate, R. J. Wilson, both J. Hallsworth and R. J. Davies had been elected to the Union's Parliamentary Panel. All three fought the Election on the nomination of the local Labour Parties in Stretford, West Salford and Newcastle North, respectively, and with the endorsement of a Labour Party that hesitated to recognise their political existence! None was successful, but at least AUCE had demonstrated its fidelity to the cause of independent working class politics.

This situation continued until the post-war years when, as we shall see, the heat and fury of inter-Union hostility died down, and AUCE returned to both the TUC and the Labour Party.

By 1918 there had been a number of changes in the leadership of the Union. The General President, R. B. Howe, died suddenly in February, 1915, and in the subsequent election he was succeeded by R. B. Padley. A. Hewitt, who perhaps more than any man could be called the father of the Union, retired from the General Secretaryship in 1916, although the Executive Council retained his services in two important capacities. He remained on the committee of the Approved Society and as editor of *The Co-operative Employee;* continuing with both activities until 1920. He was succeeded by J. Hallsworth, who was elected unopposed as General Secretary on the nomination of 164 branches. In 1915 staff was replanned on the basis of

National Organisers operating from Central Office, and Organising Secretaries for the Districts. A future General President, J. Jagger, was appointed to the Secretaryship of the Yorkshire District.

It was to be a new world after 1918. Old empires gone, new nations born, old values shattered or challenged, a second Industrial Revolution on the way. AUCE was still a young Union, but shrewd leaders and loyal members had already overcome difficulties that could have wrecked a weaker organisation. They were well equipped for the harsh tests that were to come in the twenties and thirties.

9 THE ROAD THAT LED TO NUDAW

THE first World War was to have been the war to end war. The League of Nations was to be the forum in which differences would be settled without nations wrecking their economies and decimating their peoples. Here at home, Britain, in Lloyd George's words, was to become "a fit country for heroes to live in". It was a time of noble aspirations, rich in hope after the Armistice of November 11th, 1918, but soon to be proved a false dawn in the grey years of the twenties and and thirties.

There was a brief euphoria in 1919 and 1920 when to Trades Unions and other working class organisations it seemed that they could indeed look forward to building the promised land. The collapse came in 1921 and 1922, and for every year thereafter to 1939 Western capitalism was economically stagnant and millions of ordinary people were tormented by unemployment; the evils that led to Fascism and the second World War.

Neither AUCE nor any other Union had foreseen the crash and crisis of 1920/21. Governments in the victorious powers were equally unprepared, and had contributed to the crisis by the rapid dismantling of controls in the rush to return to "normal business". For AUCE the two years were the most dangerous in its history. Disaster was only averted by the loyalty of the membership and the cautious policy of past years in building up strong financial reserves. We shall return to these hectic years in the next chapter.

First, however, it is necessary to consider a development in the immediate post-war period which greatly enlarged the Union's field of operations — the first major amalgamation. AUCE had begun with an amalgamation and in 1905 there had been one other merger when the Union took over the small National Millers' Union, whose members had mainly been employed by Co-operative mills in Yorkshire. It became the nucleus of AUCE's Millers' Branch. The real expansion through amalgamation, however, began after the war.

The special meeting of 7th January, 1917, and the ordinary meeting of the same year, had opened the door to recruitment of distributive and commercial employees in private trade, and had visualised either amalgamation or a federation of Unions catering for these workers. There were early discussions with the National Warehouse and General Workers' Union, based in Liverpool, and these led in June, 1918, to an "alliance" between the two Unions as a preliminary to possible amalgamation. In August eleven other Unions were invited to a conference to discuss amalgamation or federation — the Clerks', Bakers', Tailors', Journeymen Cloggers', Butchers', Shop Assistants', Co-operative Officials', Grocers' Assistants, Boot and Shoe Operatives', Boot and Shoe Makers' and the Millers'. The first three said they would be represented by the anti-AUCE Federation, but that, most definitely, was not acceptable to AUCE. The Shop Assistants' would only discuss amalgamation of distributive workers, but not of Unions based on or including productive workers. The Cloggers', Co-operative Officials', Grocers' Assistants and Butchers' were willing to talk, but nothing came of it. The Millers' and Boot and Shoe Operatives' said No, and the Boot and Shoe Makers' did not reply. Not a very promising start.

Nothing daunted, however, AUCE turned to other Unions and continued to strengthen links with the WarehouseWorkers'. As J. Hallsworth told a special delegate meeting in October, 1918, the time for amalgamation with this Union might not immediately be ripe but " ... it would probably be of great advantage on both sides to get to know more of one another's difficulties before the psychological moment arrived when amalgamation would become possible".

The Warehousemens' Union had been founded in 1911 and was a particularly suitable partner for AUCE under the new "open door" policy. It had members in many trades where AUCE was either beginning to organise or already had a strong position. While a working arrangement would have avoided competition between them, outright amalgamation and concentration of resources would be even more effective in strengthening both Unions.

For some time discussions with the Warehousemen's Union

continued in parallel with attempts to bring about a wider amalgamation. The Shop Assistants' waived their objections to talks and in July, 1919, they took part in a joint meeting with AUCE and the Warehousemen — three representatives from each side — which declared in favour of a merger and appointed the three General Secretaries to "prepare draft proposals for giving concrete expression to this declaration". Distributive workers were to be the basis of the new Union, but productive and allied workers in trades linked to distribution "would find a place" (to quote Hallsworth), and this seemed to satisfy the Shop Assistants' insistence on the priority of distribution. A detailed scheme was duly prepared, including a provision that the new organisation should be called the "National Union of Distributive and Allied Workers" and after a lengthy debate was adopted by AUCE at a special delegate meeting in October, 1919.

So far, so good. But historical evidence demonstrates that it is easier to establish a Trade Union or a Co-operative Society than to amalgamate them once they are in existence. In the case of the Warehousemen, "Barkis was willing". The Shop Assistants' were not convinced. So the other two Unions went ahead. In the summer of 1920 each held the necessary ballot on amalgamation, and the results were conclusive. In AUCE the vote was: For 51,562, Against 3,076, with spoilt and blank papers (627), a total vote of 55,265 out of a certified membership of 88,777. The Warehouse Union vote was: For 49,745, Against 1,395 (290 spoilt papers), a vote of 51,430 out of a total membership of 96,289. Financially, AUCE was the stronger, with balance sheet assets in 1920 of £110,245 compared with £32,702 for the Warehousemens' Union.

The objects of the new Union, apart from the obvious purpose of improving wages and conditions, included "To work consistently towards securing the control of the industries in which its members are employed". The recruitment provision was widely drawn to include "all workers eligible for its membership". Those eligible were defined as " . . . any person of either sex employed wholly or mainly in any commercial occupation in connection with the retail or wholesale trades", plus such other allied workers as the annual conference might decide. Subject to the annual delegate meeting, government was to be by Executive Council, two General Secretaries and twenty members elected from the Divisions, broadly in proportion to membership. Until the ADM of 1922 the Executive Council was to consist of the aggregate of members serving on the Executives of the two Unions at the time of the merger, who would be eligible for re-election.

While the Presidency was eventually to be an elective office, the rules provided that the first holder of the office should be J. Jagger,* subject to the same re-election conditions as those applying to Executive Council members. The two General Secretaries were to be J. Hallsworth and W. A. Robinson (who held that position in the Warehousemens' Union). They were to hold office "during the will and pleasure of the members". These, and other new rules, were adopted by a joint delegate conference on 14th/15th November, 1920, to become operative from 1st January, 1921.

One immediate advantage of the amalgamation was to widen the field in which AUCE's General Section was already seeking to recruit. Another advantage was that the Warehouse workers were already in the TUC and the Labour Party, and affiliation continued with the new Union, thus bringing the AUCE element back into the fold. The disadvantage was timing. The duties of permanent officials of the two Unions had to be co-ordinated and in some cases reorganised. Administrative systems had to be standardised. Normally these adjustments could have been made at leisure. But scarcely a month was to be spared for the two formerly separate Unions to coalesce before the economic blizzard hit the country and faced the British working class with the greatest challenge since the Hungry Forties.

The formation of NUDAW was a long step along the amalgamation road. But the new Union did not regard it as a reason to pause and rest awhile. Efforts to merge with the Operative Tobacconists' Society, the Journeymen Butchers' Federation, the National Drug and Chemical Union and the Life Assurance Workers' during the period up to 1926 (when this chapter ends) were unsuccessful. But in 1920 a new source of membership was developed among Co-operative Insurance

---

* J. Jagger replaced W. B. Padley as President of AUCE in 1919; the latter having held the office since 1915.

Society agents and other staff, the Scottish Slaughtermens' and Allied Workers Union "joined up" in 1923, as did the Amalgamated Union of Fur Workers. In 1925 the Barbers' and Hairdressers' Assistants' Union joined NUDAW and the Belfast Linen Lappers' and Warehouse Workers' Union was another recruit a year later.

In one form or another, discussions with the Shop Assistants' Union over amalgamation were continued, sometimes direct between the two Unions, sometimes under the auspices of the TUC. While discussions were taking place there was a suggestion from the provisional representatives of the new Transport & General Workers' Union that NUDAW should become a member of that body, but nothing came of the idea. Of one attempt at amalgamation, chaired by C. W. Bowerman (General Secretary of the TUC) in 1921, J. Hallsworth told NUDAW's annual meeting of that year " . . . we really believed we had got to the end of what some people have described as that feud — long drawn out — between our organisation and that of the Shop Assistants". But it was not to be. Negotiations broke down over the inclusion of productive workers in an amalgamated Union. Twenty-five more years had to pass before the two Unions finally came together.

In Chapter 3 we said goodbye to the Manchester District Co-operative Employees' Association and welcomed AUCE. We now say goodbye to AUCE. It had made a name for itself in both the Trades Union and Co-operative Movements and had earned the respect which accrues to those who hold strong principles and stand by them. In subsequent chapters we shall see how, first, NUDAW, and later USDAW, have carried those principles into the remainder of the twentieth century.

PART 3

A TIME OF DANGER AND A TIME OF GROWTH

10 THE LEVY THAT SAVED THE UNION

THIS chapter is a story of crisis and conflict. Crisis for the nation in an industrial depression which in duration and intensity transcended anything that had been known before. Crisis particularly for working people. They bore the burden in unemployment and a savage reduction in their standard of living. Crisis for NUDAW and other Trades Unions. They experienced loss of membership and crippling erosion of their funds. Conflict for those Unions, of which NUDAW was one of the foremost, which fought to defend their members' standards with the weapon of last recourse — the strike.

For the Union, the story of conflict began before the amalgamation of 1921. In the last months of the war AUCE became involved in the most widespread dispute since its formation, the antagonist being the mighty CWS. In August, 1918, there was a strike in support of a wage claim at the Longsight, Manchester, Printing Works (the CWS then printed at six centres). What began as a more or less local dispute escalated into a battle over the Union's right to represent its members. The Manchester and District Printing and Kindred Trades Federation, comprising eleven Unions, claimed that it could provide for all employees in the works (although over a long period the print Unions showed no interest in the 300 or so workers, mainly women and warehousemen, who had joined AUCE). Against this background the CWS Board refused to negotiate on the pay claim, on the argument that it could only deal with all the Unions concerned.

The CWS itself was under pressure from some of its shareholders to make Trades Union membership a condition of employment. Perhaps with this in mind, and with or without its collective eyes open to the probable consequences, the Board decided to back the P&KTF by notifying the print workers on strike that they would only be reinstated if they joined " . . . the Trade Union applicable to their respective craft". This set the fire among the heather with a vengeance. It was a basic principle for AUCE that Co-operative employees had the right to join the Trade Union of their choice, and it was determined to resist any attempt by employers to restrict freedom of choice.

The immediate challenge was over the Longsight workers' strike (although there were also disputes in one or two other CWS undertakings), and in view of the Board's decision the Executive Council called for sympathetic action by CWS branches. Members came out at food, soap, clothing and other factories. By September, 1918, 7,000 were on strike, according to one report, 10,000 according to another. There was danger of the conflict spreading to retail societies through shop workers refusing to handle goods coming from the CWS. The issue came before the Trade Union Congress, where the printing Unions had the support of Unions in the anti-AUCE Federation, and the Congress called on the strikers to "become members of their respective trade [craft] Unions".

It was perhaps fortunate for future labour relations in the Co-operative Movement that wartime legislation governing industrial disputes was still in force. Under the Munitions Acts, if there appeared to be no prospect of a strike being settled in any industry which affected the war effort — as food supply from Co-operative factories certainly did — it could be ended by Royal Proclamation. This power was invoked, and the Executive Council immediately instructed members to report for work.

Three arbitrators were appointed to determine whether the CWS had the right to prescribe the Union employees should join. They found for the CWS, their ruling being that the Board had the power to prescribe that employment should "... only be given to members of the particular Trade Union applicable to their respective crafts". AUCE was also censured for withdrawing labour from essential trades during a time of war.

It was a technical defeat for the Union and there was some feeling at the next ADM that the dispute had been allowed to escalate too far, too fast. But the ultimate victory was for commonsense, for the CWS did not again try (apart from one or two local incidents, probably due more to management than to Board policy) to interfere in its employees' choice of a Trade Union, and the Longsight workers were allowed to continue their membership of AUCE. Some, however, did not get their jobs back.

Compulsory Union membership became a condition of employment in the Society in 1919. It was based on a shareholders' resolution declaring that there should be membership of a Union "... recognised for affiliation to the Trade Union Congress". There could have been another flash-point here, for it was not until AUCE was merged in NUDAW in 1921 that the Union was back in the TUC. Wisely, however, in the intervening years the CWS did not try to interpret this provision or the arbitrators' award in a manner which would have provoked further conflict.

We come now to the post-war years. They were to be the period in which the "fit country for heroes to live in" became the subject of the bitter jibe that for a great many people it was a land in which you had to be a hero to be fit to live at all. There were to be almost two decades of high unemployment. The monthly average of registered unemployed in Great Britain was 1,543,000 in 1922 and 1,514,000 in 1939. In the intervening years the figure never fell below a million. Between 1931 and 1933 one fifth of the national work force (excluding agricultural workers and those under 16) was unemployed. It was a time of retreat, or at the best, long periods of standstill, on wages and conditions, years in which the "dole" and the Means Test became part of the folk-lore of working people. For the fully employed worker, after 1927 real wages in terms of what his earnings would buy began to improve against a falling cost of living. But the unemployed, subject to a Poor Law concept of "dole" scales and to the Means Test, derived little benefit from that source.

The experience of AUCE, and, from 1921, of NUDAW, in the immediate post-war years, can be divided into three phases, extending up to 1925. While it is an arbitrary division, it covers the two years in which it was possible to improve wages and conditions, the shock and almost the paralysis of many Unions when the economy collapsed in 1921 snd — for NUDAW — the cautious moves towards improvement in standards which began around 1923.

The whole period can be epitomised in the percentages of the

Union's benefit provision represented by unemployment or
dispute and victimisation costs during each year. They were:

	Benefit expenditure as percentage of the total on —	
	Unemploy- ment percent	Dispute/ Victimisa- tion percent
1918	1.4	30
1919	15	23
1920	12	32
1921	62	16
1922	39	27
1923	18	48
1924	16	26
1925	16	28

These figures must be seen against the fact that in 1922
benefits were reduced to meet a heavy deficiency on revenue,
and were not restored until July of 1924. The high dispute/
victimisation percentage for the otherwise "prosperous" year
of 1918 would reflect the cost of the CWS strike. Nineteen-
twenty three saw another long struggle with the CWS, which is
reflected in the high percentage for that year.

To return to the earlier years. In 1919 an attempt by the
Executive to revitalise the national wages policy of 1913 was
unacceptable to the Divisions, which were then deputed to
prepare their own scales. In due course these were presented to
all Hours and Wages Boards or individual societies outside the
Wages Boards' machinery. In most Divisions reasonably
satisfactory settlements were secured, or were being negotiated
at the end of the year. But in the North-Western Section of the
Co-operative Union a selective call-out by NUDAW in one
district led to a lock-out throughout the Section. Similar
selective action in Yorkshire, however, led to a settlement
without spreading the dispute. In these two Divisions the disputes were settled on terms "which substantially benefited
practically the whole of our members concerned." The annual
report estimated that in these and the Divisions where there had
been a settlement the new agreements represented an annual

gain of £1¼ million in wages. In all cases war bonuses had been incorporated into wages.

In 1920 there were no major national disputes but much negotiating and some conflict at Divisional or individual society level. As an illustration, the 17th October meeting of the Executive Council had before it 27 cases of disputes or possible disputes in retail societies, seven in the CWS and one in the Co-operative Insurance Society. The 48-hour working week, it was reported at the end of the year, had been established in retail societies generally, with 44 hours in the Northern Societies and many productive works.

On the whole, the future seemed bright. Then . . . the economy collapsed. The wartime impetus to full employment of workers and machines had carried forward into the short-lived peacetime boom. It began to weaken in 1920 and ran out of steam in 1921. Unemployment soared to the figures given earlier. Wages and conditions were among the first victims of the blizzard. NUDAW had been born on 1st January and by 31st December the first annual report had to say: "The year 1921 will long be memorable in Trade Union history as the year of wages reductions. The slump in trade which ensued on the artificial after-war boom was followed immediately by a concerted attack on wages and other conditions, from which our private trade members suffered at once, and of which the Co-operative Movement was not slow to take advantage".

In almost every Division of the Union there were reductions in Co-operative wage rates, in some cases twice in the year. In the general section there had been reductions in the warehouse, flour milling, sugar refining, sugar based (jam, confectionery), drug and fine chemical, soap, feed and compound trades. In several of these trades there had been two reductions in the year. The Union was represented on 29 Trade Boards and eleven Joint Industrial Councils or other Joint Trade Committees. In some cases, it was reported, Trades Boards had proved a slight check on the amount of wage cuts demanded by employers, particularly in the case of women workers. But, generally, it was retreat all along the line.

For NUDAW, however, it was a fighting retreat. The Executive's policy, endorsed by the 1921 ADM, was that "Where our own members have been and are prepared to make a stand against reductions, they have had and will find every ounce of the Union's strength behind them". During the year there were strikes at sixteen retail societies, usually over attempts to enforce wage cuts without the agreement of the Union; three against private employers; one each against the CWS and the CIS. Unemployment benefit in 1921 amounted to £122,331, almost six times the total amount paid since it began in 1896. Dispute and victimisation benefit was £31,568, approximately half as much again as the total since this benefit was introduced in 1912/13 (although of course, the 1921 figures related to the much larger membership of the amalgamated Union).

Unemployment ravaged the Union's membership. We saw as percentages earlier in this chapter the toll it levied on benefits payments. In human terms, the average weekly number of unemployment claims throughout 1921 was 3,200, and in the worst weeks, 6,738. The effect on finances was crippling. With only eight weeks experience of the new year, the annual meeting of 1921 had been warned of the deteriorating financial position and had agreed that there should be an appeal for extra voluntary contributions. But that sort of appeal is rarely successful. The best response to an emergency comes when people can feel they are all in it together, contributing equally to find a solution.

The voluntary appeal failed. The position continued to deteriorate. The Executive was concerned above all that financial considerations should not cripple the Union's ability to resist, through organisation, agitation and strike where necessary, the attack on wages and conditions. In June, 1921, it was decided by the Executive that there should be a "capital levy" of £1 per member and 10/- for associates (by then, this category included only members under 16 years of age. In their case the levy was later reduced to 5/-). Payment was to be either as a single sum or in weekly instalments.

Almost every member of the Union had experienced cuts in wages. Many were on short-time. Yet the response was magnificent. More than £57,056 was paid in levy or donations during the remainder of the year. J. Hallsworth was to declare at the annual meeting of the following year that "The amount raised by the levy in 1921 saved this organisation". Nine years later, when the Union completed its first decade, the annual report for 1930 stated that in that earlier year of crisis " . . . its destiny

then was in the balance very much more than was realised".
The present day USDAW owes much to those members of long
ago.

Finance was not the only cause for anxiety. There was also a
heavy loss of membership. At the time of the amalgamation in
1920 the total was 185,066. By the end of 1921 this was down to
104,746. The slide continued to a low point of 81,297 in 1923.
Thereafter, the climb back began, and by the end of this
chapter in 1925 the figure was 93,468 (65,873 men, 27,595
women).

The decline in the early twenties would be due to several
causes. NUDAW began with 72,267 women members. A year
later the number was down to 36,902. Many women were,
almost literally, driven out of industry during the depression.
To "clean up the books" after the amalgamation and in subsequent years several thousand members heavily in arrears were
written off the lists. These factors would account for a considerable part of the lost membership.

In addition, the enlargement of the Union had made it vulnerable in times of depression. Co-operative employment was
relatively stable. By the 1920s few Co-operators, whatever their
quarrel with NUDAW, denied that their employees should be
in a Union. NUDAW, however, was now operating in many
trades where employment was much more volatile and all or
some employers would gladly have seen Trades Unionism
destroyed. Many members probably left the Union to save their
jobs, or, if unemployed, to improve their chance of getting
another job. It was not until 1928 that the membership figure
again turned the hundred thousand, at 104,129.

To return to the early twenties. The levy alone did not lift the
financial burden. Welcome as it was, it had still left a deficiency
of £41,948 for 1921. In the following year unemployment and
dispute/victimisation benefit continued at a crippling level and
the attack on wages called for all the strength the Union could
mobilise in resistance. Reluctantly, the Executive had to ask the
ADM of 1922 to accept a reduction in provident benefits.

The proposal was a reduction of 50 per cent, except in the
case of strike pay, where the reduction was less. The rules were
to be altered accordingly. It was a tense and unhappy meeting,
facing a situation which was new to a Union that so long had

gone from strength to strength. After a lengthy debate the proposal was rejected by 30,485 votes to 23,719.

But a negative vote could not make the crisis go away. There were "off-stage" discussions and the Standing Orders Committee accepted an emergency resolution. This reinstated the proposal with the exception that, if carried, the cuts would be regarded as temporary, to operate for twelve months, and sick benefits would be reduced by 25 per cent, not 50. With these amendments the proposal was adopted by what the official report described as "an overwhelming majority".

J. Hallsworth, who was the principal speaker, probably carried the day on two main arguments. One was that to attempt by economies alone to meet deficiencies of the prevailing size would reduce the Union to a nullity, incapable of rendering adequate Trade Union services (although a rigorous programme of economies *was* being carried out). The other, and related, argument was that provident benefits only affected members, and then a minority of them, on occasion, but the task and cost of fighting to maintain wages and conditions was vital to all members "day after day".

The annual meeting of 1923 agreed to continue the reduced scales, with the proviso that the Executive could make any earlier revision, wholly or in part, towards the old scales if it considered it would be justified by the financial situation. The benefits, with some amendments to the former scales, were restored in 1924 in a new schedule submitted by the Executive and adopted by the ADM of that year, to operate from 1st July. To add to the problems of this period a break away Union was formed at Barnsley; the cause apparently being discontent over some of the post-amalgamation arrangements. Within a few years, however, it returned to the NUDAW fold.

The defensive battle over wages continued. Towards the end of 1922 and in the early part of 1923 there was a long-drawn-out strike, more or less national in scale, against what the Union contended were wage cuts imposed by the CWS in some factories without negotiation and, equally important, a claim by that Society to a free hand in operating Trade Board, JIC or "accepted" Trade Union variations in wages and conditions. The strike extended into a refusal to handle goods from the CWS in many retail societies. When the dispute was eventually submitted to the Joint Committee of Trade Unionists and Co-operators, the award more or less endorsed the wage cuts. But the Society's claim to a free hand in selecting the rates it would apply in future was rejected, largely on the grounds that it would give the right to pick and choose among a wide range of rates, and enforce its choice without negotiation with the Unions concerned.

Many workers' productive co-operatives have been formed as the result of a strike. NUDAW is probably the only Union to have gone into retailing in an extension of strike action. At Bishop Auckland in 1921, and Wallsend-on-Tyne about a year later, there were prolonged strikes against the local retail societies. With Union support, competitive societies were formed, and employed a considerable number of the strikers, the remainder continuing on benefit. They were initially successful, but eventually closed down. While they thus failed commercially their very existence probably deterred some other management committees from driving the Union to a total confrontation. (Hallsworth described the cost of supporting these societies as "an insurance premium.")

Not all the disputes of these hectic years were in the Co-operative Movement. Some notable battles were fought against private employers. In 1921 a group of firms in the Liverpool rope trade sought to impose Trade Board rates, which meant a substantial reduction in earnings. The dispute lasted from May, 1921, to February, 1922, and ended in victory. In 1922 there were successful actions against wage reductions by a Leicester firm of drug and fine chemical manufacturers and similarly against a distillery firm. In 1924 Liverpool sack and bag makers, mainly women, came out against Trade Board rates that were lower than those in any other industry covered by Trade Board machinery. It was a rough struggle, with police action against pickets, but it ended in a wage increase.

The tide began to turn in 1923/24. While there was still massive unemployment, the first shock-wave of the depression had worked itself out. Co-operative trade, which had slumped drastically between 1920 and 1921 (partly through a fall in prices), began to recover. The General President, J. Jagger, was able to claim at the ADM of 1924 that in the preceding year . . . "the retreat had almost stopped", with very few reductions in wages during the year. Nineteen-twenty-four saw slight advances in wages for a considerable number of members and an increase in membership of 8,047. By 1925 the annual report claimed "distinct success" in maintaing wages and conditions, plus a further increase of 4,124 in membership.

Nineteen-twenty-five also saw another attempt to establish improved national scales for all grades of workers in the Union. They were drawn up by the Trade Conferences and Trade Advisory Groups which for a time were part of the Union's machinery. NUDAW's experience had been, particularly in the Co-operative Movement, that wage reductions in one Section or District were invariably followed by similar applications throughout the country. Hopefully, national scales would lead to national negotiations and agreements, but whether negotiations were national, regional or local, J. Jagger told a conference at Leicester " . . . we will all for the first time be negotiating upon the same scale." The Co-operative Union, although it was believed to be in favour of national negotiations, soon had to make it clear that they were not on. Its constituents insisted that applications must go through the Sectional or District Hours and Wages Boards.

By the end of the year they had been submitted and were being actively pursued in Co-operative and some private trades. In the North-Western Section of the Co-operative Union there was another lockout, which was embittered by the attempt of some societies to induce employees to give up their membership of NUDAW. The lockout ended in an agreement to resume negotiations and if the differences were not settled to refer the issue to " . . . any new machinery that may have been set up between the Co-operative and Trade Union Movements". If no such machinery had been created within a specified period a Court of Arbitration was to be set up, comprising NUDAW, Sectional Hours and Wages Board, TUC and independent members, with a mutually agreed chairman. A somewhat similar agreement was made in the North-Eastern Section. Eventually, without arbitration, it was agreed to stabilise rates until April, 1926, but with an immediate improvement in holiday entitlement. While on the whole the North Western agreement was honourably observed, a few societies refused to reinstate Union members.

One break with the Union's past must be recorded. A Hewitt

died on 26 March, 1925. Of no man would it be said that he was the creator of USDAW but among the band of pioneers and builders who were the architects of the Union his memory holds a high and honourable place.

We have now reached the end of the most dangerous five years in the Union's history. The future would not be lacking in problems and crises but never again would they be so acute that they could threaten the Union's existence. There are not many members still around from these tense and challenging years. If they think of them at all, they must recall many occasions when it seemed that NUDAW would be swamped by the deluge sweeping through the national economy, and recall also how they and their colleagues gritted their teeth and determined that somehow the Union would survive. That it did so is a tribute to its national leadership and to the memory of now forgotten stalwarts in the branches and districts.

11 PROGRESS IN DEFIANCE OF ADVERSITY

W E have made our way through five years in which an embattled NUDAW had to be constantly on the alert to defend wages and conditions and, gradually, to improve them. That is a primary purpose of any Trade Union. But strife is not the every-day activity of a Union, even in the worst years. We must now return to many other developments through which NUDAW sought to serve its members between 1918 and 1925; years in which there was growth as well as adversity.

POLITICS

There were four General Elections between 1922 and 1924 and by the latter year the Union had four representatives on the Labour benches. But its first-ever Parliamentary seat was won at a by-election in 1921, when R. J. Davies, secretary of the Approved Society, won the largely mining constituency of Westhoughton (Davies himself was a former miner).

A year later he held the seat in the General Election of 1922, and R. J. Wilson joined him as Labour MP for Jarrow-on-Tyne. Both were re-elected in 1923, with the addition of W. Mackinder, who won the Shipley constituency. NUDAW also had official candidates in Spen Valley, Stafford and Ashton-under-Lyne, all of whom were defeated. The three sitting Members were returned in Labour's victory election at the end of 1923. Union candidates at Stafford, Spen Valley and Ashton-under-Lyne were rejected. R. J. Davies became Under Secretary of State for Home Affairs in Ramsay Macdonald's first Government.

In the notorious Red Letter election of October, 1924, Labour lost 39 seats, but the NUDAW three held their own and Ellen Wilkinson won Middlesbrough East, to bring their number up to four. She was the only successful woman Labour candidate. Altogether, it was a good achievement for a Union which, for the reasons given earlier, had been a late starter in Labour Politics.

Apart from increasing the number on the Parliamentary

Panel there were two other changes in the Union's political arrangements during the twenties. While both General Secretaries were eligible to seek election as an MP, the Executive considered that it would be inadvisable for both to be in Parliament, which could have happened with the rising tide of Labour support. Therefore, the ADM of 1924 was informed that a mutual arrangement had been made with them that J. Hallsworth should devote himself entirely to the control of industrial, organisation and administration activities and be known as Industrial General Secretary and W. A. Robinson should operate as Political General Secretary, with specific authority to seek a seat in Parliament. The second alteration, authorised by the 1926 annual meeting, increased the allocation from the General Funds for political purposes by 6d per member to 1/6d; the increase being made to provide for the servicing of four MPs and three other prospective candidates.

EDUCATION: *THE NEW DAWN*

These two must be considered together as complementary parts of the same purpose. At the time of the amalgamation it was decided to continue the journal, and the first intention was to re-christen it as "*The Distributive and Allied Worker*". But some genius on the Executive asked what was wrong with "*New Dawn*", a title symbolic of NUDAW's aspirations and virtually identical with its name? His suggestion was adopted. It was also decided that publication should be fortnightly, beginning with the first Saturday in March, 1921. L. Lumley, AUCE's first full-time organiser, was appointed as editor and publicity manager.

It was hoped to reach a circulatio⊥ of 50,000. But if there is one thing British workers will not do, it is read their own publications. They will join a Trade Union, they will strike, they will stand by their Union in bad times, they will vote Labour — but the greater number of them will not read publications that belong to them.

The *New Dawn* was one of the brightest Trade Union publications of its day. It gave extensive news of the Union, including some brilliantly written reportage on the great strike battles of the twenties. A. W. Petch, Financial Secretary and Office Manager, wrote regular articles on Union finance and administration which, apart from their national interest, were virtually

a serial textbook on branch administration. There was a strong
literary content, frequently including poetry and fiction. There
were many cartoons including contributions from Vic Feather,
a one-time Co-op. employee who later became General Secretary of the TUC, Women's Pages, fortnightly sketches of local
Union personalities, contributions from the principal national
leaders of the Labour and Trades Union Movements (and from
the Union's own leaders), articles on health, holidays, Parliamentary reports, a special section on Scottish affairs: all these
were included. But for long the circulation remained obstinately
well under 20,000. Nevertheless, *New Dawn* was probably the
most potent single factor in teaching members the Union's
conception of Trade Union organisation and introducing them
to Socialist philosophy and the humanities.

AUCE had long discussed the establishment of more formal
education, but had deferred action because of disagreements in
the Labour Movement over the political and philosophical base
from which education should be provided. There had been
links with the Workers' Educational Association, but these
ended in 1921. There was also an internal scheme of summer
school scholarships for members taking Co-operative Union
examinations. Some members, however, wanted a more clearly
defined Socialist approach to educational work, and the 1922
ADM adopted a demand for action based on " . . . the independent working-class policy of the Labour College Movement."

The National Council of Labour Colleges, which was the
body meant by the resolution, was a grouping of the London
Labour College (owned by the NUR and the South Wales
Miners' Federation), the Scottish Labour College, 51 local
non-residential Colleges, the Plebs League and some Trades
Unions. NUDAW joined, and was represented on the national
and district committees of the NCLC.

During the first World War the Union also began an association with the Fabian Society, the Labour Research Department
and the National Council for Civil Liberties.

JOINT COMMITTEE OF TRADE UNIONISTS AND
CO-OPERATORS: CONCILIATION

We saw in the previous chapter that the Union swallowed its
objections to the Joint Committee when there was no better
arbitration and conciliation machinery available. But in the

ranks of NUDAW, as of AUCE, the Committee was suspect and the search continued for a more satisfactory method of conciliation. On the initiative of NUDAW, the TUC had set up a committee representing Unions with members in Co-operative employment and since the early twenties it had been discussing with the Co-operative Union the possibility of a substitute for the Joint Committee. These talks ended in deadlock. The General Council then appointed its own investigation committee to seek a way out of the deadlock. It prepared proposals which, again, were rejected by the Unions concerned. The principal objection, so far as one can see, was that the proposals over-emphasised the validity of Trade Board and similar rates, which NUDAW and some other Unions regarded as a bare minimum, while many employers sought to establish them as a maximum. It was back to square one.

By now the General Council had run out of patience. It said, more or less, "A plague o' both your houses" to Co-operators and the Trades Unionists alike, gave notice that it was withdrawing from the Joint Committee by Whitsuntide of 1925, and in effect left the two sides to sort out the problem between themselves. Surprisingly, in one sense — considering the background of protracted disagreement — they did so. Not surprisingly in another sense, for both parties genuinely desired means of conciliation and arbitration that would be more flexible and more representative of the Unions concerned in a dispute than the old Joint Committee.

The new machinery, set up in 1926, provided for a National Conciliation Board, equally representative of signatory Unions and the Co-operative Union. Each Union and each Section of the Co-operative Union nominated panels from which they could draw six members to constitute any meeting of the Board. Four could be members of the Union or Section concerned in a dispute. The chairman for each meeting was drawn in rotation from a panel of independent persons. Decisions could be by unanimous agreement, by majority agreement if that was acceptable to both parties, or by agreement to accept a chairman's arbitration. Decisions by any of these methods were to be binding. Within seven days of direct negotiations breaking down the case must be referred to the Board, which must meet within fourteen days from the date of the reference.

H

Seventeen Unions were parties to the scheme, which covered
all retail Co-operative societies and the Co-operative Production
Federation (organisation of the worker productive/co-partner-
ship societies). The CWS was not included but later was to make
separate conciliation arrangements. The new machinery was
fully operative by 1927, and in that year NUDAW was involved
in thirteen cases. Five resulted in the Union's favour, in four
there was no decision, three were referred back to the parties
for settlement and one was withdrawn by mutual agreement.

NUDAW GETS A HOME OF ITS OWN

A notable move — in both senses of the word — came in
1920. After nineteen years as a tenant of the Co-operative
Newspaper Society with increasing over-crowding as staff and
activities expanded, the Union purchased and moved into its
own premises. The building was a large mansion with extensive
grounds, known as "Oakley", in Wilmslow Road, Fallowfield,
Manchester. It had been built in the 1870s and enlarged in the
intervening years.

Appropriately, "Oakley" is situated in a district with a long
progressive tradition. Platt Fields, which are immediately
adjacent to the building, were part of the estate of the Worsley
family, who were active leaders of the Commonwealth cause in
the Civil War against Charles II. In more recent times many
leaders of the Labour Party have spoken there at open-air
meetings. Richard Cobden, the great radical leader of the early
part of the nineteenth century, lived nearby, as did Mrs. Gaskell,
whose novels did much to educate Victorian society in the hardships of the cotton trade.

It was not, however, the first attempt by the Union to secure
a home of its own. In 1914 a site had been purchased in Denmark
Road, Manchester. Building plans were prepared but the war
put a stop to development, and eventually the site was sold.

TWO "BREAKAWAY UNIONS"

Two attempts were made in the 1920s to hive-off from
NUDAW breakaway Unions of Co-operative employees.

One was in the Co-operative Insurance Society, then just
beginning the programme of expansion which by today has
made it one of the largest insurance organisations in the United
Kingdom, with a premium income in 1978 of £238,500,000 and
6,000 agents. The Society was founded in 1867 by a number of

retail Co-operatives, individual members and the CWS. In 1913 it was absorbed by the CWS and the then Scottish CWS (now itself merged with the CWS). It made little headway, however, until after the first World War.

Insurance workers were first mentioned in the AUCE Executive Council minutes of January 13th, 1918, which authorised efforts to enrol them in the Union. A Co-operative Agents' Union already existed; in 1920 it merged with AUCE, and was established as a national branch. By 1923 the branch could report to its conference that there were 1,500 members — an increase of 1,200 since the previous conference. But all was not plain sailing. Among district managers there was a move to form a separate Union, which agents were invited to join, and some did so, particularly new men who were influenced by their managers. The TUC rejected an application for membership by the breakaway which then sought a kind of half-and-half link by joining the National Federation of Insurance Workers, which was affiliated to the TUC.

There was not, however, any real stamina in this "Union". It had neither the resources, the experience nor the general back-up which NUDAW could provide. In 1927 most of its approximately 2,000 members merged with NUDAW, a small number (mainly officials and office staff) transferring to another Union as a separate section. Effectively, however, NUDAW had (and USDAW has) one hundred per cent membership of the agency staff. Fuller details of the special structure through which agents are organised are given in Chapter 33.

The other attempted breakaway was at the Newcastle Branch of the CWS, in the aftermath of the General Strike of 1926. Membership of a Union eligible for affiliation to the TUC was by then firmly established in the Wholesale Society and the breakaway attempted to obtain recognition. It was rejected by the General Council as ineligible and the CWS Board notified its members that they could not continue in the Society's employment unless they were in an affiliated Union. Exit the Co-operative Employees' Union (as it had been called).

There was also an attempt by some retail societies to weaken the compulsory Trades Union membership clause in the CWS, a backward move which was overwhelmingly rejected by the shareholders' meetings.

OTHER DEVELOPMENTS

There can only be a brief mention of other developments of the period.

From 1918 onwards the Union renewed the campaign for compulsory Trades Union membership in retail societies. In 1921 this was the rule in 123 societies. By 1925 the number was 192. In some societies, however, it did not require compulsion to secure full Trades Union membership. Rodney Hanes, who was later to become President of USDAW, recalls that when he worked in the Eccles Society, it was their proud claim that they were one hundred per cent through voluntary recruitment.

In 1920 the right of employee members to seek election to committees of their societies was in the rules of 29 societies (in 19 of which employees had been elected). By 1925 the number was 65, with employees on committees in 48 cases.

In 1917 central funds became responsible for maintaining full-time secretaries in very large branches, the first four being Bolton, Irlam CWS, Liverpool and Woolwich. The latter branch had maintained a full-timer, G. Settatree, at its own expense since 1915. Formed in 1908 with 7 members (now just under 5,000), the first secretary of the Woolwich Branch, E. J. Bull, was one of the two new full time officials who were added to the Union's first organiser, G. Lumley, in 1908.

The Union continued to strengthen its international links, and by 1925 was affiliated to the International Transport Workers' Federation, the International Federation of Commercial, Clerical and Technical Employees, the International Federation of Trades Unions (through the British TUC) and on behalf of its members in the fur trade, the International Clothing Federation.

12 NUDAW IN THE GENERAL STRIKE — AND THE "ALMOST GENERAL STRIKE THAT WASN'T"

THE General Strike of 1926 is considered by many to have been an isolated event, almost a freakish distortion, in the history of British Trades Unionism. It should more properly be seen as part of an historical process, an almost inevitable attempt to apply in practice ideas that had influenced working class thinkers since the days of Robert Owen and his Grand National Consolidated Trades Union of 1833. Or of William Benbow, who a year earlier proposed a "sacred month" in which, by refusing to work, the common people would compel reforms in the State which would establish social and economic equality.

In his book *Robert Owen*, G. D. H. Cole describes the objects of the Consolidated Union as being " . . . to include all producers within its scope and by the threat of a general strike to enforce, first, a universal eight hours day, and soon a complete transformation of the industrial system". Thus, there were two objectives. One was to lead mankind into the Golden Age by the mass exercise of working class power. But the immediate practical objective was to be the use of the strike weapon to advance or defend working conditions and wages. By far the greater part of the Union's rules (given as an appendix in Cole's book) was devoted to methods of organisation and action to carry out this second purpose.

The Grand National had a brief and turbulent existence (the Tolpuddle Martyrs were one of its "lodges"). It was destroyed by its own organisational inefficiency and the hostility of Government. But the idea of a gigantic strike of all or most workers either for social/political or for industrial purposes lingered on — some would say, haunted — the Trades Union Movement long after the days of Owen and Benbow. It had many advocates in the decade following the first World War. Syndicalists, Guild Socialists, Communists of the period agreed on very little but all saw in the power of Trades Unionism a

force for social change as well as for the defence of wages and
conditions. The majority of Trades Unionists who belonged to
none of these factions recognised that post-war capitalism was
consolidating and rationalising into bigger national units (the
great multi-national corporations, while they existed, were then
fewer in number than they are today). The growing power of
employers was contrasted with the fragmentation of Trades
Unions. Mass action, it was argued, was the only countervailing
power the workers could mobilise.

There was not, however, any organised move towards a single
all-in national union such as Owen's Grand National, and there
was only a minority interest in the use of Trades Union power
for revolutionary purposes. Amalgamation was favoured, as
the means by which Unions could best defend wages and conditions against the consolidated power of employers. Some of
the biggest Unions of today date from those years. The Transport and General Workers' Union and NUDAW were formed
through amalgamation in 1921, the National Union of General
and Municipal Workers in 1924. Amalgamation led to increased
interest in federation through formal agreements for defence or
advance between Unions with a broadly similar industrial or
occupational base. The possibility of united action on a wider
front than that of a single Union was also reflected in the decision of the 1924 Trade Union Congress to give the General
Council considerable power of co-ordination in disputes likely
to involve large numbers of workers in more than one industry.

In one case amalgamation and federation went a stage further
by, so to speak, adding quality to quantity. A Triple Alliance
of the Miners' Federation of Great Britain, the National Transport Workers' Federation (of which NUDAW was an active
member) and the National Union of Railwaymen had been
formed in 1911 but did not emerge dramatically on to the
national scene until 1921. In theory it had the power to paralyse
the nation by closing down transport, use of the ports and the
supply of fuel for power, heat and light. (King Coal, no matter
how decrepit he had become, had not then been seriously
challenged by oil. As late as 1938 the United Kingom's consumption of petroleum was only a fraction of what it is today).
A strike by the Triple Alliance could thus have produced much
the same impact as a General Strike.

The test came in April, 1921 — and the result was a fiasco. As we have seen, 1921 was also the first year of the great attack on wages and conditions, and by no employers was it pressed home more savagely than by the mine owners. Notices ofwage reductions and a general worsening of conditions were posted at the pit heads. The miners refused to accept them, and were locked out. They had already invoked the support of the Alliance, and had every reason to believe that rail and other transport workers would come out in a sympathetic strike. A resolution of full support had been carried at a special conference of the Unions in the Alliance, moved by H. Gosling, President of the Transport Workers' Federation, and seconded by J. Hallsworth, Joint General Secretary of NUDAW. All seemed ready for the closest approach to a General Strike that Britain had yet seen. The strike was set to begin on the night of Friday, April 15th.

It was, however, to be the "almost General Strike that wasn't"! The mood of the special conference was not truly reflected in the Executive Council of the Alliance. The Council's nerve soon began to weaken. It did not have plenary powers. The last word still lay with the Executives of the affiliated Unions. Possibly, some of them feared that their members would not obey a strike call on an issue which did not immediately and obviously concern their own wages and conditions. They may have flinched from an open confrontation with the Government, which was only too obviously backing the mineowners and had strengthened its hand with an Emergency Powers Act in 1920. Whatever the reason, the strike was a non-starter. The Executive of the Alliance decided that some unofficial discussions that had taken place between miners and mineowners' representatives and MPs (which were repudiated by the miners' Union) justified them in calling off the strike at the last hour of 15th April, a date which was to become known as "Black Friday". P. Kean, NUDAW's representative on the Executive of the Transport Workers' Federation, was one of those who voted against the cancellation, and his action was approved by the Union's Executive Council.

NUDAW's membership among transport workers was small compared to that of some other Union's in the Federation. But the Union was among the most active supporters of every move to stand by the miners, and the Executive protested at the cancellation of the strike. Their plans to meet the mineowners' challenge had been thorough and realistic. NUDAW's leaders realised that to strike and hope for the best was not enough. There must be a policy to provision the strikers and sustain their morale. A plan for that purpose was drawn up by the Joint General Secretaries, J. Hallsworth and W. A. Robinson, approved by the Executive Council, sent to the Executive of the Triple Alliance and circulated to Union branches on 9th April, 1921.

It was based on the establishment of " . . . joint machinery of the Triple Alliance and the Co-operative Movement." A National Strike Food Committee was proposed, with local committees. They were to be manned, nationally and locally, by representatives of the Unions in the Alliance, the Co-operative Movement, Co-operative employees. Strikers were to be supplied with food to the value of their strike pay. Where a food was scarce, Co-operative Managers were to draw on their wartime experience to introduce rationing schemes. Co-operative Societies were to be urged immediately to move all stocks of food, fuel, petrol, forage etc., which might be "lying in railway stations, warehouses", before the strike began "so that the stores can be in our hands before the Government commandeers the larger accumulation of supplies". Whether the plan was ever considered by the Executive of the Triple Alliance is doubtful. By the time it reached them they were more concerned to avoid a strike than to find means of conducting one.

After Black Friday the miners struggled on until July, when they had to capitulate to the old strike-breaker; hunger. During the months they were out NUDAW, itself financially harrassed by the impact of the slump on cash and membership, contributed generously to relief funds.

There were many lessons to be learned from the collapse of the Triple Alliance, including particularly the need for advance planning on the lines which NUDAW had proposed. They were not taken to heart by the Trades Union Movement which, in 1926, drifted into a full-scale General Strike with little more contingency planning than in the fiasco of 1921. The lesson that preparation is half the battle in industrial disputes as in war was, however, mastered by the Conservative Party, which was in

Government in both years. It was ill prepared for a confrontation in 1921. By 1926 an armoury of legal, administrative, military and strike breaking resources was ready for action.

The "real" General Strike of 1926 also began over an attack on the miners. It had, however, been simmering since early in the previous year. The sacrifices imposed in 1921 failed to revitalise an inefficient and, in many areas, decaying coal industry. Germany, Poland and other countries were chasing British coal out of long established markets. A plan to nationalise the industry, modernise it, and among other proposals, link it to the development of electrical power (in which Britain was acknowledged to be then falling behind other industrial nations) and develop pretreatment of coal to utilise the profitable by-products and eliminate the smoke evil, was jointly prepared by the Miners' Federation, TUC and the Labour Party. It was submitted to, and rejected by, the Royal Commission on the Coal Industry which, as we shall see, was set up shortly before the General Strike. In any case, it never stood a chance with a Conservative Government in power. The forces opposed to the miners had their own Triple Alliance in the coalowners, the Royalty owners who sucked about £6 million a year out of the industry, and the Government, and for them there was only one cure for the sickness of King Coal — another twist to the screw that already squeezed the miners' standard of living.

The coalowners' intentions had been clear well before they were formally published. The April, 1926, annual conference of NUDAW anticipated the coming storm in a resolution which assured the Union's " . . . comrades in the mining industry that it stands solidly with them . . . and declares its determination to support them to the utmost of its power and regardless of the cost".

The storm broke on 30th June, 1925. Notices went up at the pit heads ending the national agreement which still existed with the Miners Federation of Great Britain, substituting district agreements, imposing heavy wage cuts and increased hours. The Miners' Federation sought the support of the TUC General Council at a joint meeting on July 10th. The support was promised, a special committee was set up to carry it out, and the railway and transport Unions agreed to embargo the movement of coal from midnight on Friday, July 31st. Neither exports nor imports were to be handled, and all deliveries of coal to commercial and industrial concerns were to cease The Unions that had flinched from action on Black Friday, 1921, made good their failure on Red Friday, 1926.

The immediate result was a retreat by the Government, then headed by Stanley Baldwin. It was not yet ready for a showdown. Only hours before the embargo was to begin it was announced that there would be a subsidy of £25 million to the coal industry. It was to last for nine months, and the owners' demands would be postponed until April, 1926.

So far so good. The threat to use mass power had worked. But it had not yet been tested in action, and an ominous deadline lay nine months ahead. The TUC's special committee was kept in being and announced its intention to " ... apply itself to ways and means of consolidating the resistance of the Trade Union Movement should the attack be renewed." But it was the Government that did the consolidating. An Organisation for the Maintenance of Supplies (OMS) was set up. The country was divided into ten regions, each under a Civil Commissioner. Arrangements were made for the enrolment of special constables and strike breakers. Preliminary plans were made for the deployment of Army and Naval forces.

A Royal Commission on the industry had been appointed in September, 1925, under Sir Herbert Samuel, and it reported in the following March. It made some useful recommendations, but it also accepted the owners' case for economies at the expense of wages and hours. The Spring of 1926 was the critical season. In April the notices of cuts in wages and debasement of conditions again went up at the pits. A lock-out from 1st May was the sanction if they were not accepted. This time there was no postponement. Government and coalowners were ready for battle, and there is considerable reason to believe that many of them welcomed an opportunity to cut the Unions down to size.

On 20th April the Government proclaimed a state of emergency. On 29th April Executives of most Unions in the TUC began to assemble for a special conference on the crisis in the Memorial Hall, Farringdon Street, London, where the Labour Party had been born twenty-six years earlier, under its original name of the Labour Representation Committee. For most of three anxious days they waited in the hope of a peaceful and humane settlement of the mining dispute. But Government and coalowners were adamant that miners' wages and conditions must be worsened. The owners would not withdraw the lock-out.

On 1st May the conference decided by almost unanimous vote that as from 3rd May other Unions would strike in support of the miners, under the direction of the TUC. On 30th April the TUC had already circulated the "first line" list of Unions to be called out " . . . as and when required by the General Council." Other Unions were to be brought out as needed at a later stage, but the strike was over before that stage was reached. The first list comprised all transport, from docks and harbours to road and rail to the then infant Civil Aviation industry; printing, including the Press; iron and steel; metal and heavy chemicals; building. With electricity and gas, Unions were recommended to co-operate with the object of cutting out power supply to industry. Unions were to "do everything in their power to organise the distribution of milk and food" and to maintain medical and other supplies to hospitals. All Unions were warned to be aware that " . . . the opponents will in all probability employ persons to act as spies and others to use violent language in order to incite the workers to disorder".

NUDAW immediately responded to the call. On 3rd May wires went to every branch directing that all members engaged in transport of every description "must cease work tonight". Branch meetings were to be called to make arrangements and Central Office was to be informed by wire of the numbers affected. In a follow-up letter signed by J. Hallsworth as Industrial General Secretary the TUC warning on incitement was repeated.

The General Strike was on, and it lasted for nine days. This is not the place to follow the story through all the discussions between the TUC and the Government, and between the TUC and the Miners' Federation, which led to the General Council's decision to call off the strike on 12th May. The strike had not collapsed through lack of support. The miners, of course, were already out. There was a full response from the "front line" Unions that were called out in support. In some cases members of Unions not immediately involved came out of their own

accord. In parts of the country Strike Committees were effectively in control of vital services. There was no evidence that the
majority of those already out were weakening, or that the
"second line" would not respond to the call.

On the other hand, the more successful the strike became, the
more was it likely that the Government would seek to break it
by police and military action against pickets and by encouraging
strike-breakers. Hundreds of strikers were arrested and imprisoned under the Emergency Powers Act. The provocative
promise of full official support of any act committed in repress-
ing the strike was virtually an incitement to violence. There
were also plans to rush coercive legislation through a Tory-
controlled Parliament. The bogey was raised that the strike was
an attack on the constitution, a charge that was vociferously
voiced by Tories who only a few years earlier had been preparing for armed rebellion in Ulster to prevent the passage of
legislation for Irish Home Rule. Although the charge against
the Unions was untrue in fact and doubtful in law it undoubtedly scared some members of the General Council.

Sit Herbert Samuel had drafted unofficial proposals for
settlement of the coal dispute which the Council apparently
assumed to have the support of the Government, although they
were rejected by the miners on the grounds that they meant a
reduction in wages and worsening of conditions. Nevertheless,
the General Council convinced itself that they were the best that
could be won, notified the Miners' Federation accordingly,
and ordered a return to work. So ended Britain's first and only
General Strike.

Before coming to the sequel one document which survives in
the archives of NUDAW must be mentioned. It is "An account
of the Proceedings of the Northumberland and Durham General
Council Joint Strike Committee", prepared in May, 1926. No
author's name is given but it was probably by C. R. Flynn, the
Union's Northern Divisional Officer, and Secretary of the
Council.

It begins with an informal discussion on the evening of 3rd
May by representatives of NUDAW, T&GWU, Northumberland Miners and Labour Research Department, held at the
Union's Divisional Office, Newcastle-upon-Tyne. This led to a
meeting the next afternoon of representatives of most Unions in

the area, which agreed to set up a local General Council and a Strike Committee of representatives from each Union or group of Unions on strike or locked out, to meet daily. Flynn was secretary of both. Thereafter comes a day by day (sometimes hour by hour) account of crises, solutions and the gradual build-up of an efficient organisation. Confusion, at first, was widespread. One transport Union had called out all men involved in food transport but had given permits for the distribution of building materials. Another Union stopped all transport of building materials but issued a number of permits for food. Permits were being issued by a great variety of local Union offices and Strike Committees and were frequently being abused. It was soon discovered that " . . . the abuse of permits was beginning to reach gigantic proportions. Unscrupulous contractors or employers were conveying any and every sort of goods under the aegis of 'food only' or 'housing materials only'.

This problem was met, firstly, by banning all permits for building materials, subsequently by banning any permits at all except a limited number for essential foods. This favoured private traders with their own cars or non-Union labour, but penalised the Co-ops, whose transport workers were solidly behind the strike. So restrictions on supplies of bread and milk to societies were temporarily relaxed and a more comprehensive solution was being worked out when the strike ended.

Strike breakers from OMS were brought in to work on unloading food ships at Newcastle quayside, where two destroyers and a submarine were moored. Port workers who had been unloading food under permits immediately stopped work. The Regional Commissioner, Sir Kingsley Wood, sought to negotiate some form of joint working, which was refused. It was denied in the House of Commons that there had been any negotiations with the Strike Committee, but this detailed narrative leaves no doubt that they did take place.

Only a small selection of items from this historically interesting document have been given here. The complete story brings out two factors. One was the lack of preparation. Describing the confusion and delays at the beginning of the strike the writer says "All these hitches . . . were clearly incidental to the fact that on the Trade Union side no preparations had been made in advance for carrying out the general stoppage". The other was the skill and speed with which the Strike Committee sorted out the muddle and improvised a large measure of control over the economy of the two counties. A similar story could be told in many other regions. However disappointing the outcome, the strike was unquestionably a remarkable demonstration of working class solidarity and ability to organise.

The miners refused to give in. They held out for six months before they were starved back to the pits on the owners' terms. Large sums were raised to help sustain them in their struggle, and NUDAW was a generous contributor. At a conference of Union Executives called by the TUC on 23rd November, 1926, to consider means of helping the miners J. Hallsworth, on behalf of NUDAW, moved that members of all Unions should be asked to contribute a 1d per working day, to which NUDAW would make an immediate grant of £10,000 on account of payments which the Executive Council was confident would be made by members. The proposal was carried by acclamation. (By 31 December, 1926, the "miners' penny" had yielded £43,785, including NUDAW's £10,000).

About 10,000 of the Union's members were out during the General Strike, two thirds being transport workers. The largest number involved was in Liverpool, with London coming next. But some members were affected in nearly all the Union's 750 branches. At the end of the year 40 members were still drawing victimisation pay due to their part in the strike.

The cost of the strike to the Union was £43,601, of which £14,000 was grants to the Miners' Federation, £500 to the Women's Committee for the relief of miners' wives and children, £17,659 dispute and victimisation benefits, £9,316 unemployment benefit, £1,000 a grant to the TUC and £1,126 special expenses. In addition, branches and officers of the Union contributed £7,157 to one or other of local and national funds.

After the miners had been beaten back, came the year of revenge. The Conservatives and their allies had won, and used their victory without mercy. As G. D. H. Cole puts it in his *Short History of the British Working Class Movement*, 1789-1927 "The Government . . . felt that the Trade Unions were down, and it could not bear to miss the chance of stamping on their face". A Trade Disputes and Trade Unions Act was hurried on to the Statute Book. The General Strike was declared illegal, as were sympathetic strikes. The right to picket was severely restricted. Limitations were imposed on the Trades Union rights of workers in the public services and on the enforcement of the closed shop by local authorities. Contracting-in was substituted for contracting-out in the case of political contributions. The Attorney General and the Courts were given wide-ranging powers to interfere in Trades Union affairs by process of legal injunction. NUDAW MPs and staff played an active part in the campaign against the Bill by the TUC and the Labour Party. But the Tories had the majority and in due course it became law, and was not repealed until 1946, as one of the first acts of the post-war Labour Government.

If there is any "hero" of the General Strike it is the British worker. He, and in many cases she, came out for no personal advantage. There was an immediate and certain loss of wages. There was no prospect of immediate gain. There was a risk that there would be no job to go back to, for a great many were victimised when the strike was over. Yet out they marched, almost two million of them, because they wanted to stand by other working people in their hour of trial. They stayed out for nine days and no doubt would have stayed out a good deal longer had they been asked. It was a demonstration of comradeship and solidarity that deserved a better result.

13 WAGES AND CONDITIONS TO 1931; THREE UNION CRUSADES TO 1939

WE now turn from the turbulence of the General Strike to the quieter conditions in which most Trades Union activity is pursued. The defence and improvement of wages and standards is the primary purpose, and we saw in an earlier chapter that during the years immediately before 1926 NUDAW had enjoyed considerable success in regaining the ground lost on the wages front in 1921/22. In this chapter we shall follow the Union's experience with wages and conditions up to the national political and economic crisis of 1931. We shall also extend the time-span beyond 1931 to deal with come causes which NUDAW pursued in all conditions, whether of crisis or normality.

In spite of the weakening of Trades Unions power that followed the General Strike, NUDAW was able to maintain most of the gains that had been made in previous years, but was unable to make any significant advance. Nineteen twenty six was more or less a year of marking time. With the long drawn our closure of the mines and the general aftermath of the General Strike conditions were not conducive to wage increases. But the annual survey of wage movements in private trade speaks of having "more than held our own", "conditions maintained", "no change in rates". Some small gains were reported. Of the Co-operative Movement it was said that apart from involvement in the General Strike " . . . the year 1926 has probably been freer from industrial disputes than any year since 1912".

Nineteen twenty seven was a similar period — "Except in isolated cases there has been no serious move on the part of the employers of our members to interfere with the existing agreements". For 1928 the story was "In spite of the continued depression in the basic industries . . . the general body of our membership have maintained their rates of wages and conditions of employment". In 1929 the Executive reported " . . . no reduction in wages of any serious amount for any section of our members" and recorded success "at many points" in improving existing agreements. Similar progress was reported in 1930. Members were rarely called on for strike action during the period. Apart from the General Strike, there was only one serious dispute (with a private firm) in 1926. None is recorded in the reports for 1927 and 1928, one in 1929 against a private firm. There was, however, a major strike lasting almost three weeks against the Co-operative Insurance Society in 1930; partly over commissions and partly over a minimum wage for agents from the day of appointment. It resulted in the establishment of a minimum of 50/-. The Union was unsuccessful, however, in securing reinstatement of a number of CIS agents dismissed after another strike.

In the Co-operative sector this period of comparative calm could probably be attributed to three causes. The retail trade of the Movement was buoyant and had increased from £184,879,902 in 1926 to £217,318,001 in 1930. The biggest increases were in London, South and the Midlands. Societies in the North and in South Wales, however, were experiencing a rough time. But there was no widespread urgency to seek economies through what all too often had been the first target of many management committees — the wages of their employees. Moreover, while NUDAW was ready to fight wherever it regarded a cause as important in principle, the days when the Union had to prove itself to the Movement by battle were past. Willingly in many cases, reluctantly in some, societies had accepted that they could no longer with impunity impose wages and conditions. The fact that the National Conciliation Board, which was introduced in 1926, did not, like its predecessor of 1915, fade out but continued to be extensively used was in itself evidence of this change for the better, even though the Union complained that the Co-operative side too often refused to accept a chairman's award when the parties could not agree.

There were, however, two black spots particularly affecting private trade members. In the aftermath of the General Strike, women workers were being sacrificed to industrial depression, both in wages and employment opportunity. And low as their wages were, they were frequently driven out of their jobs by even cheaper juvenile labour. In the light domestic productive and distributive trades 50 per cent of the workers were under

I

age of 18. The Union came across one large factory in Cheshire where girls of 15 were refused work on the grounds that they were too old to start.

The idea that the upper and middle social classes were entitled to cheap domestic servants still lingered on, and the Ministry of Labour sought to oblige by forcing women off unemployment registers into the kitchens of their "betters". As NUDAW's report for 1930 tartly pointed out, the demand for servants might be vocal but it was not unlimited and if the Ministry was challenged " . . . they would not be able to provide anything like the number of vacancies that they claim exist". The Union's own female membership in 1930 was 32,900, equal to 28 per cent of the total; a proportion at which it stood for many years.

Juvenile labour had worried the Union since the earliest days. Partly because of the threat to adult employment and wages, partly for the human and social wastefulness of recruiting young people into blind-alley jobs. The Executive Council reported in 1906 that a favourite argument against a fixed minimum wage in Co-operative service was that societies could have a number of young men just out of their time, to whom they could not afford to pay an adult wage and did not care to sack — " . . . a state of affairs largely brought about by the employment in the past of an inordinate number of young people for the sake of cheapness". A year later the annual delegate meeting called for a scheme to regulate the number of apprentices and juniors. A similar demand was made in the following year.

By 1910 the annual report was proposing that in no case should there be more than one junior to three journeymen. There was a lull during the war and immediate post-war years but in the late twenties NUDAW sought and obtained the support of the Co-operative Union for the crusade to shut off the blind alley in the Co-operative service. The Labour Committee of the Co-operative Union, working partly from information collected by NUDAW, in 1929 circularised societies urging closer supervision of the number of juniors engaged, the training of juniors employed in delivery and other departments with a view to absorption as adults, transfer of surplus labour between societies, representation to the CWS and SCWS to absorb trained workers who were surplus in retail societies and the establishment of more superannuation schemes. The problem was largely confined to bread and milk deliveries and societies were urged to examine their delivery systems, since experience in some societies had shown that the work done by boys could more economically be done by adults.

To help unemployed members in the depressed areas the Union maintained a version of the employment register set up by the old Manchester District Co-operative Employees' Association and, more positively, contacted societies advertising vacancies and supplied the names of NUDAW members. In addition, it was reported in 1928 " . . . we are in constant touch with some of the societies whose trade is most rapidly increasing, and are arranging with them to receive by transfer surplus labour from societies badly hit by trade depression".

Northern branches established a fund to pay the fares of members transferred to other societies. Northern, Midland, London and Southern Divisional Officers in co-operation with the London, Grays, Dartford, South Suburban, Birmingham, Nuneaton, Coventry and other societies — all in Co-operative growth areas — succeeded in providing for large numbers of members from the North East who might otherwise have been in the twilight world of the dole.

Membership of the Union continued to recover from the heavy losses of the early twenties. The figure was 91,488 in 1926 and 119,623 in 1931, an increase of 28,135. The Executive Council missed no opportunity of extending the range of recruitment. Mutuality, i.e. credit trading, clubs were increasing in the Co-operative Movement and the Union set out to organise and introduce agreed scales and conditions for the collectors employed on the clubs. Optical workers, for whom wages and conditions were very bad, were also organised and today form a considerable section of NUDAW. The expansion of the CIS brought an increasing number of agents into membership. Billposters were also organised. Along with other Unions, NUDAW recruited newspaper circulation canvassers, a field of employment which disappeared with the second World War, and has not since been revived by the newspaper industry. Organisation of the hotel and catering trades began, though this highly mobile occupation has proved to be one of the most difficult fields in which to enrol and retain members.

When NUDAW was formed it inherited two cherished objectives from AUCE. One was to establish Trades Union membership as a condition of service throughout the Co-operative Movement. The other was to seek full membership rights for employees, that is, the right to vote and to seek election to the management and other committees of the societies that employed them and of which they were also members. To these objectives there was added a third in the mid-twenties — the establishment of superannuation schemes for all employees. With all three, the initiative must in most cases be local and the campaigns, which we will follow to the outbreak of the second World War, were based on a high degree of co-operation between the Union's national leadership and the branches.

At the beginning of the century a few progressive societies had adopted the practice of employing only Trades Union labour. But the real drive for Union-only labour began after the first World War and as was recorded in Chapter 11, 123 retail societies had adopted this rule by 1921, plus the CWS and the Scottish CWS. The number continued to creep up slowly and by 1930 had passed the 300 mark at 304. Eight years later, on the eve of the second World War, it was 496.

In most of these cases Union labour only had been conceded willingly by management committees. In some cases, local branches of NUDAW had to invoke the authority of ordinary or special meetings of members to win the closed shop. But committeemen, who were mostly themselves Trades Unionists, and in some cases had established the closed shop in their own trades, could not readily find convincing arguments against its application to their employees.

It was a longer haul to convince societies that they should allow full membership rights. This had been a Union objective for many years. At the height of the war, the 1916 annual meeting carried a resolution " . . . strongly recommending " . . . the advisability of every branch being represented by one of their fellow employees on all society boards of management". When Whitley Councils were proposed as a means of harmonising relations between capital and labour the NUDAW annual meeting of 1918, on a resolution from York branch, called on the Executive Council to propose a scheme for the Co-operative Movement that would include direct representation of the

Union's branches on societies, boards of management. The resolution only just scraped through (22,520 for, 21,413 against), Syndicalist, Guild Socialist and other ideas for complete workers' control of industry were very much in the air at the time. and an earlier resolution at the ADM (from Midlands District Council) had affirmed that " . . . no scheme of reconstruction after the war will be adequate which does not give to the organised workers the full control of industry". This probably accounted for the narrow vote. Nevertheless, the York resolution was the basis of the Union's future attempts to gain a voice in the control of Co-operative Societies.

The old idea that since Co-operative workers could become members and, therefore, were virtually self-employed, was longgone; and in any case, in equity and logic, it could be used to justify their enjoyment of the same rights as other members. But equity and logic are not automatic persuaders. Some management committees, perhaps fearing a Trojan horse at the committee table, argued that representation would weaken their authority.

An extreme argument was that unrestricted representation could lead to boards composed entirely of employees fixing wages and conditions to suit themselves. This argument was taken sufficiently seriously in some societies for them to limit employee representation, when it was introduced, to a fixed number. There were moves to popularise Joint Advisory Councils between committees and staffs which, while desirable in themselves, were undoubtedly seen in some societies as an alternative to employees in the committee room. But experience continued to show that those societies with employee representation were no less successful — sometimes more so — than their neighbours. Although hostility began to diminish, progress was at a snail's pace. There were 72 societies where membership rights operated in 1927 (when the annual report began to publish the figures), the same number in 1928, 76 in 1929 and one less in 1930. By 1939 the number had only reached 111.

It was not until the nineteen-twenties that superannuation became a major interest of NUDAW and the Co-operative Movement. In 1920 the number of societies with superannuation schemes could almost be counted on the fingers of two hands. By 1938 the greater number of Co-operative employees, retail and wholesale, were covered by schemes (280,326 out of 346,761). In the years to 1939 the accumulated pension funds increased from £899,773 to £11,672,292. It is probable that no other major reform in Co-operative service was ever established so rapidly and, on the whole, with so little friction between Union and employers.

The beginning of the campaign can be dated from the annual delegate meeting of 1923. A cautiously worded resolution was adopted to, first, put the Union's own house in order by establishing a scheme for the staff and, secondly, to gather information on which to base campaigns for pension provision covering the members as a whole. A staff scheme had been established by 1925, based on joint contributions and a maximum pension of two-thirds of retiring salary at the age of 65. Schemes had also been introduced in some retail societies, and by 1927 30,000 employees were covered. In the same year the Co-operative Congress urged societies to make pension provision part of their employment practice. The CWS, the biggest employer in the Movement, came in in 1928 (41 years after its shareholders had rejected a proposal by the directors that there should be a pension scheme for employees.) The 1928 scheme was criticised by NUDAW, particularly on the provision made for long service employees who could have only a short period of contributions. Schemes were also introduced by the Scottish CWS, the CIS and the English and Scottish Joint CWS (which handled the enormous tea trade of the Movement).

To these, and subsequent, developments, a vital contribution was made by a national official of the Union, A. W. Petch, the Financial Secretary and Office Manager. He became an expert on the intricacies of superannuation, advising hundreds of Union branches on negotiations with their societies, frequently consulted by societies themselves. His booklet *Co-operative Employees and Superannuation Funds* gave a comprehensive survey of every known scheme in the Co-operative Movement. Model rules were also published.

It was not all plain sailing. While most schemes were satisfactory, there were occasions when the Union had to warn that some were unsound in their financial provision, and branches were urged to consult Central Office before agreeing to proposals from their societies.

There were two other weak links in the superannuation chain. One was the role of the small societies with up to 100 employees. In 1935 the Union reported that out of 790 societies in this category only 29 made provision for superannuation. In contrast, of the 36 societies with 1,000 employees or more, 32 had schemes, Federal schemes were advocated to meet the problem of the small societies, but by 1938 only 15 had been established (covering 87 societies) out of 711 societies with fewer than 100 employees. The "over 1,000 employees" group had by then increased to 40 societies, and all but one had superannuation schemes.

The other defect was the plight of older workers who came into schemes late in life. In many schemes their actuarially determined pension was insignificant and the Union had only limited success in establishing a minimum of £1.

Partly to meet these problems the ADM of 1936 urged that there should be a national scheme for the Co-operative Movement, with a minimum of £1 at age 60. As an ideal, this was admirable. But as the Executive pointed out in the following year's annual report "There is little likelihood of any of the existing schemes agreeing to co-operate ... owing to the wide diversity of conditions adopted, and the fact that local control of funds would probably be lost is also important from the employees' point of view."

By the eve of the second World War 355 societies, retail, wholesale and worker productive, had established schemes, covering 83.50 per cent. of the combined total of retail, wholesale and productive employees. While success on a similar scale could not be claimed for the private trade, the Union had received many enquiries from firms interested in making pension provision for their employees. We can fittingly end this chapter by claiming superannuation, with all the limitations of some schemes, as a triumph alike for NUDAW and for the strength of the social conscience among Co-operative members.

14 STORMY WATERS AGAIN

THIS chapter, beginning in 1931, brings us once again into stormy waters, both industrial and political. The industrial storm was to add more than a million workers to the ranks of the unemployed. In politics, the Labour Party went through the greatest crisis of its history, when three of its best known leaders not only left the ranks but deserted to the enemy.

Between 1923 and 1929 the collapse of the early twenties had levelled off into a chronic depression in the older industries such as mining, shipbuilding, cotton. Unemployment fluctuated at an annual average figure either just above or just below 1,250,000 (except in 1927, when the average was just over a million). British capitalism had come to terms, so to speak, with Slump Number One, and more than a million men and women, (plus in most cases their families) paid the price in the grinding poverty of an inadequate "dole" and the humiliations of the Means Test.

It seemed that the state of the nation could not become worse. But Slump Number Two was on the way, and bad was to become much worse. The unemployment average in 1930 shot up to 1,917,000. In 1931 it took a further leap to 2,630,000. Thereafter the figure was not to fall below 2,000,000 until 1936.

The great depression which began in 1931 was world-wide in its impact, not least across the Atlantic, where it deflated the apparently boundless prosperity which it was claimed capitalist enterprise had brought to the United States. "Buddy, can you spare a dime" became an American song that was to echo round the industrial world. A study published by the International Labour Office in the mid-thirties (based on examination of economic and social conditions in 36 countries) estimated that between 1930 and 1934 the cost of economic depression was approximately the same as that of the first World War and that industrial production had fallen by 32 per cent.

The basic cause was the failure of nations to find means of

operating their industrial capacity and international trading arrangements on a scale that would match productive capacity with consumer purchasing power. But the immediate cause in Europe was a partial collapse of the banking system, starting with the failure of a major Austrian bank in May, and bringing down banks throughout Central Europe. Britain was affected by the banking crisis. Through the rising cost of unemployment, falling national income and a diminishing yield from taxation, it was also threatened with an unbalanced Budget, and in those years, much more than now, the Budget was a jealous God who could only be appeased by the incantation "in balance".

A Labour Government, headed by Ramsay MacDonald, was in office, though not in power, at the time of the crisis; with 287 seats against 261 Conservatives. Fifty-nine Liberals held the balance. The Government had proved incapable of devising any strategy — or even palliatives — to cope with industrial depression. The Cabinet, however, accepted that it must balance the Budget and that there must be large economies in public expenditure. The content of an economies programme depends very much on the political and social views of those who draw up the sacrificial list. Incredibly, for a Labour Cabinet, the job was given to a committee under Sir George May, Chairman of the Prudential Insurance Company, and, as Clement Attlee points out in his autobiography, with " . . . a majority of opponents of Labour on it". Predictably, their proposals were based on severe cuts in Social Services and unemployment benefits. Neither MacDonald nor Philip Snowden (then Chancellor of the Exchequer) gave their Cabinet colleagues a list of the economies intended — except that they must include a 10 per cent cut in unemployment benefit. Without that, it was insisted, confidence would not be restored (i.e. the confidence of the world bankers and Finance Ministers, plus the City of London), and no other item in substitution would do it. On that issue the Cabinet rebelled. MacDonald could have gone to the country, Instead, on 25 August, he began the formation with Stanley Baldwin, the Conservative leader, of what purported to be a National Government. Snowden, J. H. Thomas and a few other Labour MPs followed MacDonald into the Tory embrace, and were expelled from the Labour Party, the leadership being taken over by Arthur

Henderson. Ramsay MacDonald remained Prime Minister in name, commanding a "National Labour Party" of 12.

It was tragedy for Labour, both electorally and to thousands of life-long Party Workers, struck in their very souls by the betrayal of men they had followed and almost revered for years — particularly MacDonald and Snowden. In September Snowden, who continued as Chancellor, introduced a "National" emergency Budget, in which economies amounting to £90,000,000 in a full year included almost 40 per cent from cuts in unemployment benefits or increased insurance contributions by workers and employers. Next came a General Election in October when the Parliamentary Labour Party was decimated. Only 56 Opposition MPs were returned, 46 Labour, five Independent Labour Party and the rest a small Lloyd George group.

Nowhere was the great betrayal felt more keenly than in NUDAW which, apart from its representation in Parliament, was widely active in local Labour politics throughout the country. Two of the Union's three MPs were defeated. Ellen Wilkinson lost Middlesbrough East and R. J. Wilson went down at Jarrow. W. A. Robinson failed to regain Shipley, which W. Mackinder had held as a NUDAW nominee until his death in 1930. At Westhoughton R. J. Davies was victorious for the sixth election in succession since 1921, and once again became the Union's sole voice in Parliament.

In the annual report for 1931 the Executive Council recorded its " . . . full support to the loyal members of the Parliamentary Labour Party, who decided to become His Majesty's Opposition rather than follow those who misguidedly sold their honour and turned their backs on the people they had led for so many years". And Ellen Wilkinson summed up the reasons for Labours defeat in an article in *New Dawn*. "What beat us was fear. The Press, the BBC, the Church and the cinema, every employer . . . set to work to create the grand "wind up". To which the ADM of 1932 added a rider in a resolution which condemned " . . . the weak, vacillating policy of the late Labour Government" and criticised the Parliamentary Party for not realising " . . . that they were slowly but surely being betrayed into a false position by their leaders".

The backlash against wages and conditions was not long delayed, and was soon to show in NUDAW, both in unemployment benefit to Union members and, on a wider scale, in demands from employers for wage reductions. Unemployment benefit for the three years 1927 to 1929 had totalled £22,723. For 1930 to 1932 the total was £45,229. By the end of 1931, in the private sector, there had been reductions in wages in the paint, colour and varnish, tarpaulin, general warehousing, drug and fine chemical, heavy chemical and meat trades, and cuts were threatened in other trades. In the Co-operative sector there had been reductions in the Cheshire and North Wales, Liverpool, Manchester and Yorkshire Divisions, and they were impending in other parts of the country. Some branches had accepted short-time working without consulting the Union, and were warned that in doing so they endangered the legal right of workers employed on weekly contracts to be paid a full week's wages when they were available and ready for work. Thirty-two cases (the highest number since the Board was formed) had been taken to the National Conciliation Board by NUDAW, in twelve of which the decision was in the Union's favour.

In 1932 and 1933 rates were partly maintained, although in 1932, as Jagger put it to the ADM of the following year, " . . . by now it had become evident that we were threatened with what was the nearest approach to a national attack on our standards that we have ever had to meet" and in most districts they had to accept reductions to some extent. In neither of these years could the Union claim that it was more than approximately holding the line. By 1934, however, the situation changed slightly for the better, restoration of cuts or direct increases being secured in some areas of Co-operative and private trade. The improvement continued at a steady pace. But it was mainly through the restoration of previous wage cuts (although there was a small "bonus" through the fall in prices). By the early part of 1938, however, there was a brake on progress. Resistance to wage claims had become stronger and a year later the annual report for 1939 stated that progress "almost ceased" in the first part of the year. By then, however, another and mightier struggle was close upon us all.

We have seen in earlier chapters that the Union had a long experience of conflict in defending wages and conditions in times of industrial depression. While there were some strikes in the thirties there was nothing on the scale of the great battles of strike and lockout that had been fought in earlier years. One reason in the Co-operative Movement undoubtedly was the existence of conciliation machinery, which had taken much of the tension out of relations between societies and Union. The peaceful influence of the Board was acknowledged in the annual report of 1934, with the words "The lightened burden of dispute benefit in recent years is due chiefly to the operation of the National Co-operative Conciliation Board."

Up to 1937 the CWS was outside the conciliation machinery, and for several years NUDAW had been pressing for both a speedier method of negotiations with the Society, and for conciliation in the event of failure to agree. At the end of 1937 the pattern of conciliation in the retail and wholesale sectors of the Movement was completed by an agreement between the Society and a committee of Unions with Co-operative membership, set up by the TUC. The agreement was based on the principle that " . . . the relationship between the Trade Unions and the Society differs fundamentally from the relationship between the Trade Unions and private enterprise". It provided that when no settlement could be reached in disputes " . . . limited solely to the Society's establishments (as distinct from general trade disputes)" the matters at issue should be referred to the Conciliation Board, and unless and until this reference had been made no strike or lockout should take place. The constitution of the Board as to appointment of an independent chairman, decision by unanimous vote, by majority or by agreed arbitration of the independent chairman was broadly similar to the conciliation scheme for the retail societies.

There were to be two secretaries, one appointed by the Society and the other by the Unions collectively. J. Hallsworth was appointed to the latter position.

The thirties were also the years of the great unemployed marches from the depressed areas of England, Scotland and Wales to London. The most famous of these was the Jarrow march between 5th and 31st October, 1936, led for 200 of the 300 miles by Ellen Wilkinson, by then MP for the "town that was murdered".

One hundred and nineteen years earlier in another time of great suffering for working people the Blanketeers had set out from Manchester on a similar march, each carrying his blanket for sleeping rough on the route; and had been denounced for "traitorous conspiracy", harrassed and many arrested by Dragoons, Yeomanry and Special Constables and finally turned back by Yeomanry as they sought to cross a river in Derbyshire. The times had changed. The Jarrow marchers were welcomed and helped all the way on the long road to London, not least by NUDAW branches and Co-operative societies.

For NUDAW members the thirties were a period of see-saw in wages, with reductions followed by a partial or full restoration but little real advance except insofar as they benefitted from lower prices. The Union's members fared better than workers in many other industries. But the real gains of the period were less in earnings than in improvement of conditions, such as the widespread introduction of superannuation schemes described in the previous chapter.

Superannuation affected Union members in all trades in which the Co-operative Movement was engaged. Sectional improvements in conditions were also won in particular trades, for groups of employees of which two examples will be given. "Working conditions" can cover almost any aspect of employment from the heating and lighting of workplaces to the physical effects of a particular job. One issue of the latter sort was taken up in the twenties on behalf of employees in the CWS and privately operated flour mills. Flour for Co-operative bakeries and for the home-baking trade of retail societies was traditionally packed in 280 lb. sacks, which were heavy to lift, awkward to manhandle and could bring about strain or other injury. On the Union's initiative in 1920 the Joint Industrial Council for the milling trade recommended millers to replace the weight by 140 lb sacks when the heavier stock was worn out.

Some progress was made in private and CWS mills but the heavier weights continued to be used by the CWS Sun (Manchester) and Star (Oldham) Mills; the Society contending that it had to supply them because they were specifically ordered by its retail customers. When approached by the Union some societies (and, apparently, some of the Union's own members) argued that these sacks were the most convenient to handle for their trade, and discounted the health danger. In reply, the Union tactfully suggested that " . . . if the decision were compulsory, means would soon be found to adapt to new conditions", and pointed out that only two CWS Mills were still using the 280 pounders, so " ... everybody else seems to have fitted in their arrangements accordingly". It was a long haul, but eventually the 280 pounders joined other mementoes in the records of industrial archeology.

Another reform that had to be patiently worked for over many years was one day off in seven for dairy roundsmen. Britain's daily delivery of milk to most homes does not exist in other countries, and is the main reason why our consumption of milk is one of the highest in the world. But it hinges on a decidedly unsocial starting hour for dairy roundsmen in particular, and for a long time there was an equally unsocial working week of seven days.

The attempt to secure one day off in seven had simmered for many years without getting very far. A questionnaire sent in 1932 to 600 NUDAW branches covering 185 societies resulted in 181 replies. They showed that only 24 societies operated a six day week (some only for inside workers). In twenty-five societies there were alternative methods, such as one day in fourteen, extra annual holidays, one day every seven weeks. When branches were asked what steps had been taken to secure the reform, it was found that in 123 societies no approach had been made to the employers. Nor did the roundsmen seem particularly concerned. Comments in the replies to Central Office included "roundsmen do not want a six-day week"; "members concerned do not wish to press the matter"; "day off obtained unofficially"; "unsuccessful in getting agreement among workers"; "competition too keen in this district".

From this rather discouraging response the Executive concluded that as yet there was " ... not a sufficiently strong desire among our own dairy membership to take drastic action to secure a six-day working week". They decided that what was required was more propaganda among the branches, to be followed by district conferences.

There were, however, militant roundsmen who *did* want the six-day week and they sponsored a resolution at the 1933 ADM criticising the Executive for not giving a strong enough lead. This was defeated, but a resolution calling for further efforts was carried. The campaign gathered momentum and subsequent annual reports had a much more encouraging story to tell.

By 1936 there were agreements in the Midland Division of the Union, the North Western Section of the Co-operative Union, and "substantial progress" towards an agreement in the North Eastern Section. Where Divisional agreements could not be secured, a number of societies had put the reform into operation as a result of the Union's activities. By 1939, when this chapter ends, the dairymen of the Movement were well on the way to securing a more civilised working week. When societies such as London, Royal Arsenal, South Suburban, Enfield Highway, Newcastle upon Tyne, Barnsley British, Stockport, Manchester and Salford, Coventry, Birmingham, Liverpool, Hull, United Co-operative Dairies (a federal body of societies in the Manchester area) — and scores more with a large dairy trade — were all on the six-day week it could safely be claimed that the reform had become established. (At the time of writing the agreement between the Co-operative Employers' Association and the Joint Trade Union Negotiating Committee is for a 40 hours working week, arranged as far as possible over five days).

With other reforms there was less success. The demand for Saturday half-day closing at 12.00 noon was frequently made but rarely conceded, probably because of the great volume of non-food trade that is done on Saturday afternoon. A campaign for Thursday payment of wages — to minimise congestion late on Friday, particularly in food shops — was building up when war broke out. The war itself was to encourage this reform, which was widely introduced to ease the problems of weekend shopping.

The general theme of this chapter has been one of constant struggle against adversity. We can end on a more heartening note. Amidst all their problems the Executive Council did not forget the men whose past effort, and in some cases sacrifice, had made the Union strong to face the problems of the times. In 1933 it was decided to make presentations to branch secretaries with a continuous record of 21 years' service. For members who could claim 30 years in the Union there were to be certificates and medals, plus concessions on retaining membership and funeral benefit on retirement. By 1934 30 branch secretaries had qualified, the longest serving secretary being

A. Shaw, of Silverdale (Staffordshire), who took up office in May, 1899. Close behind was A. Thornton, of Hebden Bridge, Yorkshire, with a record beginning in July 1901. H. N. Hunter, Pittington (Co. Durham) had served since September, 1904. It was estimated that about 1,300 members would qualify for certificates and medals. Truly, a Grand Army of pioneers. And to their number we can add the army of the future — the 74,283 new members who had joined the Union between December 31st, 1931 and December 31st, 1939.

15 AS WAR DREW NEAR

Amalgamation: Politics: "New Dawn" and Education:
Federations: Structure and Staff

NINETEEN-TWENTY-ONE saw the amalgamation between
AUCE and the Warehousemen's Union which resulted in
the formation of NUDAW. Efforts to bring about a wider
organisation of distributive and allied workers continued with
the encouragement of the TUC. By 1926 several Unions had
dropped out of the talks but three went to a ballot on a scheme
of amalgamation — NUDAW, the Shop Assistants, and the
Women Clerks' and Secretaries' Association. A special delegate
meeting of NUDAW endorsed the scheme and all three Unions
balloted their members. For Trade Unions to amalgamate
required a minimum of 50 per cent of the members to vote, and
the votes in favour must exceed those against by not less than
20 per cent. NUDAW qualified on the 50 per cent but failed —
just, by 197 votes — to secure the 20 per cent. The other Unions
did not poll the necessary 50 per cent.

During the year, there was, however, one slight consolation
for NUDAW when it took over the Irish Linen Lappers' and
Warehouse Workers' Union, based in Belfast. And, nothing
daunted by the major reverse, the Executive at the end of the
year was discussing possible mergers with the Scottish Bakers'
and Belfast Butchers' Unions. Nothing came of these talks.
But amalgamation, particularly with the Shop Assistants' Union
seemed to wax and wane in approximately four to six year cycles.
In 1930/31 and 1937 there were two more determined efforts to
bring about the merger which both Unions had sought for so
many years.

The first began at NUDAW's annual meeting of 1930, when
a resolution was submitted in favour of amalgamation or
federation " ... with any Trade Union or Unions catering
for distributive and/or allied workers ... provided that the

J

Executive Council considers that such . . . would be in the interests of our present membership". The resolution was thus widely drawn to cover the whole field of distribution and other trades. But what the delegates had in sight was not a blanket merger but one with a specific Union — that of the Shop Assistants. The qualification at the end of the resolution brought into the open discontent at the failure to make any progress along that road. There were charges from the floor and the platform that the Executive Council was, in effect, "dragging its feet" and the "interests of our present membership" phrase was suspected as a loophole through which any agreement could be frustrated. Two members of the Council said there was "procrastination" and "division" among their number. J. Hallsworth said he was opposed to the resolution on the grounds that "It gets you no further than you are today, than you were twelve months ago, or even five years ago". The charges were rebutted but they undoubtedly reflected a feeling of frustration that so little headway had been made.

Eventually, standing orders were suspended, the first resolution rejected and a substitute proposal moved "That the Executive Council be instructed to communicate with the National Union of Shop Assistants and other kindred organisations with a view to amalgamation . . . as speedily as possible". The result was to be reported to a special delegate meeting or to the next ADM. This resolution was carried by 52,303 votes to 21,774.

There was no "procrastination" in carrying out the instruction, but the ADM of 1931 showed a surprising lack of fervour for the merger it had demanded so vigorously in 1930. Agreement between the NUDAW and Shop Assistants' Executives had been reached in good time for NUDAW's annual meeting. Looking at the terms in retrospect, it can be seen that NUDAW, which was much the larger Union, had been generous in the provisions for control, finance, staff and other sensitive factors. For three years the two Executives (which were equal in number) were to form a combined Executive, with NUDAW having no numerical advantage beyond the casting vote of the chairman. At the end of three years the members would determine the size of the new Executive. The different patterns of contributions and benefits prevailing in the two Unions were to continue for a period until experience showed which was most popular with the members. NUDAW was to provide for the first three years the three principal elected officers — President, Industrial General Secretary and Political General Secretary, with the General Secretary of the Shop Assistants as Publicity Officer. Appointed members of the staffs of both Unions were to be retained on existing remuneration and status.

The proposals were debated on a simple resolution that they should be submitted to a ballot of the members, and the debate was one of the longest in the history of the Union, covering seventeen columns of *New Dawn*. All the old arguments were traversed again and again. That the Co-operative employee and the private trade shop assistant were oil and water — they could not mix . . . then why, it was asked, did NUDAW already spend time and money on trying to organise private trade distributive workers? . . . that private trade workers were unorganisable — their conditions could only be improved by legislation . . . that Co-operative conditions would be dragged down by a deadweight of private trade members . . . then why did the Co-ops repeatedly reproach NUDAW for not organising private trade? That the Shop Assistants were too concerned with provident benefits, and they were not a fighting Union. But had they not fought many doughty battles against private employers? And so on. The divisions were deep, and at the end of the day they were irreconcilable. The resolution was defeated by 50,026 votes to 37,404 — figures not all that much different from those in which the previous year's ADM had demanded immediate action *for* amalgamation.

Against that vote, however, amalgamation seemed a dead duck. But it would not lie down — for within six years a scheme not dissimilar to that of 1931 was again before the ADM.

This time it was approved by the 1937 annual meetings of NUDAW and the Shop Assistants' Union and went to the ballot required by law. And this time it was the democracy of the ballot box that defeated the project. NUDAW met both the 50 per cent and the 20 per cent requirement, Out of 170,395 members, 81,813 voted in favour, 15,931 against. The Shop Assistants' fell short on the 50 per cent count — a total vote of 27,042 out of 72,695 members, with 23,962 in favour, 3,080 against.

Amalgamation was to be out until the end of the war. But it did not mean renewed bitterness between the two Unions. They had a working agreement, which continued, and when war broke out two years later Maurice Hann, General Secretary of the Shop Assistants', was to record that he and J. Hallsworth were " . . . working in the closest co-operation . . . particularly on the question of war-time problems which are common to both Unions".

POLITICS

Over politics, NUDAW could report much greater progress up to 1939. After four years of "National" government, with unemployment still at astronomical levels, with the inhumanity of the "dole" and the Means Test, the memory of the first fleet mutiny in the Royal Navy for 134 years when, in September, 1931, the seamen of the Atlantic Fleet at Invergorden refused to put to sea in protest against cuts in Service pay, with rampant depression in industry, with all these and other arguments for a change of Government, Labour had reason to hope for electoral victory when the General Election came in 1935. For the Party the result was disappointing. Although there was a large increase in the Labour vote over 1931, the number of seats won was only 154, with four Independent Labour Party and one Communist. There was 20 Liberals. The Tories won 387 seats outright, plus 40 odd satellites (National Liberal, National Labour).

For the Union, however, the result was heartening. Ellen Wilkinson regained Jarrow for Labour, J. Jagger entered Parliament for Clayton (Manchester), W. A. Burke won Burnley, W. A. Robinson won St. Helens and the indestructable R. J. Davies retained Westhoughton for the seventh successive election. To these could be added H. Midgley, who, via the Parliamentary Panel, was a Union nominee for the Northern Ireland Parliament (which had different election arrangements from those for the rest of the country.) He was the Member for the Dock Division of Belfast.

J. Jagger, MP, gave up the position of Chief Organising Secretary, which he had held since 1929, retaining, however, the Presidency, to which he had been elected in 1919. He was succeeded by A. W. Burrows (Midland Divisional Organiser), with G. Beardsworth (Cheshire and North Wales Divisional Organiser) as Assistant Organising Secretary.

Contracting-in for political contributions had begun in 1928, when 74 per cent of the Union's membership had signed the necessary form. By 1939 the percentage was 87, a fine record for a Union whose membership was widely scattered and in many cases worked in very small groups. In 1933 the political contribution was increased from 1/6d. to 2/-d. per member per annum, amended two years later to $\frac{1}{2}$p per week.

One great shadow lay over the political scene of the thirties — the increasing power of Fascism and the threat of a second World War. Or, what was even more frightening, the apparent ability of the dictators to take over Europe without any real resistance. Benito Mussolini had seized power in Italy with a *coup d' etat* in 1922. But he was a pigmy compared with Adolph Hitler, who became dictator of Germany in 1933. Almost overnight he destroyed the once strong German Socialist, Trades Union, Communist and Co-operative Movements. His nightmare racialism and his conviction that the Germanic *Volk* were destined to become the master race, expressed in his book *Mein Kampf*, had been dismissed as the posturings of a half-mad visionary. They were soon to be seen as the day-to-day policies of a dictator ruling without any effective challenge over a powerful nation.

By the end of the thirties Germany, Italy, Austria, Czechoslavkia, Portugal, were under dictatorships, Franco was close to victory in Spain, the Balkan countries were becoming satellites of the two senior dictators and Japan was successfully pursuing a similar policy of aggression in Asia.

How to combine peace with resistance to Hitler was a problem never absent from the Labour Movement's thinking and controversies of the period. Some argued for a United Front of all anti-Fascist forces to bring down the Tory Government and seek through the League of Nations to mobilise overwhelming power against the dictators. Others contended that such an alliance of Labour, ILP, Liberals and Communists would never hold together. A better course, they maintained, was to strive for a straight Labour Government. Russia was obviously a key factor in any common front against Fascism. But there were deep suspicions in Labour ranks that the British and French Governments were lukewarm in seeking a Soviet alliance, and hoped that Hitler could be induced to divert his ambitions eastward.

Communist members in NUDAW and other Unions were foremost in demanding a pact with Russia and other potential victims of aggression. For their other diverse activities attempts were made in the Trades Union Movement to restrict the activities of Communists, but NUDAW resisted any such moves on the grounds that the rules gave power to deal with any members who sought to subvert Union policies. Western Communists in general turned a somersault after 23rd August, 1939, when the German-Russian Non-Aggression Pact was signed. The war in the West which followed was then denounced as an imperialist adventure. They back-somersaulted in 1941 when Hitler struck at the Soviet Union.

All these influences were strongly reflected in NUDAW during the tense and troubled years of the mid and late thirties. All were expressed in speeches and resolutions at successive annual meetings. For a United Front, for a general strike in the event of war, for a ban on German goods (called for by the TUC), against the wicked farce of the non-intervention agreement which denied the Spanish Government the right to buy arms, against British rearmament, denouncing the successive and successful aggressions of Hitler, Mussolini and their Japanese allies. But as freedom died in one country after another the conviction was growing that attempts to placate the dictators only increased their appetite for conquest. In 1935 the TUC and the Labour Party, in condemning the Italian invasion of Abyssinia, accepted economic sanctions and the use of force through the League of Nations to halt the aggressor. At the conference of each body NUDAW delegates had supported this decision. A number of Union branches took the unusual course of requesting a special delegate meeting where an attempt was made to challenge the Union vote at the TUC and Labour Party. But by a large majority (83,688 to 12,490) the delegates' action at those conferences was endorsed. It was unlikely that the vote troubled the dreams of Mussolini or Hitler. But small straws can signal a rising wind, and this decision by a Union with NUDAW's pacific and anti-war tradition was a sign that the wind of resistance was rising in the West.

Other causes prominent in the thirties — superannuation, membership rights, etc., — were mainly of a non-political character and have been described in previous chapters.

THE NEW DAWN: EDUCATION

In 1934 L. Lumley retired from the position of editor of *The New Dawn* and Publicity Manager. He had been a Union member since the foundation year of 1891, was President of the Oldham Industrial Branch at 21, became the Union's first organiser in 1906; a unique record. No immediate successor was appointed, the General Secretary acting as editor-in-Chief of the Journal until in August, 1935, Cyril Hamnett was appointed editor and placed in charge of publicity.

Circulation had hovered round the 13,000 mark for a long time, and did not keep pace with increasing membership. This was a matter of concern to the Executive, conscious of the fact that the pioneering generation was passing on, and that it was of prime importance to ensure that a new generation was aware of the Union's traditions and principles, and in touch with its manifold activities.

The introduction of more pages and features and a renewed circulation drive raised the print to 17,500 in 1935. A NUDAW news service was introduced in the same year to maintain contact with the Press and other media. By 1938 *New Dawn* circulation had passed the 19,000 mark and when war broke out a year later arrangements were made to supply free copies to branches for members in the Forces. A similar arrangement for employees was made with the *Co-operative News* by many retail societies and on land or on sea, from the jungles of Burma to the chilly mess decks of Atlantic convoys, the two publications kept Co-operative employees in touch with home and peacetime job.

The Union's two earlier monthly journals (*The Co-operative Employee* and *The AUCE Journal*) had been printed by the National Co-operative Publishing Society. When *New Dawn* began as a fortnightly, printing was transferred to the Labour Press, Manchester. In 1926 printing returned to the NCPS (now Co-operative Press Limited) and the Union's publication is still printed there in its present newspaper format and new title of *Dawn*. In 1928 the price was reduced from 2d. to 1d.

Educational work continued to be carried out mainly through the National Council of Labour Colleges. The scheme began modestly in 1923 when 251 NUDAW students attended one or more of the 293 classes available, 34 took correspondence courses and 540 attended lectures. A year later the number of Union class students was 1,025, 116 were taking correspondence courses, and adding in day and weekend schools, plus lectures to Union branches, the total number of students was 3,322. Five years later the total for 1930 had slipped back to 2,734, of which correspondence courses (584) were the biggest single group. By 1939 the total number of students was 4,541, almost half of whom (2,135) were on correspondence tuition.

Year by year the Union sent contingents of rank and file members to the annual NCLC and TUC summer schools. There had been suggestions that it should run its own national summer school, but that was not to come until the educational plan was revised after the second World War. Financial or other help was given to members who won TUC scholarships to Ruskin College, or to other appropriate centres of further education. For many years in succession A. W. Petch lectured at the TUC school on "The machinery of a modern Trade Union". Indirectly, the Union became involved in the Co-operative Union's very widespread provision of correspondence or class technical training for Co-operative employees, when in 1932 Co-operative educational machinery was reorganised under a National Educational Council, on which NUDAW was represented.

FEDERATIONS

As AUCE branches began to multiply earlier in the century, so, too, did Union activists in various districts begin to look for means of meeting together to discuss common problems. This desire was expressed from around 1911 in the formation of federations.

The Executive Council recognised the need and drew up model rules in 1912. The objects of a federation were to include any duties allocated by the Executive or District Committee, special attention to weak branches, pooling arrangements for representation at the ADM and other conferences to help branches which could not afford to send delegates. Boundaries were to be decided by the then District Councils, which were in each case to appoint one member to a federation committee. Funds could be raised by an affiliation fee of 1d. per member per annum, with a maximum of 2d. and in all matters concerning Union policy federations were to act on the instructions of the District Council.

The Executive Council, while willing to encourage anything which promoted democratic participation in Union affairs, appeared to have some fears that federations might develop as an alternative to the District Councils. Some members suspected they were mainly a platform for candidates in the Union's elections. So for some years federations had a sort of twilight existence, recognised as being of, but not quite in, the official machinery of the Union. Their number waxed and waned, some having only a brief existence, others settling into permanency. On the whole, however, the number tended to grow.

Many of them were doing a good job, in line with the Union's concern for democratic discussion and wide member participation. Reports of federation conferences, one day and weekend schools, annual dinners, are plentiful in the columns of *New Dawn* in the twenties and thirties. From 1921 onwards they began to press for official recognition through branch resolutions at the Union's annual meetings. It is probable that their claim was not helped by moves in the twenties to replace the Union's Divisional structure with the smaller areas of federations. The argument continued at other "annuals" until in 1934 a more conciliatory resolution was adopted asking the Executive to prepare a scheme for officially recognising federations as part of the machinery of the Union. This was done, and a year later the Union's Rules were altered to provide that "for the purpose of assisting the Executive Council and Divisional Councils ... branches may form Federations", the rules of each Council to be approved by the Executive. Financial help was given from National funds. Fourteen federations, the annual report for 1935 stated, were then in existence, three in Scotland, the rest in England.

By 1940 the number was 33, located in Ayrshire; Border (Scotland); East of Scotland; Falkirk and District; Fife and Kinross; Glasgow and District; Lanarkshire; Scottish Inter-Allied; Beds. and Bucks.; Birmingham; Bristol and District; Cheshire, North Wales and North Staffs; Cornwall; Devon; Eastern Counties; East Riding; Gloucester and Hereford; Hants., Wilts. and Dorset; Huddersfield and Calderdale; Kent; Leeds and Heavy Woollen District; Leicestershire and

East Midlands; London; Manchester; Manchester and District CWS; Northants; North East Lancashire; North Lonsdale; Nottingham; Sheffield; Shropshire and Mid-Wales; South Yorkshire; Surrey and District.

STRUCTURE AND STAFF

Little has been said up to now about the Union's staff, although it will be obvious that it must have increased in number in line with the ever-growing membership. Nor has the structure of the Union been mentioned for several chapters, and we will look at that first. In 1921 Divisions replaced the former District Councils, and by 1939 there were eleven of them — Cheshire and North Wales, Liverpool, London, Manchester, Midland, Northern, Scottish, Southern and Eastern, South Wales and Monmouthshire, South Western; Yorkshire; each with its elected Divisional Council. Among the 81 Divisional Councillors was one woman — Miss A. Brown of the Southern and Eastern Division. Membership in the Divisions varied widely, from 2,754 in South Wales and Monmouthshire to 32,471 in the Manchester Division. Although private trade membership was rapidly growing, both in numbers and the variety of trades and firms organised, the bulk of the membership in 1939 still consisted of Co-operative employees. At the top of the Union's structure was the Executive Council of 14, elected on a Divisional basis, with the two General Secretaries.

The staff enjoyed the full membership rights which the Union sought to establish in the Co-operative Movement, and officers of the Union were elected to Divisional Councils and |the Executive Council. The total staff numbered 260 at 31st December, 1939, comprising 5 Central Officials (J. Hallsworth, General Secretary; W. A. Robinson, M.P., Political Secretary; A. W. Burrows, Organising Secretary; G. Beardsworth, Assistant Organising Secretary; R. A. Campbell, Principal Chief Clerk), 3 National Organisers, 11 Divisional Officers, 66 Area Organisers, 95 Central Office Clerks, 7 other clerks, 24 Divisional Office Clerks and 49 Branch Accounts Clerks.

The large number of clerks was not a reflection of bureaucracy. It was, in fact, a measure of the highly efficient financial and administrative links between Central Office, branch officials, members' subscriptions and benefit payments. Inadequate financial and administrative systems were a weakness of many

Unions and NUDAW was and is a model in the efficiency of its control over these important factors.

From time to time there were proposals at the annual meeting that specialist organisers should be assigned to particular trades. There had been developments in this direction in AUCE, e.g. national organisers for boot repairing, the meat trades, drug and chemical. But as NUDAW, the Executive Council resisted the proposal, contending that the Union was better served by general organisers, regionally based, who, in any number required, could be concentrated on any particular problem. This was not, however, to be a permanent policy, as we shall see in later pages. Many new appointments were made to the organising staff in the thirties and more were planned when, in 1939, other and sterner tasks faced the nation and the Union.

This chapter must end with a grievous loss suffered by the Union in 1935. A. W. Petch, Financial Secretary and Office Manager since 1921, died suddenly at the age of 49, eleven days after the death of his wife. His work for superannuation schemes within the Co-operative Movement had been mentioned in an earlier chapter, and he had been a tower of strength in the administrative and financial organisation of the Union. A bronze plaque was installed at "Oakley" in memory of his services to the Union.

PART 4

INTO
UNIFORM AGAIN

National Negotiations — for War Bonuses and after;
Substitute Labour: Reinstatement; . . . and many other services

THE World War of 1939-45 differed in many respects from
the war of 1914-18. In the latter, civilians in most belligerent
countries were not directly involved, except in the immediate
vicinity of the battlefield. As we saw in an earlier chapter,
between 1914 and 1918 the AUCE recorded in its journal the
death in action of hundreds of members, but none was killed on
the home front. There had been air raids on Britain in the first
war, but they were insignificant compared with the massive
attack of the *Luftwaffe* from 1940 onwards. Our cities, particularly London, were prime targets for destruction from the air,
culminating near the end of the war in the rocket campaign
against the capital. Well over a hundred Union members lost
their lives in their homes, at work or on the streets.

In the first war the mobilisation of human and material
resources was gradual. Conscription was not introduced until
the beginning of 1916, systematic food rationing until the last
few months of the war. Britain was again at war from 3rd
September, 1939. Conscription into the Forces was already in
operation, the future call-up was regulated through a schedule
of reserved occupations. The Government soon took power to
transfer workers from civilian jobs to war industry, registration
and rationing of food, after some initial blundering, began on
8th January, 1940. Firms were "concentrated" to rationalise
the use of labour and machines. It was total war on a scale not
reached between 1914-18.

There was a profound psychological difference between the
two wars. Britain marched into Armageddon in 1914 almost in
a mood of euphoria. Men could still see war as a setting for
glory and adventure in which, as in the 1914 slogan "Business
as usual", normal life continued at home and the Royal Navy

guaranteed our shores against invasion. There was a more dour mood in 1939. Most people knew, or felt instinctively, that they faced a long and dirty struggle and those who had any doubts had them dispelled after Dunkirk.

Another vital difference between the two wars was the role of the Trades Union and Co-operative Movements and the Labour Party. They had an important part to play between 1914-18 but they were not brought in strength onto the top levels of policy making and administration. In Churchill's first Cabinet of the Second World War Labour representatives played a leading role. C. R. Attlee was to become Deputy Prime Minister. Ernest Bevin, powerful Trade Union leader and general secretary of the Transport and General Workers' Union, had the vital task of mobilising man and woman power and maintaining the support of Trades Unionists. A. V. Alexander (a member of NUDAW) was First Lord of the Admiralty, Herbert Morrison was Home Secretary and Minister of Security, Hugh Dalton was Minister for Economic Warfare. Arthur Greenwood served on the War Cabinet as Minister Without Portfolio, Sir Stafford Cripps was, first, Ambassador to Moscow and later Minister of War Production. Labour Members also served in several other positions.

All three working-class Movements had enormously increased in size since 1914. In that year there were 2,886,077 Trades Union members affiliated to the TUC, AUCE had 45,044 members, and the Co-operative Movement 3,054,297, with a trade of £87,964,229. By 1939 the number of affiliated Trades Unionists was 6,575,654, NUDAW had 194,000 members and the retail Co-operatives 8,643,233, with a trade of £272,293,748.

The enhanced importance of the Trades Union and Co-operative Movements was strongly reflected in the wartime experience of the distributive Unions. The General Secretary of NUDAW, J. Hallsworth, after thirteen years on the General Council of the TUC, had presided over the Congress at Bridlington in 1939 (reduced to two days because of the outbreak of war). Over the years he had served on a great variety of Governmental bodies and inquiries, and in particular he had become a notable figure in the work of the International Labour Office at Geneva (removed to Canada after war broke out). During the war he played a major part in many of the national committees set up to control or advise on economic, labour and social problems. A similar role was played by G. Maurice Hann, General Secretary of the Shop Assistants'. Both Unions were also represented by officials or lay members on a great number of other bodies, national and regional, set up to deal with particular commodities or services.

In both wars Governments paid lip-service to the importance of distribution but in practice denuded the shops of labour to an extent equalled in few other industries. Hallsworth warned NUDAW's annual meeting of 1939 (held at Easter, before the outbreak of war) that the number of male members under 40 years of age was so large that in the event of a war they would probably be more heavily hit by the call-up than any other Union. His forecast was correct.

The war with Germany ended on 7th May, 1945, when, at the Rheims headquarters of the Supreme Allied Commander, General Eisenhower, German leaders signed the unconditional surrender of their forces on all fronts. The war with Japan was expected to continue, but ended suddenly in the flash and blast of the two atom bombs on Hiroshima and Nagasaki. Mankind had entered a new era of destruction, too terrible for even the fanaticism and courage of the Japanese, who surrendered unconditionally on 15th August.

Throughout the war the number of members serving in the Forces was reported to each Executive Council meeting. The peak figure was 78,006 on September 8, 1945 (71,136 men, 6,870 women). This was probably the biggest proportion of any Trade Union and the total was 33,000 more than the entire membership of 1914. Up to the surrender of Japan those who lost their lives while in uniform numbered 1,529. But war still took its toll after hostilities had officially ended. Through accidents, from wounds suffered while the battles still raged, in the mopping up operations which continued in many parts of the world, lives were still being lost, and the total of fatalities reported to the monthly meeting of the Executive crept up until it reached 2,047 in October, 1946. It was a grievous loss, but at least it was much less in proportion to membership than the number who died between 1914-18. In addition, an earlier report stated that 140 members were killed in the aerial attacks on cities.

K

Members of the two distributive Unions, particularly those
in retail Co-operative food shops, factories and warehouses of
the two Co-operative Wholesale Societies, and in associated
transport, bore a responsibility equal to that of workers in
war industry. When rationing was introduced, Co-operative
registrations in one typical period (mid-1942 to mid-1943) for
sugar, butter and margarine, bacon and ham, cooking fats,
preserves and cheese represented more than a quarter of the
supply to the civilian market. For meat the proportion was 14.55
per cent and for eggs 17.93 per cent. At retail level entirely, and
at wholesale level by far the greater part, of this enormous
volume of essential food was handled by Union members,
many of them living and working under constant threat of
death or mutilation from the air, grappling with rationing
documents and changing coupon values and frequently beginning the day's work by clearing up a bomb-damaged shop.
By the end of the war 105,274 of NUDAW's 266,467 members
were women (mostly elderly as younger women were drafted
into war industry) plus, in the retail trade, branch managers,
adolescents of both sexes and pensioners returned to service.
They and their colleagues in other sections of distribution were
the heroines and heroes of the nation's wartime larder, who
ensured that the rations always came through. Trades Unionists
and Co-operators should take more pride in the fact that two
of the oldest democratic Movements in Britain thus made such
a massive contribution to destroying the arch-enemy of
democracy.

From the general we must now turn to the particular, to the
Union's policy and problems during the war. One of the most
significant developments was the beginning of national negotiations on wages and conditions for members in Co-operative
service. This has long been a Union objective, but little progress
had been made. We saw earlier that in 1925 NUDAW sought
to introduce national negotiations, but the Co-operative side
insisted that they must continue to be on a sectional, district or,
in many cases, individual society basis. With the rise in the cost
of living (the index rose by 10 points between 1st September
and 30th September in 1939) NUDAW and other Unions concerned proposed a flat rate over-all increase as a first war bonus,
with terms and conditions other than wages to be maintained

without alteration for the duration of the war. The Co-operatives agreed to negotiate on this basis, joint machinery was
established, and, to quote NUDAW's annual report for 1939
" . . . for the first time in Co-operative history, negotiations
for the whole of England, Wales and Northern Ireland were
conducted and, in the space of six weeks, a settlement was
reached". A large number of societies outside the Co-operative
Union's Wages Board machinery agreed to be bound by the
award, which thus covered the greater number of the Union's
members in retail Co-operative service (J. Jagger, in an article
in *New Dawn*, estimated the proportion as between 90 and 95
per cent).

The amounts of the first war bonus were: **MALES** — 21 and
over, 4/–d; 18 and under 21, 2/6d; under 18, 1/6d. **FEMALES** —
21 and over, 2/6d; 18 and under 21, 2/–d; under 18, 1/6d.
Similar amounts were obtained in the Wholesale Societies and
in Scotland (which, for a time, was outside the national
machinery, but joined in 1942). There were escape clauses in
this and later bonus agreements for societies which claimed
their trading position was so bad that they could not pay and,
conversely, for the Union to claim more in particularly prosperous societies. These clauses, however, were little used. In some
productive and specialist trades carried on by the Co-operative
Movement, particularly in the CWS and SCWS, separate
agreements had to be negotiated. But generally, throughout
the war, the tendency was to follow the pattern of the retail
bonuses. The first bonus was agreed by direct negotiation, but
most of the others were on the award of an independent chairman of the National Conciliation Board, a procedure which
both sides had agreed to accept when agreement could not
otherwise be reached.

There were eight more bonuses before 1945 (the fifth, in 1942,
for females only), including a special advance in 1946 linked to
the bonus. In total over the period of the war the increases
amounted to: **MALES** — 21 and over, 24/6d; 18 and under 21,
18/–d; under 18, 13/–d. **FEMALES** — 21 and over, 23/6d; 18
and under 21, 17/6d; under 18, 13/–d. The 1946 "extra",
awarded in April, added for males and females alike 4/–d at 21
and over, 3/–d at 18 and under 21, and 2/–d under 18. There
was another increase in 1947, after which the bonuses were

consolidated in the new national agreements, which will be the subject of a later chapter. In overall total, from the outbreak of war to 1947, the bonuses amounted to: **MALES** — 21 and over, 32/6d; 18 and under 21, 24/–d; under 18, 17/–d. **FEMALES** 21 and over, 31/6d; 18 and under 21, 23/6d; under 18, 17/–d.

Broadly similar bonuses were negotiated with the Wholesale Societies during the war. But one section of Co-operative workers received no war bonus — CIS agents. The argument was that since they were paid on commission and had a proprietorial interest in their books, bonuses were inappropriate.

A keenly felt grievance of branch managers and manageresses was dealt with in 1942. They had a harrowing job, with un-trained or half-trained staff, frequently changed, a constant shower of rationing and other documents (some carrying legal penalties for failure to carry out correctly their provisions). To meet their case, a scheme of plussages based on turnover was added to the amounts they received under bonus awards.

Managers of food shops, with wages related to sales, were also protected against any actual *reduction* in wages below the immediate pre-war level, which could have happened when branch sales fell because of rationing and the shortage of other foods.

For its private trade members the Union also secured wartime increases, varying over the great number of trades concerned, sometimes negotiated direct with employers' associations, frequently theough Joint Industrial Councils, Trade Boards (which became Wages Councils during the war), Essential Work Orders or other special machinery. By 1943 the Union was associated with 38 negotiating bodies, in all of which increases had been secured.

It would, of course, be impossible that this complicated process of bargaining with the Co-operatives on so sensitive a subject as wages could continue over six years without differ-ences arising between the two sides. One, oddly enough, was in the Union itself: some members simply did not like national negotiations. They argued that better results could be secured by district or individual society negotiations, and that removal of the vital question of wages from local decision weakened the interest of members in their branches. We shall return to this subject later.

The most intractable problem was one which was also
evident in the first World War — equality of payment for
women who substituted for men in the Forces or who had been
directed to other war work. The first task was to enrol the new
recruits as Trade Union members and that was successfully
carried out, payment of entrance fee being suspended to encourage recruitment. But the question of female wage rates (other
than the increases awarded on the bonus) had been left over
from the first Co-operative War Bonus agreement. NUDAW
took the initiative among the Unions concerned in proposing
detailed rates and conditions for the substitute female workers
who by 1940 were beginning to throng into the shops. Drawing
on the experience of 1914-18 — when it proved impossible to
secure the general operation of equal rates for both sexes — the
Unions proposed plussages at various ages which would give
the substitutes more than the current female rates but less than
the full male scales. Separate negotiations were proposed for
women in transport and some other services. The issue went to
the National Conciliation Board and the award of the Chairman,
John Forster, included a provision which became notorious as
Clause 2(c) and which for the rest of the war was to tangle the
subject in a knot of truly Gordian intricacy.

In effect, it provided (a) for a woman to qualify for the full
male rate it had to be proved that she was carrying out "the full
range of duties and responsibilities of the male worker for whom
she is substituted", (b) that these duties and responsibilities
differed "in their nature, character and scope" from the work
normally undertaken by female workers. For those who thus
qualified a scale was to be negotiated, and this was eventually
agreed by the Unions and the Co-operative National Wages
Council as 80 per cent of the male rate plus war bonus for the
first six months, thereafter the full rate, with the appropriate
war bonuses in each case.

But ... how did you prove, particularly in the artificial
conditions of war-time retailing, that a woman was carrying out
"the full range" (a phrase in itself almost impossible to define)
of duties performed by the man she had temporarily replaced?
There were complaints of societies operating shops with only
one adult man but still refusing to pay more than the female
rate to the women who had taken over. The central problem

was that each case had to be proved on an individual basis and
if necessary carried right up to the National Conciliation Board.
Officials of the Union admitted that in a great many cases it
was almost impossible to prove in the terms of Clause 2(c) that
a woman was carrying out exactly and in full detail the duties
of a man, even though in fact and in essence that was precisely
what she was doing. But the Union was bound by the agreement
to abide by the awards of NCB chairmen, and could only strive
to seek favourable interpretations of the clause. Branch officials
were urged to supply precise details of cases which could be
taken through the negotiating machinery. Very often this
was beyond the powers of men already harrassed by the
complications of wartime retailing, the black-out, air raids and
possibly worry over sons or daughters in uniform.

The problem, however, should not be exaggerated. The
general experience of the Union was that relations with Co-
operative employers was infinitely better than during the first
war. National action led much more rapidly to agreement than
Sectional, District or individual society negotiations had ever
done. Had the battle of the bonuses been fought piecemeal,
members in some societies could have won bigger amounts
but many would have had less and would have had to wait
longer. In the article in *New Dawn* mentioned earlier, J. Jagger
recalled that in the first war it was well into 1916 before they
obtained a bonus equal to that offered within four months of
the outbreak of Hitler's war. And in the earlier war there had
to be strike after strike before the bonus reached the pay packets
of many members.

To return to national negotiations. As the fortunes of war
began to swing decisively in favour of the Allies, the argument
took a new turn. Were national settlements to continue into
the post-war years? The question was brought to a head by two
developments. First, the Co-operative Movement was now in
favour of national bargaining when the war was over. More
immediately, a National Conciliation Board award arising from
a provision in the original war bonuses agreement had sharpened the need for a policy decision by the Union.

Clause (5) of the agreement restricted, although it did not
entirely debar, attempts to improve the basic sectional and other
agreements and scales to which war bonuses were added. This

was a strongly felt grievance in some Divisions, particularly
those which had been so ravaged by the depression of the twenties and thirties that the Union had been compelled to accept
wages and conditions much inferior to those in other parts of
the country. Early in 1945 two Divisions, Northern and
Southern and Eastern, sought to remove some anomalies by
invoking Clause (5).

In March the NCB chairman, Professor D. T. Jack, ruled
against piecemeal variation of the agreement. He found, however, that there was general acceptance that national agreements
on basic scales as well as war bonuses were desirable in principle and, he said, anomalies could be cleared up within their
ambit. The Union argued that the time was not opportune for
this change; Jack ruled to the contrary — that " . . . the parties
shall at the earliest possible date open negotiations with the
object of finding a basis for the construction of national
agreements".

A special meeting of the NUDAW Executive on 14th April,
1945, formally protested that this award went beyond the issues
raised by the Union. As, however, NCB decisions were binding
" . . . this Executive are prepared to implement the award for
the opening of negotiations . . . for the construction of national
 agreements with the National [Co-operative] Wages Council,
provided that the procedure to be followed . . . shall be based
on the fundamental principles of absolute equality of representation . . ." (There was similar action by the Shop Assistants' Union)

This decision was reported to a joint conference of Executive
and Divisional Councils on the same day. The conference was
also informed that procedure for national negotiations had
been agreed between the Co-operative side and the Unions
concerned, providing for joint secretaries and equality of
representation on the negotiating body.

The point had now been reached for the debate to move onto
the national stage of NUDAW's annual delegate meeting, and
it was already on the agenda for 1945. The issue was presented
in the starkest possible terms in a Birmingham Co-operative
Branch resolution which, perhaps sensing the way events were
moving, declared that " . . . the best interests of the membership
will be served by reverting to Divisional wage negotiations in the

post-war period". It was discussed in the longest debate of the
ADM and, as the voting showed, it was far from a foregone
conclusion that the result would be a victory for the Executive.

Moving the resolution, — Dunn said that the Co-operatives
wanted national negotiations to prevent some societies giving
more through Union pressures and "Surely, as far as we are
concerned, is it not a rule that on wage questions we get what
we can?" — Russell (Coventry) made the point that they could
get 100 per cent branch attendance when negotiations were
local, attendance began to fall off when they became sectional
and "how many do you get when negotiations (for war bonuses)
are national?" This was an argument frequently used, but
which ignored the fact that the greater number of the younger
active members were in uniform and could not attend meetings,
while many of older age had been drafted into war industry.
Other arguments voiced were that a change in wages bargaining
would lead to breakaway Unions, that national agreements
took too long to reach, that it was all a plot to weaken the
Union, that national minima would become maxima.

The case for national negotiations was presented by W. A.
Burrows. He contended that the tendency in industry generally
was towards national negotiations, a process which had been
accelerated by the war. The Union was already involved nationally for many members through JICs, Wages Councils and other
bodies. Under the old system there were more than 300 agreements in the Co-operative Movement, and, leaving out individual society agreements, there were very wide variations in the
rates for similar jobs. "Our rates are as varied as the colours of
the rainbow". As a result of national negotiations few societies
were not paying the full war bonuses. Many members in
small country societies were receiving a bonus they would not
otherwise have obtained. The average time for negotiating
national war bonuses had been 13 weeks [figures given in
another context showed that from 1936 to 1939 the average
time taken to reach decisions was almost six months]. As to
maintaining the interest of members, other times required other
ways and methods valid many years ago were no longer so in
the present. Certainly members must be consulted on wages,
and it would be done through Divisional Councils and specially
called conferences.

At the end of the day the direct negative of the Birmingham resolution was defeated by 106,041 votes to 61,209. National negotiations were on; not with unanimity of votes but at least by a respectable majority. We shall read of the post-war sequel in Chapter 19. But at this stage we must pass on to other aspects of the Union's wartime experience.

REINSTATEMENT

To the soldier awaiting rescue on the beaches of Dunkirk, to a comrade finding his way through the jungle after the rout in Burma, to the Merchant or Royal Navy seaman in the Murmansk or Atlantic convoys the subject of reinstatement in peacetime employment must often have seemed an academic issue. Survival with the odds against them required all their immediate attention. But the second world war, much more than the first, was fought by civilians. Civilians, men and women, in uniform, civilians at home under the nightly threat from the skies, civilians who, as workers and consumers, were tightly controlled from the early days of the war, civilians whose determination to win was inspired less by military ambition than by the desire to get it over with, destroy the evil which threatened the world and return to their peacetime jobs and lives.

Reinstatement was a vital interest to them. For NUDAW members, still mainly employees of the Co-operative Movement, this interest was covered early in the war by two agreements with the Co-operative National Wages Council and the Unions concerned — the Substitute Labour Agreement of April 22nd, 1940 (embodied in the Conciliation Board award, which also contained the contentious Clause 2(c) on women's wages) and the Transferred Labour Agreement of August in the same year. Much later, in 1944, Parliament passed the Reinstatement to Civil Employment Act, which laid it down that there must be at least 26 or 52 weeks (according to length of former employment) return to peacetime employment.

Both the Co-operative agreements went further than the Act. In addition to men and women in the Forces or Civil Defence, they covered enrolled conscientious objectors and workers of both sexes who were transferred to war work or left for this purpose with the prior consent of their societies. There was no limit to the period for which workers must be reinstated. War service, whether in uniform or at home, was to be without adverse effect upon position or prospects of promotion and at the rate of pay prevailing at the time of return to work. Another clause provided that changes in the sex and skill composition of staffs necessitated by wartime labour shortage should be temporary and as soon as practicable after the war there should be a return to the *status quo*. The Transferred Labour Agreement, covering employees compulsorily directed to work of national importance, was broadly similar in its provisions.

As the war neared its end the Executives of NUDAW and the Shop Assistants' Union increasingly urged branches to concentrate on the operation of the two agreements. It was the policy of both Unions that joint committees should be set up to ensure a smooth return to pre-war jobs, or, in the case of disabled members, to occupations they were able to perform. In many societies these committees were formed. But the Co-operative National Wages Council, while reiterating its intention to carry out the two agreements, was not prepared to endorse local committees. Instead, a procedure agreement was accepted by the Council and the Unions, covering intervention by the Council or Wages Boards in certain cases, while, in effect, leaving the Unions free to persuade as many societies as they could to set up joint committees.

The other side of reinstatement was, of course, redundancy for many of the employees who had taken the place of men and women in the Forces or on war work. They were full members of the Union, and in many cases had kept alive branches that were almost denuded of their basic membership. In guidance given to branches towards the end of 1945, NUDAW's Executive Council suggested a policy for the orderly run-down of temporary staffs.

Four weeks was proposed as a reasonable period of notice. Where the demobilisation dates of men and women in the Forces were known the "temporaries" should be notified that their services would not be required after a given date. Through reinstatement committees where they existed, or by direct negotiation in other cases, branches should seek to establish priorities for dismissal. Thus, pensioners who had returned to service would go first, part-time employees next, then married women with husbands in civilian employment; and so on, married men with families being last to go.

Considering the enormous number of men and women involved demobilisation and reinstatement worked smoothly. No legislation or agreement can be free of borderline interpretations and there were disputed cases, for which there was provision in the Act and in the Co-operative agreements.

SERVICE ON MANY FRONTS

It was a long war, more than a year and a half longer than that of 1914-18. It was total war, in which most aspects of working, domestic and personal life were controlled in varying degree. For NUDAW, it brought many other responsibilities than those already described, and only a few can be mentioned here, mostly campaigns in which NUDAW and the Shop Assistants' Union acted jointly.

In the early days of the War the Union sought to secure allowances that would make up the Forces pay of members to or close to the figure of normal wages. Many Co-operatives and private firms accepted this obligation but it did not become general. There was more success in persuading societies and the Wholesales to pay employees' superannuation contributions. There was much slower progress in the introduction of new superannuation schemes, many societies holding back until they knew Government policy on the proposals for social security in the Beveridge Report. In 1941, however, a new CWS scheme was introduced which went most of the way to meeting the objections to some aspects of the earlier scheme.

When the Battle of Britain began in 1940 fire watching became part of the working routine, at first on a voluntary basis, later compulsory under the 1941 Fire Prevention (Business Premises) Order. Agreements on pay and conditions for this extra duty were negotiated. There was also an agreement covering absence through injuries caused while working during an air raid "Alert", the Co-operative Wages Council agreeing that for eight weeks payments due under the Personal Injuries (Civilians) Scheme should be made up to normal wages.

Working time lost in air raids, particularly in London and other cities subject to frequent attack, was the subject of another agreement with the National Wages Council. The Legal Department was kept at full stretch, particularly with cases under the

Factories and Workmen's Compensation Acts — with every machine that would turn going full out on production for the Services, for the much reduced home market and for export there was an inevitable increase in accidents.

Members of the Union, male and female, were compulsorily transferred into all branches of war industry. A former grocer could find himself in a shipyard, or a milliner in a tank factory. Inter-Union arrangements had to be made for the mutual observance of membership cards; the basic provision being that the member's "original Union" should be responsible for all services and benefits, but would not be concerned with trade negotiations on wages and conditions. NUDAW had several of these agreements with other Unions.

During the war the Union contributed to the various funds raised to help allied nations — £1,000 to Russia, plus £4,253 raised through branch activities; £1,000 to China. Earlier in the war there had been £1,000 to Finalnd, then struggling against the might of the Soviet Union. Through one of those ironies so common in history, Finland was soon to be ranked among our enemies. At home, the Union, as part of a TUC scheme, contributed four mobile canteens for the use of the Forces.

The 1941 annual report welcomed the establishment of Joint Industrial Councils for the Distributive Trades (described as "The outstanding feature of the year"). It had long been a Union objective to seek some form of legal regultaion of wages in the jungle of distribution, even though among some distributive workers this could weaken the argument that a strong Trade Union was equally necessary. The 1941 report recorded that the Union was represented on the workers' side of the JICs for Retail Food; Wholesale Grocery and Provisions; Retail Drapery, Outfitting and Footwear; Retail Furnishing and Allied Trades; Hairdressing; Stationery and Tobacconists; Wholesale Meat; Retail Meat: Offal Section.

Finally — a tribute to the NCOs of NUDAW — the branch secretaries and officials. They could scarcely get to know the names and faces of many of their members before they were off to the Forces or war industry. In some branches it was the other way round — the members scarcley knew who their secretary was from one month to another. It was not uncommon for a branch to have two or three secretaries in a single year. It took dedication to take on the job and NUDAW was fortunate in having so many members willing to give up their leisure to serve the Union.

This chapter has been almost entirely about the Union's members as wage earners during the second World War, whether they were in uniform or carrying out their normal jobs. In the next chapter we shall look at the political and other wider aspects of the Union's role. But before moving on one decision that reflects honour on NUDAW must be mentioned. Immediately prior to the war the Executive Council decided that the services of the full-time staff should be at the disposal of members affected by the Military Service Act, and this should be available to those who held conscientious objection to joining the Forces. When war broke out, the Executive further decided that members imprisoned as COs should be excused contributions (as was the case with those in the Forces). Some COs were dismissed and in at least one case a wife was banned because of her husband's conscientious objection to war. NUDAW fought these cases with the same vigour that was devoted to defending the rights of all other members. A similar policy was followed by the Shop Assistants' Union. In neither case was the policy universally popular, particularly in the darker days of the war. Nevertheless, it was maintained, a true expression of the humanistic and libertarian traditions that run strongly through the history of both Unions.

17 NUDAW IN THE SECOND WORLD WAR — 2

Preparing for Invasion: Politics and Policies:
The Victory Election

FOR Britain 1940 was the worst year of the war. In April Hitler's forces overran Norway and Denmark. In May they poured into Holland, Luxembourg and Belgium and rapidly swept onward into France. The British Army was driven towards the coast and seemed doomed to surrender or decimation. It was saved by the miracle of Dunkirk, lifted from the beaches by an armada comprising anything that would float, from pleasure boats to warships. On 22nd June the French Government concluded an armistice with Germany.

By the Autumn all Western Europe with the exception of Switzerland was under the jackboot or, as in Spain and Portugal, was ruled by Governments that were nominally neutral but in philosophy and to some degree in practice were allies of Hitler and Mussolini. To the North East of the continent Sweden was to remain an apprehensive neutral for the duration of the war. Finland was soon to come within the German orbit. Poland had been dismembered between Germany and Russia. To the South East the Balkans were dominated by German power. From the far north of Europe to the Western coasts of France and the Low Countries every fjord and harbour, every aerodrome and landing strip, all the skill and technology of the most industrialised of the continents, were at the disposal of the Nazis for invasion or for submarine blockade of our food and raw materials. It seemed inevitable that for the first time since 1066 Britain would be invaded by an army who came not to raid but to conquer and possess.

One spectacular victory and one silent victory saved us from joining the rest of Europe in servitude to the Nazis. In the Battle of Britain Fighter Command of the Royal Air Force broke the efforts of the *Luftwaffe* to control the skies over the

Channel and the invasion coast. All the world watched that battle far up in the skies. Few people in those days thought of the other powerful deterrent to invasion that lay in wait northward of the Channel. Among those haunted by that silent presence, however, were the professionals of the German Admiralty, who knew that they could not prevent the Royal Navy, at whatever cost in ships and casualties, from destroying the larger part of an invasion armada while it attempted to ferry the *Wehrmacht* across the Channel. More than one hundred years earlier, when Napoleon was expected to invade, the British Admiral St. Vincent declared "I do not say that the French cannot come. I only say that they cannot come by sea". In the *Kriegsmarine* they probably remembered that saying when they cautiously advised their impatient master of the dangers of attempting a sea-borne crossing against a powerful and determined battle fleet.

But this knowledge lay in the future. During that hot summer of 1940 we could only cheer the bravery and skill of the RAF and hope for the best while preparing for the worst. The Battle of Britain was succeeded in August by battle against civilian morale. The Battle of Britain could be watched from the ground. The battle of the cities could only be heard and endured. Few cities, London in particular, escaped nights that were hideous with the drone of the bombers, the crash of anti-aircraft fire and the rumble and flames of falling buildings.

The coast from Berwick-on-Tweed to Portland had been declared an invasion area, with large scale evacuation, compulsory and voluntary, of civilians. The trade of many Co-operative societies withered away, causing redundancy among staffs, most of them Union members. To continue its role of consumer supply, the CWS had divided the country into areas with detailed plans for continuing supplies to or from any area that might be invaded. Some of its departments had already been moved out of London, although in the event most supplies to the Metropolitan and Southern societies continued to be handled from the capital throughout war. In *New Dawn* of 20th July, 1940, A. W. Burrows reported that the Unions had reached an agreement with the Co-operative National Wages Council for evacuated or redundant labour to be absorbed by societies in safer areas.

The first wartime annual delegate meeting of NUDAW was held at Blackpool on May 5th, 6th and 7th, 1940. The "phoney war" mood that had prevailed since 1939 had been given a sharp jolt by the Nazi successes in Norway and Denmark. But the worst was yet to come. Only three days after the meeting ended Hitler launched his attack in the West. Before the ADM met again the British people — and not least Trades Union members responsible for supplying the home market — had survived one of the most critical years in our long history.

We saw in Chapter 15 that before the war began there was division and confusion in the Union (as in the Labour Movement generally) over the action necessary to halt the advance of Hitler, Mussolini and their Japanese allies. These differences continued in a different form to be reflected in the annual meetings between 1940 and 1945. Communist, ILP and Pacifist members and some who belonged to none of these groups but wanted a more Leftward Labour policy continued to put forward their varying interpretations of events. There could be no doubting that the generality of the Union's members, the Executive Council, the MPs and the full-time staff realised that the war was being fought for the survival of democracy, free institutions and in particular free Trades Unions and Co-operatives. If Hitler won, they would disappear, as they had already gone wherever Nazi rule was imposed. But NUDAW was very much an open democracy. The voice of dissent had the right to be heard at the annual Parliament.

Communist members could act in concert without infringing Union rules, but one resolution of the 1940 ADM, carried by 81,445 votes to 52,264, attacked the use of the Union for Communist propaganda. A stop-the-war resolution at the same meeting reflected an ILP and Pacifist viewpoint. It called on the TUC and the Labour Party " . . . to cease helping and supporting the present Government and to use all their energy to bring about cessation of hostilities". It was only narrowly defeated (For 58,358, Against 62,908). A resolution opposing the electoral truce was carried, as was one opposing conscription. There was also a demand for better pay and allowances for the Forces (in one form or another this demand was repeated at all war time annual meetings). In 1941 a call for a "People's Socialist Government", conscription of wealth and "a vigorous

Socialist peace offensive" was rejected. Not that delegates were necessarily opposed to these objectives. But the proposal was seen as an indirect attempt to belittle the Labour Party's participation in Churchill's wartime coalition. Resolutions demanding a declaration of war aims and Union support for the People's Vigilance Committee set up by the Communist Party, were also defeated.

The 1942 meeting carried a protest against a Government ban on the publication of the *Daily Worker* but rejected a demand that the Government should " . . . invite representatives of all nations to a conference to discuss an immediate armistice". It adopted a resolution calling upon the TUC and the Labour Party to campaign for "elected councils" through which members of the Forces could express their "economic and political demands". A further call for the establishment of a "workers' Socialist Government" was rejected. In 1943 an attempt was made to obtain Union support for a Communist Party application to affiliate to the Labour Party — defeated at the ADM by 102,122 votes to 66,173. (A similar resolution in 1946 was lost by a much bigger majority — 144,798 to 31,700). The Beveridge report was welcomed in 1943, a resolution critical of the report rejected, the meeting demanded action to deal with the housing problem, and deprecated the support given by some Labour leaders to Lord Vansittart's campaign for punishing the whole German people for the crimes of Nazism. Finally, it sent a message of congratulation to General Eisenhower and all ranks of the Allied armies on " . . . the magnificent victory in Tunisia over the forces of Fascism and Nazism".

In 1944, with victory in sight, the emphasis was on winning the peace. A resolution calling on the United Nations to " . . . take such steps when victory is won as will ensure that Germany will never again be enabled to throw the world into war" was amended to cover both Germany or " . . . any other imperialist power". The decisions of the Teheran Conference (of Churchill, Roosevelt and Stalin), the Anglo-Soviet Treaty of Friendship and the Soviet-Czech Treaty were cited as examples of the agreements required to ensure peace. A demand that the electoral truce be ended was defeated by 66,545 votes to 58,293.

The 1945 ADM was held on May 2nd, 3rd and 4th. Again it

L

met in Blackpool. The 1940 wartime meeting had been held
there in a year when national survival seemed doubtful and
victory impossible. But once again Britain had saved herself
by her exertions and Europe by her example. The meeting was
held during the week of German surrender on all fronts. This
historic event was celebrated by a declaration in which the
ADM paid "heartfelt tribute of gratitude and admiration to
the Armed Forces and Mercantile Marine of the United
Nations whose valour and sacrifice have brought the struggle
against the barbaric forces of the Nazis and Fascists in sight of
its successful conclusion. It declares its whole hearted support
to the policy of the TUC that there should not be a peace
settlement which will perpetuate the hatred and antagonisms
which have torn the world asunder, but by a firm resolve to
lay down such political and economic conditions as will afford
the fullest possible guarantee that order and law will be maintained throughout the world." It went on:

"For Germany and also Japan military defeat and surrender
must mean retribution and atonement, war criminals of every
rank and status must bear the full penalty of their crimes, with
the dissolution of all Nazi institutions and the re-establishment
of full democratic rights. For all countries which have been
plundered and devastated by the Nazis, restitution in suitable
forms shall be exacted and territorial frontier changes carried
out to ensure the stability of the states bordering Germany and
strengthen European peace".

It should not be assumed from this rapid survey that the
annual meetings of the war years were entirely dominated by
political issues (although there was a suggestion in 1944 that
" . . . no political matters should be discussed prior to the
completion of the industrial business of the meeting". It was
rejected on the grounds that it was impossible to draw a line
between Trades Union and political activities). In practice, industrial issues, particularly questions of wages and conditions
and the mass of statutory rules and regulations governing
working and other conditions, took up most of the time at each
ADM. Members were also alert to the way in which science and
technology were opening up new fields for Union activity and/or
public ownership. One resolution of the 1946 ADM called for
the nationalisation of the ophthalmic optical trade in view of

its importance to the National Health scheme. The same meeting carried a resolution urging the TUC to set up a National Council to bring together all unions catering for scientific and technical workers which, among other purposes, would study and report on the role of scientific workers in rebuilding the national economy.

Midway through the war death removed a man who, as delegate and as General President, had been an outstanding figure at the ADM for many years. On 9th July, 1942, John Jagger, MP, died in a road accident while on his way to his duties as Parliamentary Private Secretary to Herbert Morrison, then Home Secretary. Since 1919 he had been General President, first of AUCE, then of NUDAW following the amalgamation of 1921, holding this high office longer than any other incumbent, before or since. He was succeeded as Acting President by P. Cottrell, who was in due course confirmed in office by vote of the membership. A "Jagger Memorial Fund" of £1,000 was subsequently set up by the Union to be administered by the TUC for the purpose of developing Trades Unionism in the colonies.

Before leaving the politics of the war years one other distressing event must be recorded. During 1944 the Executive Council had been informed by the St. Helens Labour Party of their "profound dissatisfaction" with the services of W. A. Robinson as their MP. He had retired from the position of Political General Secretary in 1942, but retained his Parliamentary seat. (The position of Political General Secretary was abolished by the annual meeting of 1943.) Following the St. Helens approach, a meeting of the Executive in May made the painful decision that they must ask him to resign the seat, and the National Executive of the Labour Party was notified accordingly. W. A. Robinson declined to resign and the Executive subsequently withdrew a retaining allowance and certain other allowances made to him as a Union sponsored member.

This action was later referred to the House of Commons Committee of Privileges and the President and A. W. Burrows (who was at the material time Acting General Secretary) appeared before the Committee. After hearing a full explanation of the circumstances the Committee reported in June that there had been no breach of the privileges of the House. It had long been recognised, said their report, that there were members who received financial assistance from associations of their constituents or other bodies and "A body which provides such assistance must normally be free and entitled to withdraw it". There had been " . . . no attempt to influence the action of the Member in the House of Commons in voting or speaking".

Victory in war was soon followed in Britain by Labour's greatest-ever victory at the polls in the General Election of July, 1945. Churchill had wanted the Coalition to continue at least until the end of the war with Japan. The Labour Party Conference (presided over by Ellen Wilkinson) would not have it. The Election was on. It was to be the "never-again" election; expressing the determination among men and women at home and in uniform that they would never go back to 1939.

In their tens of thousands and in their hundreds of thousands they turned out to cheer Churchill on his much-publicised election cavalcade through Britain. To cheer him as a war leader, the man who had put into burning words the peoples' will to fight. But they rejected him as a man for peace and particularly they rejected the Tory Party which he led, the Party which they identified with the dreary years of national decline, and of hardship and humiliation for millions of ordinary people. Labour had played a major part in the success of the wartime Coalition Government. In "Let us face the future", the Party sought a mandate for strong, positive policies for rebuilding Britain on firmer and healthier foundations. The voters gave the mandate, more than eleven and a half million of them, approximately two million more than the total Tory vote. There were 393 Labour MPs, and 20 who would normally support the Party (ILP etc.).

USDAW, which contributed £5,000 to Labour's Election Fund, went into battle with four sitting Members and entered the new Parliament with seven MPs. Those who already held seats and were again returned were E. Walkden (Doncaster), W. A. Burke (Burnley), R. J. Davies (Westhoughton) and Ellen Wilkinson (Jarrow). The three new MPs were A. Robens (Wansbeck), H. Boardman (Leigh) and T. Scollan (Western Renfrew). In the first Attlee Government Ellen Wilkinson was Minister of Education with a seat in the Cabinet, W. A. Burke was Assistant Postmaster General, A. Robens became Parliamentary Secretary to the Minister of War Transport (Alfred Barnes) and E. Walkden who had been PPS to the Minister of National Insurance in the Coalition Government, was appointed to a similar position with the Minister of Food (Sir Ben Smith). H. Boardman also became PPS to the Minister of Labour (George Isaacs).

Eleven members not on the Union's Parliamentary Panel were elected as Labour or Labour-Co-op candidates. They were A. V. Alexander (Hillsborough, Sheffield; Labour-Co-op), J. Baird (Wolverhampton, East), H. W. Bowden (Leicester, South), Mrs. E. M. Braddock Liverpool, Exchange), P. Daines (E. Ham North; Labour-Co-op), N. Dodds (Dartford; Labour Co-op), E. Grierson (Carlisle), W. Hannan (Glasgow, Maryhill), P. L. E. Shurmer (Sparkbrook, Birmingham), T. C. Skeffington-Lodge (Bedford), L. Tolley (Kidderminster).

It had been a long war, the first (and one can only pray, the last) ever fought on a world-wide scale. When it began, two of the five Continents, Africa and Asia, were still largely under Colonial rule. The British Trades Union and Labour Movements were still weakened by their defeat in the thirties. NUDAW was still predominantly a Union of Co-operative employees, the second Industrial revolution was just beginning. All this had changed. Africa and Asia were on the march to freedom and the right to make or mar their own future. The Labour Party was established in Government. The Trades Union Movement was to assume a power not only in industry but in the State that it had never known before. USDAW had emerged as a large and growing general Union. The Co-operatives, after some post-war years of decline, began a new period of advance. And over it all was to lie the gigantic question mark with which nuclear power has faced mankind.

18 GOODBYE TO NUDAW, WELCOME USDAW

A T the end of both World Wars the Union increased in size and scope through amalgamation. The 1921 merger with the Liverpool based Warehousemen's Union not only more than doubled the membership of the old AUCE but opened up a wide field of recruitment among general workers. Twenty-five years later, in 1946, two more amalgamations again brought increased membership and widened the scope for recruitment. The principal merger was with the National Union of Shop Assistants, Warehousemen and Clerks, and the other with the Journeymen Butchers' Federation of Great Britain.

For NUDAW's Co-operative members the link with the Shop Assistants' was an emotional as well as an organisational event. For more than fifty years the two Unions had lived uneasily together, frequently competing for membership in the Co-operatives, sometimes at daggers drawn, sometimes in guarded alliance, inevitably duplicating machinery and costs in seeking to serve the same body of workers. Discussion on amalgamation had begun as far back as 1904. The subject had rarely been absent from Executive or ADM agenda of one or both Unions in the intervening years and we have already seen several false starts along the road. Now the goal was in sight. By 1946 NUDAW had much the greater number of Co-operative members and was the dominant influence in the retail societies and the Wholesales. The Shop Assistants were stronger in private distributive trades and in particular had a wide range of agreements with multiple firms. But the entire membership of both Unions was still only a small part of the total number of distributive workers.

The idea of amalgamation simmered quietly on during the early part of the war but came to the boil in 1944. In a statement on post-war policy to the annual meeting of that year the NUDAW Executive gave a high priority to obviating inter-Union competition by seeking amalgamation with "certain organisations". This was approved by the meeting. Effectively, it meant the Shop Assistants', although, hopefully, other Unions would be included. At the end of the year the Executives of NUDAW and the Shop Assistants' were well on the way to agreement. By November the terms had been settled and at its meeting of 16/17 December NUDAW's Executive decided to recommend them to the ADM, and circulate to branches for preliminary discussion. Meantime, conversations had been taking place with the Butchers' Federation, but for convenience we will complete the NUDAW - Shop Assistants' amalgamation before coming to the second merger.

The terms agreed between the two Executives were not radically different from those that had been unsuccessful in 1931 and 1937. The title was to be "Union of Shop, Distributive and Allied Workers", thus including something of the original title of both organisations. In scope, the new Union was to begin with the existing membership of its two constituents, with its future development to be " . . . in the organisation of workers employed in the wholesale and/or retail distributive operations and in the catering trades, administrative, clerical, supervisory and general commercial employees, and all such productive and manipulative workers who are employed in separate establishments or in premises ancillary to distributive departments as may be determined from time to time, with proper machinery set up to serve adequately the various occupational needs as well as the general interests of the members".

The central political funds of the two Unions were to be merged, and all other central funds were to go into a single general fund. For contributions and benefits the scales operative in NUDAW were to continue for the members of that Union " . . . and for all new members recruited in the Amalgamated Union". Shop Assistants' members were to have two options (a) to continue on contributions and benefits applicable at the time of the amalgamation; or (b) they could transfer to one of the scales applicable in the Amalgamated Union (i.e. the NUDAW scales).

The first — provisional — Executive Council was to consist of the existing Executive Councils of the two Unions at the time of the merger. For NUDAW this comprised twelve territorial members and the President, all with voting rights, plus the

General Secretary and A. W. Burrows, non-voting members. The Shop Assistants' had thirteen voting members and G. Maurice Hann (General Secretary) as a non-voting member. The President of NUDAW was to be President of the Amalgamated Union during the transitional period.

The Provisional Executive was to hold office for two years, provision being made for filling vacancies, and before the expiration of this transitional period arrangements were to be made " ... for the amalgamated membership to decide the future composition and method of election of the Executive Council".

J. Hallsworth was to be the General Secretary with G. M. Hann and A. W. Burrows as Assistant General Secretaries, subject " ... only to the direction of the General Secretary". There was provision to make full use of the specialised private trade and multiple shops experience of the Shop Assistants' Union. In these fields of distribution, Union activity would continue to be superintended from Dilke House, London — the headquarters of the Shop Assistants' — by G. M. Hann. The central office of the new Union was, however, to be at "Oakley", Manchester. The permanent staffs of both Unions were to be taken over at wages and other terms of service "not less favourable than those obtaining at the date of decision to amalgamate".

Both Unions had detailed arrangements for territorial and vocational contact with members and it was provided that existing arrangements for conferences, divisional councils and federations of branches prevailing in either or both should be adapted to serve for the Amalgamated Union. *New Dawn* and the *Distributive Trades Journal* of the Shop Assistants' were to continue "until such time as the Amalgamated Union has decided what shall be the future Journal/s needed therefore". Similarly, existing educational facilities would be continued until the new Union had decided upon a comprehensive scheme.

One benefit from the long delay over amalgamation had been that most of the differences between the two Unions had been identified, thrashed out over the years and acceptable compromises envisaged. The scheme of merger that has been summarised did not attempt too quickly or too sharply to alter established practices in either Union. Time was given for the two Executives to get to know each other and establish a corporate identity, the subscription and benefit scales familiar to existing members of the Shop Assistants' were undisturbed for those who wanted it that way, decisions on such matters as Journals and education were left for later discussion when the new Union had settled down. Above all, the titanic struggle of the war had prepared the minds of men and women for change and, among distributive workers, for an end to old rivalries that indirectly helped to perpetuate the weakness of Trades Unionism in their field of employment.

This new mood was reflected in the ADM of 1945, held at Blackpool on the 2nd, 3rd and 4th May, by which date the proposals had already been adopted by the Shop Assistants' conference. The NUDAW meeting voted on a resolution, moved by J. Hallsworth, to adopt the proposed basis of amalgamation, submit it to a ballot of members as soon as practicable, and if that secured the necessary majorities, hold a joint special delegate meeting with the Shop Assistants to adopt rules and fix a date of operation. There were only three speakers from the floor, none opposing the proposals, which, on a show of hands, were carried by 446 votes to 8. But in moving the resolution Hallsworth mentioned several special problems arising from the war (which at the date of the ADM was expected to continue for an indefinite period against Japan once it was ended in Europe). NUDAW still had approximately 80,000 members in the Forces and the Shop Assistants' about 30,000 scattered in almost every corner of the world and on the high seas. To conform to the law, at least 50 per cent of the members must vote and the number in favour must exceed those against by 20 per cent. The first percentage would be no easy task when it was difficult or impossible to reach many members. Therefore, said Hallsworth, the Executive would not rush the ballot.

In the event, both wars were over before the two Unions ballotted their members in 1946. Both, however, had sought to obtain the greatest possible number of addresses of members in the Forces or Civil Defence. NUDAW already had this information for members receiving regular copies of *New Dawn* from Central Office. Branches were urged to send all the Forces addresses they could obtain to Central Office and to keep up to date with alterations.

An article in *New Dawn* of 3rd November, 1945, announced that ballot papers and explanatory circulars would be despatched to branches on 1st March, 1946, to be distributed to each member. Branch committees, particularly those with large memberships, were directed to plan team work distribution to ensure that all members knew the case for amalgamation. Forces members whose addresses were available would be covered direct from Central Office, the ballot cards to be returned by a date approximately two months later than that stipulated for the return of the civilian ballots. As a slight compensation for the work involved in distributing and handling this mass of paper there was to be an allowance to branches of 1d for each ballot paper returned. It was suggested that branch committees should allocate the allowance to shop stewards or other branch officials in proportion to services rendered in thus oiling the wheels of the ballot machinery. Branch meetings should also be called to discuss the amalgamation proposals prior to the ballot.

Altogether, more than 208,000 ballots were sent out in bulk by NUDAW, and 14,000 posted to members in the Forces or on National Service. Similar strenuous efforts to secure a large and favourable vote were taking place in the Shop Assistants' Union. Polling in NUDAW branches began after 1st March, 1946, and the last day for the return of ballot papers to Central Office was fixed as Friday, 12th April, or 21st June for the Forces vote.

And now — the stage was set. How would the cast perform? Given the two Unions' long history of "amalgamation — almost but not quite" there must have been some nail-biting at "Oakley" and Dilke House as the ballot papers began to come in, either in the slim envelope of a small branch or the bump of a parcel from one of the great city Co-ops. But all was well. Both Unions satisfied the two voting provisions of the Act, with comfortable margins in the case of the 50 per cent required to vote, and overwhelmingly in the case of the majorities in favour of amalgamation.

The actual figures were:

NUDAW

Ballot cards issued	—	222,864
For amalgamation	—	133,176
Against amalgamation	—	6,915
Majority in favour	—	126,261

NAUSAW & C

Ballot cards issued	—	106,282
For amalgamation	—	69,660
Against amalgamation	—	2,516
Majority in favour	—	67,144

Of NUDAW's Forces membership 43,603 either could not be contacted or did not vote.

The next step was the joint delegate meeting of the two Unions, held at Blackpool on Sunday, 10th November, 1946, to clothe the infant USDAW in provisional rules in readiness for its official launch into the world on 1st January, 1947. Complete revision of rules was to come later. There was one note of sadness at the November meeting. As we have seen, J. Jagger, for long an advocate of unity,would have been in the presidential chair but for the accident in which he lost his life. Another well known figure missing from the meeting was G. M. Hann, who had retired from the General Secretaryship of the Shop Assistants' to become a member of the Industrial Court. P. Cottrell, President-Designate of the new Union, ably steered the meeting through a somewhat intricate agenda.

All went well at the joint meeting and on 1st January, 1947. The **Officers** and provisional **Joint Executive Council** of the new Union were: President, P. Cottrell; General Secretary, Sir Joseph Hallsworth (who had been knighted in 1946); Assistant General Secretaries, A. W. Burrows and J. D. Hiscock (who took the place of G. M. Hann. Aged 42 at the time of his appointment, Joe Hiscock, as he was best known, had already been an official of the Shop Assistants' Union for 25 years.); Chief Organising Officer, G. Beardsworth; Chief Administrative Officer, R. A. Campbell. **Executive Council,** From former Shop Assistants' Union: J. Carruthers (Clydebank), B. C. Davies (Bridgend), H. Gunson (London CWS), W. Harvey (Reading), F. Jackson (Harrogate), D. McGibbon (Springburn, Glasgow), H. C. McGinty (Manchester Optical), W. Marsh (Salisbury),

S. Mills (Birmingham), H. Moore (Glasgow East), Miss
M. Scott (Newcastle), Miss C. Smith (Leith), H. M. Tribe
(West London Co-operative). From former NUDAW: J.
Cunnick (Manchester Equitable), W. S. Jones (Birkenhead
Co-operative), W. H. Marshall (Irlam CWS), R. T. Milloy
(Kilmarnock), F. J. Newman (Bristol Retail), R. B. Seabrook
(Chelmsford), W. H. Stacey (Birmingham Co-operative), S. F.
Thrower (Woolwich Mutuality), J. White (Throckley, Northum-
berland), F. Williams (Stockport Co-operative), I. Williams
(Aberdare), H. Worfolk (York).

The definitive rules were not adopted until 1948, the provisional period being used to unify administrative and other
procedures of the two former Unions and to prepare a rule book
based on the terms of the amalgamation agreement and other
necessary provisions. One contentious feature of the proposals
considered at a special rule-making delegate meeting on May
9th and 10th, 1948, typified the strong democratic tradition of
NUDAW, and is worth recording in some detail. The proposal
was that branches with fewer than 250 members should be
grouped for the purpose of representation at the ADM. In
moving, A. W. Burrows, the Acting General Secretary, acknowledged that this was a complete break with the former
NUDAW practice of direct representation, although the Shop
Assistants' combined direct and indirect representation, and
for them the change would not be so marked. Even before the
amalgamation, he argued, NUDAW's annual meeting, with
1,148 delegates and Divisional Councillors in 1947, was too big
to be an effective deliberative assembly — and in the new Union
there were almost twice as many branches (2,144).

But the delegates were not convinced. An amendment from
Walsall branch proposed that each branch should have one
delegate up to 500 members, with additional numbers for those
with a larger membership. The proposer — James, could see
no reason why the Union should be afraid of numbers when
there were even larger attendances at the Labour Party Conference, the Trade Union Congress and the conferences of some
other Unions. Small branches were often the liveliest. Another
speaker enquired why it should be assumed that "... at 800
you are an intelligent lot, at 801 you are a mob". A Liverpool
Butchers' delegate from a branch with under 200 members said

they could have some special trade problem which they wished to bring to the ADM, but under the proposed rule they might have to ask a hairdresser or a grocer to put the butchers' point of view. It was also argued that there was no reason why small branches should not voluntarily co-operate in selecting a delegate (this provision is in present rules of the Union). Executive Councillor McGibbon sought to avert defeat by pointing out that of 360 branches with from eleven to thirty members, 344 were not represented. But the meeting would not have it. The proposal was defeated on a show of hands and the amendment carried. It is still the rule of the Union. Probably the right decision was made. Grass roots democracy is not perfect but it does embody one essential freedom — the right to be heard if you so desire, however small your voice may be.

The new rules reduced the Executive Council from twenty-four plus President and General Secretary under the provisional arrangement to eighteen plus President and General Secretary. But by 1949 there were new occupants of the two latter offices. Percy Cottrell died on 2nd February, 1948. R. T. Milloy, a Union member since 1913 and Executive Councillor since 1930, was appointed acting President but at the ensuing election, W. (Walter) E. Padley was elected by the former NUDAW membership (as new rules were not yet operative), later confirmed by the entire membership of USDAW.

To complete the list of changes at the top, Sir Joseph Hallsworth resigned in May, 1947, to become a member of the National Coal Board. It would be a painful decision for him to make, for we have seen how intimately his life had been bound up with the Union. But he was also a convinced believer in social ownership and with USDAW now well established as the major distributive Union he no doubt felt that he must work for the success of the principle in which he so strongly believed. A. W. Burrows was appointed as Acting General Secretary. He retired in the Autumn of 1949, handing over the Acting Secretaryship to J. A. (Alan) Birch, who was subsequently confirmed in the position by vote of the members. A former active member of the Warrington branch and a Liverpool Divisional Councillor, Alan Birch, as he was known in the Union, became a Union Area Organiser and at the time of his election had been a National Organiser since 1943.

Percy Cottrell was the third President to die in office. He had held the position for only six years but had been a Union member since 1899. His working life from the age of ten had been spent with the small Delph Co-operative Society, perched on the Pennine Moors between Lancashire and Yorkshire. He had been secretary of the Society since 1923. The new President was well known in the Union as a skilled debater, a dedicated Socialist (for many years in the ILP) and an active Union member who had served for ten years on the Southern and Eastern Divisional Council. For two years he was at Ruskin College, Oxford, on a TUC scholarship, gaining the University Diploma in Economics and Political Science.

The amalgamation was "the end of the beginning" for Trades Unionism among distributive workers. And the story reaches its final chapter with the election of the first definitive Executive Council of USDAW in 1949. The Council included, of course, the two newly elected officers mentioned earlier. The other members were (with Divisions in brackets — note that some larger Divisions had two representatives):— F. Williams (Cheshire and North Wales); W. S. Jones (Liverpool); G. B. Hunter, R. Hanes (London); W. H. J. Marshall, J. Cunnick (Manchester); W. H. Stacey, F. H. M. Nichols (Midlands); J. White (Northern); A. Sutherland (North Scotland); D. McGibbon (South Scotland); W. L. Peck (Southern and Eastern); I. Williams (South Wales and Mon.); W. A. Parfitt (South Western); E. Rollinson, Edna Falkingham (Yorkshire).

So ended the long, often weary, road to amalgamation of the two pioneer Unions of shop workers. There were still alive founders of the Manchester District Co-operative Employees' Association of 1891 and no doubt of the men who founded the Shop Assistants' Union in the same year. Near the end of their days, they could feel satisfaction that from microscopic beginnings they had helped to build the largest Trade Union of distributive and allied workers in the Western World.

We come now to the merger with the Butchers' Federation. It is not to be belittled because it was smaller in size than the principal amalgamation, for it brought into a single Union specialist workers in one of the most important distributive trades. In this case, however, a simpler procedure was followed. The method was a transfer of engagements, which did not call for the fixed voting percentages required in an amalgamation, simple majorities of those present and voting at the appropriate meetings being sufficient. The 1945 annual meeting of NUDAW unanimously adopted a resolution for a scheme of fusion " . . . as constituting the instrument of transfer required under the Societies (Miscellaneous Provisions) Act, 1940". But when the Federation delegates met at a special delegate meeting there was a hitch which threatened the merger.

It was mainly over the future organisation of branches. The scheme provided that, according to local circumstances, branches of the Federation would either continue a separate existence, merge with branches of NUDAW consisting solely of meat trade workers or become part of composite branches along with other classes of distributive workers. Probably through fears that this would destroy the craft basis of their trade, Federation delegates rejected the scheme. Assurances were given by NUDAW that there would be no compulsion; any merger of branches would be through persuasion. With this safeguard a second special meeting adopted the scheme, which was further endorsed by the vote of branch meetings.

On contributions and benefits the terms were similar to those agreed with the Shop Assistants' Union — existing members of the Federation to continue on present scales if they wished, with the option of transfer to NUDAW scales, all new members to join on the NUDAW scales. A National Committee for the meat trades membership of the Union was to be set up to deal with trade matters and advise the Executive Council. Organisers of the Federation would continue as such as part of USDAW's staff. The merger with the Butcher's Federation was followed by two other meat trade organisations joining USDAW in 1947 — Manchester Abattoir Workers' Association and the Glasgow Slaughtermen's Association.

With all the complications safely negotiated, the National Union of Distributive and Allied Workers, the National Amalgamated Union of Shop Assistants, Warehousemen and Clerks and the Journeymen Butchers' Federation of Great Britain — let us enjoy the full resonance of those names for the last time — passed into history. As a turning point, their merger ranks with, and was a continuation of, the decisions of 1915 and 1917 which, as we saw earlier, converted the

Amalgamated Union of Co-operative Employees of those years from a body mainly concerned with Co-operative shop workers into a general Union open to all workers in distribution and associated trades. That decision could never be fully implemented while the two main distributive Unions weakened each other by competition. January 1st, 1947, was the day of a "new dawn" of opportunity to mobilise the still scattered and exploited army of distributive and allied workers.

PLATE I

LIFE IN THE SHOP WHEN VICTORIA REIGNED

A DEPARTMENT STORE OF 1891 IN LONDON'S
WEST END

PLATE II

REVOLT BEGINS IN SHOPS AND OFFICES

The masks were not a theatrical stunt; these clerks of 1913 could have been sacked for parading.

Sandwich-board protest against living-in. Third on right is PC Hoffman, Shop Assistants' Union pioneer.

MANCHESTER AND BOLTON UNITE TO FORM AUCE

The joint committee of the Manchester District Co-operative Employees' Association and the Bolton Co-operative Employees' Trade Union, which formed AUCE in 1895. In centre, wearing the top-hat of his trade (he was manager of the Working Hatters' Co-operative Association) is J. Dyson, first President of AUCE, with A. Hewitt, first Secretary, on his right.

PLATE III

PLATE IV

FIRST GENERAL SECRETARIES, AUCE AND NUDAW

A. HEWITT
March, 1891 to April, 1916
Full-time from Feb., 1899

SIR JOSEPH HALLSWORTH
April, 1916 to Jan.,1921; Joint G. S. NUDAW
Jan., 1921 to Dec., 1923; Industrial G. S. Dec.,
1923 to Nov., 1942; G. S. Nov., 1942 to Dec., 1949

*FOUR PRESIDENTS

W. A. ROBINSON
Joint G. S. NUDAW Jan., 1921 to
Dec., 1923; Political G. S. Dec., 1923
to retirement from staff Nov., 1942

T. HOWE
June, 1897 to Feb., 1915 *Died in office*
*J. DYSON, March, 1891 to June, 1897
is on Plate III.

R. B. PADLEY
Aug., 1915 to April, 1919

J. JAGGER
April, 1919 to July, 1942 *Died in road accident*

PLATE V

STRIKES IN THE EARLY DAYS

Above: A strike of AUCE members at Lincoln Co-op in 1913 ended after 6 weeks on terms satisfactory to the Union.

Right: Employees of Beavans, at Byker, Newcastle-upon-Tyne drapery firm, join in a strike organised by the Shop Assistants' Union.

PLATE VI

MEN GO TO WAR IN 1914...

...WOMEN TAKE OVER IN THE SHOPS

PLATE VII

UNION BADGES, PAST AND PRESENT

Badges of the National Union of Distributive & Allied Workers, the Shop Assistants' Union and USDAW. Some are in brilliant colours, a tribute to the craftsmen who designed and made them, and it is not possible to do justice to them in black and white. They were commonly worn by Union members in times past but badges are less frequently seen today.

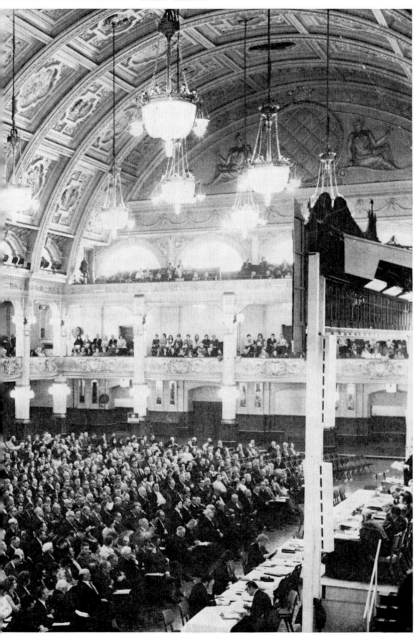

"OAKLEY", FALLOWFIELD, MANCHESTER, USDAW's CENTRAL OFFICE

The original building is on the left, with most of successive additions to the right.

PLATE X

PLATE XI

THE SECOND WORLD WAR, 1939-1945

Ration books meant that there was a fair distribution of basic foods but were frequently a headache for the housewife and USDAW's members in the shops.

Clement Attlee, soon to be Prime Minister, acclaims Labour's victory at the General Election of 1945.

PLATE XII

THREE GENERAL SECRETARIES, 1949 TO 1979*

SIR ALAN BIRCH
Dec., 1949 to Dec., 1961
Died in office

LORD ALLEN
May, 1962 to July, 1979

W. H. P. WHATLEY
July, 1979, to date

SIX PRESIDENTS, 1944 TO 1979*

P. COTTRELL
May, 1944 to Feb., 1948
Died in office

W. E. PADLEY
June, 1948 to Oct,. 1964

R. B. SEABROOK
Feb., 1965 to April, 1965
Re-elected May, 1967 *to May*, 1973

R. HANES
April, 1965 to May, 1967

J. D. HUGHES
May, 1973 to April, 1977

S. TIERNEY
April, 1977 to date

*Both these positions were at times held by an acting member until elections took place. Only those directly elected are given here.

PLATE XIII

THE UNION'S SUMMER SCHOOLS

Above: Beatrice Webb House, Holmbury St. Mary, where the first
school of each year is held.
Below: Students at the second series advanced school, held each year
at Ruskin College, Oxford.

PLATE XIV

THE UNION IN THE TUC

USDAW is the sixth largest Union affiliated to the TUC. It is also a member of the Scottish TUC, Wales TUC and the Northern Ireland Committee of the Irish Congress of Trades Unions. Two General Secretaries, Sir Joseph Hallsworth and Lord Allen, were presidents of the British Congress.

USDAW delegates vote at Congress . . .

. . . and at the TUC Women's Conference

DIVISIONAL OFFICES AND OTHER PROPERTIES

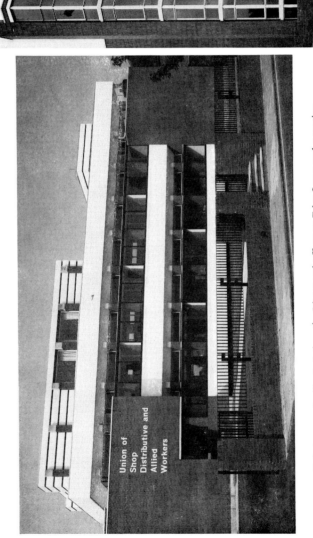

Only two can be illustrated — the Liverpool offices at Edge Lane and a section of Concord House, Leeds, a joint project with the General and Municipal Workers' Union.

PLATE XV

PLATE XVI

THE VOICE OF THE UNION IN PRINT

Dawn, the present colour printed tabloid newspaper of the Union, is its fifth journal since the establishment of the Manchester District Co-operative Employees' Association. Other were *Gleanings for Members, The Co-operative Employee, AUCE Journal* and *New Dawn*. Shop Assistants' Union publications, eventually merged in *New Dawn* were *The Shop Assistant* and *The Distributive Trades Journal*.

19 THE FIRST PEACETIME NATIONAL AGREEMENT:

THROUGHOUT this history we have followed NUDAW's efforts to improve wages and conditions in the Co-operative Movement and also to establish some degree of uniformity. Twelve chapters ago we saw the first cautious probings of the Manchester District Co-operative Employees' Association to find out what was actually being paid in 1892. In the following years the Union won many victories with wage rates and conditions but made little headway towards uniformity. Until 1946. On 2 October of that year the Joint Trade Union Negotiating Committee for the Retail Co-operative Movement and the National Wages Board of the Co-operative Union Ltd. signed their first ever peacetime national agreement on basic rates. NUDAW — only two months away from becoming USDAW — had been the principal member of the Trade Union Committee, and A. W. Burrows, the Union's Organising Secretary, was the main architect of the agreement and also the spokesman for NUDAW and the other Unions involved throughout just under a year of negotiations.

Two weeks after the signature, on the pay day of the week beginning 14th October, the wages packets of Co-operative shop workers, branch managers and manageresses, clerical, dairy and transport workers were heavier. Some very much heavier, for one purpose of this historic agreement was to smooth out local anomalies, many entrenched in custom and practice, some imposed regionally during the depression years.

And it all happened almost by chance! We saw in Chapter 16 that it was the binding decision of a Conciliation Board chairman in 1945 that led the Union's Executive Council almost reluctantly to begin discussions on a national agreement, and the best that could be said of the 1945 ADM was that it tepidly accepted the principle by defeating a proposition to resume Divisional negotiations after the war.

War weariness may have had something to do with this

M

apparent reluctance to support a reform which the Union had sought in the past. Certainly, to turn a decision in principle into detailed agreements would be one of the most complex tasks that any Trade Union had faced. There were about 300 (some reports said 200) separate agreements with the retail Co-operative Movement which had to be reshaped into a uniform pattern. There were 1,037 retail societies in 1946, varying in size from a few hundred members to tens of thousands, each of them an independent entity. All would have to agree before the new national scales could operate. A little hesitation in plunging into that maelstrom could be understood, and when the series of national agreements surfaced in August, 1946, the contents gave some measure of the concentrated work by Union and Co-operative negotiators that had gone into their composition.

In the draft proposals there were around 3,000 variables according to job specification, age or (in the case of branch managers and manageresses), sales; Many, of course, were small age/wage steps or variations in skill or responsibility, such as an ascending scale for transport workers according to carrying capacity of vehicle. But all would be carefully scrutinised and frequently argued over from the two sides of the negotiating table. This enormously detailed settlement had been reached through a Joint Committee of the Unions and the Co-operative National Wages Council (later to become the National Wages Board) and in particular through a joint sub-committee of twenty. Of the ten representing the Unions, NUDAW appointed four members, the Shop Assistants' two and other Unions four. This sub-committee conducted the actual negotiations with the Co-operative side, beginning its work (after some preliminary sparring over procedure) on 3rd September, 1945, and holding 26 two-day meetings before agreement was reached on 9th August, 1946.

The first progress report on the sub-committee's work was given at a joint conference of NUDAW's Executive and Divisional Councils in Manchester on 20th October, 1945. A. W. Burrows reported that after some resistance the Unions had accepted as inevitable that there should be grouping of societies and grading. It was envisaged that there would be four groups — Metropolitan, Provincial A, Provincial B and a "temporary" group (eventually designated as Provisional). This group was for small societies where current wages went so far below a group scale that there could be financial difficulties if there was an immediate jump. The actual grouping of societies would be arranged through the Sectional Wages Boards of the Co-operative Union and the Divisional Officers of the Unions concerned. The Unions were pressing for a 40 hour week, but if one reads the conference report aright Burrows was not optimistic that it would be conceded (nor was it). There was also deadlock over equality of adult male and female rates. They were, however, optimistic that the two weeks holiday would be obtained. On actual wage rates, the Unions were concentrating on eliminating the low rates then prevailing in some Divisions.

So far so good. The negotiators continued to slog it out in many a "smokefilled room". They must frequently have been dizzy in following the permutations of age, wage, group and even terminology (for instance, first assistants were called "second hands" in Scotland and "foremen" in the Northern Section). There was occasional light relief. A. W. Burrows tells the story of an argument over payment for weekend ostling duties (there were still many horses in transport in the forties). Five shillings for these duties was claimed. One of the Co-operative side quoted the case of an old pensioned horse, the last in the society, of which the ostler was very fond. So much so that he came in each weekend to tend it. "If you want 5/- for looking after that horse", he said, "you might as well take the confounded animal." But one by one obstacles were overcome and in the early part of 1946 the main agreement covering general distributive and ancillary workers had been worked out and NUDAW referred it to the democracy of the membership in a series of Divisional delegate conferences (details of the agreement are given in Appendix I).

It must be rare for Trade Union negotiators to produce an agreement that is satisfactory to all their constituents. NUDAW members ran true to form. There were complaints, very strong in London, that the proposed basic rates were too low. Ex-servicemen in particular seem to have maintained that the Co-operatives had lagged behind rising wage standards during the war, and were continuing to do so. Some members were

concerned that the war bonuses had not been consolidated into
the basic rates. A. W. Burrows and G. Beardsworth (the
Assistant Organising Secretary) met these points at all the
Divisional conferences. It is probable, however, that many of
the complaints reflected the feeling that even if you consider
your negotiators have on the whole done a good job, there is
no harm in prodding them to try and do better.

Nine of the eleven Divisional conferences were reported in
New Dawn during March and April, 1946. London and Cheshire
and North Wales rejected the proposals. London because of
" . . . the inadequacy of the wage rates at the adult age for both
men and women", the other Division presumably for the same
reason (its conference was not directly reported, but the hostile
decision was mentioned at the ADM). For the other Divisions
the reported verdicts were:

Southern and Eastern, accepted by an "overwhelming
    majority".
South Wales and Monmouthshire, carried "with only
    one branch dissenting".
Liverpool, carried on a show of hands.
Manchester, carried 107-19.
Yorkshire, carried 106-1.
Northern, carried 126-43.
Scotland, carried 127-13.

For some reason no reports were published of the Midland
and Western Divisional conferences. But the mandate was clear
and it was basic to the whole concept of national negotiations.
General distributive workers formed much the larger part of
the Union's Co-operative membership, and had they rejected
the proposals there would have been little hope for national
scales for branch managers and manageresses, clerical, transport and milk workers. These were completed by the summer,
and endorsed by a further joint conference of the Executive
and Divisional Councils on 24th August for reference to the
Divisions, London voting against. At similar conferences of
the Shop Assistants' Union the proposed agreements were
discussed and eventually ratified, with some dissentients.

All the agreements were built round the same framework —
the grouping of societies into the four categories of Metropolitan, Provincial A, Provincial B and Provisional.

The main general distributive workers' agreement covered male
and female shop assistants in all departments (except hairdressers and cafe workers); cash desk workers; leading assistants; first assistants in grocery and provision, butchery, green-
grocery, fish and dry goods departments; ancillary workers such
as head warehousemen, male warehousemen, packers, porters,
cleaners, lift attendants and cellarmen; female packers, cleaners,
lift attendants and warehouse workers; travelling shop workers.

Thr *branch managers' and manageresses'* agreement covered
male and female grocery managers; male managers of butchery
branches; tobacco manageresses of separate shops detached
from grocery; bread and confectionery manageresses; male or
female manageresses of all departments other than those
mentioned and pharmacy; grocery and butchery travelling
shop managers with responsibility for stock control, leakage
and other factors. The *clerical* agreement covered male and
female clerks, calculating machine operators, shorthand
typists and section heads.

The *transport* agreement covered one-horse carters; four
categories of drivers of mechanically and electrically propelled
vehicles ranging from those with a carrying capacity of up to
15 cwt to those with a capacity between 3 and 5 tons; junior
drivers and "all other workers"; adult and junior bakery
rounds workers; coal workers. For adult *milk* workers, rates
were prescribed for roundsmen, rotary roundsmen, head
sterilisers and pasteurisers, foremen, and for assistant roundsmen, pasteurisers, sterilisers and "all other male workers".
There were scales for adult and junior females other than
roundswomen. Scales for adult transport workers, mainly or
wholly employed on milk work (other than roundsmen) were
similar to those in the transport agreement. Additional amounts
were listed for night work.

All agreements specified that the rates did not include national
war bonuses. All except that for clerks were for a working week
of 44 hours. For the clerks it was 40 hours. The clerical agreement also went up to age 26, most others which prescribed an
age/wage scale, to 23. In general, overtime was to be at time-and-
a-half, with double time for Sundays or Statutory holidays.
But the ostler and his horse were not forgotten. Weekend ostling
was to be at the rate of 1/- per horse per visit, with a minimum

of 3/- per visit. For milk workers any overtime could range up to double time in certain specified circumstances.

All five agreements provided for up to twelve days annual holiday, according to length of service. The question of wages during sickness was deferred until after the enactment of the National Insurance Bill, and pending negotiations that would then take place the former agreements continued to operate.

It would require an impossible amount of space to give the actual wage rates in full detail. They were, as Burrows repeatedly insisted, not designed to give all-round increases (wage increases were still being negotiated as war bonuses) but to even-out anomalies, establish standards that members in many societies could never have won on the old basis of sectional or local negotiations, and provide that at least within each group members doing the same job received the same pay. As a guide to the new scales, the table in Appendix I gives the top male and female rates for shop assistants *inclusive* of War Bonus, and for grocery branch managers and manageresses the rates without bonus added.

The general distributive agreement had already been approved at the earlier series of conferences. The agreements for transport, milk, clerical workers and branch managers and manageresses now went through a similar rigorous examination at separate meetings in September for each occupational group. In many societies there were also preliminary discussions at branch meetings. The agreements were accepted in all except two Divisions. At long last a pattern of order and discipline had been carved out of chaos in one important field of the Union's activities.

It was not likely, however, that any agreement covering so much ground could continue for long without amendment, and in 1947 there was considerable turmoil on the wages scene, partly over the national agreement, partly over war bonuses. Although the two were linked they will, for convenience, be dealt with separately.

London was the centre of the strongest protest against the national scales. There were unofficial strikes and the strong feelings among the workers concerned persuaded the Metropolitan Wages Board to seek and obtain the permission of the Co-operative National Wages Council to negotiate an increase for the five Metropolitan societies (London, Royal Arsenal, South

Suburban, Enfield Highway, Grays). There was a similar situation at Bristol and it was soon known that a number of Group A societies were giving outside-scale increases under one guise or another. In these circumstances an attempt was made to negotiate a Super A Group, but after long argument no agreement could be reached on the criteria for such a group.

In May the Unions had claimed a tenth war bonus, designed in part to secure a minimum wage of £5 for the lowest paid workers (a broadly similar claim was simultaneously made for private trade workers through the four principal JICs for the retail trade). The Conciliation Board chairman awarded USDAW members approximately one-third of what had been claimed, and by the end of 1947 there was simmering discontent that no progress on wages and conditions was being made, either through the National Agreement or war bonuses. At this point the two began to coalesce.

In January, 1948, the joint Unions applied for consolidation of bonus into the basic national scales and for an advance to all employees of 7/6 weekly for those over 18, 5/– for those below that age (more or less the balance of what had been claimed in May). Again it was emphasised that one reason for the claim was to establish a basic minimum of £5. It was mid-summer, 1948, before the two sides had hammered out an agreement. Negotiations were complicated by the fact that the Co-operatives, in response to a direct appeal by the Chancellor of the Exchequer, Sir Stafford Cripps, were voluntarily operating a series of price cuts on basic foods, and there was some resentment that they were simultaneously being pressed by the Unions for a wage increase. But the Unions had a strong case on grounds of the cost of living and comparability with other industries. When agreement was reached consolidation had been effected and, in the words of the official statement " . . . the parties have endeavoured to approach the claim for a £5 minimum for the lowest paid workers".

For shop assistants, increases at various ages brought the consolidated rates at age 23 to:

		Men	Women
Metropolitan	—	113/–	85/6
Provincial "A"	—	105/6	81/–
„ "B"	—	102/6	79/–

Approximately similar increases were given to other groups — branch managers and manageresses, warehousemen, porters, packers, etc., clerical workers, transport workers, milk workers. The agreement also tidied up previous arrangements for paying wages during sickness without deduction of National Health Insurance benefits, a national scale of sick pay entitlement being substituted, based on length of service. The Provisional Group, which covered only a minute number of employees, was to be abolished after 1st January, 1949. Finally, it was agreed that superannuation payments and benefits which in most societies were based on the pre-war basic wage, would so continue unless there were agreed local arrangements for a different basis, actuarially approved.

Negotiations on grouping were a continuous process and by the end of 1949 more than 90 per cent of provincial Co-operative employees were on Group A rates.

From the first war bonus of 1939 it had taken almost ten years to establish a national wages pattern throughout the Co-operative Movement. Nothing has been said in this chapter about the Wholesale Societies, but in general they followed the lines of the retail agreements, both with war bonuses and now with consolidation. Wages negotiations were never likely to be easy, but both Union and Co-operative negotiators must have sighed with relief that at last the basic groundwork had been laid. However much they might disagree in the future, they had ensured that there should be a base for an approximate equality of rewards.

PART 5

PROBLEMS
OF THE PEACE

20 A NOT SO BRAVE NEW WORLD

THE war was over. But between 1945 and the mid-fifties the problems of peace were never-ending as they overlapped each other in rapid succession. At times it seemed that Britain's war-ravaged economy would collapse under the strain. The tension of these years was reflected in USDAW and we must now sketch in the national background against which the Union had to operate.

Even the weather was against us. In the winter of 1946 the country was buried beneath mountainous snow. Coal was frozen at the pitheads, transport immobilised. Electricity for industry had to be severely reduced in many areas. Along with other periodicals, *New Dawn's* issue of 22nd February, 1947, could not be published because of the fuel and power crisis. The wettest March on record brought floods, destruction and loss of life, and when at last it seemed that the storm gods had relented they returned with snow in April.

In July, 1946, bread, which had never been rationed in Britain throughout the war, went on ration to release cereals for the hungry millions who had become the responsibility of the victors with the collapse of Germany and Japan. Supplies continued to be rationed until the middle of 1948. In August and October, 1947, there were cuts in other food rations and in November potatoes were rationed (rationing was not completely ended until 1955). With overseas assets liquidated to pay for the war, and with enormous debts in addition, Britain staggered under a further blow when American aid under Lend-Lease was withdrawn in 1945. A dollar loan was negotiated in 1946 but it soon began to disappear under the pressure of rising world prices and the multiplying needs of an ailing economy.

A more fundamental solution to the problems of Europe as a whole came in 1947 when General G. C. Marshall, then American Secretary of State (who, during the war, was the organising head of America's military effort) proposed the plan for European recovery that was known by his name. The Marshall Plan, which was authorised by the United States Congress in March, 1948, was denounced by Communists and some Labour people as dollar imperialism but undoubtedly it provided the means by which Europe, Britian included, hauled itself from the edge of the abyss.

Life goes on under the worst conditions and as well as agonising problems there were great achievements. The United Nations had been launched and was hopefully welcomed as a successor to the League of Nations, welcomed nowhere more wholeheartedly than in USDAW and the British Labour Movement generally. If it has not lived up to those hopes it has at least been more successful than its predecessors as a forum in which international disputes can be defused, and in particular where East, West and the Third World can talk to each other. As Churchill once said "Jaw, jaw is better than war, war". In the dark and frozen days of February, 1947, Prime Minister Attlee made the historic announcement that power would be transferred to Indian hands not later than June, 1948. On 23rd June of that year Lord Louis Mountbatten, the last Viceroy, gave up his imperial role to the two new States of India and Pakistan.

Here at home life slowly crept back to something like normal conditions. After six years there were lights in the streets again (the blackout had been relaxed in September, 1944, and ended in April, 1945). Football resumed some of its former glory (though not, alas, to regain the international superiority of which we had once been proud). In April, 1946, the first Grand National since 1940 brought the crowds to Aintree and in June the one hundred and sixty third Derby — the first since 1939 — was won by Airborne at odds of fifty to one. In July that quaint annual mixture of Old School Tie, tea on the lawns and tough athleticism came back to Henley, after seven years in which Leander and other ties had been food for the moths.

Death also made its regular accounting and two writers whose influence had been world wide, particularly in turning the minds of men and women towards Socialism, died during the period — Bernard Shaw (1950) and H. G. Wells (1946). So, too, in 1946, died Will Thorne, the man who as much as anyone had founded what is now the General and Municipal

Workers' Union, and "Jimmy" Maxton, one of the best known
leaders of the Independent Labour Party. Sidney Webb (Lord
Passfield) who, with his wife Beatrice (died 1943), had done so
much to shape the thinking of the British Labour Movement,
died in 1947. But the loss most keenly felt by USDAW members
was the death on 6th February, 1947, of Ellen Wilkinson, MP
and Minister of Education, the Union's first woman officer, one
of its first MPs and a fiery torch-bearer of Socialist idealism
for most of her life (the Union retained the Jarrow seat when
E. Fernyhough won the by-election). A happier event was the
knighthood conferred on Joseph Hallsworth in 1946 after thirty
years as General Secretary and forty-five in the service of the
Union.

For USDAW, 1946 was the year of the two great achievements already discussed; the National Wages Policy in the
Co-operative Movement and the amalgamation with the Shop
Assistants' Union. To these could be added at the beginning of
1945 the Bevin Act which enlarged the power of Wages Councils (formerly known as Trade Boards) to fix statutorily enforceable wages and conditions. Several of these Councils were
introduced into the distributive trades, on all of which the Union
was represented. It was also represented on the Wages Councils
for many other trades (such as milk, aerated waters, laundry)
and a wide range of Joint Industrial Councils.   Where changes
to Wages Councils took place, however, the result was not
always an unmixed blessing. When it came to recruitment, many
short-sighted workers argued that they did not need a Union, as
"the Government" now fixed their wages. It was to be a long
hard slog to convince them that the Councils only fixed minimum rates, and only through Trade Union power could they
ever hope to build higher earnings onto the Wages Councils'
minima.

The years between 1946 and 1950 saw the first great measures
of nationalisation which were the economic side of Labour's
far-reaching social reforms. Taking in most cases the vesting
days (i.e. when the public corporations or other form of control
became operationally responsible) the succession was: Bank of
England and Civil Aviation, 1946; Coal, and long distance road
haulage and Cable and Wireless, 1947; Electricity and Rail,
1948; Gas, 1949; Iron and Steel, 1950. More than half a century

of Socialist agitation reached a climax with the nationalisation
of these basic industries and services.

USDAW welcomed the change and for several years sought
to bring the distributive trades under some form of public
ownership. The Union had long maintained that the uncontrolled
opening of new shops, and the plethora of intermediaries
between manufacturer and consumer, wasted more in national
resources than was saved for consumers by the theoretical
advantages of a competitive free-for-all. In addition the Union
contended that price competition between shops was largely
financed by the low wages of distributive workers.

During the war, distribution to the consumer was controlled
by rationing, registration with a chosen shop, and the points
system for unrationed goods. Shops were controlled through
licensing under the Location of Retail Businesses Order of 1941
and the Register of Withdrawn Traders established in 1943.
These Orders were partially revoked at the end of 1945, although
licensing still continued for food retailers (soon, however, to be
diluted by the right of anyone to open a food shop who could
show 25 registrations for one of four rationed commodities).
With the general scarcity of goods in 1945/6 there was no
immediate rush of new businesses. But the door had been
opened. The Union feared that if nothing was done to control
new entrants, distribution would be back in the old jungle,
only slightly controlled by town planning legislation, and shop
workers would be the first to suffer. The Union's Objects Rule
included (as it still does) a clause "To work consistently towards
securing the control of the industries in which its members are
employed" and this in itself was a mandate to seek participation
in the nationalisation programme of the Labour Government.
The first move, however, was over the licensing of shops.

The Shop Assistants' Union, prior to the amalgamation, had
advocated the continuance of licensing to be carried out by a
revised version of the licensing bodies that had operated under
the Location of Retail Businesses Order. NUDAW's Executive
Council joined in the debate at the beginning of 1946 with a
lengthy statement in *New Dawn*. It began with the question:
"Can economic planning be accomplished under a capitalist
system?" and reached the conclusion that it cannot. In any
case, Britain was " . . . only on the threshold of socialisation".

The Labour Government, it went on, was dealing with a few basic industries through nationalisation. Even this would take much time and "We cannot just stand aside waiting in the queue for the turn of the distributive trades to be socialised". Therefore, the Executive supported a continued system of licensing. Not, however, by special bodies set up under the Board of Trade, as the Shop Assistants' Union had suggested. NUDAW proposed that the power should be exercised through local authorities, which already could control the number of retail outlets in new development areas, and through their statutory duty to administer the Food and Drugs Acts, Shops Acts and other legislation had an " . . . exact knowledge of these areas that cannot be gained otherwise." The local licensing committees should, however, " . . . be augmented by representatives of the traders and of the Trades Unions of distributive workers". With both existing and new traders, wages and conditions " . . . must be not less favourable than . . . laid down by Trade Union agreement for the district".

It was recognised that there could be difficulties in determining *what* was the appropriate agreement — Co-operative or private trade (where the latter existed) and on this subject the Union's conclusions were, to say the least, on the vague side. The Executive also insisted on the right of consumers to " . . . purchase Co-operatively or through private trade" and, particularly in new housing estates, that the Co-operative Movement must not be barred (as not infrequently happened in areas controlled by Tory Councils).

The statement was introduced to the 1946 ADM by J. Hallsworth and was adopted, surprisingly, considering the importance of the subject, without discussion. However, there was more interest in the subject than this quiescence appeared to indicate. Resolutions in favour of licensing continued to be sent in for the ADM agenda and the Executive continued to enlarge and strengthen its preliminary ideas of 1946. A much fuller document on *A Planned Distributive Economy* was submitted to the ADM of 1950.

It repeated the charge that distribution was too costly, unnecessarily increased the cost of living, and absorbed too much labour at a time when " . . . the nation needs the maximum number of workers on production. If there were more workers making things and fewer workers were needed to distribute them efficiently the standard of living . . . could be higher". The central problem was that there were too many shops and too many middlemen, and without fundamental change " . . . substantial economies cannot be made". The document then went on to grasp the nettle that lies in front of any attempt to rationalise distribution — the consumer's right in a free society to freedom and variety of choice.

It was accepted that in trades where taste, fashion or personal service were concerned " . . . freedom of consumer choice is essential". Nationalisation on the lines of coal mining, gas or electricity would be harmful " . . . except possibly in the case of standard commodities."

Therefore, more than one type of undertaking was necessary, provided that none could " . . . exploit the public or the worker, viz, that they were non-profit making and subject to democratic control". The Co-operative Movement, being non-profit making and democratically controlled, would thus continue to cater for its voluntary membership. That was as far as the statement went in trying to define by structure, by geographical area or by trade the different types of undertaking that should carry out distribution. Those were " . . . matters for future consideration", but municipal trading and State purchasing of some commodities were mentioned as possibilities. Wholesaling was discussed in rather more detail. While accepting that this function was necessary for many commodities, the Executive contended that there was too much duplication and too many intermediaries. There should be an investigation, trade by trade, to determine the appropriate route for goods from producer to retailer, and wholesalers should be licensed only if they conformed to such conditions as buying direct from the producer, holding stock, breaking bulk, etc. Many of the so-called middlemen and dealers, it was argued, would be sieved out by this test.

Detailed proposals were made for the milk and coal trades, which were considered to be ripe for immediate public ownership and control, with protection for the Co-operative Movement to compete with the public undertaking, thus maintaining consumer choice.

This plan was adopted by the 1950 ADM with one dissentient.

An attempt was made to amend the proposals by demanding that distribution and a considerable part of associated productive industry should be nationalised under a public corporation (the Co-operative Movement being excluded). This was defeated, as was a proposed reference back for discussion by branches and Divisions. The Executive's proposals, won a notable victory in the larger forum of the Labour Party. At the Party's 1950 Conference USDAW presented a resolution much on the lines of the two statements. The Party Executive opposed the resolution, in particular the suggestion that the number of shops should be restricted. Dr. Edith Summerskill, who spoke for the Executive attributed this idea to "doctrinaire economists" and said that she believed there should be competition between shops — not exactly the most cogent argument from a Socialist platform. But the conference did not agree with her and on a show of hands the resolution was carried by a large majority. A composite resolution carried at the TUC of 1951 also embodied the Union's criticism of wasteful marketing and distributive methods.

On the whole, however, the Executive's patient efforts over many years had not made much headway on the national scene. But they had at least forced the issue on the attentions of the Union itself and the Labour Movement in general. Apart from the national forum, the future of distribution had been discussed widely at the conferences of the Union's Divisions, at one-day and weekend schools arranged by Federations, at the annual summer school and, outside the Union, at Co-operative schools and conferences, Trades Council and local Labour Party meetings. USDAW's initiative had also contributed to discussions that took place between the Co-operative Movement and the Labour Party on the role of the Co-operatives in a collectivist economy.

By 1951, however, the Executive decided, probably with an eye on the Labour Government's already heavy commitments on nationalisation of basic industries, that it has done all that was possible, that there was no likelihood of " . . . fundamental action . . . in the immediately foreseeable future" and that decisions on the details of nationalisation could be deferred " . . . until after experience is gained from activities of a similar kind in other fields". This advice was adopted by the ADM.

N

As this is being written in 1978 there have been 27 years of the "immediately foreseeable future". Those years have seen vast changes in distribution; through self-service into super-markets, into hypermarkets, into discount houses, into huge shopping precincts, into a great increase in credit trading interlocked with finance capital. The number and variety of products, basically identical in everything except their plastic wrappers or containers, has enormously increased. A large industry is dedicated to the task of persuading the shopper that brand X is better than brand Y. Far from being sheltered by competition, consumers have had to band themselves into voluntary protective associations. Governments of both parties have found it necessary to establish statutory bodies for the same purpose. The wages and conditions of distributive workers have been partly protected by the existence of USDAW itself and the fall-back of Wages Councils. But shop workers still rank low in the table of earnings. Britain undoubtedly has an efficient distributive system, possibly the most efficient in Europe. But it is arguable that we do not need so great a number and variety of shops and stores and brands to maintain either efficiency or the consumer's freedom of choice. Perhaps it is time for USDAW to again turn its attention to the future of distribution.

The years covered by this chapter also saw the beginning of a national debate that still continues. The post-war public expected and demanded rising personal standards of living in addition to the wide-ranging social provisions introduced by the Labour Government in the National Health Scheme and other "services of life". The problem that no government has yet solved is to bridge the gap between these expectations and the apparent inability of the British economy to meet them through production and exports.

The issue first emerged in its post-war form in 1947. In two White Papers the Government warned that the country was drifting into a level of inflation that would damage both the standard of living and an already shaky balance of payments. In the White Paper *Personal Incomes, Costs and Prices* there was a call for restraint in wage claims as one means of checking inflation.

This was a new concept at the time. But, writing more than thirty years later, it is depressing to note how little the basic argument has altered and how far from solution the problem is. In 1948 the Chancellor, Sir Stafford Cripps, and Prime Minister Attlee expounded the same unpalatable facts about national housekeeping that we heard from Chancellor Healey and Prime Minister Callaghan during the Labour Government that ended in 1979. The debates on the problem at the annual meetings of USDAW (as of other Unions) during the late seventies were in essentials an echo of 1948.

For USDAW the White Paper was bitter medicine. Distributive workers were still near the bottom of table of wages and earnings and many of the productive and service workers in the Union were no better off. The Union was torn between two loyalties. Its support for the Labour Government was unshakeable. For most of its existence it had advocated Socialist planning of the economy and the Government had made the first moves along that road. It was difficult to argue that wages should be excluded. On the other hand, Britain was still a mixed economy, Socialism was only beginning, and it was impossible for a free Trade Union to remain inactive when so many of its members were on a bare subsistence level.

In February, 1948, the Executive Council issued a statement declaring that " . . . to freeze wages whilst the cost of living continues to rise would only lead to new industrial disturbances". It urged rigorous control of prices, limitation of profits and recognition " . . . of the necessity for a minimum wage throughout industry". A special conference of Union Executives gave qualified support to the White Paper in March. In the same month the USDAW ADM carried a resolution endorsing the Executive's statement with, however, the inclusion of words declaring that criticism of wages policy did not diminish support of the Labour Government.

By 1950 the first attempt at wages policy had ended. USDAW's annual meeting in April again declared its opposition and condemned the action of the Executive Council in casting the Union's vote at a special 1950 conference of Executives in favour of TUC wages policy. The General Council's case for continued restraint was rejected by the TUC itself in the Autumn. As readers will know, however, the problem that first emerged in 1948 has refused to go away and today is aggravated by heavy unemployment. We shall meet it again all too often in future chapters.

The late forties and the early fifties saw the breakdown of the wartime co-operation between the Soviet Union and the Western nations. Hopes for continued co-operation had been institutionalised in the United Nations and other international bodies. These have served since 1945 to moderate mutual suspicion, and at times outright hostility, but have not yet been strong enough to maintain genuine friendship and co-operation. This is not the place to trace in detail the story of those troubled years. But a brief description must come into a history of USDAW because of the cold war's impact on the ADM and on the Union's stance at the conferences of the Labour Party and the TUC, particularly when the Labour Government launched out on a massive programme of re-armament.

The break between East and West began over the growing conviction in the West that the Soviet Union was determined to extend its power and influence by every means open to it, not excluding the use of force. The first counter-move by the Western nations came in 1949, with the signing of the North Atlantic Treaty, of which the North Atlantic Treaty Organisation (NATO) was — and still is — the military arm.

In Korea, which had been a satellite of Japan, a Communist North faced a South under American control. Open war began with a Northern invasion in 1950. This was condemned as aggression by the United Nations, and under American leadership a UN force was formed to expel the invader. China was later involved on the side of the North, which, less directly, was supported by the Soviet Union. For three years the world teetered on the edge of a greater war, until the conflict in Korea was ended by the cease-fire of 1953. There was no thaw in the cold war, however, to which another degree of frost was added with the agreement in 1954 to incorporate West German forces in NATO.

In this deteriorating situation Britain embarked on a hurriedly drawn up programme of rearmament, announced by Prime Minister Attlee on 3rd August, 1950. It was designed to cost £3,400 million over three years, and would raise defence expenditure from 8 to 10 per cent of the national income.

The conflict of ideology and mutual mistrust had also

affected the international Trades Union Movement. The World
Federation of Trade Unions had been a hopeful development
of 1945. But as the wider conflict increasingly intruded on its
activities the TUC and other national federations withdrew
in 1949 on the grounds that the WFTU was being misused as a
forum for Soviet propaganda, in which the representatives from
Communist countries were spokesmen for their Governments
rather than for Trades Unionism as such. At the end of the year
a conference in London led to the formation of the present
International Confederation of Free Trade Unions.

USDAW's Executive Council endorsed withdrawal from the
WFTU, and a critical resolution was heavily defeated at the
ADM of 1949. The re-armament programme, however, brought
the Union into conflict both with the Labour Government and
the TUC. In ADM resolutions and in speeches, particularly by
Alan Birch and Walter Padley, the Union accepted that Britain
must play its part in precautionary measures for Western
defence. But it was argued that an increase in spending on
defence of the scale envisaged was beyond the country's
resources, and could only disrupt its all-too slow recovery.
The Union consistently maintained this attitude, alike while
Labour was still in power and when the Tories came back in
1951.

Feelings ran high. The TUC, in a statement on rearmament
in 1952, more or less accused USDAW and Unions that took a
similar stand of being among those whose " . . . first loyalty
exists outside this country". The statement defended the re-
armament programme, but accepted as a reasonable condition
that the programme might require adjustment in the light of
what was industrially practicable. Alan Birch, in a reply sent
to the TUC and published in *New Dawn*, pointed out that this
latter qualification was " . . . diffiuclt to reconcile with out-and-
out rejection of all criticism of the original programme". In
answering the inference that the Union was "playing the
Communist game" he said that Trades Unionists, while appreci-
ating the need for collective resistance to aggression " . . . are
not convinced that our rearmament programme was originally
planned with a full realisation of its economic effects and they
see . . . a danger of our becoming so preoccupied with the
military 'answer' to international problems as to find ourselves

committed to a military 'solution'."

It was a confused and unhappy situation. USDAW's criticism probably had a great deal more support than was ever expressed in votes. But loyalty to the General Council was stronger, and at the 1952 TUC a Union proposal to reduce the arms programme was heavily defeated.

There were three General Elections during the first half of the fifties — in 1950, 1951 and 1959. In the first Labour just scraped back, in the second it was defeated and was not to regain power for thirteen years. There are times when a word or a phrase can sway the public mood and if ever that was true it was in the election of 1951. Labour had saved Britain from disaster by controlling the economy, stimulating exports and encouraging the re-equipment of our war ravaged industry. The Tories and most of the newspapers used every trick in the armoury of politics and print to brand this as a policy of needless "austerity" which wantonly deprived the people of a better life. Even with this evocative appeal they only just made it in terms of votes. Labour's poll in 1951 was actually bigger than that of Churchill and his followers — 13,948,385 Labour/ Co-op against 13,724,418 for the Tories and associates. But the distribution of the votes gave the latter a majority of seats — 321 Conservative, 295 Labour/Co-op, six Liberals and two "others". The Tories retained their grip in 1955.

At the 1950 Election, held in February, eight Union candidates were returned. Five were existing MPs — A. Robens (Blyth — a new constituency due to redistribution), A. W. Burke (Burnley), E. Fernyhough (Jarrow), H. Boardman (Leigh), R. J. Davies (Westhoughton); three were new — W. E. Padley (Ogmore), R. E. Winterbottom (Sheffield, Brightside), G. Craddock (Bradford, South). T. Scollan lost his seat at Renfrewshire, West.

Al Robens was appointed Parliamentary Secretary to the Minister of Fuel and Power and later was to become Minister of Labour and National Service; H. Boardman was reappointed as Parliamentary Private Secretary to the Minister of Labour.

At the General Election of 25th July, 1951, all the sitting members were re-elected, with the exception that J. T. Price (head of the Union's Legal Department) had replaced R. J. Davies at Westhoughton. After holding the seat without a break since 1921, the politically almost immortal RJD had retired. J. T. Price winning at the by-election and the subsequent General Election. Davies, the first and for many years the best known of the Union's MPs, died in 1954.

In the May election of 1955, ten of the members of the Parliamentary Panel fought constituencies and eight were elected. They were A. Robens (Blyth), G. Craddock (Bradford, South), W. A. Burke (Burnley), H. Boardman (Leigh), W. A. Padley (Ogmore), R. E. Winterbottom (Sheffield, Brightside), J. T. Price (Westhoughton), E. Fernyhough (Jarrow). W. A. Burke had presided over the Labour Party Conference of 1953. USDAW donated £15,000 to Labour's General Election Fund.

From issues of national policy, which USDAW could influence but where it did not have the power of decision, we now turn to Trade Union activities within the Union's control. One of the most important was the increase in the machinery for specialist consultation on wages and conditions with its members in different trades. In part this development was linked with the recruitment campaign in private trade that followed the amalgamation. Divisional and federal conferences of a general character had been held for many years. But up to 1939 there is no evidence in *New Dawn* of systematic consultation on the problems of specific trades. Although not all meetings would be reported, only two specifically trade conferences are recorded in 1930 — for flour millers in Scotland, and for London shop stewards. There were three in 1935 (a national conference of flour milling branches, one for Midland boot repairers and one for Yorkshire transport workers) and five in 1939 (E&S Joint CWS workers — jointly with the Shop Assistants' Union — London bakery roundsmen, national meat trades, Scottish creamery workers, Yorkshire chemists).

During the war transport difficulties, air raids and the absence of so many members restricted the scope for consultation. But by 1946 a new policy was evident, with national conferences for the bacon curing and check and credit trades; Divisional or regional conferences for dental technicians in the South West, Northern and Yorkshire (joint) and North Western Divisions; milk recorders in Southern and Eastern; Retail Co-operative milk workers in the same Division and laundry workers in South Wales. Thereafter in the post-war

years the development of consultation was continuous and in
1950 a National Conference Structure report was adopted by
the ADM. By 1952 the trades or individual employers covered
by conferences, national or divisional (in some cases both)
were: soap, candle and edible fat; bacon curing; check and
credit; catering; insurance (CIS); CWS branches; retail
Co-operative; dental technicians (Midlands); dairy; NAAFI;
optical; research and laboratory assistants; retail meat; retail
private trade (non-food); retail private trade (food); chemical;
Co-operative boot and shoe; hairdressing; laundry; milling;
wholesale meat; wholesale grocery; food manufacture and sugar
confectionery. Nor is this list complete, for in some trades
conferences were held at longer intervals than a year, and do
not appear in the 1952 list.

Parallel with the trade meetings was an even wider range of
general conferences and schools organised by Divisions,
Federations and sometimes by large branches. Add the extensive
educational work carried out by the Union and it will be seen
that USDAW was embarked on a comprehensive programme
of contact with members as individuals and as wage earners
in a particular trade.

Much else of concern to USDAW members was happening
in the not-so-brave new world which we entered in 1945. But
it must wait on another chapter while we next consider the
first results of the amalgamation between NUDAW and the
Shop Assistants' Union.

21 PROBLEMS OF RECRUITMENT

The First Breakthrough in the Multiple Grocery Trade: Wages to 1955

THE Union of Shop, Distributive and Allied Workers began life on 1st January, 1947. The birth of the new Union was celebrated with pride but also with an optimistic vision of the immediate future that was to be harshly qualified by events. The Union, it was predicted, would speedily breach the double bastions of hostility from private trade employers and the apathy of their employees. At the last of NUDAW's own annual meetings a million members was spoken of as the target. At the first delegate meeting of the new Union the target became a million in five years. The figures were over-optimistic but not necessarily absurd. Very large numbers *were* recruited. But there was a "worm i' the bud" and we shall soon see how it gnawed at the bright hopes of 1947.

First, however, the spectacular programme of celebration that marked the launch of the new Union on 9th February. The King's Hall at Belle Vue, Manchester, was packed with 5,600 people for an "organising and celebration" concert. For weeks beforehand volunteers had been canvassing shops and stores and distributing leaflets throughout nine miles from the centre of Manchester. The event was publicised as " . . . part of the vast organising campaign to obtain a £5 per week minimum wage for a five day week of forty hours for all shop workers and to celebrate the formation of one Union of Shop, Distributive and Allied Workers". Well known radio and concert artistes of the period were engaged — Anne Ziegler and Webster Booth, Carrol Gibbons, and others. In spite of the savage winter of that year the hall was packed under P. Cottrell's chairmanship and with J. Hallsworth putting the case for Trade Union organisation of shop workers.

More than half a century earlier a handful of members of the

Manchester District Co-operative Employees' Association had
held their first annual meeting at Belle Vue. Some would still
be alive, as would pioneers of the Shop Assistants' Union, and
although their presence was not reported, a few could have been
there on that night of rejoicing — and what memories it would
bring back! Similar events were held in the Royal Albert Hall,
London, and in Birmingham.

So the great crusade was launched. But the first results were
disappointing. The new Union had begun with 343,137 members; 210,178 males and 132,959 females (38.75 per cent of the
total). By the end of 1948, however, the Executive had to report
a drop in membership of 1,471, and a year later there was a
further drop of 1,363. A net increase of 7,434 for 1950 and 1951
together was more than cancelled out by a total drop of 8,693
in 1952 and 1953. The balance of members between the sexes
was changing. Between 1951 and 1955 male membership fell
by 12,836, female membership increased by 11,234.

What had gone wrong? Not in the balance of membership
between men and women (the Union's purpose was to organise
workers, regardless of their sex) but in the hopes of rapid and
maintained overall growth? The first part of the answer lay in
the nature of the distributive trades that were the special target
of the early recruiting drive. They were "in and out" trades,
particularly in the private multiple store chains. The shop
worker recruited this week could have drifted into a completely
different job a few weeks later. Women workers, according to the
1951 census, were about two-thirds of the number in the grocery
and provision trade and an even higher proportion in general
and mixed retail businesses. They left to get married, or if they
continued to work for a time, eventually left to start and bring
up a family. There were a great many part-time married women
who were much more difficult to organise than full-timers.
Conscription was still in force and the Union found that in
many cases young men called up were replaced by boys. Many
members left distribution for better paid jobs in industry,
building, transport or commerce.

Another adverse factor lay in the machinery of the Union
itself, or, rather, in almost unavoidable defects which weakened
the ability to hold recruits once gained. There were 123 Area
Organisers and seven National Officers in 1961; not a very large

army to tackle and service the huge and scattered labour force of the distributive trades. Moreover, as Alan Birch reminded the 1948 ADM, the Organisers also had to service the large existing membership in productive and service trades.

One of the most acute difficulties was the regular collection of subscriptions from thousands of new members. This could efficiently be organised in a large Co-operative society, or CWS factory (in both of which Trades Union membership was a condition of employment) or in a large private department store or warehouse. It was a different matter when new members were scattered over hundreds of shops, and could live and work remote from a Union branch. Some new private trade members faded away because they saw no quick results in wages or hours (a practice for which the Executive had criticised some Co-operative employees as far back as the annual report of 1892!). The fixing of wages through Wages Councils and JICs diminished the interest of shop workers in Trades Union membership — illogically so, but, then, when was logic the sole motivation of human conduct? The distribution of leaflets and the holding of meetings proved to be an imperfect method of recruitment. An article by W. J. Davies in the *New Dawn* issue of 10th July, 1948, said that in the Central London area a distribution of 10,000 leaflets brought only 40 people to a meeting, 30 of whom were already members.

It will be noted that few of these problems were new. There was no mystery about the difficulty of organising shop workers scattered over tens of thousands of shops or about the volatile nature of distributive employment. The former Shop Assistants' Union had a long experience of both these factors, NUDAW (with its relatively stable Co-operative membership) had less. What was new was the scale on which the Union was now operating. It was seeking to organise without limit the last of the great trades of which it could still be said that it was unorganisable. And the frustrating fact was that the Union was very successful in recruitment — but then lost most of the new army through desertion.

The actual figures were at once impressive and disappointing. A. W. Burrows told the ADM of 1950 that in the previous two years 190,000 new members had been enrolled but 175,000 had lapsed, mainly for the reasons given earlier. A. Birch reported

to another Divisional conference in 1950 that nationally they
had enrolled 80,000 new members in 1949 but " . . . no increase
was shown above the 1948 figure". An investigation by Central
Office had indicated that between two-thirds and three-
quarters of the lapses were inevitable, due to members leaving
the trade, retirement, marriage or other factors beyond the
control of the Union. Maybe so, but taking Burrows' figures of
190,000 recruits, and on the assumption that the loss rate was
an inevitable three-quarters, 47,500 recruits had "deserted" in
two years for other than inevitable reasons.

Potentially, what the Union was facing was a problem of
success. The fruits of success, however, could only be won by
overcoming four preliminary problems, none new in kind but
all now greater in scale. They were:

1. To strengthen organisation and contact with members,
   both in their capacity as individual Trade Unionists and
   as workers in a particular section of distribution or a
   related trade.
2. To carry out a strategy on wages and conditions that
   would visibly yield results unobtainable except through
   Trade Union action.
3. To mobilise active members as voluntary "recruiting
   sergeants" and particularly to involve strong and long
   established Co-operative branches in organising their
   fellows in private trade.
4. To accept as a fact of life that "in and out" was endemic
   in retail distribution and some of the trades related to
   distribution.

During 1948, and to a lesser degree in subsequent years, the
Executive Council, Divisional Councils and Federations, full-
time staff and active members devoted themselves to these
problems with an intensity rarely equalled in the Union's
history. Articles and letters in *New Dawn*, speeches at the ADM
and other conferences analysed the problem and came up with
a variety of solutions.

A report on the Scope and Organising Policy of the Union
was presented to the ADM of 1948 by the Assistant General
Secretary, J. D. Hiscock. In moving the adoption of the report
he explained that, in broad outline the strategy on wages and
conditions in private trade was based on a two-pronged attack.

Once the Wages Councils had issued their first Wages Regulation Orders, which were statutorily enforceable, the Executive Council, in consultation with the Divisional Councils and officers concerned, would select national multiple firms with significant standing in the multiple trades for concentrated campaigns aimed at securing Trade Union agreements on wages and working conditions above the statutory minima in the Wages Council Orders. In effect, the aim was to establish a two-tier structure of collective wage regulation — the legally enforceable minimum and above that the superior provisions of a Trade Union agreement. It was a strategy, he emphasised, that would call for maximum efforts by all concerned — Executive and Divisional Councils, full-time officials and active lay members, for such a campaign could be expected to meet with powerful resistance from the employers.

There was little disagreement with this as strategy. Since, however, it depended for success on recruiting and retaining thousands of private trade employees, the subsequent debate at the ADM, in Divisions and Federations and in the columns of *New Dawn*, broadened to include organisation. It is not possible to cover the whole span of ideas and arguments ventilated during the great debate but a selection is given in paragraphs which follow.

At the ADM of 1948 it was argued that the Union should not begin recruitment in any area until a team of shop stewards or collectors had been organised. In the words of J. D. Hughes, later to become Chief Organising Officer and President of the Union, unless you thus " . . . mend the bucket . . . you are putting in the water and it is running away".

R. Silk (Houndsditch and Whitechapel), in a letter to *New Dawn*, agreed that collectors or shop stewards were vital. But generally they did not exist in small units. Most recruits lived far from their places of employment, they " . . . cannot or will not bother to attend a branch meeting" at or near their place of work. He proposed that new members should, if desired, have the right to attend and pay contributions at any branch convenient to their home, while retaining membership of the branch to which they were recruited.

In an article J. R. Elliott suggested the Union should concentrate all activity for a period on the wholesale grocery,

drapery, footwear and other trades, build up a strong organisation at the source of supply and use the threat to cut off
supplies when tackling wages and conditions in the shops.
S. R. Pearson (Grimsby (S) Branch) argued for compulsory
Trade Union membership by law as the surest way to rake in
these contemptible workers, "the take all and pay nowts".
A. Cohen urged that there should be more single-trade branches
and Divisional activities to hold the interest of new members
according to their trade, instead of including them in general
branches of many trades. The appointment of paid collectors
was already being discussed in 1948, but E. Parker objected in
New Dawn on the grounds that " . . . we shall make progress
only on the basis of voluntary effort by rank and file members".
He also agreed with a trade rather than a mixed membership
basis of organisation.

From the powerful Royal Arsenal (Woolwich) Co-operative
Branch F. R. White voiced the opinion that they would never
recruit on a mass scale by expecting full-time Organisers to do
the job in the multitude of retail shops and stores, nor by
piecemeal individual canvassing. His proposal was that in every
Division they should seek to establish multiple stores branches
based on Woolworth, Marks and Spencer and similar firms
which, like City Co-operatives, were large concentrated units,
with identical problems and capable of effective organisation.
Recruitment would be carried out by existing branches in
every Division through " . . . a core of keen members" who
would campaign among the local chain store workers. Full-
time Organisers " . . . engaged in the unenviable task of
'organising the private trades'" would co-ordinate the local
groups. Established branches would help the new groups until
they could elect their own committee and operate independently.

A. Waistow (Sheffield General No. 1) pointed to the argument that "The Government now fixes my wages" (through
JICs and Wages Councils) which was often used by shop
workers as a reason for leaving or staying outside the Union.
He proposed that immediately a statutory or agreed scale
minimum had been adopted, USDAW and other Unions
concerned should begin to agitate and recruit for a Trades Union
scale above the minimum. Also, no new branch should be
formed completely from new recruits. Where there was an

established branch they should attach new members from the multiples. Branches should be reorganised on a residential basis, regardless of places of employment, should be limited to 1,000 members and should be divided into trade categories for the discussion of common problems.

So the debate continued. But there was action as well as argument. By 1951 seven full-time collector-canvassers were operating in certain Divisions (there were thirteen by 1955). As described in the last chapter, there was a large increase in specialist machinery for consultation with members in different trades. The Union had more or less come to terms with the fact that it could not avert a heavy turnover of membership and was concentrating on means of cutting the loss to the minimum.

A new approach to the problem of contributions began in 1953. The Executive Council reported that the Audit and Special Investigation Department was negotiating with Co-operative Societies and private firms for the deduction of contributions from wages (the "check off", as it is known). A year later the Department (its name now abbreviated to Audit Department) had concluded a number of agreements, the first being with Newcastle upon Tyne Co-op. Today the greater part of the Union's members pay their contributions in this manner.

We saw earlier that the Union's strategy was to super-impose Trade Union agreements on Wages Council minima. The opposition to this policy by multiple firms and their organisations was every bit as strong as J. D. Hiscock had warned would be the case. The Union had to walk warily. But by 1951 it was ready for action. The Wages Council for the Retail Food Trades (England and Wales) had settled its first Wages Regulation Order at a low level. After consultation with the South Wales and Monmouthshire Divisional Council and the Divisional Officer, B. F. C. Weston, it was decided to concentrate on a Welsh subsidiary of the International Stores combine — a grocery multiple with national ramifications.

The subsidiary selected for action was the Direct Trading Company and a few other Welsh subsidiaries of International. Wages and conditions were unsatisfactory and Union attempts to negotiate were constantly rebuffed. Shop managers and staffs were ready for a showdown if that was the only way to secure improvement. An application to the controlling company for an agreement above the Wages Council rates was summarily rejected. Intervention by the Conciliation Department of the Ministry of Labour failed to bring about a change of attitude. Following a ballot of members there was a general stoppage of work throughout the Welsh valleys and other areas, beginning on 27th August. Since food rationing was still in operation, customers registered with Direct Trading had to transfer their registrations to other shops — a consequence which was not without its effect on the company.

It was said earlier that the Union had to walk warily in selecting the first ground for battle with the increasingly powerful multiple retailers. One of the factors in deciding to open the campaign with the Direct Trading Company was that USDAW also had complete organisation in London in the central distributing warehouses which serviced the shops of the entire International combine. London members had already indicated their readiness to strike in support of South Wales. By the end of the first week formal authority was sought from the Executive Council for supporting strike action in the London warehouses.

That was the turning point. International Stores might have been ready to fight a localised battle but it was not prepared to see the trading operations of the whole combine brought to a stop. At the request of the company the Ministry of Labour intervened to bring the parties together on 13th September. With a representative of the Ministry in the chair, the Union and the Multiple Grocers' Association (acting for the company) met. The Association argued that it would create serious difficulties for the company if it was singly picked on to sign a Union agreement, and offered as an alternative that there should be negotiations at an early date for a collective agreement to cover all the signatory firms in the Association. The Union negotiators, led by the Assistant General Secretary, made it clear that by then the dispute with the International company had gone too far. The Union was ready to negotiate an agreement with the Association but the dispute in South Wales must be settled first if an extension of the strike was to be averted. The meeting was told that shop stewards in the London warehouses had instructions that failing word to the contrary by midnight, work was to cease the following morning.

There would be some anxious clock watching by both sides as the hands crept towards midnight. But International did not want a total confrontation. Agreement was reached, bringing managers and staff in the Direct Trading Company and the other companies in South Wales and Monmouthshire up to the level of the current retail Co-operative agreement. Arrangements were also made for early discussions with the Multiple Grocers' Association. By the end of the year J. D. Hiscock was able to report a settlement with the Association which provided for wage rates substantially higher than the Wages Council minima, and for improved conditions.

It was a major victory, a text book exercise in co-ordinated planning and execution by members. Executive and Divisional Councils, officials and outside sympathisers (of whom there were a great many). Even *The Times* supported USDAW's case in a second leader of 13 September, 1951.

Although the victory in Wales was rightly described as " . . . a landmark in the advance of the Union's policy" by W. E. Padley in his New Year message of 1952, it was not, of course, the only major activity on the wages front during the immediate post-war years. Some of the improvements won for members have been mentioned in previous chapters. As the cost of living continued to rise and distributive workers lingered at the bottom of the wages scale the target of a £5 minimum became £6, then £6.10s, then £7.10s, and by 1955 the ADM was demanding an increase of 15 per cent. Subsequent negotiations did not reach a 15 per cent settlement, but over the whole period up to 1955 the Union was successful in securing annual increases for most of its members, Co-operative and private trade; either through direct negotiations (as with the Co-operatives, including the Wholesales) and some private employers, or through Joint Industrial Councils, Wages Councils or other national wage fixing bodies.

In a typical annual report (for 1953) there were 34 pages giving details of settlements on wages and conditions. The overall tendency can be judged by brief quotations from the introduction to the wages section of several annual reports. For 1950 it spoke of a " . . . general advance in many rates". For 1951 the " . . . upward movement of wage rates generally was greater than in any previous year. In 1952 " . . . wage

o

increases have been won in practically all the trades and industries with which the Union is concerned". There was a similar report in 1953. In 1954 the attempt to secure a 15 per cent increase in Co-operative and private trade was unsuccessful, but resulted in substantial advances. The proposed increases were submitted to and adopted by a vote of members at branch meetings. By 1955 the report was " . . . increases have been recorded in every trade".

Recruitment and lapses continued to concern the Union, particularly during the sixties, when there was massive re-organisation, and consequent redundancies, in the Co-operatives, retail and wholesale, and unemployment was once again becoming a problem for the nation and for Trades Unions. As we shall see later, recruitment was to be the subject of an exhaustive examination by a special "Committee of Investigation". While the Committee did not solve the problem, it was to give the Union a more realistic view of the road to the future than the rosy vision of 1947. And in the meantime, USDAW was proving by results that it genuinely served the interests of shop and allied workers, whether or not they were members of the Union.

22 FORWARD MARCH AGAIN

D URING the war there had necessarily been a halt to many of the Union's efforts to improve conditions. Campaigns of the thirties had to be put aside for more urgent tasks. They were renewed when peace returned and are the subject of this chapter, together with new battles that had to be fought and new developments in the Union's services.

With superannuation, the most important of the pre-war campaigns, there had been more or less a standstill. The percentage of Co-operative employees, in retail, wholesale, productive and special societies, covered by pension schemes was 84.59 in 1939 and 85.77 in 1945. The number of retail societies with schemes, however, increased from 378 to 423 and the proportion of *retail* employees covered from 82.89 per cent in 1939 to 84.21 per cent in 1945. In the first of these years only 106 of the 695 societies with up to 100 employees had schemes, by the end of the war the number was 127 out of 660.

The reluctance to form new schemes was mainly due to wartime conditions and, after the Beveridge Report was published in 1942, to uncertainty over future provision of State pensions. But in 1941, after long agitation, the CWS scheme was revised to the benefit of about 38,000 employees, many of them retired. The alterations followed closely proposals made in a Union publication *The Case for Better Pensions in the CWS, Ltd.*

From the end of the war there was steady progress. By 1955 95.76 per cent of all Co-operative employees were covered by pension schemes. But small societies still remained a problem. They constituted most of the 416 societies, with 15,986 employees (4.24 per cent of the total) which still made no pensions provision. An enquiry by the Union in 1955 showed that 165 independent schemes and eleven federal (covering 172 societies) had carried out total or partial consolidation of war bonuses. Full consolidation had taken place in the CWS, E&SCWS and

CIS. Aggregate funds of all schemes amounted to £53,377,938 in 1954.

When the war began 502 retail societies employed only Trades Union labour. Scotland, which was the fourth Division in number of members, was well in front with the number of Union-only societies — 120, more than twice the number of the much bigger Manchester Division. By 1945 499 societies, and by 1955 564, were one hundred per cent Trades Union; Scotland still being well ahead.

Full membership rights had been won in 118 societies by 1939. The number had increased to 146 in 1945. Thereafter progress was rapid; to 257 societies in 1955, covering 68 per cent of retail employees. It was the smaller societies with up to 5,000 members which obstinately resisted this democratic innovation. Out of 597 in this membership bracket only 46 had introduced full rights for employees by 1955.

In 1947 the *Distributive Trades Journal* which had been published by the Shop Assistants' Union (for many years under the title *Shop Assistant*), was incorporated in *New Dawn* from the first issue of February. *New Dawn* itself had previously been restyled in typography and layout. It continued to merit the praise it received as one of the brightest of Trades Union journals. There was a thorough coverage of the Union's far-ranging activities. Particularly useful for active members were case studies of the distributive and related trades byT. Cynog-Jones (Research Officer). In 1953, for example, the Census of Distribution was analysed in seventeen articles and another ten were published on the major distributive combines. For branch officials the regular articles on legal subjects by H. G. Pridmore constituted a textbook in serial form on subjects that could affect Union members. The literary quality continued to be high and *New Dawn* must have introduced many Union members to the giants and the lesser luminaries of literature. The journal serialised such working class classics as *The Raggered Trousered Philanthropists* by Richard Tressell (the pen-name of Robert Noonan). Circulation of *New Dawn* was about 25,500 in 1947. A peak of 27,600 was reached a year later. But after an increase in price from 1d to 2d in 1952 circulation began to fall away.

C. (Cyril) Hamnett, the editor, was also publicity officer and produced a steady flow of impelling recruitment leaflets. His responsibilities included contact with the Press, national and regional. In that capacity he developed close links with the political and industrial correspondents, an association which secured for USDAW a wider and better-informed presence in the Press than was enjoyed by many other Unions. In 1947, continuing the Union's long association with the Co-operative Press Limited, he was elected to the Board of that society in the succession to A. Robens. In 1953 R. A. Campbell, Chief Administrative Officer, who had served the Union for forty years under three General Secretaries, retired. He had largely been responsible for the investment of accumulated funds, which underpinned the finances of the Union. On his retirement there was a threefold reorganisation of his function. C. Hamnett became Administrative Officer, but continued his supervision of the Journal and publicity, T. Whittaker was appointed Clerical Officer supervising clerical staff throughout the Union, and L. Cain, while retaining the position of Central Treasurer, was given wider responsibility for the Union's financial arrangements.

In 1948 the Executive Council carried out its obligation under the amalgamation agreement to draft an education scheme for the new Union, to be considered by the next annual meeting. It comprised six main clauses: (1) To establish an educational fund of 5d per member per annum (increased to 7d in 1952). (2) To continue the existing link with the NCLC. (3) To continue the association of the former Shop Assistants' Union with the Workers' Educational Association and the WEA Trade Union Committee. (4) To focus attention on "domestic educational matters", which were defined as (a) branch administration; (b) the structure, function and industrial relations of the Union, including the very wide range of wages negotiating machinery in which USDAW was concerned; (c) industrial and economic questions, including " . . . the place of distribution in Labour Britain".

Clause 5 provided that the Union should continue to support the summer schools to which it normally sent students (TUC, Labour Party, NCLC, Co-operative Union, WEATUC). Under Clause 6 Divisional Councils and Federations would be encouraged to run one-day and weekend schools, with approved speakers, and a suitable grant would be made in each case. Finally, a national one-week's school would be run by the Union itself .(The first school was held in 1950 at Beatrice Webb Memorial House, Dorking, with Cyril Hamnett as organiser, a role he continued to fill for many years).

This scheme, which was adopted by the 1949 ADM, was sound in one respect, less so in another. It provided for a wide diffusion of the sort of education in political and social policy that could be acquired at one-day and weekend schools (there were 53 Federations and fifteen Divisional Councils in 1949). But schools, meeting for a few hours, with intervals of several months between "sessions", were not suited for the systematic study of the "domestic" educational matters which the Executive regarded as important. For systematic education the Union relied on an outside contractor, the NCLC. That body had played a great part in Trades Union history. But the times were changing. A large general Union such as USDAW, covering a great variety of disparate trades, had a growing need for specialist training of members. In the firms organised by the Union the growing influence of shop stewards had to be matched by systematic training if they were to operate effectively. Knowledge of procedure and negotiating techniques, of work study and other procedures that could affect earnings and conditions, could not be effectively acquired at occasional one-day or week-end schools. Branch secretaries, too, required specialist training. These factors were soon to lead to a further development of the Union's educational policy.

In 1953 the ADM recommended that representatives from sister Unions abroad, particularly young people, should be invited to the summer school. The following year there were two students from Holland and one from Denmark, the beginning of a practice which has continued down to the present time. USDAW representatives also attend the schools of Continental unions.

International links were quickly renewed after the war and by the middle fifties the Union was affiliated to the following Internationals: Transport Workers, Food and Drink Trade Workers, Commercial, Clerical and Technical Employees, Industrial Organisations and General Workers' Unions, Hotel, Restaurant and Bar Workers, Garment Workers. J. D. Hiscock was on the Executive of the International Federation of Commercial Clerical and Technical Workers, and later became its acting President. Fraternal delegations to annual meetings were exchanged with overseas Unions, In the same period national affiliations were:—

British TUC	NCLC
Scottish TUC	WEA
Irish TUC	WEA Trade Union Committee
Labour Party	Labour Research Department
Scottish Council of the	United Nations Association
Labour Party	Royal Institute of International
Northern Ireland Labour	Affairs
Party	Scottish Council of
National Joint Committee	Development and Industry
of Working Women's	British Workers' Sports
Organisations	Association
National Council of	Fabian Society
Labour Colleges	Movement for Colonial
British Institute of	Freedom
Management	*Women's Service Library of
Industrial Welfare Society	the Fawcett Society
National Federation of	British-Asian Socialist
Professional Workers	Fellowship

The last named body had been formed in March, 1953, on the initiative of the Labour Party National Executive. Clement Attlee was Honorary President. Some of these were "sympathetic" affiliations with a nominal subscription (e.g. to the Women's Service Library). Others reflected the moves towards Colonial freedom that were widespread in the fifties and sixties (there were frequent resolutions at the ADM demanding that the freeing of India and Pakistan should be followed by similar measures in other Colonial territories).

New Appointments to the organising staff continued to be made. In 1939 there were 66 Area Organisers, eleven Divisional Officers, three National Organisers, and five Central Officials. By 1951 there were 123 Area Organisers (the number included MPs) and seven Collector/Canvassers (thirteen in 1955), with seven National Officers and three Central Officials.

---

* Formerly the London and National Society for Women's Suffrage.

The 123, of course, included staff of the former Shop Assistants' Union. One new Area Organiser appointed in 1946 was A. W. H. Allen (now Lord Allen), who later was to become General Secretary. Following the merger in 1947 the number of Divisions (and Divisional Officers) for the enlarged Union was for a period increased to seventeen, later reduced by stages to eleven in 1963. At that figure it remained until 1969, when a further reorganisation reduced the number of Divisions to the present figure of eight. For the Union's own staff a scheme of voluntary retirement at 60 to 64 was introduced in 1945, and a five-day working week in 1947; provision being made to cover events which might arise on a Saturday. In the same year arrangements were made to affiliate to the Irish TUC on the basis of Northern Ireland membership.

A national campaign for Saturday half-day closing was launched in the Autumn of 1948 and the annual report for the year announced that 493 retail Co-ops (out of 1,032) were completely closing food shops on Saturday afternoon, while many others were working various sorts of rota. In "at least six towns" all private trade shops were also closing. As the future was to show, however, these figures were not typical of what was likely to happen when there was a complete return to a free market. Most goods were still scarce in 1948 and it was a very foolish or unlucky housewife who left her weekend shopping to a Saturday afternoon. We shall return to shop closing hours in the next chapter.

A special Delegate Meeting in October, 1952, increased contributions to all scales by 1d per week and also introduced large increases in the rates for dispute and victimisation benefits. In proposing the alterations Alan Birch said that pre-war contributions at the most popular scale represented about 2½d in the £1 of wages; in 1945 (when they were increased by 1d), the proportion was about 2d; and on the new proposal would be a little over 1½d. The weekly wage of shop assistants had increased from around £3.5.0d in 1939 to £6.9.0d in the period.

A new wing was added to "Oakley" in 1951, and was opened in June by Lewis Lumley, who had by then completed the remarkable record of 60 years' membership of the Union and its predecessors, holding membership card No. 5 of the Manchester District Co-operative Employees' Association.

This chapter ends with two tributes. One to a man famous in the Union's history, the other to thirty members, most of whom achieved no more than local fame.

In 1950 the ADM approved the establishment of an annual Sir Joseph Hallsworth residential scholarship at Ruskin, renewable for a second year if the student was satisfactory, and in 1951 applications were invited for the first scholarship. There were nine applicants, five were interviewed and the award went to E. A. Webb of the South Suburban (London) branch (at the Golden Jubilee of Ruskin in 1949 £1,000 had been given to endow an USDAW Room).

In 1945, immediately after the end of the war, the Executive published and paid tribute in *New Dawn* of 28th July to a list of members of more than fifty years standing who had joined the Union in the pioneering days of the Manchester District Co-operative Employees' Association. There are, of course, others who have since achieved a membership of half a century and, with a break during the war, the Union already recognised membership of thirty years and more with the presentation of badges. Awards were also made to branch secretaries with more than 21 years' service. But only the thirty remained of those who had helped to establish the Union when it was still a plant with a doubtful future. Their names and the Co-operative Societies in which they had worked as "servants" (in the nomenclature of the time when they joined the Union) were as shown in the table on the following page.

They have all gone now and most of the Co-operative Societies in which they served have disappeared through amalgamation. They were the last of the pioneers.

Branch	Name	Date of Joining	Years of Continuous Membership
Blackburn	Atkinson, J.	1894	51
Huddersfield	Wright, J. J.	1894	51
	Collier, H.	1894	51
	Marsden, H.	1894	51
Leigh (Lancs)	Hunter, F.	1894	51
Middlesbrough	Lynn, F.	1894	51
Oldham Industrial	Broadbent, A. E.	1892	53
	Elliott, J.	1893	52
	Horrocks, J. H.	1894	51
	Kendall, J.	1893	52
	Lawton, F.	1894	51
	Lumley, L.	1891	54
	Mee, P.	1894	51
	Tetlow, C. E.	1893	52
	Thompson, H.	1893	52
	Wormald, J. H.	1891	54

Branch	Name	Date of Joining	Years of Continuous Membership
Pelaw CWS	Forster, F.	1893	52
Preston	Fowler, W.	1894	51
Rochdale	Blomley, J.	1894	51
	Clegg, G.	1894	51
	Guest, J	1894	51
	Turner, J.	1894	51
	Whinray, J.	1894	51
Seaton Delaval (Northd.)	Adams, W.	1894	51
	Gibson, T. W.	1894	51
	Kneebone, J. C.	1894	51
	Kneebone, R. A.	1894	51
Sherburn Hill (Durham)	Knox, R.	1894	51
	Lowther, T.	1894	51
	Jennings, E.	1894	51

23 SHOP HOURS — 1

The Long Struggle for Legislation

ATTEMPTS to reduce the excessive hours worked by shop assistants began in the early years of Queen Victoria's reign. But the aged Queen had been in her tomb for eleven years before the first reform of any substance reached the Statute Book in 1912. Apart from the Co-ops, where wages and hours had improved by the end of the century, the hundreds of thousands in the private trade were little better off than their predecessors had been on that June morning of 1837, when Victoria woke up to find herself Queen of Great Britain and Ireland. In a great many cases, they were probably worse off, for competition had become much fiercer during the century and the wages and hours of shop workers were sacrificed to the cut-throat struggle for custom.

The more energetic among the workers, a minority of the multitude of self-employed shopkeepers and some progressive department store owners did not tolerate this servitude without challenge. In the case of private trade shop assistants, however, a considerable degree of snobbery, a feeling that they were socially superior to manual workers, and an even larger measure of apathy, delayed for a long time the day when the more intelligent of them accepted that Trades Unionism was an essential tool of reform. There were many efforts from early in the century through local Early Closing Associations and the initiative of individuals to introduce voluntary agreements on closing times. But one bad apple could spoil the barrel and an almost unanimous local agreement could collapse on the refusal of one or a few retailers to observe the agreed closing hour. The response of their competitors was "if they stay open they'll steal our trade" — so all stayed open.

The obvious solution was statutory regulation, which had been invoked to end the employment of women and children in the mines, and to control many of the more brutal aspects of factory employment. But most of the small shopkeepers shied away from the thought of compulsory regulation and middle-class reformers were for long convinced that in time persuasion would win the day. It was the age of *laissez faire*, in which the conventional wisdom held that a man had the right to do what he liked with his own, including his labour, and if he chose to work until his legs would scarcely hold him and his eyes could scarcely see, that was his affair. You could try to persuade an employer to ease the burden, but if he refused, well, he, too, was doing what he liked with his own business.

Eventually, however, the Early Closing Association, which was the leading non-Trades Union advocate of shorter hours, accepted that only statutory regulation could bring about reform. But division among the supporters of early closing and the hostility or indifference of Parliament still had to be overcome. Time after time Sir Charles Dilke (the headquarters of the Shop Assistants' Union were named in his honour) and Sir John Lubbock (later Lord Avebury) brought in Shop Hours Bills, actively supported by the Shop Assistants' Union and by AUCE, and time after time their efforts ended in whatever was the receptacle for unwanted legislation. There were some slight improvements in the law relating to the employment of women and children. A Shops Act of 1904 gave local authorities the power to impose a closing hour not earlier than 7 p.m. except on one day when it could be not earlier than 1 p.m. But the Act was so hedged around with reservations as to be virtually useless. It was not until 1912 that there was real progress.

Before coming to the Shops Act, which was operative from the beginning of that year, it is desirable to consider the problems which reformers hoped to solve by legislation. Overwhelmingly the most important was to impose a legal limit to the hours shop assistants could be compelled to work. That necessarily meant the inclusion of one-man businesses which employed no labour, for if they were exempt, as it was frequently argued that they should be, they would enjoy an unfair advantage over retailers who were also employers. The second target for reformers was to give legal force to the weekly half holiday which was already observed in many retail shops, and to safeguard against cheating through employers juggling with the

hour at which the half day should begin. The third problem
was to hold the line against any general extension of Sunday
trading which was only feebly controlled by an Act of 1677.
All these factors, sometimes, singly, sometimes together,
figured in the Shops legislation that began with the Act of 1912.
Finally, in all cases it was necessary carefully to scrutinise the
exemptions which it was accepted could be necessary in any
general regulation of the distributive trades.

The Act marked a real advance. But as it made its long and
weary journey towards the Statute Book (it took two years to
get through Parliament) it was pushed and pulled from every
point of the compass, and ended up as a series of compromises.
There was something for those who favoured legislation and
for those who were opposed to it, those who sought a comprehensive measure covering hours, the weekly half holiday and
welfare regulations and those who wanted only a cautious
piecemeal approach, for those who believed there should be very
few exceptions and those who, if they had had their way, would
have exempted almost the entire range of retail trades. Thus,
proposals to limit the number of hours that could be worked
weekly soon disappeared from the Bill.

But the weekly half holiday (with exemptions that we shall
come to later) became compulsory in a clause that "Every shop
shall . . . be closed for the serving of customers not later than
one o'clock in the afternoon on one week day in every week"
(the Unions had proposed twelve noon). Shop assistants,
however, were not to be free until one thirty, presumably to
allow time for clearing up the shop. Local authorities were
given the power to fix the day on which shops were to be closed,
and could either fix the same day for all shops, or vary the day
according to the different classes of trade, different parts of
their district or for different periods of the year.

Exemptions, however, were numerous. Where a local
authority had reason to believe that most of the shopkeepers of
"any particular class" in any area wished to be exempted from
the half day, either wholly or by fixing a later hour, the authority
would, after consultation with or vote of the shopkeepers (no
mention of the assistants!) exempt the class from the provisions
of the Act. In holiday resorts the local authority had power to
suspend the half day closing for not more than four months in

any year. Compensation for this loss of the half day was to be
not less than two weeks paid holiday in every year. Nine trades
or activities were exempted from the provision of the weekly
half holiday, including the sale of intoxicating liquors, newspapers and magazines, meats, fish, milk, cream, bread, confectionery, tobacco, medicines.

While the Act did not fix a statutory limit to weekly hours
worked, it gave local authorities powers to make "closing
orders", which could not be earlier than seven o'clock in the
evening on any day of the week. Parliament appears, however,
to have had some doubts whether — given the general composition of local authorities in 1912 and their failure to use the
Act of 1904, restricted as it was — there would be much zest
for the use of this power. So it made provision for a gentle prod.
A "substantial number of occupiers of shops and (in this clause)
shop assistants" could ask the Secretary of State to appoint a
competent person to hold a local enquiry and if he was satisfied
that a closing order should be issued he could prepare a draft
order for the acceptance or otherwise of the Secretary of State.
The Shop Assistants' Union made frequent and skilful use of
this provision to secure more civilised closing hours. So — the
Act protected the half holiday for most shop assistants, and took
a timid step towards the control of hours. Not a lot, but at least
a beginning.

It took a world war to galvanise the Government into any
general control of shop hours. To economise on heat and light
during the war of 1914-18, and because of the general shortage
of goods for the civilian market, a Government Order made
under the Defence of the Realm Act (DORA) introduced
nationally compulsory closing in winter at 8 p.m., with a late
night of 9 p.m. on Saturday. There was a considerable number
of exceptions, mainly covering the sale of perishable goods.
This Order was extended to the summer, and continued until
August, 1920. In practice a great many shops were by then
already closing earlier than the times given. And the entire
world of shopkeeping, having tasted and enjoyed the sweets of
leisure, did not want to lose them. Even the National Federation
of Small Traders' Protection Associations had no wish to go
back to unrestricted hours. The public, too, had become
accustomed to the new closing times. Parliament, now including

an increasing number of Labour MPs, was more responsive than
it had been in the past.

So control of closing times to 8 p.m./9 p.m. was continued
by a temporary Act in 1920 (when war regulations expired).
This limitation was renewed annually until 1927, when the
House of Commons appointed a Departmental Committee to
consider whether the temporary provisions should become
permanent. The Shops (Hours of Closing) Act of 1928 followed,
and enshrined in permanent legislation a general closing time
of 8 p.m. with 9 p.m. on the late night. Holiday resorts could
fix later hours for up to four months, but shop assistants who
were affected were entitled to corresponding holidays with pay.
Both the Shop Assistants' Union and the then NUDAW
campaigned in support of the Act, although they were unsuccessful in efforts to reduce closing hours to 7 p.m./8 p.m.
Another Act in 1934 further limited the working hours of young
people, and provided for the improvement of heating, lighting,
ventilation and sanitary conditions for all shop workers. It did
not, however, specify standards that must be observed, the
requirements being couched in the vague form of "suitable and
sufficient".

During the second World War closing hours were again
controlled by Government Order under temporary wartime
legislation, although, of course, the hours in the basic Shops
Act still remained at 8 p.m./9 p.m. By the end of the war, however, there was a general feeling that the statutory closing times
were too late and in addition that health and safety factors
should be improved not only in shops but in many other un-
regulated occupations. It was estimated that about eight million
people were in jobs where the provision for health, safety, etc.,
was minimal or non-existent. To study the situation and make
recommendations the Government set up a committee in 1946
under the chairmanship of Sir Ernest Gowers. Its comprehensive
purpose was to enquire into the closing hours of shops; health,
welfare and safety in places not covered by the Factories or
Mines and Quarries Acts; and hours of employment of young
persons.

Those were the halcyon days of reform. Labour's great
programme of social welfare and nationalisation was beginning.
Trades Unionists in many occupations looked forward to a

shorter working week. USDAW — as the Union had then
become — believed that shop assistants should share in the
better times. In particular it believed that the shorter hours
already prevailing in a great many shops through Union action
or custom and practice should not be under the constant threat
from predatory retailers seeking to invoke the statutory closing
hours of 8 p.m./9 p.m. The kernel of the evidence, written and
oral, which USDAW submitted to Gowers on hours was that
the closing times should become 6 p.m. and 7 p.m. on the late
night and that the power of local authorities to suspend shop
closing hours provision should be withdrawn.

The Union waited with confidence for news that reform of
statutory hours was on the wing. The greater the shock when,
with the argument that "It is now the public's turn for consideration", Gowers launched a bird with a crippled wing. In
its interim report of May, 1947, the Committee recommended
that 8 p.m./9 p.m. should go, but should be replaced by a
general closing time of 7 p.m., with 8 p.m. on the late night.
Both the proposal and the innuendo that shop workers were a
pampered lot angered the Union, and, indeed, a great many
private retailers who had no wish to be at the mercy of any
competitor prepared to return to the bad old days of chronically
late closing. Several other of the Committee's interim recommendations were, however, supported by the Union, in
particular the proposal to withdraw the power of local authorities to exempt from the weekly half holidays any section of local
traders who petitioned for the right to do so. But the Union
deplored a recommendation to increase from four months to
five the period in which the half day could be suspended in
holiday resorts.

From the Executive Council and throughout the Union there
were protests at the proposed new closing hours. At many
meetings the question was aked: How could a Labour Government have landed itself with a committee that proposed a little
that was good but so much that was reactionary? A deputation
from the Union met the Home Secretary (Chuter Ede). The
Government had received the report but it showed no inclina-
tion to legislate, possibly because it was impressed by the
hostility expressed by Trades Union, Co-operative and private
trade interests. In 1949 Gowers issued a second report dealing

with that part of its remit relating to health, welfare and safety of workers other than those regulated under the Factories and Mines and Quarries Acts, and with the hours of young persons. USDAW's annual report for the year welcomed the health, welfare, etc., proposals as far as they went, but was dissatisfied with those concerning the hours of juveniles, which fell short of the proposals which USDAW and other Unions concerned had made through the TUC (many of these proposals were included in the Office, Shops and Railway Premises Act, 1963, which was strongly supported by the Union on its passage to the Stature Book. So at least part of Gowers reached home base).

Nothing was done about the recommendation on hours but there was major "tidying-up" legislation in 1950. The Shops Act of that year consolidated the Shops Acts 1912 to 1938, including most of the provisions mentioned earlier. It is mainly this Act which currently governs closing hours, which remained at 8 p.m., with 9 p.m. on the late night one day a week.

Under the 1950 Act local authorities could still make closing orders different from those in the Act, though not earlier than 7 p.m. and 8 p.m. on the late night. No person could be employed on Sunday "about the business of a shop" unless he or she received compensating holidays.

There was a wide list of exemptions and partial exemptions, and in holiday resorts local authorities could permit Sunday trading in food and other commodities for not more than eighteen days in the year. The Act continued the provision for revoking a closing order by ballot of shop-keepers, and establishing a six-day trading week. The remainder of the Act was concerned with health, safety, meal times and breaks and hours of young people.

With one small exception there has been no shops legislation since 1950, the exception being the Shops (Early Closing Days) Act, 1965, which tightened up protection for the weekly half holiday (renamed the "early closing day") but continued the power of local authorities, in certain circumstances, to exempt shops in some areas from the early closing provision.

From USDAW's standpoint, the 1950 Act was a mixed bag, consolidating as it did some good measures, some not so good, some downright bad. But throughout this period the Union's main objective was to secure shops legislation that would lower

P

closing hours and narrow the range within which those hours, including the half day, were vulnerable to exemptions granted by reactionary local authorities. Sunday trading was not then the challenge which, as we shall see later, it was to become.

Year after year in the fifties and sixties, sometimes on its own, sometimes in conjunction with the TUC, at the annual conference and in the House of Commons, the Union pursued the Government along the corridors of power, and came away with prevarication as its answer, or with smooth half promises. J. D. Hiscock, the Assistant General Secretary, was the Union's specialist and principal spokesman on shop hours, backed up in the Commons by the Union's MPs whenever opportunity offered.

In 1953 the omens seemed to be hopeful. It was known that the Home Office was preparing drafts, largely based on Gowers, for amending shop hours legislation, and including general closing at 7 p.m., with 8 p.m. as the late night. The Union stood by its demand for 6 p.m. as the general closing hour, with 7 p.m. on the late night. Nevertheless, with new legislation there was always the hope that a successful amendment in Committee would be accepted by the Government. But whatever the drafts contained, they were still in the files of the Civil Service at the end of 1953.

A year later a powerful deputation from USDAW, retailers' organisations and the Early Closing Association met the Home Secretary and urged on him the Union's 6 p.m./7 p.m. proposals. Again, nothing happened. In 1955 T. W. Cynog-Jones, the Union's research officer, supervised exhaustive research into the closing hours actually operating. Returns were received covering private multiples and small shopkeepers in 296 provincial towns and cities, and 463 Co-operative Societies. These showed that throughout the country the general closing hour which actually prevailed was between 5 p.m. and 6 p.m. In grocery, only 3 per cent were later than 6 p.m., 73 per cent closed at 5.45 p.m. or earlier; in meat 2 per cent were later than 6 p.m. and 73 per cent closed at 5.45 p.m. or earlier; in drapery and department stores 65½ per cent closed at 5.45 p.m. or earlier and only 1½ per cent were later than 6 p.m. Principal exceptions were newsagency and confectionery/tobacco, where 21 per cent of the former and 30 per cent of the latter were open after 6 p.m.

Of all the trades surveyed (and only a selection has been given here) only newsagency and confectionery/tobacco bothered to have a late night at all. Still the Government was unmoved.

In the Queen's speech to the new Parliament elected in 1955 there was no reference to Shops legislation and the TUC sought a meeting with the Premier, Anthony Eden. USDAW was represented on the deputation which was assured that the Government intended to legislate on Gowers in general (which it did in the 1963 Act), while on shop hours in particular it was the intention to introduce a Bill in 1955-56. Victory seemed just over the horizon, with USDAW hopefully preparing to argue for the substitution of 6 p.m./7 p.m. closing for the 7 p.m./ 8 p.m. of Gowers. But that hopeful horizon was soon to recede.

The Bill was published during the winter and, as anticipated, contained the Gowers proposal on closing hours with, however, continued power for local authorities to revise them downwards, or upwards if justified by special circumstances. Although falling short of the Union's requirements, J. D. Hiscock reminded members in a *New Dawn* article that at least the proposals were one hour better than the existing law. There were other improvements in the Bill, such as stronger protection for the weekly half holiday and meal intervals.

Although it was a Government Bill, there was considerable opposition, in the Press, and in that last homestead of the backwoodsmen, the House of Lords. There were Peers whose own shopping was probably mainly done by servants who agonised over what they saw as a threat to the consumer's right to shop around the clock. USDAW issued a statement in answer to criticism that the Bill's proposals would penalise the consumer. On the contrary, it said, "They are necessary in the interests of the consumer, the shop worker and the shop keeper who wishes to keep reasonable hours. Without them, the highly competitive nature of retail trade will lead to later and later closing times for all shops and longer and longer working hours for those who work in them". It pointed out that the shift system was impossible in three out of four shops because of the small numbers of staff employed.

All seemed to be going well. But for USDAW it was soon to be a case of "Put not your trust in Tory promises". For suddenly the Bill was withdrawn on the excuse of lack of Parliamentary time. The Government had ratted on the Prime Minister's promises. The Union's protests were long and loud, in Parliament and in the country. The Government's decision was condemned at the TUC, the Labour Party Conference and the Co-operative Congress. But to no avail. Shop closing hours, so far as the law was concerned, were to stay at the level fixed in the first World War. And there they stay to this day.

We have now reached the mid-fifties, with USDAW fighting for shorter hours within a pattern of retailing that had not altered in essence since Victorian times. But the pattern was changing. The battle over hours was moving onto new ground. In the next chapter we shall look at new problems that are facing the Union at the present time.

24 SHOP HOURS — 2

The Changing Face of Distribution:
and the New Challenge of Sunday Trading

IN previous chapters the story of the Union's growth, policies
and problems has been carried forward in stages, covering
developments over successive periods of time. With shop hours,
however, it will be more convenient to the reader to complete
the story in two instalments, from the beginning of Victoria's
reign to the days of Elizabeth II. We now move into the seventies
and a new challenge to USDAW's traditional attitude to closing
times and the working week, together with special pleading by
vested interests to open up Sunday as a trading day for most
foods and a wide range of other products.

It is almost three decades since the Shops Act of 1950.
Since the end of Hitler's war there has been a great reduction
in the number of shops. The supermarket and the hypermarket
have largely taken over the grocery trade in both the private
sector and the Co-operative Movement. A Union report to
which we shall shortly return has forecast that by 1980 there
will be few grocery counter shops left of any size. The same
tendency towards size is evident in the spread of large discount
houses in the consumer durables trades.

Two trends have been pulling in opposite directions. Trade
Union action by USDAW has been successful in reducing shop
working hours to 40 a week or less (USDAW is currently
campaigning for a 35 hour week). In recent years the opposite
trend has been for many retailers, particularly in supermarkets
and discount houses, to seek to extend the trading week to
somewhere round sixty hours. In this situation some Union
members have argued for a two-part policy. The Union should
continue to fight for a reduction in the total number of hours in
a standard *working* week. There should, however, be greater
flexibility in meeting the pressure for a longer *trading* week in

which a standard working day would be maintained or reduced and there were plus payments, overtime rates or other concessions for days in which there was a later closing time, or in which unsocial hours were worked.

This conflict between the standard working week and the trading week surfaced nationally in the report of a working party on shop trading hours and the working week, called for by the ADM of 1974. The working party consisted of six officers — the Union's President, J. D. Hughes, John Phillips, the Assistant General Secretary, J. Flood, W. H. F. Whatley, T. F. Callinan and W. J. Jones; four lay members, W. Barrow, L. Hazell, T. Lawless and Mrs. P. H. Doyle, and also D. McGibbon and W. Tait of the Executive Council. Their report comprehensively covered the changes in retailing practice and their conclusions, together with the recommendations, are summarised in the paragraphs which follow, more or less under the headings in the report.

CHANGING TRENDS

The number of retail shops, it was stated, had fallen in the decade 1961-71 by 10 per cent to 485,000; grocery and provisions by 27 per cent to 108,000, "Other food dealers" by 18 per cent to 94,000, confectionery, tobacconists, newsagents by 23 per cent to 54,000. Households goods stores increased by 20 per cent to 74,000.

Multiples had decreased by 6,000 to 67,000, but in the five years 1966-1971 had increased their turnover by 58 per cent "illustrating quite clearly the movement towards larger shops in the retail multiple chains".

Co-operative stores had decreased, under the drastic reorganisation programme which began in the sixties, from 29,000 in 1961 to 15,000 in 1971 and the tendency was for them "to concentrate their trading in an increasing number of large general stores".

WORKERS

Sixty per cent of shop workers were women and one in three of these were part-timers. One in four of all shop employees were part-timers.

A survey of sales staff carried out for the Distributive Industry Training Board, based on information from 1,600 firms, had illustrated the "in-out" nature of shop employment. About

200,000 were recruited as sales staff in the year to October, 1971, but at the end of the year only 110,000 remained with their original employers. There was also a heavy loss (7 per cent) of managers.

SHOP OPENING HOURS

Investigations by the Union's Divisional Officers revealed an increasing movement towards late night opening up to 8 p.m. on two nights a week, while in discount houses — Co-operative and private — more extensive opening hours applied. There had also been a large increase in the number of six-day trading areas.

"In a number of Divisions the extended trading hours have been adopted in agreement with the Union at local level in return for improved working arrangements for the staff. These provide for improved five-day working week arrangements, overtime payment for late night working, etc. In certain cases full-time staff work a normal 40-hour week or less — the staffing on the late nights being done entirely by part-time labour or voluntary overtime or a combination of both".

In non-Unionised firms it was assumed that late night opening had been arranged on terms acceptable to the staff concerned.

THE WORKING WEEK

Most Union members were on a standard week of 40 hours or less. Most shops operated on a six-day week, on a cyclical basis, with a periodic long weekend of Saturday, Sunday and Monday.

PRINCIPAL RECOMMENDATIONS

1. "The former policy of seeking to maintain a rigid closing hour of 5.30 p.m. or 6 p.m. for all shops is no longer practicable."
2. "As shopping habits alter . . . greater flexibility and liberalisation in the weekday closing times of shops needs to be accepted — subject to there being no extension of the employees' normal standard working week".
3. There was no evidence to justify opening of shops beyond 8 p.m. and the provision of the 1950 Shops Act was still appropriate.
4. The statutory half-day should be maintained.

PAYMENT FOR UNSOCIAL WORKING HOURS

Recommendations (1) and (2) were amplified by proposals

for plus payments for unsocial (e.g. late evening) hours. They
were:—
    (i) That the Union should seek to establish a defined standard
working day of from 9 a.m. to 6 p.m.
    (ii) Time outside the standard day should be covered by
overtime and/or unsocial hours payments " . . . notwith-
standing that the total hours constituting the working week
have not been absorbed or exceeded".
    (iii) Additional payments to all full-time staff for hours
worked on a Saturday.
    (iv) Provision within agreements for "daily overtime".

SUNDAY TRADING

On Sunday trading the report reaffirmed the Union's opposition to any extension beyond that already permitted and
against the extension of Sunday markets. Legislation should
extend to Scotland, where Sunday trading was not illegal.

John Phillips, in moving the report at the 1974 ADM
declared that the crucial issue was: how could a five-day
working week of 40 hours or less be operated " . . . within the
context of an approximate sixty hour opening or trading week
which is currently operating in many sections of distribution?"
They could maintain present policy of resisting any change, or
they could recognise the change in trading methods and prepare
their own proposals " . . . in such a way as to serve the best
interests of the membership". He pointed out that in practice
they had already established in agreements with many employers the principle of premium payments for Saturday working
and for hours worked between 6 p.m. and 8 p.m.

The debate on the report was one of the longest at the 1974
ADM and the general tenor was against the recommendations.
Mrs. C. Leishman (Midlnds Divisional Council) questioned the
inevitability of a longer trading week and said the Union should
be concentrating on a decent basic wage rather than overtime
or unsocial hours. Mrs. D. Vaughan (Birmingham, Lewis's)
quoted women shop workers at a recent meeting in the Midlands
as saying "Our hours now are unsocial enough. We have to
rush home to get the old man's tea; we do not want any more
of that". F. S. Beney (Area Organiser, Midlands) said extra
money for unsocial hours would be passed on in prices. Since
shopworkers themselves would have to pay the extra, they

would be working longer hours and be no better off. In support of the recommendations T. P. Callinan (Eastern Diivsional Officer and member of the working party) contended in the face of interruptions that the later closing times were a fact and "... you must face the realities of the situation". In his Division they had obtained premium payments for staff who were willing to work after 6 p.m., and the payments were made whether or not the total hours worked were within the 40 hour week.

Delegates were not convinced, and the report was defeated. But a vote does not make a problem disappear. With or without Union agreement on compensatory payments, late night closing has continued. Moreover, shops legislation in general has been under increasing attack, and as this is written in early 1979, there is a new threat — the third since 1968 — to reduce the already frequently ignored restrictions on Sunday trading. The organisation of the shops inspectors (the Institute of Shops, Health and Safety Acts Administration) has prepared a Bill which could open a great many more shops on Sundays and it was introduced in the House of Lords on 13th March, 1979.

The Bill substitutes for Schedule 5 of the 1950 Act a new list of transactions for which all shops may be open on Sunday. The new list includes the sale of all kinds of food, including butchers' meat, for consumption on and off the premises. Another major schedule enables *any* local authority to allow shops within their area to open for sale on Sunday of a much wider range of goods than is at present permissible. The additions include souvenirs, articles for bathing or fishing, toys and fancy goods, cosmetics, stationery, photographic requisites, tents, caravans or trailers. Under existing legislation this power applies only to holiday resorts, for a limited range of products and services, and then only for 18 Sundays in any one year.

Other non-food articles, such as clothing, footwear, consumer durables, are not mentioned in the Bill. But once the gates were opened for food shops, it is obvious that non-food retailers would soon demand a similar right to open on Sundays, and the seven day retailing week would be complete.

We have already seen that USDAW's working party pronounced against Sunday opening. Even before the Bill was

mooted the Union was engaged in guerilla warfare against the
"hit and run" market traders who come into a neighbourhood
on Sundays, establish their stalls in defiance of a variety of
legal provisions, and then depart to pastures new, or continue
to return to the same locality if, as is too often the case, the
local authority turns a blind eye.

The Union went quickly into action against the Bill.
Branches were alerted in a memorandum from John Phillips
which analysed not only the adverse effects on the lives of shop
workers but also the increase in prices to the consumer through
higher costs for labour, heating, light and other services that
would inevitably follow Sunday opening. Private traders,
including the National Chamber of Trade, also registered
opposition.

In the columns of *Dawn* members of USDAW were urged to
mobilise against the measure, and when the proposals reached
the Lords on 19th March, 1979, the entire centre spread of the
newspaper was devoted to a text and pictorial report of the
debate.

The Bill was introduced by Lord Ponsonby, a member of
USDAW and former member of the Union's Parliamentary
Panel, facts which Lord Allen commented on with some
astonishment when he made the principal speech in opposition.
Lord Ponsonby argued that the numerous anomalies that had
developed under existing legislation constituted a strong case
for revision of the law. Other speakers accepted that there were
anomalies and frequent failure by local authorities to enforce
the existing legislation. They contended, however, that these
defects were a case for clarifying and strengthening the law
rather than, so to speak, pouring the baby out with the bath
water.

Lord Allen pointed out that the vast majority of workers had
Saturday and Sunday for family and social activities. But for
shop workers "Sunday is the one day of the week which offers
the opportunity of a common rest day with the family". Young
people "of which the distributive trades take the greater proportion as school leavers" would bitterly resent having to work
on Sundays as well as Saturdays.

Over 70 per cent of the labour force in distribution consisted
of women. A high proportion were married, with families and

domestic responsibilities. For them the social disadvantages of Sunday opening would be most acute. Staffing difficulties were already severe in retailing and the effect of the Bill would be that many would leave the trade rather than put up with Sunday working in addition to Saturday. He went on:

"There is no evidence of a genuine or widespread demand on the part of the majority of the shopping public for extended shopping facilities on Sundays beyond those already permitted under current legislation. If you ask people 'Would you like to see the shops open? — then of course you get the answer, 'Yes' . . . But if you ask 'Would you, as a housewife, be prepared to pay more . . . over the counter' . . . then I think you will get a different answer". But the proposals would increase costs, and the increase would go into prices. He continued.

"If shops are to be kept open around the clock for seven days a week, no over-all greater volume of goods would be sold, for the housewife's purse is not elastic. It would simply mean that the same volume of sales would be spread over a longer period with increased labour costs and overheads. Extended trading hours must in the long term . . . involve regular overtime, increased staff, shift work or all three." But as over 70 per cent of shops in the United Kingdom employed less than four persons, including working proprietors and manageresses, the application of a shift or rota system would be totally out of the question.

He emphasised that increases in costs as a result of the Bill would fall on the consumer and challenged supporters of the Bill whether they were " . . . seriously suggesting that it would be in the national interest to legislate for increased retail prices on the questionable ground of a supposed demand as yet unproven for a seven day shopping service."

Lord Sainsbury, who made it clear that he was not speaking on behalf of the great retailing firm with which is name is associated, also opposed the Bill, primarily on humanitarian grounds, and secondly on economic grounds. He did not believe, as had been argued, that the Bill would have only a limited effect. From his knowledge of retailing he thought the Act would lead to a steady increase in Sunday opening by food shops and supermarkets because of fear that competitors would take their trade, and this would happen despite possible difficulties in obtaining staff or having to pay higher wages. Nor did he believe that the community had the right to expect more shop workers and more small shop owners to forego their Sunday rest.

The Bishop of Norwich and the well known Methodist, Lord Soper, also opposed the Bill, as did Lord Blease, another USDAW life peer who was formerly Northern Ireland Officer for the Irish Congress of Trade Unions. Lord Lyell welcomed the Bill for the Conservatives, Earl Grey for the Liberals.

For the then Labour Government Lord Faversham declared a position of neutrality, saying "We shall do nothing to restrict the progress of the Bill and we shall . . . take note of reactions to it both inside and outside Parliament". On a vote 22 Peers expressed themselves as "Content" (i.e. in favour of the Bill) and 11 as "Not Content".

The Union's opposition was forcefully expressed at the 1979 ADM, held almost mid-way through the General Election of that year. But the Conservative Party, under Mrs. Thatcher, won the election. Their spokesman in the Lords had already welcomed the Bill. Opposition will continue during further stages in the Lords and in the Commons if the Bill reaches that stage. Nationally and in the country the Union will have many allies in Co-operative and private trade in continuing agitation against what, basically, is change for the sake of change, without any solid evidence that it meets a widespread public need. Religious bodies can be expected to protest at this increasing secularisation of Sunday. But given a Conservative Government likely to be in power for several years, a future historian may have to record a major setback in the long campaign for civilised working hours in the distributive trades.

PART 6

PROGRESS AND CONTROVERSY

25 THE FIFTIES AND SIXTIES

IN this and the immediately following chapters we shall carry the Union's story from the early 1950s to 1965, years in which memories of the war receded and the post-war world was born. Most of the war leaders had gone, through death or retirement. Stalin had died in 1953, Roosevelt much earlier in 1945. Churchill gave up the Premiership in 1955. C. R. Attlee, his Labour Deputy in war time and his successor as Premier for the Parliaments of 1945 and 1950, retired in the same year. The new men who succeeded the war leaders could have been expected to enjoy a long run of power or the pursuit of power. But they were an ill-starred generation. Churchill's successor, Anthony Eden (later Lord Avon) wrecked his career in 1956 in the brief and unsuccessful Anglo-French war with Egypt over the Suez Canal. Aneurin Bevan, at the age of 63, died in 1960. Hugh Gaitskell, Attlee's successor, died in 1963 at the age of 56, and Harold Wilson was elected as Party leader. Morgan Phillips, Secretary of the Labour Party, died a few days before Gaitskell. J. F. Kennedy, elected President of the United States in 1960, was killed by an assassin's bullet three years later.

The military occupation of Western Germany ended in 1955. A year later the German Federal Republic opened diplomatic relations with the Soviet Union. But it was a period of fragile peace, as was seen in the Korean war and the brief military adventure of Suez. The latter was a particularly bitter experience because it diverted the attention of the world from the almost simultaneous Russian invasion of Hungary and the abuse of Soviet power to stamp out an early attempt by a Communist state to liberalise Marxist dogma and practice.

They were the years when science and technology increased the ability of mankind to soar into outer space or to commit nuclear suicide on a global scale. In Britain they were the years of the Campaign for Nuclear Disarmament and the Aldermaston March, two gallant enterprises that achieved considerable influence but were not successful in changing national policy. We have since learned to "live with the bomb" in a mood of fatalistic optimism that it will never be used, or alternatively, by closing our minds to its existence.

Industrial production and world trade had revived, although Britain soon began to be outpaced by other European countries. Six of them (Belgium, France, Western Germany, Italy, the Netherlands and Luxembourg) had launched the European Economic Community (the Common Market) in 1958. Britain was divided (and still is) over the issue of membership. Japan, having failed disastrously to establish by military means the so-called Greater East Asia Co-prosperity Sphere, was gaining a wider dominion in many fields of world trade. It is fascinating to read, in light of current events in Britain, that in 1957 the production of motor vehicles in the United States was 7,200,000, in Great Britain 1,149,000 — and in Japan 45,000.

Conservative Governments were in power for the thirteen years from 1951 to 1964. Their disastrous influence on the British economy and on labour relations do not enter into this chapter but will be seen when we come to USDAW's role in the political and wages policy issues of the fifties and sixties.

For the Union this period saw several changes at the top level of executive and political service. Some were predictable through the operation of the retirement age. The most shocking to Union members was the death of the General Secretary, Alan Birch, in Manor House Hospital, London, on 13th December, 1961, at the age of 51. He had been in the hospital earlier in the year but seemed to have recovered and to be well on the way to resuming his role in USDAW and the TUC. But it was not to be. Most of his comparatively short life had been spent in the Union. He joined as a junior on the clerical staff of Warrington Co-operative Society. Thereafter, as branch secretary, Liverpool Divisional Councillor, Area Organiser, National Officer, he progressed to the General Secretaryship when Sir Joseph Hallsworth left for the National Coal Board in 1949. He had been knighted in the Birthday Honours of 1961. Others who departed without the poignancy of early death were Margaret Bondfield (81) in 1953, J. R. Leslie (81), former General Secretary of the Shop Assistants' Union, in 1955, and P. C. Hoffman in 1959, three who had done much to pioneer the Shop Assistants' Union and wage the battle against the iniquitous living-in system.

In the election in 1962 which followed the death of Sir Alan Birch, Alfred Walter Henry Allen, better known in the Union as Alfred or Alf Allen, was elected as General Secretary. Born in 1914 in Bristol, his career had been along similar lines to that of his predecessor — early membership of the Bristol Co-operative Branch, Area Organiser in Liverpool and later the South West, National Officer at Central Office in 1951, eleven years later elected General Secretary by a very large majority. In a by-election following the death of Sir Alan Birch, Alfred Allen was elected to the General Council of the TUC, and re-elected at the subsequent Congress. He continued to serve on the Council until his retirement in 1979, when he was Chairman of the powerful Economic Committee.

Another change at the top was the retirement, for health reasons, in June, 1964, at the age of 60, of J. D. Hiscock who had served USDAW and previously the Shop Assistants' Union for 42 years. He had been Assistant General Secretary since the amalgamation and had played a leading part in Union campaigns to win wage agreements in the private sector of retailing and wholesaling. He was awarded the OBE in 1952. In the international field he was acting President of the International Federation of Commercial, Clerical and Technical Employees at the time of his retirement. The new Assistant General Secretary was J. Phillips, who was promoted from the position of National Officer in which he had dealt mainly with the retail distributive private trade, catering and check and credit trades. Aged 48, he had seen long service in the Shop Assistants' Union as well as in USDAW.

The memory of Sir Alan Birch was commemorated by a Union scholarship in his name at Ruskin College, tenable for two years. A great many Union branches were associated with the scholarship. There was also a moving tribute by Walter Padley, MP, at the 1962 annual meeting, to which Lady Birch responded.

The new General Secretary was introduced to the ADM of that year and declared that the immediate tasks before them were to replace the current minimum wage of well below £10 (which was then the Union's target) by a basic weekly rate that was an adequate reward for a week's work, together with attainment of the five-day, 40 hours, working week and equal pay for men and women — three objectives with which he was to see substantial progress during his term of office.

Changes also took place in the Presidency of the Union. When the Labour Government was returned in 1964, the new Prime Minister, Harold Wilson, appointed Walter Padley, who for sixteen years had been President, as Minister of State for Foreign Affairs. R. B. Seabrook was elected to fill the remainder of Padley's term. An Area Organiser in the Southern and Eastern Division since 1937, "Dick" Seabrook had also been an Executive Council member since 1957. In the subsequent election of 1965, however, Rodney Hanes was returned as President. A Lancashire man, he had long been based as an Area Organiser in London, and had served on the Executive Council since 1949. In 1960 he married one of the few women members to be elected to the Council, Miss E. Falkingham, who, under her married name, was awarded in 1963 the annual TUC gold badge for service to the Movement. She had been a Union member for 38 years and until her marriage worked in the private distributive trade in Leeds. The badge was presented at the 1963 TUC. Rodney Hanes held the Presidency until 1967, when R. B. Seabrook was re-elected.

Another well-known member left the Union's service in September, 1960. Alfred Robens, MP for Blyth constituency since 1945, was appointed Chairman of the National Coal Board. As Lord Robens he became widely known as a vigorous opponent of the short-sighted policy — pursued by Governments of both Parties — of running down the coal mining industry on the assumption that the oil producing countries would obligingly continue to supply the West with cheap fuel. At the subsequent by-election in November, 1960, E. J. Milne, an USDAW Area Organiser in Scotland, retained Blyth for Labour.

From personalia we now turn to policy. The sixties in particular saw the beginning of a breakthrough with a reform that had been official Union policy since the amalgamation of 1947 — the five-day working week for retail distributive workers. Many progressive employers recognised the cogency of the Union's argument that with full employment the distributive trades would find it increasingly difficult to enlist new recruits for a lifetime of Saturday working with no compensatory benefits. But private trade organisations, as distinct from individuals, dredged up from Victoriana an old, old argument — that reform was a matter for individual employers. They ignored a century of experience that if one or two employers rejected a reform, the rest, in self defence, would follow suit.

In 1955, Trevor Bowen, chairman of the John Barker store organisation, had publicly suggested that the trade must face up to the five-day problem. USDAW's Executive Council was quick to respond with a supporting statement and invitations to the Retail Distributors' Association, the Multiple Shops' Federation and the Multiple Shoe Retailers' Association to discuss the subject with the Union. The National Chamber of Trade was also approached. The general response, however, was insistence on individual action. The Union declared that this left no alternative but to go ahead with regional or single firm campaigns in every suitable area, and an article in *New Dawn* of October 29th, 1960, affirmed that " . . . in the absence of any kind of joint recommendations nationally, this is the course which we shall have to pursue." Department stores, which were one of the few fields of large scale distribution which had not negotiated comprehensive voluntary agreements on wages, etc., were to be given special attention.

The Union continued the campaign on two fronts — pressure for negotiation with Trade Associations, and on individual employers. Two store firms, Bentalls in South London and the John Lewis Partnership, with 21 shops in London and the provinces, decided of their own volition in 1960 to introduce the equivalent of a five-day week. Other firms were reported to be operating or contemplating similar arrangements.

The Union won its first individual agreement in 1961. It was with the powerful Lewis's group of department stores, and related to the company's Manchester store. The agreement provided for a six full-day trading week and a five-day working week, based on a staff rota cycled over periods of three weeks, giving one day off each week and so arranged that in each span of three weeks there was one week with Saturday, Sunday and Monday off. This arrangement was possible because Manchester was one of an increasing number of cities in which most department store and other traders in city centres were exempted from the observance of an early closing day.

A year later there was a similar agreement for the staff at the firm's Birmingham store. In that city the Chamber of Commerce had recommended retailers wishing to trade for six days to consider arrangements for five-day working, and USDAW members backed up the recommendation with meetings and poster parades. Agreements were made with other Lewis's stores as and when municipalities granted exemption from early closing.

Progress was being made. But, to misquote Abraham Lincoln, you cannot satisfy all of the people all of the time, and at the 1962 ADM the Central London Hairdressers' branch were successful with a resolution expressing concern at the slow progress towards the five-day, 40-hour week. By 1963, however, the Executive Council reported an advance that should have satisfied the sternest of its critics. It was an agreement on a five-day working week for the multiple grocery trade in England and Wales, the culmination of some two years of negotiation, long periods of frustration and one stage when a series of conferences in the trade declared the Union's members to be ready for "a head on collision" if results were much longer delayed. As J. D. Hiscock described it in *New Dawn* the experience had been not unlike the long saga of the first Co-operative national agreement, with the difference that in the latter case both parties were willing negotiators, while it was some time before the multiple grocers were willing to sit round the negotiating table. About 100 firms were involved, with thousands of shops, ranging from supermarkets to small counter service branches. There could be no uniform standard that fitted every case and the agreement provided a variety of alternative ways in which the five-day week could be operated, the central factor being that however it was done, there must be an additional full half-day of leisure.

A year later, in the autumn, the General Secretary (who traditionally led negotiations with the Co-operatives on behalf of the joint committee of Unions concerned) reported another victory — a five-day — forty-hour week agreement for retail shops with the National Wages Board of the Co-operative Union. At local level the agreement was to be translated into opening and closing hours through negotiations between retail societies and the Trades Union branches concerned. In most societies weekly working hours were reduced by two. This agreement also stated that both parties had taken into consideration "the urgency of improving the Co-operative Movement's share of the national retail trade to enable present wages standards and conditions to be maintained and improved upon".

We temporarily leave the five-day week campaign at this point. It was no longer a dream. Distribution was still rife with exploitation of the worker, but the curse of excessive hours was being lifted.

During the nineteen sixties the Executive Council was increasingly aware of the need to reorganise the Union's arrangements for member-education. The number of agreements with trade associations of employers and with individual firms was increasing. So, too, was the number of trades and services in which the Union operated. To service these developments trained and experienced shop stewards and collectors were required at the grass roots level of store or factory. Moreover, the large turnover in membership (which is the subject of the next chapter) required constant effort to educate recruits in the social and political objectives of the Union and of the Trades Union Movement in general. As was pointed out in Chapter 22, the education scheme adopted in 1949 was well-fitted to provide social/political education but much less so for training in Trade Union organisation and administration.

In 1958 a new programme was introduced, and still continues as the basis for the Union's educational work. A special report by the Executive Council to the ADM of that year declared that in addition to contributions to national bodies, for pooled facilities to the Trades Union Movement as a whole, " . . .specialised services maintained by the Union itself are also indispensable". The report made six basic proposals:—

(1) In addition to the established one-week summer school there should be a second school annually of a more advanced nature, for which students who had attended the first school would be eligible.

(2) Between fifty and sixty Union Federations were already organising one-day or weekend schools, individually or jointly with other Federations or Divisional Councils. In South Wales

and Monmouthshire there had been experiments in linked schools, with the same body of students attending a series of lectures. Federation schools were mainly financed by branches. To stimulate interest it was proposed that they should be given greater help from central funds.

(3) Facilities should be provided at Central Office for the training of voluntary branch officers and intensive courses should be organised. The educational staff should be increased.

(4) Full use should be made of the Union's entitlement to nominate members for places on the one or two week courses which the TUC had begun to provide at its training college in London.

(5) Places should continue to be taken and allocated on a Divisional basis at the summer schools of the TUC, Scottish TUC, Workers' Educational Trade Union Committee, the Co-operative Union and the Labour Party.

(6) Various other grants or facilities should be extended.

The scheme introduced in 1949, said the report, had been financed by an annual allocation of 5d per member, increased to 7d in 1952. During the preceding six years about £10,000 a year had thus been allocated to education, plus an amount which was not segregated in the accounts for administration, expenses of Union officers addressing Federation schools, the income from the sum invested to finance the Sir Joseph Hallsworth scholarship at Ruskin and that part of the TUC affiliation fees which went to finance the TUC training college. About £7,000 of the total went in part on payments to national bodies for direct services, and more than £5,000 of the sum represented affiliation fees, of which £4,300 consisted of affiliation to the NCLC at 3d per member.

The NCLC had sought to increase the fee to 4d, to which the Union could not agree. Instead it proposed that payments should cease to be on a per capita basis but should be made for services actually rendered, such as correspondence courses; a method which operated with several other Unions. The NCLC, however, had stated that this form of association was no longer available. The Union Executive therefore proposed to dis-continue affiliation from the end of 1958.

After so long a link between the two bodies it was natural that when the report reached the ADM, and was moved by

Alan Birch, there should be some opposition to breaking the link with the NCLC. A fear expressed by some delegates was that it would diminish political education. But the fact was that while the Union had grown enormously since affiliation began there had been no similar progress in the use that members made of NCLC facilities. In 1938 3,511 members took part in one or some of the facilities provided by the NCLC, 1,911 of them taking correspondence courses. In 1957 the total was 3,141 of which 785 represented correspondence courses. ADM delegates accepted that times had changed, new methods were necessary and they adopted the report.

The decision was quickly followed by the appointment of the Union's first full-time Education Officer, Peter Rosenfeld, who took up the position in October, 1958. He is still in office, and we shall see later how the Union, under his guidance, began to develop the well organised educational scheme that it operates today.

Another historic decision of the 1958 ADM meeting was to change the date of the annual meeting. It had long been at Easter, Standing Orders prescribing that it must be held on Easter Sunday, Monday and Tuesday or at Whitsuntide, whichever was the more practicable. An Executive Council statement proposed that while Easter should still be named Whitsuntide should be deleted and the alternative should be " . . . on the last Sunday in April and the two subsequent days". A principal reason for the change was the size of the conference and the problem of securing accommodation for between 1,100 and 1,200 delegates, and 400 to 600 visitors. Only three centres in the United Kingdom were suitable, at all of which there was competition from other organisations for accommodation at Easter. In addition, Easter is, of course, a movable feast and arrangements for conference documentation had to be altered from year to year. The proposed alteration, the statement said, would still permit a return to Easter if that was justified by experience.

Old habits die hard and the meeting was not totally en- amoured of the proposal, particularly in Scotland, where the new date could clash with municipal elections. But the difficulties involved in sticking to Easter or Whit were self-evident to many delegates with experience of the ADM, and after some objections the proposal was carried by a large majority. A proposal to return to Easter was defeated at the 1961 ADM, the April date survived a further examination in 1962, and continues to be the Union's practice.

There were three General Elections in the period covered by this chapter — in 1955, 1959 and 1964. In the first two the Conservative Party was returned with a substantially higher vote than Labour: 1955, Conservative 49.7 per cent, Labour 46.4 per cent: 1959, Conservative 49.4 per cent, Labour 43.8 per cent. The balance was the other way in 1964: Labour 44.1 per cent, Conservative 43.4 per cent. In that election Labour won 317 seats, the Conservatives 303 and the Liberals 9. In all three elections USDAW candidates did well. The 1955 result was given in Chapter 20, but will be repeated to complete the picture of the period covered by this chapter.

Union members elected to Parliament in—

1955: A. Robens (Blyth), G. Craddock (Bradford South), W. A. Burke (Burnley), A. E. Hunter (Feltham), H. Boardman (Leigh), W. E. Padley (Ogmore), R. E. Winterbottom (Sheffield, Brightside), J. T. Price, (Westhoughton), E. Fernyhough (Jarrow).

1959: All the above re-elected except W. A. Burke who did not stand. G. W. Loughlin won South Gloucestershire, a new seat for the Union.

1964: All re-elected with the exception that E. J. Milne was Member for Blyth. H. Solomons won Hull North, a new seat for the Union.

The Union continued to give generous support to Labour's General Election funds. In 1964 the amount was £55,000 in two donations.

Other events of the fifties and sixties can only briefly be mentioned. The Union regularly entered candidates for the TUC Gold Medal awards, and during the period women members outnumbered men by three to one in receiving the coveted distinction. One, Mrs. Hanes, has already been mentioned. The others were, first, Miss Alice Brown, of the Guildford Branch, in 1959. She had worked in the Movement for fifty years. The other was Miss M. I. Groves, Blaina branch, in 1961. The man was H. Winipenny, St. Helens (S) branch, who received the men's award in 1960. The TUC itself, after years in which it had occupied eight different sets of rented offices in Central London, obtained a home of its own when it moved into newly built headquarters in Great Russell Street, London, in March, 1958.

The Union, with its long links with the Co-operative Movement, and its large Co-operative membership, welcomed the report of an Independent Commission set up by the Co-operative Congress of 1955 under the general oversight of Hugh Gaitskell, and with Anthony Crosland, then out of Parliament, as Secretary, USDAW had submitted recommendations to the commission on the subject of labour relations. The report, which was presented to the Co-operative Congress of 1958, proposed major changes in Co-operative policy and trading practice, many of which were later implemented. A conference of Unions with members in the Co-ops, retail and wholesale, was organised by the TUC on the suggestion of USDAW and set up a committee to consider the proposals, Alan Birch being secretary. The Union's members were urged by the Executive Council to work to secure the support of their own societies for the Commission's proposals.

The Union gave financial and moral support to the ICFTU International Solidarity Fund, set up at the beginning of 1958, with the principal purpose of helping Trades Unionism in under-developed countries; each Union being asked to raise contributions equivalent to 1/6 per member over three years. A practical example of the Union's international spirit was an interest-free loan of £10,000 to the Belgian Commercial Employees' Union in 1961, for the relief of distress during a General Strike.

In 1963 the Union began a practice which still continues — the provision of financial assistance for the attendance of young members as visitors at the annual delegate meeting.

We saw many chapters ago that A. Hewitt, the Union's first secretary, worked as a proof reader at the Co-operative Newspaper Society (now the Co-operative Press Limited) before becoming full-time secretary of the Amalgamated Union of Co-operative Employees and for a long period the Union's Offices were in the Newspaper Society's premises. The link has continued ever since, in representation on the Press Board to which A. Hewitt was elected in 1903, and in printing of the

Union journal and other publications. Cyril Hamnett, who
became Administrative Officer of the Union in addition to
having responsibility for *New Dawn* and publicity, was chairman of the Co-operative Press from 1952 to 1977, having been
elected to the Board five years earlier. In that capacity he
devoted endless time and energy to maintaining and building
the circulation of the Sunday *Reynolds News*, the principal
newspaper of the Co-operative Press (the title derived from
George William MacArthur Reynolds, an early Victorian
Chartist and Socialist who was also a novelist of considerable
quality). National newspaper production is a notoriously high-
cost industry, and the paper was kept going mainly by voluntary
contributions from the Co-operative Movement. The title was
altered in September 1962 to *Sunday Citizen and Reynolds News*
and to finance publicity for a relaunch Trades Unions were asked
for help. USDAW responded magnificantly with a contribution
of £10,000, and with further grants of £1,500 in 1966 and 1967.
But the odds today are against a small national newspaper (or
many big ones, for that matter, judging from post-war experience) and the paper appeared for the last time in June, 1967.

After many years' membership the Executive disaffiliated
from the Labour Research Department in 1962. This action
was challenged at the ADM of that year but was defended on
the grounds that the LRD was dominated by the Communist
Party, was proscribed by the Labour Party whose constitution
the Union was expected to observe, and in addition adequate
research facilities were now available through the TUC and
USDAW's own research department. The Executive's action
was endorsed on a card vote.

In 1963 USDAW launched a new publication of its own,
specially designed to back up recruitment among employees in
retail distribution. Entitled *Employee in Shop and Store* it was
issued quarterly and supplied free to Area Organisers, collector-
canvassers, voluntary branch officials and other key members in
shops and stores. Printed in web-offset by the Co-operative
Press, it served a useful purpose but eventually was discontinued
because of difficulties in distribution.

26 RECRUITMENT AND LAPSES

The "Committee of Investigation"

AT the annual conference of 1947 J. D. Hughes had warned that unless USDAW "mended the hole in the bucket" new members recruited in private trade would pour in at one end and run out at the other. His remedy was to ensure that before the Union began to recruit there should always be a shop steward or collector available to maintain contact with the new members and secure the payment of Union dues.

In the following years many measures were adopted to "mend the hole", including full-time collector-canvassers, additional organisers, appeals to active members to help in holding recruits, experiments by existing branches with schemes to interest new members, educational programmes for shop stewards, youth groups, the development of special trade conferences. But lapses on the scale which annually occurred continued to be a source of frustration to the Union.

The problem was almost entirely in the field of private trade employment. Membership in the Co-ops was established and stable. But the new Union, as USDAW then was, sought to break through to the hundreds of thousands of distributive workers who had so far been impervious to the Trade Union appeal.

Between 1954 and 1958 there was a steady though usually comparatively small increase in net membership each year; the biggest figure being 4,791 in 1954 and the smallest 798 in 1958. As a percentage of total membership, however, lapses remained persistently high. Even in a "good" year like 1954 the percentage was 28.7. Between 1950 and 1963 it never fell below 24 per cent and in 1961 it was 31.33 per cent. Divisional figures reflected the same tendency. Taking 1962 (a "good" year — there was a net increase in membership of 4,667), only one of the ten Divisions had a lapses rate as low as 23.29 per cent, while five were over 30 per cent.

The actual "in-out" figures (taken from a special report to which we shall shortly return) from 1950 to 1963 are shown in the following table:

Year Ending	Membership	New Members Enrolled	Lapsed	Lapsed Members as a percentage of Membership
1950 ...	342,789			
1951 ...	347,737	... 99,043	... 94,095	... 27.05
1952 ...	345,990	... 86,233	... 87,980	... 25.42
1953 ...	339,044	... 86,162	... 93,108	... 27.46
1954 ...	343,835	... 102,693	... 97,902	... 28.47
1955 ...	346,135	... 107,236	... 104,936	... 30.31
1956 ...	348,855	... 102,994	... 100,274	... 28.74
1957 ...	352,333	... 98,279	... 94,801	... 26,90
1958 ...	353,131	... 88,525	... 87,727	... 24.84
1959 ...	351,465	... 84,597	... 86,263	... 24.54
1960 ...	355,271	... 106,287	... 102,481	... 28.84
1961 ...	351,371	... 106,201	... 110,101	... 31.33
1962 ...	356,038	... 107,698	... 103,031	... 28.93
1963 ...	354,701	... 101,199	... 102,536	... 28.90

This situation was not, of course, one which the Union was likely to shrug off. It was acknowledged that "in-out" was a characteristic of the distributive trades. But even allowing for this, the "out" element seemed more than reasonably could be expected. In almost every year from the first debate on recruitment and lapses in 1948 resolutions on the subject appeared on the agenda for the annual delegate meeting. Some related to recruitment in general, some to special groups such as women workers, others urged the appointment of more organisers.

While everyone deplored the scale of lapses, there was argument as to whether or not the problem was being over-exaggerated in terms of the actual number of workers who were potential recruits to USDAW. At the 1963 annual meeting, at which the issue came to a head, Walter Padley, from the chair, had a word of caution for "well-meaning comrades" who talked of two or three million members. The real task was formidable enough " ... without daunting ourselves with imaginary statistics".

The annual meeting had before it a resolution from South London which noted that in 1961 the Union recruited 106,201 members but showed a net loss of 3,900. It called on the Executive Council to appoint a committee to examine Union activities and make recommendations with a view to reducing loss of members, the committee to give special attention to the sections of distribution most likely to be fields of recruitment.

There was some feeling that the resolution was an implied criticism of the Executive and officials, although this was strongly denied by the mover, W. H. Kendall. The General Secretary, in replying to the debate, accepted this disclaimer but argued that as the subject of recruitment and lapses was constantly before the Executive, and there could be few aspects of the problem with which they were not familiar, the resolution did not really introduce anything new except the appointment of a committee. However, the general opinion was that a specific inquiry would concentrate the mind of the Union on a problem that was a constant irritant, and the resolution was accepted with a few dissentients.

In due course the committee was set up by the Executive Council. It consisted of W. E. Padley, MP, Union President, W. S. Jones, H. M. Nunns, J. E. Priest, R. B. Seabrook (Executive members), A. W. Allen, General Secretary, J. D. Hiscock, Assistant General Secretary, and T. W. Cynog-Jones, Research Officer. J. D. Hiscock resigned when he retired from service, in June, 1964, and his place was taken by his successor, J. Phillips, while W. E. Padley resigned on his appointment as Minister of State for Foreign Affairs in the Labour Government of 1964. At its first meeting the committee defined its scope as being the wholesale and retail Co-operative trade and the wholesale and retail multiple and private trades; milk and bread distribution being within this scope. An interim report was presented to the 1964 ADM. It was mainly concerned with the procedures adopted by the Committee in carrying out its task, or with research work in progress, and need not concern us here. The final report to the ADM of 1965 was one of the most comprehensive studies of a basic problem that any Trade Union has presented to its members. It did not come up with a clear-cut solution to the problem of lapses, for none existed. It did equip USDAW for the first time with a more accurate picture of the many varying reasons why members left the Union, the extent to which these reasons could be countered, and a long list of recommended courses of action.

The first part of the report described the procedure followed by the committee. There were two lines of approach, one on recruitment, the other on lapses. With the former, written inquiries were made on:—

(1) Recruiting Co-operative employees —
     sent to 778 branches, of which 603 replied.
(2) Methods employed in recruiting —
     to Divisional Officers.
(3) USDAW propaganda material —
     to Divisional Officers, Area Organisers and Collector-
     Canvassers.
(4) Area Organisers' Duties —
     to all Area Organisers.

For research into lapses, the record cards of members lapsing
from the 225 branches administered at Union offices were
analysed for the quarter ending September, 1963. Letters were
sent to 21,284 persons who had dropped out during the quarter.
Arrangements were made with 146 branches to follow up
members when they changed their employment. All branches
received a letter inviting individual members to give their views
on recruitment and lapses, and the invitation was prominently
repeated in *New Dawn*.

Once this programme had been set in motion, the committee
members set out on their travels. Every Division in the Union
was visited and meetings held with the Divisional Council and
with the Divisional Officers, Area Organisers, and Collector-
Canvassers. The committee also had discussions with the
Central Office officials, National Officers and heads of Departments.

Part 2 of the report concentrated on figures of recruitment
and lapses and analysed the potential in which new members
could be sought, beginning with the 3,421,000 people recorded
by the Ministry of Labour as engaged in the distributive trades
in July, 1964. Taking the Census of Distribution, 1961, as its
measuring rod, the committee concluded that deduction of
self-employed people and their families reduced the number of
paid employees in the trades to 2,800,000. This was not, however, a realistic potential. It included a great number of part-
timers: Saturday-only sales staff, errand boys such as schoolboy
newspaper deliverers, market traders, the one or two employees
of small independent shopkeepers.

For a realistic assessment of recruiting possibilities the
report began with the Census of Distribution figures for employment in retail Co-operatives (195,144), multiples with ten or

more branches (633,029) and large independent retailers (217,292). The total for these three groups was 1,045,465. In this section of the report it was pointed out that Co-operative membership of the Union was shrinking through the declining trade and consequent rationalisation of many societies. The peak employment figure for Co-operative Societies as a whole was 292,562 in 1958. By 1963 the number had fallen by 32,758. After making adjustments for part-timers (although many of these were considered to be potential Union members), and also for the wholesale food and retail trades, the committee reached the conclusion that a realistic maximum potential for Trades Union recruitment was about 1,000,000. But this figure had to be shared with other Unions that recruited in distribution (six were mentioned), and the potential for USDAW was unlikely to be more than 800,000. On this basis, the Union, with 354,701 members at December, 1963 "... has recruited a rather higher proportion of its real potential than is realised".

Turning to lapses, the report stated that of the 21,284 lapsed members who received the questionnaire mentioned earlier, 7,273 (34.2 per cent) replied. Their reasons for giving up membership were summarised as follows:—

	Per cent
Gave up employment	29.2
Took employment in a trade outside the scope of USDAW	55.8
	85.0
Took up employment in a shop where a collector does not call	4.4
Dissatisfied with USDAW	1.6
Some other reason	5.6
Reclaimed into membership of USDAW ..	3.4
	100.00

To quote the report: "The striking fact is that 85 per cent of these lapses were unavoidable. This figure is greater than many believed. In the meetings in the Divisions, officials and Divisional Councillors were asked if they had any figures of this kind. Guesses were made ranging from 23 per cent to 80 per cent ..."
The Committee was told that "... harm is done to the Union

when local leaders overstate the proplem of lapses. Confidence in the Union is undermined if it is believed that 100,000 workers 'throw their card in' every year . . . it is of importance that the membership should recognise that 85 per cent of the lapses are due to people leaving work altogether or leaving employment within the scope of USDAW".

Part 3 of the report dealt with the central problem — reducing the avoidable 15 per cent of lapses. The two main factors which led to the loss of members who could have been held were given as (1) a breakdown in the arrangements for collection of subscriptions, (2) loss of contact with the Union when members removed to another job. To deal with these problems the committee drew the obvious conclusions that (1) all branches " . . . must accept the importance of ensuring that adequate collection arrangements are maintained" and (2) that contact must not be lost with members who joined another employer. It was also emphasised that members themselves had a responsibility to ensure that they paid their dues and notified the Union when they changed their employment, but "regrettably, it seems clear that some members have no such clear understanding of the value of Trade Union membership".

In interviews up and down the country the committee was told that it was becoming increasingly difficult to find good voluntary collectors with a sincere interest in the Union. Commission at the rate of up to 5 per cent was already paid to collectors, but a widely held view was that the amount paid was not the real problem — interest in the Union was a stronger motivation with a good collector. Branches could determine the rate of commission, which was drawn from local funds, and the committee recommended that there should be "a flexible attitude" towards payments, according to "the needs of the situation" and local financial resources.

It was also emphasised that to deal with cases in which a voluntary collector in a store left, or was ill, there should be a deputy, or two collectors in large establishments. Branches should keep close contact with their collectors, support them with advice and guidance and take steps to ensure that the branch was notified when a collector left his job — members could be lost if the position was unfilled for several weeks.

About one-third of lapses were due to members losing contact with the Union when they left their immediate employment. The committee estimated that about 5,000 members a year were lost when they changed jobs in the distributive trades. Many could have been retained by efficient follow-up. Unfortunately, the general experience seemed to be that only sporadic efforts were made to follow a member from job to job. Several suggestions were made to improve the situation, such as the provision of forms on which shop stewards and collectors could notify the branch of the members' new employment, and branches were urged to appoint a membership secretary who would be responsible for follow-up. The report recognised, however, that this was often a thankless task. The 146 branches which has co-operated in a follow-up experiment found that in general the response was poor. Nevertheless " . . . the problem must be regarded as a major challenge to the Union".

It will be noted that these recommendations were mainly concerned with what were basically routine matters of local administration. But it is at those local levels that the strength and future of an organisation are often determined. Although the report did not say so, it seems apparent that as the Union had grown in size and the great variety of trades in which it operated, there had been some loss of the local zest and interest of earlier years and a considerable measure of apathy in many branches.

Part 4 turned to the question of recruitment, beginning with the Co-operative sector. The committee was disturbed to discover that while Trade Union membership was a condition of employment in most societies, at any one time " . . . a fair number of Co-operative employees are not within our ranks". This showed up wherever a contributions deduction scheme (the "check off") was introduced, when " . . . invariably a number of employees are found who are not members of the Union". In the eighteen months to June, 1964, deduction schemes were arranged with fifteen societies, producing 1,448 new members who should have been in the Union from the beginning of employment. The figure equalled 22 per cent increase of membership in the branches concerned (By June, 1964, schemes were in operation in 476 branches covering 136,059 members. Twenty of the branches, with about 6,000 members, were in non-Co-operative employment.)

R

To ensure full membership in those societies where it was a condition of employment the committee listed eleven methods which had successfully been followed by different branches. All branches were recommended to study the full list and introduce the methods that would be most effective in their local circumstances. Five activities were given as particularly important.

(1) That Divisional Officers assist branches to ensure 100 per cent membership.

(2) That all branches consider the appointment of a membership recruitment secretary.

(3) That 15 year old employees be recruited as associate members.

(4) That membership cards be issued to all members covered by deduction schemes.

(5) That Divisional Officers ensure that periodically a card check was carried out wherever Union membership was a condition of employment.

The report made it clear that it was not an end in itself to ensure that all Co-operative employees observed Trade Union membership. There was also an obligation on branches to help new members to become Trade Unionists in the full meaning of the term, so that they had a real appreciation of the Union's purpose. In particular, branches with deduction schemes should still appoint a full quota of shop stewards to maintain contact between the branch and individual members.

Part 5 began by defining the multiple and private trades as the principal future recruitment potential for USDAW. There was, however, considerable difference in the Divisions on the extent to which recruitment had been successfully carried out. In some Divisions membership had reached a high level in the main trades. In others it was strong only in particular firms in certain trades. Union membership was most complete in the traditional multiple firms in food, footwear and tailoring, but even within such firms there were wide variations as between one Division and another. The same was true of department stores and wholesale warehouses.

Changes in the methods of distribution had brought about geographical variations in the pattern of retailing. Some Divisions had been hit by the closing of small branch shops by multiples, with consequent loss of membership. The Allied Suppliers group was quoted as a case where 1,170 branches have been closed in the six years 1957-1962, and only 427 new branches had been opened. The new supermarkets and large food stores had developed geographically at a different time and pace.

The nature of the appeal which should be made for Union membership in private trade was analysed; a fairly general view of Divisional Officers being that effective campaigns were based upon a specific issue and not on the general Trade Union appeal. Comments included " . . . when trying to recruit in a new field, the effective campaigns were based upon a specific issue and not on the general Trade Union appeal" . . . "A recruitment campaign must be purposeful — a wages claim, five-day week, etc. A campaign must have a reason, otherwise it is aimless" . . . "Private trade recruitment is not on the general issue. Special efforts and campaigns are related to specific issues" . . . "Campaigns are undertaken on the general issue and on a specific issue. The latter has produced the best results". One Divisional Officer, however, said that he had never found that wage negotiations provided a particularly good platform, partly because of the remoteness " . . . as between the JIC and the workers concerned", partly because " . . . people expect Trade Unions to embark on wage negotiations [it is] part of the normal pattern, and not something to arouse exceptional interest".

On the latter point the committee commented that in statutory or other form of wage regulating machinery affecting distributive workers, particularly Wages Councils which covered most of the retail trades, it was USDAW that initiated wage claims and Union officials led the negotiations for the workers' side.

This power of initiative was in itself a means of defence and attack on wages and its effectiveness depended largely on the scale of Union membership in the trade concerned. Branches and Organisers were also urged to drive home the additional argument that strong Union membership could lead to voluntary Union agreements which were essential to reach the next stage of something " . . . over and above Wages Councils".

The committee summed up its study of recruitment in the private trades by recommending that the priorities lay in the supermarkets, department stores and variety chains' There was, however, a " . . . continuing responsibility to maintain and extend recruitment in the traditional multiple shops" and in the multiple grocery trade automatically to extend this into the supermarkets. The wholesale grocery and textile trades were ranked as second priorities. The latter, it was said, in the large cities offered "particular opportunities".

Methods of organising the private trade potential were the subject of Part 6. For obvious reasons the committee did not fully "show its hand" in a publication which could have a wide circulation, but various details of methods which had been successful were supplied to Divisional Councils and organising staff. Some general proposals were, however, published. They included:—

Attempts should be made to get the consent of management to give out or post notices. This had the advantage of showing the staff that the Company was not anti-Union.

In the large establishments recruitment could be facilitated if there was inside contact with someone who had a knowledge and understanding of the Union.

Also in large establishments, organisers should try to obtain facilities for meetings on the premises at the commencement of a recruitment campaign. A number of firms, it was said, were willing to give such facilities.

Members of other Unions should be asked to encourage wives, sons or daughters employed full-time or part-time in distribution to join USDAW. Help in this and other ways should be sought through Trades Councils and Labour Parties. (Ironically, it was reported that some husbands who were themselves active Trades Unionists discouraged their wives or families from joining or taking an active part in USDAW).

Many firms which were potential recruitment areas operated in more than one Division. Effective campaigns must be conducted simultaneously over the whole area in which a firm operated, which called for central direction and co-ordination.

National direction raised the question of national or multi-divisional mobilisation of Area Organisers for some campaigns, according to the parts of the country in which a particular firm operated. This, in turn, brought up the related problems of Organisers' duties while they were away from base, and the extent to which some of those duties could be carried out by part-time branch officials. The temporary transfer of staff into other Divisions for a specific purpose was already an established practice, but the report visualised an extension of the practice for campaigns in the increasing number of national multiples. The three related problems of central direction, temporary transfer of organising staff, and continuity of organisers' local duties were considered in Parts 7, 8 and 9.

There was general support for the principle of direction. As one of the comments made to the committee put it "In the past ran unco-ordinated campaigns. Made progress in one Division, but not elsewhere. This led to disillusion and the collapse of the membership". Another comment was "Central Office will have to take command and direct Area Organisers and not allow Divisional Officers to give different instructions". Objections were based mainly on the opinion that experience had shown campaigns to be most effective when linked to local issues.

On the use of Area Organisers the committee discussed but rejected the formation of a mobile team. Instead, it recommended that the Executive Council should consider arrangements to " . . . make available in each Division" staff who could participate in multi-Divisional campaigns. The fear that work in the Divisions would suffer while Organisers were away from base led to a number of alterations being suggested. One was that regional rather than national campaigns should be carried out, which could reduce the time an Area Organiser was outside his territory. Another was to "consider the using of effective rank-and-filers, get them time off and pay them loss of wages". The committee, however, stood by a recommendation on transfers for urgent campaigns and in Part 9 it devoted several pages to the subject under the heading "Easing the Load on Full-time Staff by Securing the Help of Rank and File Members".

It was reported that information and opinions collected by questionnaire, by discussion at the meetings in the Divisions and by letters from members was: "(1) That Area Organisers spend so much time servicing members and on collecting contributions that they have only little time for the actual job of membership recruitment; (2) Too few rank-and-file members play a part in the day-to-day work of the Union". The committee found it "difficult to accept this assessment [and] they hope it is a too gloomy view". It declared, however, that these two conclusions raised a problem basic to the future of the Union and — "... it was of the utmost importance that immediate action be taken to increase rank-and-file participation in the work of the Union".

Inquiries showed that one-third of the Area Organisers spent more than one day a week (or its equivalent) collecting contributions, and 86 per cent spent some of their time collecting. In addition Collector-Canvassers were employed in some areas. Two systems of collection were in operation: in one case collection in a shop by someone who worked there, in the other collection from a parade of shops. The latter was the more difficult to organise, but both systems were successfully practised in many areas. The quality of Collectors was vital. To interpolate a quotation from Oliver Cromwell into the committee's report, collectors must be like Cromwell's Ironsides, men and women who "knew what they fought for, and loved what they knew". As the report pointed out, they *were* USDAW to the members, and were expected to know the relevant agreements on wages and conditions, and the general policy of the Union. Seven suggestions were made for assisting collectors:

(1) Some form of "briefing" upon appointment.
(2) An information broadsheet, or other means to ensure that they were in touch with Union developments in their trade or firm.
(3) A simplified collecting system.
(4) A simple banking system.
(5) Prepaid envelopes or postcards to call on the Area Organiser when necessary.
(6) Employer to be asked to provide facilities.
(7) Payment of a realistic commission, to be settled according to local circumstances.

Further consideration of spare-time collectors — retired members or married women — was also recommended.

Part 9 also contained a lengthy section on the desirability of a procuration fee for recruiting new members. On this there were "very mixed" feelings among officials and Divisional Councillors, ranging from outright opposition to qualified approval. The committee's own recommendation was highly qualified — "... that there are circumstances where the payment of a procuration fee would be justified ... but do not consider that such a payment should be made as a regular continuing policy".

Servicing was a problem for Area Organisers. Some branches required a lot of time, in others branch officials did much of the work themselves. Area Organisers frequently had to act as branch secretaries. The committee supported the view that this system should be ended, and the Executive Council should insist that Area Organisers "... create an effective branch administration, and train rank-and-file members to do it". The formation of trade committees in large branches, supervised by the branch committee, was recommended as a means to spread the duty of servicing members.

Part 10 dealt with "Information, Publicity and Advertising". This, said the report, was a problem facing all Unions but it was particularly acute in retailing. Branches were fragmented because members worked in small numbers in separate shops. In the multiple trades there could be a feeling of isolation — the next branch of a firm could be many miles away. The "in-out" nature of the trade aggravated the problem — the Union could not assume that members knew what had happened "a year or two ago", so basic information had frequently to be restated. The Union was responsible for "a massive output of informative circulars, leaflets and other publications." But it was failing to get its message through to *all* its members — "Conveying information from the branch to the rank-and-file members is the fundamental problem that today challenges the Union".

Reading between the lines of the report, it would seem that the committee was baffled by a problem that is not confined to USDAW — that of maintaining interest and participation with a mass membership. Some suggestions were made. To minimise the time spent in reading information circulars from Central Office, a brief summary of the main points should be attached. Staff representatives should be encouraged to take part in the work of a branch and could help in ensuring that information

reached members who did not attend branch meetings. Some
Divisional and Area Officers periodically produced local
bulletins about wage negotiations, etc., and frequently these
were posted on staff notice boards. The committee also supported proposals that there should be a wider distribution to
officials of information about firms that operated in more than
one Division.

New Dawn was regarded as "excellent for the good member
but maybe too serious for the others". This was not regarded
as a criticism because "there is a real need for a serious Union
journal". But it needed to be supplemented "by other lighter,
more newsy publications."

The great variety of leaflets produced by the Union was
praised, both for their information and recruitment value.
The committee was satisfied that the Union received a full
measure of publicity in the national and local Press. It urged
every branch to appoint a local publicity and Press officer and
recommended that Central Office should supply basic briefs to
help in preparing local news stories or letters to the editor.

This has been a lengthy chapter but even so it has only
summarised the mass of material in the report. The document
went out to branches in good time for the annual meeting of
1965, where it was the first major business following adoption
of the annual and auditors' reports.

Alfred Allen moved adoption. For obvious reasons, as he put
it, he did not traverse the mass of data and recommendations
already in the hands of delegates. He did, however, call attention
to three points. Firstly, the problems that had caused them so
much concern " . . . have not just emerged now, or within the
last couple of years". They had been with them for a much
longer period of time, slightly different in character but basically
the same. They were being felt much more sharply because of
the rapidly changing structure of distribution and a decline in
the trade of Co-operative societies, with its consequential
drastic effect on Union membership. Secondly, he emphasised
the "irreparable harm" done to the Union if the public and
other Trades Unionists were left with the belief that 100,000
workpeople withdrew because of dissatisfaction with the service
given by the Union. "The report gives the lie to that".

His third point was to place USDAW's experience "against

the background of other Trades Unions". He quoted figures from the journal of the Electrical Trades Union of March, 1965, in which it was stated that 1963 figures showed 874,000 women to be in the electrical engineering industries while the Union's female membership in that year was 22,347. The *Daily Telegraph* of January 22nd, 1965, was cited as reporting a statement by the General Secretary of the Amalgamated Engineering Union that although the AUE had a million members, it only just managed to keep recruitment ahead of losses; the figures for the previous year being 143,000 recruits for a net gain of little over 2,000.

There was one resolution and an amendment linked to the report. The resolution, from South West London, called for a sustained campaign to reach a membership of 500,000 by 1970, for regular contact with other Unions involved, and for the Executive to set up a campaign development committee with a full-time senior officer to plan and supervise campaigns in all sectors of retailing.

This was moved by Mrs. L. C. Thurgood, who argued that it was a necessary step to "complete the job" described in the report. The amendment from Chester No. 1 urged an examination of the cost and value of Collector-Canvassers. The debate was comparatively short, probably not through lack of interest but because the report itself had covered so much of the ground. T. Kay (Manchester Central CWS Transport) argued for the appointment of women organisers. D. Huxstep (Booksellers and Stationers) emphasised the vital role of the rank-and-file and urged a policy based on "a substantial increase in wages." A. Pyatt (Manchester Divisional Council) said the proposed campaign committee showed lack of confidence in the Investigtion Committee and the Union's back-up organisation. W. F. H. Kendall (London Divisional Council) argued that increasing rank-and-file participation was not enough. To get a breakthrough in private trade they needed full-time Organisers.

The South-West London resolution was referred to the Executive, the Chester amendment had fallen through lack of a seconder, and the report was adopted unanimously.

So ended this study in depth of a problem that had long haunted the Union, and to some extent still does. The report did not produce absolute solutions, for the problem is endemic in modern retailing. It did give guidelines and a realistic measuring rod for the future.

The report did not, however, (probably because it was outside the Committee's terms of reference) consider another source of recruitment which historically has been a factor in the growth of USDAW — amalgamation with Unions of a similar character. Apart from the recruitment of workers who are not in any Union, there is undoubtedly scope fot further growth through mergers such as that which took place with the Scottish Bakers' Union in 1977.

27 THE POLITICS OF WAGES — AND FIVE STRIKES

W AGES and conditions in Britain are traditionally settled in free collective bargaining between employers and workers, who are represented by their Unions. For industry generally negotiations are sometimes with an individual firm, but more commonly with an employers' association, or through a Joint Industrial Council or Wages Council. In nationalised industries and services they are with the appropriate State corporation. The various Unions of public service employees negotiate through organisations set up for the purpose by local authorities or Government. When negotiators fail to agree, there are in many cases provisions for arbitration. But in whatever manner negotiations are carried out it is a hard-won and cherished Trades Union principle that there should be free bargaining between the two sides.

The Government's role was for long considered to be one of non-involvement, standing on the sidelines or offering conciliation services. Tory Governments sometimes all too obviously stepped from the sidelines to the side of the employers. But until recent times, Governments did not attempt to regulate the overall national pattern of wages or seek openly to influence the decisions of negotiating bodies or arbitrators.

The change in post-war years began in 1948, when, as we saw in Chapter 20, the Labour Government appealed for restraint on wage increases. This appeal had only a limited success. There was a lull until the fifties, when the three successive Tory governments between 1951 and 1964 opened a long campaign to control the rate at which wages advanced. The Labour Government of 1964 sought a similar objective though with a very different order of priorities in regard to the economy in general. In this chapter we shall follow USDAW through the still continuing controversy engendered by this change of policy in both Parties, and through much agony of spirit when the desire to support a Labour Government conflicted with the needs of members in the many low-pay trades that are organised by the Union.

Before coming to USDAW's problems it is necessary, however, to attempt a brief description of the circumstances which led both Parties onto a new course. After all, Governments do not avidly seek to become the arbiters of so contentious an issue as wages. That is a problem which politicians could happily be without. But in recent years the state of the national economy has left them with little choice. Once the post-war sellers' market had ended, it was soon apparent that Britain's industrial record was lagging behind that of other countries. We had made a good beginning under the Labour Governments of 1950 and 1951. The fruits were wasted in the free-for-all of the successor Tory Governments. Industry declined, Productivity was low. Money poured into new office blocks, of which we now have the finest collection in Europe, many of them still empty. Asset stripping became a substitute for new factories and new technologies. We imported (and still tend to do) more than could be paid for by experts. These facts were common knowledge and brought about recurring crises in the balance of payment on overseas trade and in the value of the pound. Harold Macmillan said of those years that we had "never had it so good". Maybe, in some ways, But it was by eating up the seed corn.

Tory Governments had good reason to panic when the results of their free market free-for-all began to show up in the late fifties and early sixties. Once upon a time (but no further back than the twenties and thirties) economic difficulties could be met by leaving it to industry to enforce wage cuts and close down factories, while the financial Establishment juggled with the Bank Rate and Governments complacently looked on. But these regulators no longer worked. Trades Unions were too strong and public opinion would no longer meekly accept industrial depression and massive unemployment.

Not that the Tory Governments of 1951, 1955 and 1959 did not try hard within their direct power to make the nation swallow the mixture as before. By manipulating Bank Rate and restrictions on credit they further aggravated the poor showing of British industry. They ran down the social services built up by the two Attlee Governments. But on wages they had themselves to swing the hatchet formerly left for employers to wield. They tried to impose a policy of "pay pause". They tried a "guiding light" as a criteria by which those who negotiated or arbitrated on wages could reach their decisions. It ranged from zero awards to 2½ per cent. They intervened in the awards of Wages Councils. They appointed a so-called independent council of Lord Cohen (chairman), an accountant and an economist (soon derisively named "the three wise men") to review prices, productivity and the level of incomes. Hugh Gaitskell described its first effort a "not a scientific report . . . but a political tract". They even talked of planning and their one achievement of this sterile period was to set up the National Economic Development Council (Neddy), at which employers, Unions and the Government could discuss the problems of the economy. The TUC joined on the grounds that it was at least one positive move towards better direction of the economy, but with the reservation that its representatives would not be expected to preach wage restraint.

USDAW's attitude to the shifts and expedients of Tory policy during this period can be summed up in two words: unqualified hostility. The Union's case against the Government was summarised in this extract from Walter Padley's New Year message of 1958, in *New Dawn* of 11th January. "It is important that we should see wages policy in its right setting, i.e. against the background of Government economic policy. The supreme indictment is that from 1951 its attempts to redistribute the national income against the wage earner, via the Budget and legislation such as the Rent Act, along with its doctrinaire preference for high Bank Rate and credit restriction instead of selective planning controls, has led to inflation and has cut the rate of economic growth by one half. If the Government deliberately puts up the cost of living as an act of policy, wage applications are bound to follow from the Unions . . .".

At the ADM of the same year he pointed to the other side of the problem which would arise if and when a Labour Government, too, found it necessary to follow a wages policy " . . . real wages consist in the goods which money will buy . . . increases in real wages depend largely on the growth of production and efficiency in distribution (though redistribution of wealth can still make a contribution to greater equality). It follows from this that when we have secured a Labour Government, which pursues policies of economic planning for full employment, then . . . it will be the duty of all of us in the Trade Unions to co-operate . . . to ensure that wage increases are matched by economic growth and economic growth is matched by wage increases . . . unless this problem is squarely faced and solved by our industrial and political Movements, all our ambitious plans . . . will be endangered".

An emergency resolution which was adopted in 1958 embodied the chairman's criticism of Tory policy and endorsed the Executive Council's policy of making wage applications to offset the declining standards of living of Union members. The meeting also carried a resolution from Aberdeen proposing a joint Labour Party/TUC inquiry into whether a wages policy could be compatible with a free Trades Union Movement.

Padley's speech and the first of these two resolutions typified the attitude of subsequent annual meetings. In 1961 the Executive Council issued a strong statement in opposition to the "wages pause" which the Chancellor, Selwyn Lloyd, sought to introduce. The Union, it said, would continue to launch claims at the appropriate times " . . . regardless of the considerations outlined in the Chancellor's statement, which are not accepted as valid under present economic and social conditions". The Executive declaration also objected to the Minister of Labour referring back decisions of Wages Councils. This, it said, was direct discrimination against the lowest paid members of the wage earning population, since these Councils had been set up by Statute to protect workers at the bottom of the wages table.

We now come to 1964 and the return of the first Labour Government for thirteen years. The Government was elected on 15th October and immediately concentrated on the economic problems it had inherited, including increase in and distribution of the national income. Shortly before Christmas a Statement of Intent was signed by the Government, the TUC, the Association of British Chambers of Commerce, the British Employers' Confederation, the Federation of British Industries and the National Association of Manufacturers. It declared the Government's economic objective to be " . . . to achieve and maintain a rapid increase in output and real wages combined with full employment". The Government pledged itself to implement a plan for economic development, increase productivity, develop policies to promote technological advance in industry, get rid of restrictive practices and prevent the abuse of monopoly power. It undertook to set up machinery to " . . . keep a continuous watch on the general movement of prices and of money incomes" and to correct any excessive growth in aggregate profits " . . . as compared with the growth of total wages and salaries".

The TUC and the employers' organisations undertook to co-operate with the Government in carrying out this policy. In particular they agreed to attack obstacles to efficiency " . . . whether on the part of management or of workers" and to co-operate with machinery which the Government was to set up to keep under review the general movement of prices and money incomes of all kinds (this machinery was established in 1965 in the Prices and Incomes Board, later abolished by the Heath Government.)

For many members of the Union this would be a time of heart searching. The Government's plans would introduce a new factor into wages bargaining. Free collective negotiation was enshrined in their traditions. Their predecessors had fought to establish the principle in the Co-operatives. Many members of the present generation had engaged in similar battles with private employers. Would this hard-won right now be diluted? But the quiet voice of memory would speak up to remind them that for the entire existence of NUDAW and USDAW they had also fought for social planning and control of the economy. At annual meetings of the recent past they had repeatedly endorsed this policy as the constructive alternative to Tory free-for-all. As we saw in earlier chapters, the Union itself had drafted plans for the planning of distribution. Now they had a Labour Government dedicated to the same purpose. Could wages be excluded when other major factors in the economy were to be planned?

The immediate issue came before the annual meeting of 1965 on an Executive Council resolution accepting in principle the Statement of Intent, pledging full support to the Labour Government in mobilising the economic resources of Britain, declaring that " . . . the policies pursued by the Government, with continued emphasis on expansion and full employment and the rejection of deflation will materially assist in creating the right economic conditions that will make an incomes policy acceptable to Trade Unionists". It also affirmed the belief that a general plan for economic development would result in a rising standard of living for workers in distribution and other trades.

Alfred Allen, who moved the resolution, made three crucial points. They had opposed, and still opposed, wage restraint. but they believed that economic planning would promote expansion and create conditions in regard to wages " . . . in which Trade Unions can more effectively do their primary job of improving the real standards of the people we are representing". It would require a great effort by Government and the nation to solve Britain's problems, and the Trades Union Movement must play its part. "To shirk from this effort now after years of exhortation in support of the need for a higher and more stable rate of economic growth under the direction of a Labour Government, would be worse than defeatist".

Various amendments and separate propositions were on the agenda. To reserve the right of the Union to continue with a wages policy (Birmingham Co-operative), to reject any policy of wage restraint (Metropolitan Fur Skin Dressers), to insert in the resolution a demand for redistribution of existing wealth and the curbing of private economic power (Coventry), to oppose any form of co-operation either directly or through the TUC with the Government on an incomes policy which would prevent free negotiations (South East London). Only the Fur Skinners' proposition was carried. The Executive Council resolution was carried with only two dissentients.

This chapter ends in 1965. For the time being we must leave USDAW's first contribution to the Great Debate on Labour Governments and a national wages policy. It is a problem that has continued to dominate the affairs of all British Trades Unions since 1965, and we shall return to it later.

One other political event of 1965 must be recorded. It was the first occasion when the ADM was visited by a British Prime Minister, Harold Wilson being a guest at the opening session. The report of the proceedings records that he "entered the conference hall to a standing ovation".

The policies of Governments on incomes were not, of course, the only way in which the Union was involved in wages questions during the period of this chapter "Ordinary" negotiations on traditional lines absorbed much of the Executive Council's attention, that of officials and of the ADM. We saw in Chapter 21 that up to 1955 annual increases were reported each year, varying, of course, from trade to trade or whether they were the result of direct negotiations with employers or the awards of Wages Councils. The pattern was much the same in the following ten years.

Advances in wages were, however, secured against the background of an increasingly militant annual delegate meeting, and increasing concern throughout the Union that distribution and many related trades lagged so far behind the general level of industrial earnings. While increases were regularly won they did not materially narrow the gap for the greater number of members.

By 1959 a £10 minimum was the target but was already regarded as inadequate. In 1960 London Co-operative branch was successful in a call for a " . . . complete review of the retail Co-operative national agreements". D. McCallum, who moved, said that even if they got the £10 minimum shop workers would still be something like £3-10-0d behind typical earnings in industry. The resolution was carried. At the same ADM W. G. Devonald (Barrow-in-Furness), was, however, sceptical of resolutions which fixed amounts and time limits for securing improvements in wages and hours. All the Executive could do was " . . .get the maximum for you". T. A. Jones (Cardiff CWS) made a similar comment — "Let us keep this £10 minimum wage before us as a target . . . but do not tie the hands of our negotiators".

So it continued. The Union could, and did, secure increases. By 1962 it was in sight of the £10 minimum for adult males in the retail Co-operative Movement (£9-13-0d) and in multiple footwear (£9-16-6d). But the rate was still under £9-10-0d in multiple grocery and meat and £9-10-6d in tailoring. And even where these figures were increased by commissions they were still a long way short of the average industrial wage of £15. In all cases, women's rates were very much lower.

In a debate at the 1965 ADM Alfred Allen summed up the problems and the achievements of the past decade. The first problem was to keep wages at least in line with rising prices.

s

"Only in a few cases have we been able to overtake the increases in prices which . . . have debased, if not destroyed entirely, the hard-won achievements in pay levels some months earlier". That was a continuing battle, and once again the Executive could report that all the main voluntary agreements had been improved since the last annual meeting and there had been changes in rates in the principal Wages Councils for the retail trades.

The second problem was the five-day, 40-hour week, and he said, they could be proud of the progress made against the inherent difficulties of operating this reform in retailing, with its diversified trading interests. "The differing circumstances of trades and localities makes it impossible, and indeed undesirable, to try to lay down a uniform pattern of shopping hours." But employers were coming round to the Union's view that the retail trades must be prepared to face up to five days/40 hours if they were to compete for and retain the best type of worker.

The third problem was training. A well trained labour force was essential to an adequate career and wages structure in distribution. There was too much labour wastage, and this " . . . affects the kind of wage standards we hope to get, and will get . . .".

Strike action is the other side of negotiations. We have seen in previous chapters that USDAW has never flinched from calling members out when the Executive considered the cause was just and there was no hope of a peaceful settlement. But it has not sought combat. There were few strikes in the period covered by this chapter. In two cases, however, the Union was in conflict with powerful national organisations and in two other cases with companies of international fame.

In 1956 the 7,000 CIS agents in USDAW (the only Union which organised the Society's agency force) voted that they would not canvass for or accept any new business after 1st May. This decision followed long and unsuccessful attempts to negotiate improved remuneration or, failing agreement, to set up joint Conciliation Board machinery such as that which had for long existed in the Wholesale Societies (which were themselves the joint owners of the CIS). The ban lasted for four months, when the Society agreed to the establishment of a Conciliation Board similar in constitution to that of the CWS.

When the Board met the two parties could not agree and the issue was referred to the Independent Chairman, Sir John Forster, QC. His award, operative from 1st January, 1957, fell short of the Union's claim but represented a material advance on existing remuneration.

The Union's second opponent was Woolworth, and the battleground was South Wales and Monmouthshire. USDAW had been organising the company's employees in the area and in 1961 sought improvements in wages, working conditions and facilities for the collection of Union dues. Woolworth refused to negotiate, the girls marched out from many stores — and almost immediately the Company announced the introduction of a revised wage scale involving substantial increases throughout their 1,060 stores in the United Kingdom. Since only a few stores were on strike, one could safely say in terms of wages that never had so many owed so much to so few. The strike ended with an agreement that in stores where a strong Union organisation had been established there should be arrangements for the collection of contributions. Also, all store managers were to be informed by the Company that Union membership was a matter for the individual to decide and no pressure should be brought on members of the staff to join or not to join.

In 1962 USDAW recorded what was said to be the first strike in a supermarket in the United Kingdom. It took place in the Scottish town of Airdrie, where the firm concerned gave a week's notice to two senior employees that they must go because of high wages costs — a few days after two juniors had been engaged! The management refused to substitute "last in, first out" and the sixty assistants ceased work (five of them non-Union members who joined both the strike and the Union). A second supermarket of the firm came out in support and other shops were ready to do so. At this point management capitulated on the understanding that the stoppage would not be extended. A suggestion that the two dismissed members should be reinstated and the two juniors (both girls) should be dismissed was rejected — both girls were out with the strikers! The strike ended with the withdrawal of notices to the two adults and an agreement that if redundancies were necessary they should be on the basis of "last in, first out" (with the exception of specialist staff and managers).

The Union's most ambitious national campaign came in 1965. The target was the House of Fraser group, a fast expanding department stores chain which from its base in Scotand had acquired a great many leading retail stores in London and other cities. It refused to meet the Union on the grounds that any negotiations should be through the appropriate Trade Associations. At a Press conference to launch the campaign on 1st March, Alfred Allen said that the Union's demands were for shorter hours, improved wages and a five-day working week. In some cases, he said, the Company was operating the inadequate Wages Council rates, in others rates that were a few shillings above the statutory minima. He contrasted this situation with the large profits made during the expansion of the group between 1948 and 1963. A wage application had been made but at present the Union had no agreement or negotiating status.

The campaign was impressive in its scope and enterprise. There was large scale advertising in the national and local Press. A converted double-decker bus toured the country as a mobile propaganda unit. Large numbers of leaflets were distributed, plus a special campaign newspaper. The General Secretary held regular Press conferences. Officials were concentrated on the cities where House of Fraser had stores. There were one-day strikes at South Shields, Darlington, Newcastle, Middlesbrough and Dumfries.

The Company refused to negotiate a voluntary agreement. It did, however, unilaterally revise its schedule of basic rates to provide substantial increases. Once again, with or without recognition, the Union had brought more into the pay packets of members and non-members alike. Eventually, in July, there was a sort of twilight recognition through an exchange of letters providing for a Union-Company review of wage rates as and when Wages Council rates were revised, facilities for collectors and a procedure for the progression of grievances at store level through to management. Subsequent annual reports of USDAW record a steady development of negotiating rights with the Company.

The other strike of 1965 was against Foyles, the world-famous London bookseller. It was a complicated affair, spread over seven weeks, with workers being called out twice before the Union succeeded in establishing a wages scale acceptable to the members concerned.

We now leave one of the most hectic peacetime decades of the century. It began with the soon to be deflated euphoria of "never had it so good" and ended in a national mood of disillusionment and fears for the nation's future. In the Trades Union Movement it raised new problems which have not yet been solved, and to which we must return in subsequent chapters.

28 "BAN THE BOMB" — AND CLAUSE 4

IN the early sixties the Labour Party and the Trades Unions, nationally and at constituency and branch levels, were involved in two controversies over which opinions were so strongly divided that for a time, in the words of Walter Padley, there was a state of "civil war" within the Movement. The greater of the two issues, world-wide in its significance, was the demand that unilateral nuclear disarmament should become the official policy of the Labour Party — "Ban the Bomb", as it was popularly known. The other issue was domestic, and concerned proposals to revise Clause 4 of the Objects Rule of the Party. In both controversies USDAW members were participants.

There had been resolutions on atomic weapons at the Union's annual meetings in the years immediately following the end of the war. They were, however, general in character, directed at the three nations (USSR, USA and Britain) which then possessed nuclear capability. Thus, at the 1950 ADM there was a call for the destruction of stocks of atomic bombs to be carried out under United Nations supervision, and in 1954 (after the development of the hydrogen bomb) for the immediate cessation of experiment with and production of atomic and hydrogen weapons.

Those were the years of the Campaign for Nuclear Disarmament, based on an appeal that Britain should set an example to the world by unilaterally abandoning The Bomb. There were a great many CND adherents in the Labour, Trades Union and Co-operative Movements and in all three, the former generalised appeal for international action hardened into a demand for unilateral action. Few people except perhaps a few besotted generals would be likely to oppose world-wide agreement to abandon nuclear weaponry. But in the working-class Movements and in the country generally there was an acute and genuine difference of opinion over whether Britain would serve the cause of world peace by acting alone.

For USDAW, other Trades Unions and the Labour Party the issue came to a head in 1960. The USDAW annual meeting adopted a unilateralist resolution on a card vote of 112,760 For, 93,736 Against. The mover, C. B. Norwood argued that the possession of nuclear weapons was neither a defence against nor a deterrent to attack; possession of The Bomb was in itself a magnet to attract attack. USDAW's conference foreshadowed an even more dramatic decision when the Labour Party met at Scarborough, where an almost evenly split vote carried a unilateralist resolution against an appeal from the Party leader, Hugh Gaitskell. The USDAW delegation voted unilateral, in line with their ADM decision.

The Labour Movement was in disarray. Most of the Press hopefully forecast that the Party was about to split. Conservatives, accustomed to decorously sweeping their own quarrels under the mat, chuckled at the folly of Socialists who argued great issues in the open. In practice, respect for Labour was probably enhanced by the insistence that such a life-or-death issue should be debated for all to see and hear. But the immediate consequence within the Party was a high degree of bitterness between men and women who for many years had shared common ideas on Labour policy and principle.

Hugh Gaitskell was attacked for his declared intention to fight for a reversal of the unilateralist vote. It was a situation that could not be allowed to continue. As Richard Crossman put it in presiding over the 1961 Conference "The great test of a democratic organisation is whether it knows the time to stop arguing and take a decision". There were demands from all sections of the Movement that unity must be restored. The Bomb was a gigantic and hideous problem but must not be allowed to dominate the Party to the exclusion of the many economic and social problems on which it was united.

To seek a basis for unity a Committee of Twelve was set up, representing the National Executive of the Labour Party, the General Council of the TUC and the Parliamentary Party. Richard Crossman and Walter Padley were among the four members of the Committee appointed by the National Executive. A lengthy policy document was drafted and published on 22nd February, 1961.

It outlined an essentially multilateral approach to nuclear disarmament; called for (1) negotiations on general disarmament with neutral countries taking part, (2) agreement to ban nuclear tests, (3) establishment of a non-nuclear zone in Central Europe; affirmed that "The West cannot renounce nuclear weapons so long as the Communist bloc possesses them" but "The West must never be the first to use the H-bomb"; and declared that Britain should " . . . cease the attempt to remain an independent nuclear Power, since this neither strengthens the Alliance nor is it now a sensible use of our limited resources". A fourth passage included a call for reforms in the United Nations, admission of China and an agreement between the West and the Communist powers to neutralise Africa and Asia from the Cold War.

Crossman and Padley drafted amended proposals which accepted several of these points, including membership of NATO, but rejected any defence strategy based on NATO forces being the first to rely on the use of so-called tactical nuclear weapons in the field, since, as Padley put it, "some of them have the explosive power of the bomb which dropped on Hiroshima". It was also proposed that the Labour Movement should press for a radical reconstruction of NATO, with five objectives, which included an end to the present dependence on nuclear weapons, no American nuclear bases in Europe and "the best possible NATO control of what must remain an exclusively American nuclear deterrent". On the basis of these changes the Russians should be offered a plan for disarmament in Europe, including a nuclear-free zone.

The "official" statement was adopted by the General Council of the TUC, the National Executive of the Labour Party and the Parliamentary Party (though on the National Executive by a narrow majority, 15-13 against the Crossman-Padley draft). It became the majority recommendation.

Nothing daunted, USDAW's annual meeting of 1961 adopted the Crossman-Padley proposals by 153,510 votes to 80,334 for submission to the Labour Party conference later in the year but with the proviso, made clear by Walter Padley from the chair, that this would not be done if the successive conferences of other Unions throughout the year showed that support was mobilising behind the majority proposals.

The annual meeting also reversed the unilateralist declaration of the previous year. The decision to do so was based on an Aberdeen resolution that " . . . unilateral disarmament by Great Britain, with its inherent implication of withdrawal from NATO, would create a much more dangerous situation. Until lasting peace can be established by international control, Great Britain must continue to support the principle of collective security through membership of NATO, using its influence towards effective control of nuclear weapons." The Government was urged to take the initiative in preventing the spread and testing of nuclear weapons, and to obtain agreement on measures for multilateral disarmament. The resolution was moved by T. Fyfe, whose case centred on the maintenance of peace through deterrence " . . . the restraining knowledge that certain aggression will result in retaliation".

In the event the Crossman-Padley proposals never did reach the Labour Party agenda. As the year advanced it became obvious that the Unions whose votes would be decisive were opting for the majority statement. Defeat would have been certain. But even more decisive, there was no point in challenging proposals on which the Party could be united and which in important emphasis, but not in fundamentals, were not all that much different from the Crossman-Padley alternative.

Therefore, USDAW's Executive Council acted on the warning given by the President at the 1961 ADM — they did not send forward the resolution then adopted for submission to the Labour Party conference. This decision was challenged in letters from branches and at the 1962 annual meeting. But Walter Padley made it clear that the Executive had fully carried out the Mandate of 1961 — submission only if it was obvious that opinion was mobilising behind Crossman-Padley. The majority statement was adopted at the 1961 conference of the Labour Party. Multilateralism became official policy. The problem had not been settled, but neither had it been allowed to split the Party. And that, perhaps, was as far as one could expect to go in this dangerously imperfect world.

The Clause 4 issue agitated the Party over much the same period as the debate on unilateralism. It began in 1959, after Labour had been defeated at the General Election of that year. The annual conference had been overtaken by the Election, and a two-day meeting was held at Blackpool in November, the Party's electoral defeat being the principal topic.

Clause 4 read (as it still does) "To secure for the workers by hand or by brain the full fruits of their industry and the most equitable distribution thereof that may be possible, upon the basis of the common ownership of the means of production, distribution and exchange, and the best obtainable system of popular administration and control of each industry or service". It was argued that the Clause implied an over-insistence on nationalisation and this had contributed to electoral defeat. Hugh Gaitskell, speaking, he said, for himself alone, urged the need to revise a constitution "written over 40 years ago". He pointed out that the Party had for long accepted a mixed economy and it should be made clear that nationalisation was not "the be-all and end-all" of Labour policy.

In the controversy that followed it was not so much Clause 4 itself that was at stake. It was the fear among many Labour activists that if the somewhat archaic language of the Clause was abandoned it could be the beginning of a retreat from Socialist objectives. The debate was sharp and sometimes bitter, involving, said Morgan Phillips, the Party Secretary " . . . a good deal of ill-will and suspicion". Again, it was as much as anything demands from the grassroots of the Party that saved the day. There was nothing intrinsically wrong with the disputed wording. There could be a case for refining and amplifying its meaning. There was equally a case for leaving well alone. And that was precisely what was done; Clause 4 still appears under the Subscriptions columns of every Labour Party membership card.

The Clause has, however, been more clearly defined. At the suggestion of Walter Padley a "Declaration of Aims" was adopted to clearly express the meaning. It "reaffirmed, clarified and amplified" the Clause and stated that common ownership, in addition to nationalisation, included consumers' and workers' Co-operatives, municipal enterprise and public participation on the lines of, for example, the present National Enterprise Board.

So ended two dangerous and bitter years. The basic unity that is the true strength of the Labour Party had once again triumphed over issues that in a more fragile movement could have led to disintegration.

29 INTO THE SEVENTIES

THE last three chapters have dealt with the larger issues of national and Union policy; the problems of recruitment and lapses, Government intervention in wages bargaining, the threat of nuclear weapons to the future of civilisation. USDAW could influence these issues, but its voice was only one among many. We return now to the less spectacular subjects within the Union's own control during the middle sixties and into the seventies; in particular to problems of Union structure which were prominent in this period.

First, however, membership. The special report of 1965 had analysed the reasons why so many members were unavoidably lost each year, and had proposed measures to deal with the considerable number of cases where lapsed members could have been retained. It was, however, some time before the counter measures were effective. There were decreases of 12,941 in 1966, 15,252 in 1967 and 10,024 in 1968. The drift was checked in 1969 with an increase of 5,374. There was a further increase of 13,503 in 1970, a hiccup in 1971 (decrease of 10,518) and thereafter steady growth up to the last available annual report, for 1978. When the special committee's report was published in 1965 membership was 349,230. In 1978 it was 462,178, with the half-million well in sight.

The biggest single cause of the losses in the sixties was the decline in Co-operative employment that followed the rationalisation of both the retail and wholesale sections of the Co-operative Movement. Although there were outstandingly successful retail societies, the Movement in general, retail and wholesale, had been slow to adjust its structure and trading methods to the revolution that was taking place in marketing and retailing techniques. It began to modernise and concentrate its resources just in time and one consequence of delayed action was a rapid run-down in employment. Between 1947, when USDAW came into being, and 1975 approximately 56,000 Co-operative members were lost by the Union, most of them in the latter part of the period. USDAW was concerned in two ways; through the loss of jobs, and through the Union's historic links with the Co-operatives, not only as a source of membership but as part of the working-class movement. For both these reasons the Union encouraged rather then made any attempt to block the rationalisation of the Co-ops.

In the annual report and in other ways the Executive Council urged members to support the creation of bigger retail societies through amalgamation, including the establishment of regional societies. Union officials met CWS directors to discuss methods of increasing the sale of goods produced by USDAW members in CWS factories. A special conference of CWS branches at Manchester in July, 1967, while concerned at lack of consultation on the closure of factories and depots, expressed the desire of Union members to play a part at all levels in constructive policies to build up the Society. The Union was realistic in its attitude to the problems of reorganising the retail Co-ops. Thus, in many societies, local improvements on national agreements had been negotiated over the years, and at the ADM of 1972 Birmingham Co-operative Branch proposed, among other things, that there should be a standing Union committee to see that these were maintained when regional or other large societies were formed. The General Secretary pointed out that it was the job of local branches, which had secured these agreements in the first place, to see that they were maintained. The proposal was referred to the Executive.

STRUCTURE OF THE UNION

The Union was also examining its own structure in this period. Over a span of approximately three years, it twice pulled up its grass roots, so to speak, took a long hard look at them, and decided in one case that they should be replanted in new soil, in the other that, on the whole, they were best left where they were.   The big change was a programme to reduce the number of Divisions, adopted by a special meeting at the ADM of 1969.

There had been little alteration in the Divisional structure since the amalgamation of 1921. The basic structure went back even earlier, for it largely followed the boundaries of the Co-operative Union's Sections. That pattern had been adopted by AUCE and was appropriate to times when the Union was composed almost entirely of Co-operative workers. By the nineteen sixties, however, the Co-operatives, while still the biggest single section of the Union, were no longer preponderant in the membership, and the great private multiples from which new members were mainly recruited recognised no regional boundaries.

The drift of population from Scotland and the North of England to the Midlands and the South East was also distorting the pattern of USDAW's membership within the existing Divisions. Alfred Allen, in moving the alterations at the special delegate meeting, pointed out that the smallest Division represented about 4 per cent of the membership, 7 of the then 11 Divisions accounted for 50 per cent, and the other 50 per cent was in four Divisions.

The eleven then existing Divisions (with 1969 membership in brackets) were: Cheshire and North Wales (13,631), Liverpool (31,786), London (37,200), Manchester (33,788), Midlands (48,164), Northern (22,302), Scottish (43,064), Southern and Eastern (32,139), South Wales and Monmouthshire (14,592), South Western (15,956), Yorkshire (23,765).

The new pattern proposed by the Executive Council reduced the number of Divisions from eleven to eight, increased the number of members on each Divisional Council from eight to ten and provided that the Executive Council of 16 should consist of two members from each Division, plus President and General Secretary.

A map showing the prospective new boundaries was available to delegates at the special meeting and aroused opposition from two directions. Apart from the Manchester area, the two oldest Divisions in the Union were Yorkshire (originally known as Airedale) and Northern (mainly the area between the Tweed and the Tees). With good North-South communications, and, for much of their Western boundaries, with the line of the Pennine range to divide them from the other part of Northern England, these two logically could form a North-Eastern Division from the Tweed to the Humber and Northern parts of Lincolnshire. But each had a strong sense of regional identity and, in the case of the Union, of historical priority. They did not oppose the restructuring of the Union, but a Yorkshire spokesman who was probably expressing also the "Geordie" view of Northern, supported an amendment from the London Blackfriars (Sainsbury) branch which, among other proposals, would have retained the two Divisions.

The main objection of Blackfriars was that restructuring would divide the capital North and South of the Thames, whereas, it was argued, London was a single entity, and the major employers with whom the Union negotiated ignored the barrier of the river. Another amendment reflected the Welsh desire to retain national identity. All the amendments were either withdrawn or defeated, and the Executive's proposals on Divisional structure were adopted.

The special meeting also carried proposals for increases of 3p in each of the principal scales of contributions, for variations in the scale of benefits, and various other matters.

In due course the Executive Council carried out the restructuring and decided on the titles of the eight new Divisions. They are given here, with their 1978 membership in brackets: South Wales and Western (45,866), North Western (57,485), Eastern (56,362), Manchester (59,367), Midlands (77,381), North-Eastern (64,158), Southern (41,357), Scottish (60,202). The latter Division included 7,702 members of the former Scottish Union of Bakers and Allied Workers, which transferred its engagements to USDAW on 1st January, 1977.

The 1969 changes rearranged the territorial basis of the Union's structure. But other ideas were already in the air. USDAW had diversified into many trades, whose only common factor was that they were mostly related to the supply of personal and household goods or services. Was it desirable that this "diversity in unity" should be reflected in specialised trade representation on the governing bodies of the Union? At the ADM of 1971 G. Cree, on behalf of the CIS National Branch, suggested that they should consider the possibility of " . . . national sections of members having their own by-laws and administration". This was referred to the Executive which appointed a sub-committee to examine the question.

The sub-committee had a two-part task. Firstly, to suggest changes in structure that might be desirable. These, it was decided, would be presented to the ADM of 1972 as a preliminary to discussion by Executive and Divisional Councils and by branches. Secondly, in the light of the national debate, the sub-committee would submit firm proposals to its parent Executive which would decide whether or not to make recommendations to the ADM of 1974. This somewhat involuted process was duly carried out, beginning with a discussion document presented to the 1972 annual meeting.

The existing structure, said the sub-committee, had been created in the fifties to follow the then existing pattern of national negotiations. But the trend of development was towards more separate company agreements. This meant that some of the national trade conferences had " . . . less and less relevance to the more important questions affecting wages and conditions of employment in the various trades". To meet this situation there had been an increasing tendency to hold *ad hoc* conferences covering nationally based companies, such as Burton, Lewis's, Fine Fare and others. Parallel with this development there was pressure for a greater degree of national unification within particular trade groups, the milk trade being cited as an example.

The sub-committee recognised the advantages of dividing the Union's membership according to trade. But historical and administrative factors severely restricted the pace at which this policy could be carried out. In Co-operative and some other branches a variety of trades were linked in branches based on a common employer. To split them into specialised groups for grocers, butchers, dairy workers, etc., would fragment many branches, would increase administrative costs and would raise insuperable problems where a common employer operated the check-off through computer systems. In any case, the problem was partly being met by trade group committees within common employer branches.

Secondly, said the sub-committee, they had to recognise the special place of the Co-operative membership, and in that sector national negotiations were still of paramount importance. Therefore, it was considered essential to continue the annual conference for the retail Co-operative trade, but to ensure that all sections covered by national agreements were represented it would be desirable to increase from eight to ten the number of delegates from each Division. There was also full justification for the continuation of the annual conference for the retail private trade. For fifteen other trades or groups of trades it was proposed that biennial conferences should be held.

The second part of the sub-committee's terms of reference had been to consider the electoral machinery of the Union, to meet the desire for wider representation of different trades at Executive Council level. A complicated plan for electing the Executive Council in part on a trade basis was suggested. It was not adopted, but gives a picture of the Union's diversified scope:—

Section	Principal Trades	Proposed Executive Council Representation
Co-operative	Retail Co-op CWS	2
Food Distributive	Food Wholesale Grocery	1
Non-Food Distributive	Non-Food	1
Commercial	Mail Order CIS Agents Check and Credit Football Pools SATA	1
Food	Food Manufacturing Biscuit Milling	1
Service	Milk/MMB Catering NAAFI Hairdressing Laundry	1
Meat	Retail Meat Slaughtering Bacon Curing and Meat Processing	1
General and Industrial	Glass Container Rubber Manufacturing Surgical Dressings Optical Dental Technicians Chemical Soap and Candle Miscellaneous	2

It was also suggested that if the proposals on structure were adopted, the Union should consider holding the delegate meeting biennially, and that " . . . to reflect the changing pattern of membership" the title of the Union should be altered to "Union of Distributive and Allied Workers (UDAW)".

The discussion on the document at the 1973 ADM, although brief, on the whole was favourable. The next stage, after fuller discussion throughout the Union, was at the ADM of 1974. The sub-committee, having tested opinion on its suggestions during the year, made its recommendations to the Executive, which adopted two:—

(1) To accept the recommendation to continue the policy of seeking company agreements;

(2) To review trade conferences with a view to holding them biennially, except for the Retail Co-operative and Private trades, which should continue to be held annually.

The Executive's report was accepted. For the time being the Co-operative and Private Retail Conferences were held but in 1980 they are to be merged. That in itself will be a footnote to history, marking the end of almost a century in which wages, conditions and mutual suspicion divided retail distributive workers in Co-operative and private trade. Biennial trade conferences are now becoming general, and the number of *ad hoc* single employer conferences is increasing.

It might be considered that the Union had laboured mightily and had brought forth a mouse. That would be to misjudge both the purpose and the value of the exercise. USDAW is still growing and changing in the basis of its membership. There will undoubtedly be changes in trade structure before the century ends, and they are already beginning. One change foreshadowed at the 1979 ADM was that the annual meeting may be extended by a day to deal with the increasing pressure of business. But a massive restructuring of the Union's organisation and electoral arrangements before there is a clearer picture of the future pattern of membership and of worker-employer relationships would probably have done more harm than good.

INTRODUCING SATA

One new development of specialised organisation was, in fact, already taking place and will explain what to some readers

T

may have been a mysterious alphabetical inclusion in the proposed Executive Council constitution that was mentioned earlier. The Supervisory, Administrative and Technical Association (SATA) had been established by the Executive towards the end of 1970. It was part of the Union but (like the CIS Branch) with a separate identity to attract the specialist workers covered by its title. By 1971 it was reported to be making steady progress, with recognition by several large companies.

Earlier in 1970 a similar organisation, the Association of Sales, Technical Representatives and Agents, which had been independently established, applied to come under the USDAW umbrella as a separate section. Because of internal disagreements it broke away in 1972, but the bulk of the members transferred to a new SATA branch administered from the Union's Central Office. As this is written, SATA is in the course of preparing a national and divisional branch structure for consideration of the Executive Council, and a more vigorous recruitment policy is planned.

NEW DAWN SHADES INTO DAWN

Of one Union veteran in 1973 it could be said "The King is dead, long live the King". *New Dawn*, for almost 53 years the voice of USDAW, was itself restructured. The editor since 1966 had been H. G. Pridmore who, on the retirement of Cyril Hamnett, succeeded him as Administrative Officer and also as journal editor and publicity manager. To meet rising costs the journal was changed from fortnightly to monthly publication in 1967. By 1973 it had been decided by the Executive that to maintain communication with a growing membership USDAW required a mass circulation publication in tabloid format, the newspaper format that is most popular today. It was to be printed by web-offset, a process which gives a clearer printing impression than traditional letterpress production, and also provides for a wide use of colour. Printing continued at the Co-operative Press, which had been early in the field with the introduction of web-offset. The editor was, and is, Patrick H. Jones, who had been appointed in 1973 to the new position of head of the Publicity and Public Relations Department, after a wide experience with provisional newspapers and in PR for commercial and public utility organisations. *New Dawn* had gone, but the name lived on in the new title of *Dawn*.

Publication began in September, 1973, with a circulation of 56,000, issued free to members. By the end of 1978 the figure was 149,872. The readership will be greater, for many copies are passed from one member to another. The Union's link with the Cooperative Press continued through the membership of the Press Board of the Administration Officer, H. L. Booth.

POLITICS

There were four General Eections in the period covered by this chapter — in 1966, 1970 and 1974 (two). In 1966 Labour was returned to power with a clear majority of seats over all other Parties; in 1970 the Party was defeated; in the February election of 1974 it had a working majority over all other Parties; and it won again in October but with the minute overall majority of six. USDAW sponsored candidates won eight seats in 1966 but in 1974 (October) the number was down to five, as follows:—

1966

E. J. Milne (Blyth), G. Craddock (Bradford, South), C. W. Loughlin (Gloucestershire, West), H. Boardman (Leigh), E. Fernyhough (Jarrow), W. E. Padley (Ogmore), R. E. Winterbottom (Sheffield, Brightside), J. T. Price (Westhoughton).

1970

All the above, with the exception that T. W. Torney replaced G. Craddock at Bradford, South.

1974 — FEBRUARY

S. Tierney (Birmingham, Yardley — a new seat for the Union), C. W. Loughlin (Gloucestershire, West), T. W. Torney (Bradford, South), E. Fernyhough (Jarrow), H. Boardman (Leigh), W. E. Padley (Ogmore). Through death and other reasons the Union did not have candidates in the formerly held seats at Blyth, Sheffield (Brightside) and Westhoughton.

1974 — OCTOBER

All the above, with the exception that a Union candidate did not contest Gloucestershire West.

STRIKES

The Union was involved in several strikes during this period. But the purpose of strikes was altering. They were less concerned with wages, more with recognition, the closed shop or with general conditions. We will look at some local and one spectacular national conflict.

In the earlier part of 1969 the staff of British Home Stores in Swansea came out against what they contended was the refusal of the company to grant facilities for the collection of dues and other Union contact with members. The local issue was soon settled and led to a general recognition and procedure agreement, under which the company recognised USDAW as the sole Union to represent those members of the staff who wished to join a Union.

At the long established tea firm of Twining two-thirds of the staff were in USDAW and in 1969 they stopped work in support of their claim for a closed shop. The strike ended on the third day with a formula that included membership of the Union as a condition of employment. The firm made the handsome gesture of paying wages and bonus to the strikers.

In April, 1970, the dismissal of two young girls, Patricia Warby and Sheila Sizer, led to a four months struggle against "Brierleys", a discount store group. The two had joined USDAW's Peterborough private trade branch and although their Union membership was not the formal reason for losing their jobs they were nonetheless sacked. Their colleagues came out in protest. Other Unions supported the strike, the management offered to recognise USDAW but refused to reinstate the two girls. Eventually the case went to arbitration, and the award was that they should be reinstated with the same status as prior to their dismissal and should be paid the earnings lost during the period. Patricia and Sheila duly returned to work and one must hope that the extensive Press, radio and television coverage of the strike would make many non-Union shop workers think again about the value of Trade Union membership.

In February of 1973 there would be some raised eyebrows in the exclusive shopping area of London's Jermyn Street. There in the heart of that area of high quality (and prices) were eleven men and women carrying banners. Banners that bore the name of USDAW and proclaimed that the eleven hairdressers were on strike against Ivan's, a highclass men's salon. They had earlier joined the Union's Central London Hairdressers' branch and had already won wage increases and an extra week's holiday. Other grievances had been left for later discussion. But nothing had happened and the staff gave notice that they would confine their duties strictly to hairdressing and refuse to do such work as repairing electrical equipment, cleaning chandeliers, polishing brass, labelling and filling bottles. They were told that if they did not do their "usual" duties they would not be allowed to work. They downed scissors and combs and came out. They were out for a few days, when the employer conceded several of their grievances, with others to be discussed before the end of February.

The most spectacular strike of the period was against the CIS. The Society had expanded to become one of the largest insurance organisations in Britain but relations with its agents and, successively, with NUDAW and USDAW, left much to be desired. Although Conciliation machinery had been established in the Co-operative Movement in 1926 the Society did not adopt this peace-making service until 1956. Even then, as we saw in Chapter 27, it did not agree to the establishment of a Conciliation Board until the agents imposed a ban on new business for a period of five months. Other disputes in following years were settled by awards of Conciliation Board chairmen. One, however, dragged on from 1965 to 1968 and some members were so dissatisfied with the eventual award that for a period there was a partial breakaway from the Union, particularly in Belfast and Liverpool.

By 1969, L. H. Watson, the National Officer who acted as secretary of the Agents' Branch, would report smouldering discontent in the agency force. It came to white heat over a claim for an expense allowance. By definition, an insurance agent must be mobile, both in body and in his means of communication. Costs of travel, postage, telephone and other expenses were eating into commission income. There was a small travel allowance for country agents, but this was regarded by the CIS as a concession and was not part of the agent's agreement. A claim was made for a general expense allowance of £3 weekly, which, said the Union, should properly be the Society's contribution to the average expense of £6 weekly incurred by agents on CIS business.

The claim went to conciliation, where the CIS proposed that it should be wrapped up with other variations in terms of service. USDAW refused to agree to a Chairman's Award on this wider basis; contending that whatever the merits of these other proposals, the sole immediate issue was expenses. Deadlock was followed by strike action on 11th June, 1970.

The strike lasted for eight weeks. It was in itself a remarkable feat of organisation. As G. Cree (chairman of USDAW's CIS branch) put it to the 1970 ADM "To shut a dock gate, close a factory door or even shut up shop in the retail trade, is comparatively simple — it is a collective act. To have 8,000 men individually resolved not to call on and give service to 3½ million people whom they know personally, requires a courage and conviction far exceeding normal standard".

There were mass marches and demonstrations outside CIS headquarters in Manchester and other cities. In London the embattled agents marched en masse to put their case to MPs. In Manchester 4,000 of them demonstrated, plus 400 District Office clerks. CIS District Offices were picketed. Many agents who had joined the breakaway came back into the ranks. There was support from other sections of CIS employees. A *CIS Agents' Journal* had been established in January, 1970. Fred F. Cullen, the Editor, not only produced a lively and hardhitting publication. During the strike he issued a weekly duplicated "supplement" packed with information and encouragement for the far-scattered army of agents.

Protracted negotiations failed to reach a settlement. Eventually Alfred Allen suggested that Victor Feather, General Secretary of the TUC, should be asked to attempt to break the deadlock. At Congress House ,on 29th July, under Vic Feather's chairmanship, Union negotiators again met the CIS, with the agents' National Branch Committee also on the premises for consultation. After a total of 39 hours, ending at 2 a.m. on Friday, 31st July, they reached agreement to refer the expenses issue to an independent arbitrator, and also on some of the other proposals in dispute. It was almost certainly the best that could be won, and for the first time it established expenses as a negotiable right. But feelings were strong and it was only narrowly endorsed by the agents — For, 3,050; Against, 2,464.

The arbitrator's award was 15/-, plus for country agents the existing travel allowance. There was provision for adjustment to meet changes in prices of such services as transport, telephone or in commission scales. The award was well short of the Union's claim. But as Fred Cullen pointed out in his "Supplement" — "Regardless of its amount, we have established an agency expenses allowance . . . as part of our terms of employment. Without the strike we would never have broken down the Society's stubborn resistance".

PERONALIA

There were many changes in the Union, and in two cases Life Peerages were conferred on Union members. In 1976 the Executive, on the recommendation of the General Secretary, created the post of Chief Organising Officer, in a plan to sharpen the Union's drive for expansion. J. (Jim) D. Hughes was appointed. He had 20 years full-time service with the Union, and was a National Officer at the time of his appointment. In 1973 he defeated R. B. Seabrook in the election for the Presidency, and in 1976, while continuing to serve as the Union's President, he retired from the position of Chief Organising Officer. He did not stand for the Presidency in 1977, and was succeeded by S. (Syd) Tierney, who holds the position at the time this book is published. National Officer W. H. P. Whatley succeeded as Chief Organising Officer.

Cyril Hamnett, who had retired in 1966, went on to become chairman of Warrington New Town Development Corporation and a Life Peer in 1970.

In 1968 T. Cynog-Jones ended his long service as Research Officer. The Research Department was merged with the Organising Department to form a new Research and Economics Department and Diana Jeuda was appointed as Research Officer.

Herbert G. Pridmore retired from the position of Administrative Officer in 1976. He had served the Union for 47 years in various positions, and was an expert on pension matters. His father, G. H. Pridmore, had been a leading figure in the Union for more than four decades. On the retirement of "H.G." the duties carried out by the three central administrative officials were reallocated between H. L. Booth (formerly Clerical Officer), who was redesignated Administration Officer) and A. W. Hilton (formerly Central Treasurer) who was redesignated as Central Treasurer and Executive Officer.

In 1974 Alfred Allen became a Life Peer and was also Chairman of that year's TUC. Four years earlier he had become President of the International Federation of Commercial, Clerical and Technical Employees (FIET), one of the international Trades Union bodies in which USDAW has long played a prominent part. In 1973 he presided over the organisation's triennial conference, held in London and in 1976 over the Helsinki conference. At the TUC he had the pleasure as President of presenting the TUC award for youth to Union member Frank Yaffe, who was joint winner.

Death, as ever, removed some stalwarts of USDAW's history, including two who had played outstanding parts in building up NUDAW. Sir Joseph Hallsworth died in 1974 at the age of 89. A. W. Burrows, formerly Assistant General Secretary and for a period Acting General Secretary, died in 1966.

OTHER EVENTS

Nineteen-sixty-eight was the centenary year of the TUC and it was also the coming-of-age year for USDAW. The Union participated widely in the celebration of the centenary and had its own celebration when George Woodcock, General Secretary of the TUC opened further extensions to "Oakley".

The Distributive Industry Training Board was set up in 1968 and included three USDAW members. As this is written, John Phillips, recently retired from the Assistant General Secretaryship of the Union, is chairman of the Board. Two Union members were also appointed to the Food, Drink and Tobacco Training Board.

In 1974 the Legal Department obtained a Common Law settlement of £21,500 for J. Eckersley — the highest yet achieved. A slaughterman member of the Bolton Co-operative Branch, damage to his right hand severely restricted the work he could do. By 1977 Common Law settlements through the Department had reached £595,645, and the total sum recovered for members by legal action that year was £712,657.

Maternity leave agreements were secured with some employers. An example in 1974 was an agreement with Colgate-Palmolive Limited for up to 12 weeks leave, after which mothers could resume work without any less of grade or seniority. In 1976 maternity leave became a right under the Employment Protection Act, but USDAW was able to make agreements with the Co-operative Employers' Association — as the national Co-operative wages negotiating body had then become — for provisions in advance of the Act.

Also in 1974, on the initiative of a Union branch, Littlewoods

Pools Division introduced a pre-retirement scheme through which all grades of full-time staff with a minimum of ten years' service could enjoy a progressively shorter working week without loss of pay.

In the autumn of 1973 Victor Feather, just retired from the General Secretaryship of the TUC, became a Life Member of USDAW. He had joined the Union almost 50 years earlier when he began work with Bradford Co-op.

In 1972 the Union first advertised for an O&M/Work Study Officer, and an appointment was made early in the following year. Work on the Union's own administration had been carried out earlier by consultants, and had been continued by A. W. Hilton, then Central Treasurer, later to become Central Treasurer and Administrative Officer. Derek Arkinstall was appointed and four years later left to take a University course for his Master's Degree. He was succeeded by Vivian Lowe, the present O&M Officer.

In 1967 the Executive Council agreed to a request from the International Federation of Commercial, Clerical and Technical Workers to provide organising assistance for the development of Trades Unionism in the Far East. Charles Brady, an Area Organiser in Yorkshire, was released for this work for two years.

The years from the mid-sixties into the mid- and late seventies had been a period of real progress for USDAW. But, as we shall see in the next two chapters, they were also a time in which new challenges faced the Trades Union Movement in general, and USDAW in particular.

PART 7

TRADES UNIONISM UNDER ATTACK

30 A BRIDLE FOR THE UNIONS?

SINCE the early sixties industrial relations, under-investment and low productivity have been high in the list of Britain's domestic problems. This chapter is concerned mainly with the first. Disagreement between employer and employed over the division of the national product, whether the employer is the State, the municipality, a public corporation or a private firm, is to be expected. But other free countries seem better able than Britain to stop short of open conflict, which frequently is damaging to both sides and increasingly imposes hardship on the community as a whole.

In such a situation there has, of course, to be a scapegoat and Trades Unionism has been an obvious nominee for the role. Yet with all their power it is not the Unions which make the decisions on national policy that fan the embers of discontent in industry; decisions on investment, wages freeze or restraint, taxation, price controls, subsidies, factory closures, the introduction of new technologies, consultative or dictatorial management. Trades Unionists are often as much sinned against as sinning. And to misquote John Donne, each one of them is part of the mainland of mankind and for him, too, the bell tolls when wrong industrial decisions are made or, what is sometimes worse, no decisions are made at all.

However, it it not the purpose of this book to attempt an analysis of our poor industrial relations. There is an extensive and growing literature on the subject and the only conclusion so far reached is that we have not yet found a workable answer to the problem. To return to USDAW, its own involvement, and its attitude to the policies of the Labour Governments of 1964-1970, Heath's Tory Government of 1970 and the two Labour Governments of 1974. Chapter 27 brought us to the Statement of Intent in 1964 by the Wilson Government, the TUC and representative organisations of employers. It was hoped that this would be the beginning of a new era, in which

greater energy would be infused into Britain's industrial performance, there would be fewer strikes and a buoyant economy
would enable Unions to carry out their role of improving the
living standards of their members.

It was, however, to be a false dawn. The Government soon
decided that the economic indicators gave evidence that the
economy was "over heated". To bring down the temperature it
was considered necessary in the Spring of 1965 that there should
be economies in national expenditure, while increases in wages,
other incomes, and prices must be restrained. As strikes still
continued to be a problem, a Royal Commission on Trades
Unions and Employers' Associations was appointed under the
chairmanship of Lord Donovan, to examine the whole territory
of industrial relations. In the summer of 1966 a standstill on
prices and incomes was imposed for six months, to be followed
by a period of six months "severe restraint". In one form or
another supervision of, and checks on, increases in wages and
other incomes continued for most of the period up to the General
Election of June, 1970, when Labour was defeated and Edward
Heath became Prime Minister.

Like other Unions, USDAW was prepared to accept that
wages could not be left out of the policies through which a
Labour Government was seeking to revitalise the economy,
although, as we shall see, there was increasing disillusionment
as time went on. What neither USDAW nor other Unions would
accept was an attempt by the Government to bring Trades
Unions within a new framework of law, affecting the right to
strike and subjecting Unions and their members to new legal
penalties.

The Donovan Commission had reported in 1969. It largely
rejected demands for legal curbs on unofficial strikes; and for
improvement in industrial relations it looked to more realistic
systems of wage bargaining that would take into account the
increasing tendency for negotiated settlements to be based on
plant or company.It made a great many other recommendations,
some of them favourable to Unions, but including provision
for legal supervision and intervention in some aspects of Trades
Union activity. In general, however, it was a cautious report,
which recognised that legal intervention could play only a
marginal part in improving industrial relations.

The Wilson Government, however, had decided on legislation, and its intentions were foreshadowed in a White Paper *In Place of Strife*, published on 17th January, 1969. The intended legislation would have established a statutory right to be a member of a Trade Union, powers to compel employers to recognise Unions, and in the case of unofficial strikes, powers to order a return to work for 28 days (the "conciliation" or "cooling-off" period) and to instruct employers to restore the status quo during this period. A proposed ballot before an official strike took place was dropped in the Bill which followed the White Paper.

Much of the White Paper was acceptable in itself. What angered the Trades Union Movement was the dilution of free negotiations by new legal processes. The Government's proposals brought lawyers and the law into a wide field of industrial relations where, the TUC contended, unfettered negotiation and conciliation were more likely to produce mutually satisfactory agreements than the hair-splitting of legal argument. Particularly offensive was the proposed creation of new institutions which would have power to order strike ballots, impose financial penalties in some cases, and in certain circumstances to attach the earnings of workpeople who offended.

USDAW's attitude was expressed by a resolution of the Executive Council in March, before the actual Bill was published. It declared: "That whilst recognising the value of proposed Government legislation to strengthen Trades Union organisation . . . [the Executive] expresses its strong opposition to those sections of the White Paper which seek to impose restraints upon Trade Unionists and their Officials. It further pledges full support to the TUC General Council in any action it deems necessary to secure the withdrawal of the Government's proposals in relation to strike ballots, cooling-off periods and financial penalties . . .". The April meeting of the Executive also urged the General Council of the TUC to convene a special Congress, at which the Council should submit alternative proposals to obviate the need for Government action. There was strong criticism of the Government at the ADM of 1969. R. B. Seabrook, from the chair, summing it up in the advice to Harold Wilson and his colleagues: " . . . be guided by those you have known to be your friends for so many years. If you refuse to do so, then you must accept full responsibility for the consequences".

The special Congress was held at Croydon on 5th June, 1969, and rejected legal intervention and penalties by an overwhelming majority — 8,252,000 to 359,000. For the greater part of the next two weeks members of the General Council were almost camping out at 10 Downing Street as they sought a basis of agreement with the Prime Minister and Mrs. Barbara Castle, the Secretary of State for Employment and Productivity.

Eventually, a "solemn and binding undertaking" was drawn up in which the Council undertook to intervene where a dispute had led or was likely to lead to unconstitutional action. Where they considered it unreasonable to order a return to work, the Council would seek to promote a settlement. But if they considered there should not be a stoppage "before procedure is exhausted" they would "place an obligation" on the Unions concerned to obtain immediate resumption of work so that negotiations could proceed. Expulsion from Congress would be a last resort should an affiliated Union or Unions reject the advice of the Council. This was accepted by the Government. The first attempt at tighter statutory supervision of Unions was stillborn. But another was almost in sight.

Before coming to the Heath Government, however, we must review USDAW's policies during the years when Labour was seeking to control the level of wage increases. There is not enough space to go through in detail the Government's varia- tions on the basic theme, but the resolutions of successive annual meetings and one or two quotations reflect the changing mood of the Union.

Nineteen-sixty-five, as we saw in Chapter 27, was the year of qualified acceptance of wages policy. In 1966 the ADM again accepted the need for a Socialist incomes policy with price stability, rapid economic growth and the reduction of inequal- ities of wealth and income. Nineteen-sixty-seven reaffirmed support of a prices and incomes policy as opposed to the alternative of a free-for-all, but regretted the decision to operate a freeze and near freeze on all wages, which, it said, was bound to fall most heavily on lower paid workers. By 1968 the ADM was both supporting and attacking wages policy. Two resolu- tions called for opposition. Two reaffirmed support (one with various qualifications) and in both cases endorsed the procedure through which the TUC itself was then vetting wage claims.

By 1969 *In Place of Strife* was on the agenda and there was growing disillusionment with the economic and industrial relations policies of the Labour Government. One resolution expressed firm opposition to repressive legislation against the right of Trades Unions to press claims for a living wage and declared that collective bargaining was essential to an economic system where there was no overall planned growth in incomes. A second spoke of an increasing gap between the aims and policies of the Labour Party and those of the Labour Government, which, it said, could only be repaired by the adoption of Socialist policies. But USDAW ,as ever, was loyal to the Party and having expressed its dissent the ADM also called on Executive, officials and members to do all in their power to secure the return of a Labour Government at the then impending election. This resolution recognised areas of disagreement but believed that regard must be paid to the progress that had been made in difficult circumstances. By the ADM of 1970 the General Election was only a few weeks off and the meeting pledged unconditional support to the Party in a resolution declaring that with an election in sight it was not the time to debate " . . . left-wing ideals" but to " . . . show the country that the Labour Movement is united". A second resolution pledged "total support" for Labour. On the wages issue, however, the meeting carried a resolution declaring "strong opposition" to the Government's policy on prices and incomes.

One or two quotations will illustrate the feeling behind these various declarations. At the TUC of 1966 Alfred Allen left the platform to support a resolution moved by T&GWU against the pay freeze. USDAW, he said, remained a firm supporter of the Labour Party but "The Union could not support the idea of a wage freeze when it knew from past experience that Trade Unionists never caught up with lost wages; that prices still continued to rise and profits and rents could catch up subsequently".

In its document on *Wages and Economic Policy* for 1967 the Executive Council reiterated the Union's support for a prices and incomes policy based on an expanding economy but totally rejected a policy based on the assumption " . . . that the share of the national income going to working people will remain the

U

same." In particular, as a Union with many low paid members, they were concerned to ensure that the " . . . standards of some workpeople should move forward faster than those of others and that those who should receive special consideration above others are those who are known to be in the ranks of the low paid. To date the Executive Council are far from satisfied that the small percentage of the population who are at present in receipt of a disproportionate share of the nation's income, including non-wage income, have been notably affected by incomes policy as it has operated so far".

In his Presidential New Year message of 1969 R. B. Seabrook said that "The Government's own policies have alienated many of those on whom a Labour Government ought naturally to be able to rely. We can only hope it will speedily find alternative policies which will enable it to recover in good time the support of those essential to its survival at the next election". Exactly a year later Alfred Allen wrote in *New Dawn* " . . . the Government has been wrong in placing so much emphasis in the past upon restraint of incomes. It should be giving its undivided attention to encouraging growth and productivity so that enough wealth is created to allow our people to earn the wage increases they so rightfully deserve."

The widening gap between USDAW, other Unions and the Government must, of course, be seen against the overall national background. Britain's industrial performance continued to be poor, in spite of efforts to improve efficiency and stimulate greater enterprise. There was no take-off in productivity and while productivity agreements were encouraged too many of them were cosmetic exercises rather than genuine projects to reduce unit costs. The old, and to be frank, frequently illusory, belief that "British is Best" seemed to have surrendered to a conviction that what is foreign is better, expressed in floods of imports, particularly of consumer goods. The balance of payments wobbled on an unstable tightrope.

The Labour Government could be criticised for lack of consistent and firmly pursued action for radical change, too many calls for sacrifice which were not backed up by policies which convinced workpeople that restraint now was a worthwhile price to pay for better times tomorrow. But the Government was struggling against very heavy odds. It did tighten up the economy and it did improve the "social wage", that part of income which is represented by health and welfare services, education and housing, pensions and other cash benefits. But the social wage, though real in its effect on our lives, is not yet accepted on the shop floor as part of income, and it is doubtful whether it has ever yet influenced a wage claim or other decisions of a Union.

Now the Heath Government of 1970-74 comes on the scene. Through various "Phases" of pay policy control of wages continued. The new Prime Minister was also determined not only to grasp the nettle of industrial relations but to give it a much firmer tug than had been planned by the Labour Government. In 1970 the Government published an Industrial Relations Bill which again set the Trades Union Movement ablaze. Like *In Place of Strife*, this Bill offered some of the concessions to Unions which had been recommended by Donovan. But it linked them to a degree of legal supervision and penalties that the Unions found more offensive even than those proposed by the Labour Government.

The concessions included legal enforcement of an "agency shop", a form of compulsory recognition which could be secured by Unions that conformed to certain conditions. In general terms, the agency shop could be established against hostile employers through a complex legal procedure, plus a majority vote of the workers concerned. It could also be ended by a further ballot if not less than twenty per cent of the firm's employees petitioned for this to be held. A worker who objected could avoid membership of a Union which secured an agency shop agreement by paying the equivalent of contributions to a charity or by paying Union contributions but refusing to become a member. The interpretation of these sections alone — and the clauses which qualified them — could have provided a rich harvest for lawyers.

The agency shop was the carrot. Behind it was the stick. A new register of Trades Unions was to be established, and to qualify for benefits under the Act, such as the agency shop, Unions must be entered on this register and become subject to the wide powers over their rules which were vested in a new Chief Registrar of Trade Unions and Employers' Associations. A new Industrial Relations Court was to be set up, of equivalent status to the High Courts, with powers to act on many industrial issues, such as legally enforceable collective agreements (for which provision was made in the Act) and on a variety of what were called "unfair industrial practices" that were scattered throughout the Act.

As Victor Feather, by then Secretary of the TUC in succession to George Woodcock, put it the Bill " . . . intends to take responsibility away from working people and give it to lawyers and officials. A central feature . . . is the proposal to register Trades Unions. In other words, a Union must have a State licence to operate and it can only have the licence if it conforms to the Government's idea of good behaviour". The TUC also pointed out that the Registrar " . . . while he will not formally be a servant of the administration he will undoubtedly be susceptible to influence from that quarter. It is a small step from the enforcement of Trade Union rules to the determination of their content . . .".

The opposition of the TUC, in which USDAW played a leading part, was long and vigorous, in the Country and in Parliament. Another special congress was held at Croydon on 18th March, 1971, by which date it was virtually certain that the Bill would become law. Proposals of the General Council were adopted: (1) "Strongly" advising that affiliated Unions should not register under the impending Act. (2) that the Parliamentary Labour Party should be asked for assurances that the Act would be repealed by the next Labour Government, (3) that affiliated Unions should not enter into legally binding agreements, (4) that Trades Unionists be advised not to serve on the Industrial Relations Commission (which had been set up by the Labour Party to assist in improving the general quality of worker-employer relations) and to withdraw from local Industrial Tribunals.

By the date of the TUC in September the Industrial Relations Act was already on the Statute Book. The Croydon decision was endorsed. But so, too, was a composite resolution sponsored by the AUEW (Engineers Section), the T&GWU and the Amalgamated Union of Building Trade Workers. This referred to the fact that since Croydon certain Unions had indicated that they would not implement the decision on deregistration, and called on the General Council to "instruct" (against the "strongly advise" of Croydon) affiliated Unions not to register. This was carried 5,625,000 to 4,500,000, a majority of 1,125,000, while the vote for Croydon was 4,915,000 to 4,634,000, a majority of 281,000. USDAW voted against the composite, Alfred Allen saying that it went much further than Croydon and at that specially called meeting Congress had made its decision.

The battle was on. And for USDAW a year of controversy was imminent. It will be the subject of the next chapter.

31 IN OR OUT OF THE TUC?

NINETEEN seventy two was the most critical year since the General Strike of 1926 for the British Trades Union Movement. For USDAW in particular it was a year when it could have found itself outside the TUC for the second time in the Union's history.

The Industrial Relations Act became law in 1972. All Unions registered under the Act of 1871 (as USDAW was) would be transferred to a provisonal register, and, unless they gave notice to the contrary, would later go on the new register provided for in the Act. If a Union gave notice to deregister it would, in the eyes of the law, become "an organisation of workers" subject to the risks and penalties of the new legislation but denied the rights conferred on registered Unions. For every affiliated Union that had not already made its decision the question of the hour became: do we follow the decision of the TUC and deregister or do we register, risk being expelled from the TUC and count on the Act being repealed by the next Labour Government?

USDAW had presented a united front in fighting as vigorously as any other Union to prevent the Act reaching the Statute Book. But when that campaign failed to move the Heath Government, the Union became a house divided. A strong section contended that they should register to protect the funds and operations of the Union, take such benefits as the Act provided, seek out and widen the loopholes that can be found in most legislation, and continue to agitate for repeal. The agency shop provision figured particularly in this thinking. Some Co-operative branches, and some in private trade, that had established Union membership as a condition of employment feared that their negotiated but voluntary closed shop could be "captured" by registered Unions seeking to establish legally authorised agency shops at the expense of USDAW. Conversely, it was argued that the right to establish an agency shop would make it easier to enrol those workers who took all the benefits won by Union action but refused to pay for the service by joining USDAW — the "free riders" as they were called.

A decision had to be made by the end of the year and the Executive Council decided to support deregistration. At the annual meeting of 1972, held at Eastbourne, the afternoon session on April 30th was declared a special meeting to consider a proposition by the Executive for an alteration of rules that would have made USDAW " . . . a Trade Union not registered under the Industrial Relations Act, 1971". To this the Nottingham Castle branch submitted an amendment which deleted the vital word "not".

The Executive proposition was moved by the General Secretary. He restated the historic case against subjecting Trades Union processes to legal decisions, but accepted that "opinion in the Union and probably in many Unions, was . . . genuinely and sincerely divided about the wisdom of deregistering". He examined the fear that the agency shop might attract members away from USDAW to registered Unions but suggested, on the evidence, that it was possible to exaggerate this danger. "Even if [other Unions] register, it would certainly not follow automatically that employers would recognise them and concede agency shop arrangements, nor that they would be able to establish these rights through the National Industrial Relations Court". It could, he contended, equally be argued that fear of losing members could become a reality if they did register, were then expelled from the TUC and lost the protection of the Bridlington Agreement (the procedure through which the TUC mediated on disputes over recruitment between affiliated Unions).

Some branches, he said, might argue that the Union should defer a final decision until they saw what was done by other TUC affiliated Unions. The best answer to that was that up to a few days previously 91 Unions with close on eight million members had already taken action on non-registration, while 32 with a membership of over 600,000 had opted for registration. (The total membership of the TUC was then 9,894,881).

The Nottingham Castle amendment was moved by J. O'Hagan. "Whether we like it or not", he said, "the Industrial

Relations Bill is now an Act and is part and parcel of the laws that govern us". They should not let their heads be governed by their hearts but by " . . . the practical realities that face our Union". Had those who supported deregistration considered " . . . what the courts can do when it comes to awarding damages against an unregistered organisation?" The options were to deregister and put funds and membership at risk, " . . . to gamble with the very existence of our Union. Or you can vote for this amendment and use those parts of the Act that will be advantageous to our members".

The debate that followed was one of the longest in the history of an annual meeting which had seen some marathon speech-making in its time. Twenty-two speakers from the floor came to the rostrum, to whom could be added the General Secretary and R. B. Seabrook, who, in his presidential address, had made clear his own support for deregistration. Even through the medium of cold print, read several years after the event, the quality of the debate comes through as an exercise by men and women who spoke only after they had thought deeply on a serious problem. There was some repetition in the arguments for and against registration, but that was inevitable when the issue was so clear-cut. From the hundreds who did not speak there was an attentive hearing, occasional interruptions but little of the witless heckling that in some organisations attempts to deny free speech. Only a few speeches can briefly be mentioned here, but in the extracts which follow an attempt has been made to balance them pro and con.

W. J. Jones (Joint Divisional Officer, South Wales and Western Division) demanded "Are we, as a Union, to provide the Tory Government with the breakthrough which they have for so long sought?"

Mrs. A. Wise (Birmingham Dry Goods) declared "This battle is not of our making and it is quite impossible to find a way of evading it".

F. Yaffe (Manchester Dry Goods No. 1) gave the advice "Register . . . if all Unions register we can fight the Act within the law".

G. Anderson (Dyce Bacon) " . . . the very basis of democracy is acceptance of the rule of law. If we are to maintain . . . the basic freedom of the individual . . . then it follows, of necessity, that we observe explicitly the laws of the land".

D. G. Davies (Area Organiser, Eastern Division) argued that the fundamental issue was not registration, it was " . . . whether we play our part and assist in maintaining the unity . . . of the Trades Union Movement by adhering to the policy of the TUC . . . or alternatively by going it alone and threatening that unity".

A. Black (Edinburgh and Leith SCWS) said one of the basic purposes of the Act was to split the Trades Union Movement. If USDAW registered it would be the first step to causing a split inside the Movement.

B. Connelly (Edinburgh St. Cuthberts) said the Union had to recruit over 100,000 new members each year to keep going. "Under the penalties of deregistration it would be almost impossible to recruit over 100,000 per annum".

J. V. Bailey (National Officer) reminded the Conference that one of the former Unions of USDAW [the Amalgamated Union of Co-operative Employees] was expelled* from the TUC and "came back with honour and dignity". He referred to the eight million members of Unions supporting the TUC and asked how many of them were consulted " . . . in the same way as we are consulting the membership here".

So the debate continued, much on the lines indicated by the brief extracts that have been given. When it came to the vote, the amendment from Nottingham Castle was carried, 118,000 For, 111,005 Against. As a two-thirds majority was required for a change of rule, the amendment was lost. The Executive proposition was then put to the Conference and was defeated, 93,812 For, 151,299 Against. USDAW was in limbo, still in the TUC, but with a large immediate question mark over its continuing membership.

Following the annual meeting the Executive Council and officials set themselves to make the best of the ADM vote. The Executive made an early decision, which was announced to the ADM, that it would not use the machinery of the Industrial Relations Court for what might be regarded as improper membership gains at the expense of other Unions that were

* As we saw in an earlier chapter, AUCE was not expelled from the TUC, but left of its own accord.

deregistered, and that the Union would not profit from any tax concessions that might arise from continued registration. They would be passed over to the TUC. The Union remained on the register of Trade Unions under the 1971 Act; to which, failing notice to the contrary, it had automatically been transferred in view of its previous registration under the 1871 Act. Branches were advised of the conditions applicable to a registered Union. The General Council had been advised of the decision at the special delegate meeting. Subsequently, under the rules of Congress, USDAW and other Unions that had made similar decisions was summoned to meet the General Council and in the case of USDAW the meeting took place on 17th July.

By this date opinion in the Trades Union Movement generally had become firmly committed to deregistration. Some Unions had already experienced the penalties provided for in the Act. At the time of USDAW's ADM it could be argued that there was still uncertainty on whether there would be a general move off the register. There had been hints at the ADM that Unions which has declared their intention to deregister might change their mind. If that argument had ever been tenable it was no longer so by mid-July.

USDAW's representatives argued their case before the General Council. But the verdict was peremptory. Two days after the meeting the General Secretary was notified that the Council had decided " ... that continuing registration of your Union under the 1971 Industrial Relations Act was contrary to the declared principles of Congress and therefore your Union should be suspended forthwith from membership of Congress". It had, however, also been decided to recommend to the 1972 Congress that the General Council should be authorised to remove the suspension if the Union complied with the Congress policy of non-registration before 31st December, 1972. At Eastbourne on 30th April expulsion had been a possibility. By 19th July it was well on the way to becoming a fact.

A special meeting of the Executive Council was held on 30th July. It decided (although not with complete unanimity, as we shall see) that the imminent *fact*, as compared with the speculative possibility of expulsion from the TUC constituted a change of circumstances that justified the calling of a special delegate meeting on 20th August. The assembly hall of the recently opened new headquarters of the CWS in Manchester was booked and the summons went out to the Union's 1,134 branches. For USDAW, it was the first ever special delegate meeting, although, as we have seen in earlier chapters, such meetings had been quite frequent in the days of AUCE.

It was a tense and sober gathering that assembled in the ornate hall of New Century House on 20th August. Only a mile or so away was the hall where the TUC had been formed in 1868; today, the oldest, and probably the best known Trades Union federation in the world. Great and powerful as many individual Unions now are, the TUC, as well as its practical purpose, has an almost mystical significance as the symbol of the hopes and fears, the victories and the defeats, of many generations of working people. No delegate that morning wished to see USDAW outside a body that had meant so much to his class, and in which his Union had played a distinguished part. Each could only act according to his convictions but it is probable that even those who continued to stand by registration did so in the belief that any break would be only temporary.

In opening the meeting, the President, R. B. Seabrook, declared that their experience had confirmed what they said at the time, that the Industrial Relations Act would not improve industrial relations but would make them worse. "The Government itself admits this, because it is actively considering and preparing changes in the Act . . . Our own failure to carry out the policy decided by the TUC, to which we were a party, has been seen by other Trades Unionists as helping the enemy . . .". He described Trades Unionism as " . . . a Movement for the transformation of our society into a juster, happier, far more prosperous and more progressive society" in which men and women were no longer prepared to be " . . . employed or unemployed at the whims of employers or investors or at the dictates of an out-of-date economic system". He went on: "Where is USDAW to be in all this? Are we to be on the sidelines . . . complaining because our members are not benefitting as we would like them to do from the results of the changes? Or are we to be part of that Movement, as we always have been up to now?"

The issue was put squarely in the only proposition before the meeting — "That the Executive Council be authorised to take any steps necessary to maintain the Union's affiliation to the Trades Union Congress." This was moved by the General Secretary. He described the progression of events which, since the ADM, had culminated in the notice of suspension. The Executive, he said, understood the fears of some members that deregistration would expose them to poaching by other Unions and would threaten the Union's closed shop agreements in the Co-ops and elsewhere. But they disagreed with the reality of these fears, and with the concurrent hope that the agency shop would enable the Union to catch up with the free riders. The TUC itself was equally confirmed in the view that it was faithfully carrying out the instruction of the special Congress in September " . . . a decision, whether you like it or not, taken democratically in the same way as many others over the hundred years of its history".

The TUC and the Labour Party, he said, had broadly agreed the outline of legislation that would replace the Act and strengthen the position of the individual worker and of Unions in a variety of ways. Inside the TUC USDAW would have an opportunity to play its full part in the process. "Outside, we would be ignored".

An early speaker in opposition was J. E. Priest (Walsall), who had seconded the resolution to register at the Eastbourne ADM. He contended that nothing had changed since then. "We knew that we would be suspended because of the precedent that had been established" (in the case of the Seamen's Union).

G. Anderson (Dyce Bacon) asked " . . . are we seriously suggesting that the decisions of the ADM are conditional upon acceptance by the TUC General Council?"

G. H. Cree (CIS Agents), after describing the problems in seeking an agency shop agreement with the CIS, reminded the meeting that an agency shop was not immutable — one fifth of the employees in a firm could challenge its continued existence at any time.

T. R. Hayes (Area Organiser, Midlands Division) reminded the meeting that they had been able to establish the closed shop in many cases without resort to legal powers. "So we are coming out from under the umbrella of the TUC in order to get the agency shops which there is no guarantee of getting anyway, and when we have had 100 per cent membership branches for many years ... without any Act at all".

Two former Presidents spoke, one for deregistration, one against, and one member of the Executive Council expressed his dissent from the Council's proposal. Walter Padley, MP, pointed out that if USDAW was expelled the TUC would be bound to ensure that some organisation within the Congress was set up to organise shop and distributive workers. R. Hanes (Royal Arsenal Co-operative) urged the meeting to continue with the policy that was set out at the ADM. Executive Councillor J. C. Callahan declared that the full consequences of deregistration were foreseen at Eastbourne and accepted by the membership. Nothing had changed since "except this move today to try to get us to stand on our heads".

Altogether, there were 34 speakers, including the President and General Secretary. The speeches generally followed much the lines of those at Eastbourne, with rather more emphasis on the agency shop. At the end of the day the voting was 132,248 for the Executive proposal, 105,793 against.

A year later the issue was revived at the annual meeting. West Yorkshire Co-operative branch submitted a proposition calling for reinstatement on the register " ... within 14 days of the conclusion of this ADM". The report of the meeting states that "The proposition was defeated overwhelmingly".

USDAW was still in the TUC. Rightly so, for "splendid isolation" would have been a sorry role for a Union dedicated to the principle that only in unity do working people find their true strength.

32 WOMEN IN THE UNION

IT is probable that there were women among the 800 members who joined the Manchester District Co-operative Employees' Association in its foundation year of 1891. The Lancashire base of the infant Union contained many Co-operative Societies operating in trades such as millinery, dressmaking, drapery, which were exclusively or partly staffed by women. Lancashire women had a long tradition of independence of mind and action, stemming from generations of skilled employment in the manufacture of cotton textiles, and those in Co-operative service were unlikely to have ignored this new movement for reform of wages and hours among their male colleagues.

Whether they were in at the beginning or not, the Committee of the Amalgamated Union of Co-operative Employees — as the MDCEA had become — began in 1898 to list women separately in the statistics of membership. In that year, as we saw in Chapter six, they numbered 127, with 96 in the Northern District, 29 in the Manchester District and 2 lonely pioneers in Airedale (later to become the Yorkshire District).

For the record, the Societies in which they worked were: *Northern:* Annfield Plain 23; Birtley 11; Bishop Auckland 7; Blaydon 2; Blyth 2; Easington Lane 1; Carlisle 1; Haswell 5; Jarrow 1; Murton 2; New Brancepeth 2; New Washington 10; Seaton Delaval 1; Sherburn Hill 2; Stanhope and Weardale 3; Station Town 3; Tantobie 1; Tow Law 2; Wallsend 4; West Stanley 12; Willington 1. Most of these Societies were in County Durham. *Manchester:* Burnley 1; Droylsden 8; Middleton and Tonge 3; Bulwell 2; Oldham Industrial 1; Pendleton 1; Stockport 1; Toxteth 1; Ulverston 3; Westhoughton 3; Wigan 1; Winnington 2; Worcester 1; Workington 1. Most of these were in Lancashire. *Airedale:* Halifax 1; Hebden Bridge 1.

Two years later, when the new century began, the number had increased to 171, with Northern still in the lead (120),

Manchester 42, Airedale (by now renamed Yorkshire) 3 and a new Midlands District 6. It was not until 1980 that the figure passed the thousand mark to reach 1,020 (the Union's total membership was then 23,122).

The first reference to women members in the text of the annual report was in 1909 when the Executive Council proudly announced an increase for the year of more than fifty per cent — from 1,020 to 1,594. This, said the report, was partly due to the " . . . efforts of the Women's Co-operative Guild to enrol as Trades Unionists the women employed by Co-operative Societies, and to secure for them better wages and conditions of labour". Special joint committees of the Guild and the Union had been formed in the Districts. The thanks to the Guild were well deserved. But nearly three quarters of a century later we can add a tribute to the women already in the Union. Many of them must have worked hard among their colleagues in persuading them to follow up the Guild's advocacy in the only way that mattered — by signing up with AUCE.

By the outbreak of the First World War in 1914 the total was well over 5,479. A precise figure could not be given, said the report for that year, because fewer than half the Union's branches had completed the necessary forms. When the war ended in 1918 the Union was getting complete figures, and they showed 36,422 female members out of a total membership of 87,134, equal to 41.8 per cent. Of these women, 32,539 were employed in the Co-operative Movement and 3,883 in private trade (AUCE was by then carrying out the "open door" policy of recruiting outside the Co-operatives).

This vast increase was, of course, due to the recruitment of men for the Forces or war industry. We saw in Chapter Eight that equal pay for "substituted females", as the new members were somewhat ambiguously called, first became an issue during the war of 1914-18. We shall return to the subject of equal pay later in this Chapter.

As men came back from the Forces after 1918, inevitably there was a reduction in the number of women members. To some extent, however, this was counter-balanced through the amalgamation of AUCE and the Warehouse Workers' Union in 1921, as the latter Union had a considerable female membership. Moreover, the war had broken the traditional pattern which more or less limited the employment of women to textile manufacture, the garment trades and a few other industries, some sections of retailing and domestic service. In addition, new technologies were being introduced in industry, and distribution itself was on the eve of big changes. Unfortunately, most of these developments were to be based on the premise that women would continue to be a source of cheap labour.

By 1921, the female membership of NUDAW was 36,902 (35 per cent of the total): a figure it was not to reach again for thirteen years. The run-down began when the great slump exploded in the economy during the early twenties. The total membership of the new Union fell by 20,273 between 1921 and 1922 and of this loss 10,666 were women members whose proportion of the membership fell to 31 per cent. As the Union fought its way out of the trough of industrial collapse, the number of members gradually recovered and topped 100,000 in 1928. Women then represented 28 per cent of the total, and although their number continued to increase the proportion remained at this percentage until 1938, when it increased to 29.63 per cent.

The twenties and thirties were bad years for millions of male workers. They were desperate years for women who had to seek employment to live. In the savage wage cuts of the twenties the reductions in women's rates were generally greater than those for men. Women were hounded out of unemployment benefit on any pretext that could be deduced from increasingly discriminatory regulations. Many were threatened with loss of benefit if they would not go into domestic service. Strong protests by NUDAW to the Ministry of Labour in 1923 led to an understanding that no woman who could claim to be a skilled or trained worker should thus be penalised by local adjudicating committees.

Throughout the mid-twenties in particular, cheaper juvenile labour was used to replace adult women. Trade Boards and Joint Industrial Councils, particularly in trades largely dependent on women workers, were one line of defence against deteriorating conditions and generally NUDAW was able to beat off attacks on minimum rates in trades where this machinery existed. Thus, an attempt in 1927 by employers on some of

these bodies to increase the age/wage base from 18 to 21,
which would have meant large reductions for many women
members, was defeated. But taken together, those two decades
were a bleak time for working women. Only those who were
wise enough to seek the shelter of a Union such as NUDAW
could count on some measure of protection.

We are now at the eve of the Second World War. Once again
women poured into the shops and, once again, the Union
worked strenuously to organise them. By 1945 they were 39.51
per cent of the Union's membership, a proportion very similar
to that of 1918. But there was a dramatic difference in the
experience which followed the two wars. After 1918 women
membership had sharply declined. After 1945 it continued to
grow, both in absolute terms and as a percentage. Ten years
after the end of the war the 1955 percentage was 45.54 (total
Union membership, 346,135). Ten years later it was 49 per cent
(total membership 349,230). In 1970 it passed the halfway mark
at 51.8 per cent. By 1975 it was 59.3 per cent and by 1978 60.8
per cent (281,180 out of a total membership of 462,178).

REPRESENTATION ON EXECUTIVE AND DIVISIONAL COUNCILS

So much for the arithmetic of women in the Union. The
figures inevitably raise two questions. What part did women
members play in the democracy of NUDAW and, today, of
USDAW? How far are they represented in attendance at
branch meetings, on Divisional and Executive Councils,
Federations, at the annual delegate meeting? There is a single
answer to both questions. Women do not as yet play a part in
the Union that remotely measures their number. This is not a
problem confined to USDAW; it is common to other Unions
that organise women workers. Nevertheless it is a problem that
has concerned USDAW for many years past, and still awaits a
solution.

On a national scale the Union has comprehensive relations
with those organisations that concentrate on the problems and
aspirations of women in industry. Since 1920 it has been
associated with the National Joint Committee of Working
Women's Organisations, and it plays an active part in the
annual TUC Conference of Unions Catering for Women
Workers, the similar conference of the Scottish TUC, the

v

National Conference of Labour Women and other bodies concerned with the status and interests of women. A Women's Department was established in 1917 under Ellen Wilkinson (who had been appointed as the first woman Organiser two years earlier), with the twin tasks of increasing membership and encouraging the recruits to take an active part in Union affairs. She was also the Union's representative on the National Joint Committee.

We have seen in previous chapters that women members could be as militant and determined as their male colleagues when strike action was necessary. In both World Wars they kept going some branches that had been denuded of men. But, particularly after the first war, this involvement did not carry over to any large extent in the post-war years. The 1922 annual report deplored that "Many women who were enthusiastic on committees during the war seem now to regard their job as done and they leave the Union administration to the men". Statistically there are no comprehensive figures covering the level of activity by women members. But one measurement can be made from the lists of Executive and Divisional members published in the annual reports.

In the thirty years existence of the Manchester District Co-operative Employees' Association and the AUCE only three women appear as District Councillors. The best known, was Miss H. Kidd, who served on the Southern Council from 1913 to her death in 1917. An employee of the Women's Co-operative Guild, she had been an active member of the Union since joining in 1912. Although District Councils were so reduced in membership during the first war that elections had to be suspended for a time, only two other women served, both in 1918, when Miss Clark succeeded Miss Kidd on Southern and Mrs. Flynn is listed on the Northern Council.

Altogether 53 women had served on District/Divisional Councils between 1891 and 1977. But only six of them are listed in the period between 1918 and 1942: and of these three resigned without attending any meetings. Women members did not begin to make an impact until during and after the Second World War. There were, however, two long service records in the earlier period. Miss A. Brown was elected to the Southern and Eastern Divisional Council in 1922 and continued until

1957. Between 1922 and 1926 she was the only woman on a Divisional Council. Miss E. M. North joined the Cheshire and North Wales Council in 1936 and continued to 1946.

In the Second World War it was 1942 before women began to reach the Divisional Councils in any number. In that year four were elected to the London Divisional Council and one each to Manchester and Yorkshire. By 1945 they were serving on the Midland, London (two), Yorkshire, Cheshire and North Wales Councils. The numbers fluctuated during the post-war years, with a slight overall tendency to increase. Throughout the fifties there were only four years when as many as four women served on Divisional Councils. There was a slight advance in the sixties, when for three years the total was six women Councillors. In the seventies, however, double figures of representation began, with nine women in 1972, fourteen in 1973, sixteen two years later and in 1978, when 90 Divisional Councillors served for all or part of the year, fifteen of them were women. And as this book was nearing completion in the early part of 1979, 22 women were elected to Divisional Councils in the elections of that year.

So much for Divisional representation. We have now reached the more rarified level of the National Executive Council, and very few female names are recorded on the roll of membership. The first two came onto the Council indirectly in 1947. They were Miss M. Scott and Miss C. Smith who were on the Executive of the Shop Assistants' Union at the time of the amalgamation and, as we saw earlier, the Executives of both Unions formed a joint body for a period of two years after the merger, ending in April, 1949.

In 1949 the first two were joined by Miss Edna Falkingham, who had been on NUDAW's Yorkshire Divisional Council since 1942. From 1950 to 1961 she was the only woman on the Executive (for the last seven months under her married name of Edna Hanes). Irene A. Shears joined her in April, 1961 and by 1962 was herself the only woman still serving. She continued on the Executive until 1969. In 1965, however, Mrs. Christina E. Page was also elected. She had been on the Eastern Divisional Council from 1959 and after 1973 she, too, became the sole woman in what has been called the "cabinet of the Union". In 1979 she was joined by two others — Louisa Woolston, of

Stockport Co-operative Branch, and Elizabeth Wardle, of Manchester General Branch.

Mrs. Page also holds one record that is so far unique in the history of the Union. She is the first woman to have presided over the Annual Delegate Meeting. The 1979 ADM was held during the General Election, and "Syd" Tierney, the President, after presiding on the opening day, vacated the chair to continue the Election battle in his constituency of Yardley, Birmingham. Mrs. Page took over for the remainder of the meeting. She filled the role with a distinction equal to any of her male predecessors. In the same year she was awarded the women's Gold Badge of the TUC.

EQUAL PAY FOR EQUAL WORK

Equal pay for equal work is a subject of vital interest to all working women. It is a subject that has figured more often than any other on the agenda of the annual delegate meetings of USDAW and its predecessor, NUWDAW. J. Hallsworth, in 1917, was advocating that equal pay for equal work was essential. In both World Wars it was the Union's objective but we have seen that even in a "sellers' market" for labour it was never fully attained. The issue first began to appear at the ADM in the twenties and thirties. Between 1930 and 1976 more than forty resolutions demanded this act of justice for working women. Most of the earlier resolutions were a straightforward demand for the rate for the job. Later, however, they began to specify a percentage of male rates that should be sought in future negotiations. As time went on the annual meeting became restive at the pace of progress. A 1960 resolution called for 90 per cent of the male rate for dry goods manageresses and female supervisory grades and asked for a progress report on equal pay to be made to the 1961 ADM.

This report took the form of a survey of 81 trades (or special areas of trades), covering Retail Co-operative, Multiple, Wages Councils, JICs, individual employers, and, inside the Co-operative sector, the CWS and the Scottish CWS. One hundred and sixty jobs were specified, such as shop assistants, manageresses, clerks, roundsmen and women, transport workers. For each job the women's rate as a proportion of the male rate was given for 1938 and 1960 or, with the Co-operatives, typical provincial rates were chosen, since in the earlier year there were no national agreements. Only a selection of the figures can be given here but in general they showed that while there had certainly been progress there was still a long way to travel before equality was reached, and the pace of progress varied considerably from trade to trade:—

PROPORTION OF FEMALE TO MALE RATES IN:
RETAIL CO-OPERATIVES

	1938	1960
Grocery Shop Manageresses	57–68%	90%
Grocery Shop Assistants	56.7%	72.3%
Dairy Roundsworkers	73.1%	100%
Bakery Roundsworkers	58.5%	100%

MULTIPLE GROCERY

	1938	1960
Manageresses	83–84%	85–92%
Shop Assistants	61.8%	70.7%

DEPARTMENT STORES

	1938	1960
Lewis's, Shop Assistants	71.4%	72.1%
Owen Owen, Shop Assistants	71.4%	72.1%

RETAIL WAGES COUNCILS AND JICs

Drapery, Outfitting, Footwear:

	1938	1960
Manageresses	83–84%	85–87%
Shop Assistants	64.5%	73–99%

Food (England and Wales):

	1938	1960
Manageresses	82–88%	86–91%
Shop Assistants	64.5%	73.4%

NAAFI

	1938	1960
Warehouse Workers	53%	76.9%

While there had been considerable improvement, the report acknowledged that they had still a long way to go. It was pointed out that " . . . the definition of functions and the fixing of the rate for the particular job regardless of whether it is performed by a woman or a man are involved". This entailed structural revisions of agreements " . . . in which the Union's women membership, together with the men, must be prepared to play their full parts in evolving the kind of structure in which the principle of equal pay for equal work can be applied".

The report, which was adopted, was moved for the Executive Council by Mrs. Edna Hanes. One of her points was that while women in national and local government service had won equality, they had to fight for it with demonstrations and

marches "if our women are really in earnest they, too, should
demonstrate actively and as a first step take a more active
interest in our own Trade Union". Mrs. C. E. Page, not then on
the Executive Council, opposed the document and demonstrated disapproval by tearing it up. "It might be better if we
went on strike and then perhaps we could get some action" she
said.

The ADM continued to show a lively discontent at the pace
towards equality. A resolution of 1963 congratulated the
Executive on an increase negotiated for male members but
deplored the acceptance of increases for females as tending to
" . . . extend rather than shorten the gap". It called on the
Executive not to accept any future increases which did not
assist in achieving the rate for the job.

C. B. B. Norwood, who moved, said "We pay service to the
notion [of equal pay] with our lips, but the women members
of the Union are entitled to ask whether, in fact, we have
achieved very much more than that". Mrs. Page said she was
staggered by the argument that equal pay was something women
had to win for themselves. "It is a vital Trade Union matter,
and it is important to all our membership". One-tenth of all
women workers now had equal pay but it took them fifty years
to get it. Women in USDAW were not prepared to wait that
long.

Alfred Allen, who replied to the debate, said that Executive
opposition to the resolution had nothing to do with equal pay,
which they supported 100 per cent. What concerned the
Executive was the practical difficulty in carrying out the last
part of the resolution. They were often put in the dilemma where
an employer was prepared to stop at an increase of 8/- or 9/-
for women and if they wished they could stop at that point for
men, too. But the employer could say "I am prepared to go a
couple more shillings for men". Members would not thank them
if they turned down the offer of another two or three shillings
for men because they could not push up the female increase as
well.

The men, however, seemed in a mood to make a sacrifice for
unity, as the resolution was carried, 121,691 to 108,286.

So the debate continued, with the Union frequently reporting
advance or, in some cases, complete success in the campaign

for equality. In 1969 92 settlements provided for equal cash increases for men and women and 17 for greater increases to women. Out of the 51 national settlements in 1970, in all but one case the increases for women were larger than for men. This annual report pointed out, however, that as yet there was not equality of opportunity; too few women were appointed to supervisory or management positions. In 1972, when a Government-imposed pay freeze, followed by severe restraint, came into operation the Office of Manpower Economics made special reference to the very rapid progress towards equal pay in the distributive sector compared with industry generally. By the middle seventies the campaign was broadening to include demands for equality of opportunity as well as of pay.

The drive for equality by USDAW was not restricted to those trades and employers with which the Union had direct relations. USDAW played a leading part in keeping the issue before the TUC. It sponsored or supported resolutions at the women's annual conferences organised by the TUC and the Labour Party. It secured a pledge from the Labour Party Conference of 1963 that the next Labour Government would ratify Convention 100 of the International Labour Organisation, which called for equal pay for men and women. As it turned out it was a Tory Government that ratified the Convention in 1971. Very quietly, however, — only one newspaper reported the event — as though the Government feared that too much publicity would bring hordes of women workers pouring into Downing Street to demand equal pay now.

When Labour returned to office in 1974 equal pay legislation was carried a stage further in the Sex Discrimination Act of 1975. In that Statute women workers won a battle. But not the war. Many employers are ingenius in finding means to observe the letter of the Act while repudiating the spirit. Through grading, job designation and other devices women can still find themselves doing what is in essence the same job as men without receiving the same rate of pay. The great increase of women part-timers in distribution provides an opportunity to evade the intention of the Act. Moreover, in industries where almost all the workers are women and there can be no comparability with men's rates, equal pay can mean no more than equality in underpayment. It is still true that there is little equality in opportunities for promotion.

Acts of Parliament can lay the groundwork for improved conditions. It still needs Trades Union organisation, vigilance and action to ensure that the ground is fully cultivated. There is still a long way to go before USDAW and other Unions enrolling women workers convince the greater number of working women that in unity is their only strength. But despite all the problems, the potential today for a larger membership and a greater personal involvement of women in Trades Unionism is probably greater than at any time this century. USDAW can be counted upon to continue in the forefront of the march towards full equality.

THE SHAPE OF USDAW TODAY

CHANGE is a constant process for organisations as well as individuals. In this history we have followed USDAW through many changes in the past; in structure, in the composition of its membership, in relations with employers. There will be more in the future as the Union adapts itself to new conditions in industry and commerce and in the trades which it organises. We can guess at but cannot know what the future will bring. What can be done in a history is to give a bald and partly statistical account of the Union's corporate structure and leading personnel at a fixed point in time. To do so is the purpose of the present chapter, the "frozen" dates being in some cases December, 1978, in others June or July, 1979.

BRANCHES

The bed-rock of the Union is in the branches, and at the end of 1978 USDAW's 462,178 members were mustered in 1,212 branches, scattered throughout every part of the United Kingdom. From Lerwick in the Shetlands to the Western extremity of England in Cornwall, on the Isle of Man and the Isle of Wight, an USDAW member is never far from a Union branch. Some have only a handful of members, others count their numbers in thousands.

They cover a bewildering variety of trades and services. Retail food distribution in supermarkets, hypermarkets and smaller stores, food manufacturing and processing, clerical, creamery and dairy, confectionery, bakeries, chemicals and drugs, transport, tailoring, menswear, furniture, footwear, provident agents, mineral waters, department stores, discount houses, mail order, variety chains, booksellers and stationers, cash and carry, the wine trades, catering, soap manufacture, tea blending and packing, abattoir and butchery, warehouses and distribution centres, laundries, breweries: these represent only a section of the list of branches, covering the more obvious fields for a general and distributive workers' union.

Less obvious but also represented are insurance agents, dental technicians, optical workers, hairdressers and stylists, club stewards, workers in football pools, in specialist bulk distribution, Milk Marketing Board technicians, household delivery services, metal box making, glass making, NAAFI, industrial sand, rubber. With one possible exception, USDAW is the most diversified of the general Unions.

The greater number of branches had up to 100 members at the end of 1978. But 130 had a membership of between 500 and 1,000 and 81 were between 1,000 and 2,000. The "giants" of the Union, with 2,000 members or more were:

London Co-op	(11,371)	Sheffield	(2,351)
Royal Arsenal Co-op	(7,457)	Hull	(2,320)
British Mail Order	(6,872)	Portsea Island Co-op	(2,300)
Birmingham Co-op	(6,768)	Manchester Equitable	
Insurance Section	(6,628)	(Co-op)	(2,235)
Greater Nottingham		North Midlands Co-op.	(2,215)
Regional Co-op.	(5,038)	South Suburban Co-op.	(2,213)
Nottingham Castle (Boots)	(4,370)	North Eastern Co-op.,	
Leicester Area Co-op	(3,901)	Tyneside	(2,288)
Sheffield and District PT	(3,639)	Southampton & Wessex	(2,180)
Manchester General	(3,596)	Littlewoods (Oldham)	(2,173)
Littlewoods Pools	(3,434)	Belfast Co-op.	(2,089)
South West Area	(2,746)	Belfast No. 3 (Retail Multiple)	
Manchester Retail Food	(2,721)		(2,003)
Scottish Bakers, Glasgow	(2,714)	Birmingham Woolworth	(2,051)
Retail Co-op, Glasgow	(2,673)	St. Cuthbert's Edinburgh	
Tesco Retail (Eastern		(Co-op).	2,049)
Division)	(2,463)	Halifax Biscuits (United	
Strathclyde Allied S	(2,382)	Biscuits)	(2,048)
Manchester Central	(2,391)	Bristol Co-op. Retail	(2,022)

This list is indicative of the major national employers, such as the Co-ops and the multiples, in which the Union organises, sometimes exclusively so. But the figures do not give the whole picture nor, indeed, in most cases, do they measure the larger part of the membership in the firms concerned. In the case of Tesco, Woolworth and other companies employees in smaller branches took in many more, while others could be in mixed branches where their numbers were not sufficient to form branches of their own. The total Littlewoods membership is very much greater than the figure for the branch mentioned.

In the Co-operative Movement there were still 204 independent retail societies at the end of 1978 (counting Co-operative Retail Services as one; although its branches have a considerable degree of operational independence). Co-operative employees constituted the largest single group of branches, some going

back to the earliest days of the AUCE. Here again, however, a
single figure can be misleading. In the North Eastern Co-operative Society, for instance, the branch given qualifies on the
2,000 or more figure as one of the Union's giants, but three
other regional NECS branches (for Mid-Durham, Northumberland and Teesside) bring the total number of Union members
in the Society to 6,936.

By the end of 1978, 80 per cent of the Union's membership
was wholly or mainly integrated with contribution-deduction
arrangements (the check-off) through which employers deducted
Union contributions at source.

Apart from the general run of branches there are a number
of special Sections in the Union, each subject to the ADM and
the Executive Council but with considerable authority and
influence in its own field. They include:—

SPECIAL SECTIONS
1. THE INSURANCE SECTION
(FORMERLY CIS NATIONAL BRANCH)

The Co-operative Insurance Society (CIS) was founded in
1867. It began as a company (the law did not then allow
Co-operative Societies to undertake insurance) but was converted into a society when a new Industrial and Provident Society
Act in 1893 made the change possible. The Society had both
Co-operative Society (including the CWS) and individual
shareholders. Following agitation in the Co-operative Movement that insurance, like banking and other services, should
be part of an all-embracing CWS, it was taken over in 1913 by
the CWS and the then Scottish CWS. In 1918 the CIS itself
took over the Planet Friendly Assurance Collecting Society,
founded in 1905 by a group of Birmingham Socialists and
largely based on penny a week collections through agents.
This merger marked the beginning of the Society's march to its
present position as one of the largest insurance organisations in
Britain.

We saw in Chapter 11 that the Union's Executive Council
(possibly influenced by the takeover of Planet) began in 1918
to consider the organisation of insurance agents. Planet agents
joined the Union, although for a time some remained in a small
existing Union. Progress at first was slow, but by 1920 the annual
report stated that " . . . managers and agents employed by the

CIS . . . have formed sections inside our organisation". Insurance branches were listed in three Union districts, Northern, North Western and South Wales and Monmouthshire, with a total of 190 members, 12 of them women. By 1921 (when the Divisional structure was in operation) the number was 391 in six Divisions — Northern, Manchester, Liverpool. South Wales and Monmouthshire, Midlands and South Western.

A year later a new basis for CIS members had been introduced. They were all included in a National CIS Branch, based at the Union's Central Office. But to provide for local participation and involvement in national policy a new structure was developed, which still operates. The Branch is headed by a National Committee and holds an annual national conference with wide powers of decision on matters affecting agents in their role as semi-independent "contractors", with a capital interest in their books (which amounts to many million pounds in total). Leading up to the National Committee is a nation-wide array of 220 local groups, or branches, each based on a District Office of the CIS. These groups, in turn, are grouped under Area Councils, and for each Area the local groups elect a representative to the National Branch Committee

Propositions are initiated in the Groups and via the Area Councils can go to the Annual Conference. The National Committee, as a constituent of USDAW, itself can initiate propositions at the Union's ADM.

There is in existence a National Union of Insurance Workers which embraces the "house" or company Unions. All the Unions with an insurance membership, and which are affiliated to the TUC, are members of the Confederation of Insurance Unions. In 1971 the title "National CIS Branch" was altered to "Insurance Section", one objective being the hope that various sections of the existing National Union of Insurance Workers would consider joining USDAW. Some, however, have gone to another Union.

The USDAW Section is one of the few organisations of insurance agents which has the back-up services and overall strength of a large Union behind it. This factor has added considerably to the collective strength of the CIS agents. So, too, has the group structure. It is not easy to maintain contact in an occupation where each worker operates on his own, usually from his home, and the groups have been invaluable as a meeting place and source of unity. Since 1970 they have been strengthened by the publication of the *CIS Agents' Journal (USDAW)*.

One of the Union's National Officers, W. (Bill) Cowan, acts as Secretary of the Section. He is himself a former agent, one-time Scottish representative on the National Committee and a veteran of some of the battles with CIS management that have been described in earlier pages. The Chairman is Joe Peacock. The present membership of the Section is 6,628.

2. SATA

Chapter 29 recorded the formation of SATA — the Supervisory, Administrative and Technical Section of the Union. By the end of 1978 there were 102 branches. Of these 16 were in the Milk Marketing Board (in which the Union had operated for many years before the establishment of SATA), six were in football pools firms and four in Woolworth.

The branches are grouped in their respective Divisions and at the time of writing are engaged in establishing a national committee and structure which, under the Executive Council, will be responsible for developing this field of the Union's activity. S. Tierney, who is also President of the Union, and is one of the team of National Officers, is National Secretary of the SATA Section and in each Division an Area Officer has been assigned special responsibilities for recruitment and development in this new field of membership.

3. SCOTTISH BAKERS' SECTION

The long established Scottish Union of Bakers and Allied Workers became part of USDAW by transfer of engagements in 1977, and now forms a separate section within the Scottish Division. At the end of 1978 it had 62 branches, located throughout Scotland from the Highlands and Islands, the industrial areas and the Borders. While there are many small branches, the total enrolment includes large memberships in Glasgow (2,714), Edinburgh (1,343), Aberdeen (832).

Alex Mackie, who was General Secretary of the SUBAW, became a National Officer of USDAW until his retirement in September, 1978. Other SUBAW staff are now part of the Union's total staff. The Executive Council of SUBAW became the National Committee of the Scottish Bakers' Section of

USDAW, under the chairmanship of A. Douglas at the time of
the merger and subsequently of Alec Smith when the former
completed his two year term of office.

OTHER SECTIONS

Apart from the Sections already mentioned, there is one for
dental technicians, one has recently been formed for transport
workers and in South Wales there is a "Welsh Union of Club
Stewards" that is part of USDAW. It comprises eight branches
Neath and District, Merthyr, Newport and District, Rhondda
and District, Swansea, Blackwood, Mon., Bridgend, Cardiff
District.

In some areas the Union also has other club employees in
membership, principally bar staff and cleaners.

BRANCH FINANCE AND POWERS

The Rules on these two subjects are detailed and no attempt
will be made to give them fully. But a few salient points can
be given. The Rules provide that $17\frac{1}{2}$ per cent of contributions
shall be deducted to finance branch activities, the remaining
$82\frac{1}{2}$ per cent going to the central funds of the Union The first
call on the local funds must be to defray expenses incurred in
the work of the branch, such as conferences, delegations, payment of officers, etc. Any surplus after providing for these and
other necessary expenses may be used, together with any extra
funds raised by local efforts or voluntary levies, for the promotion of educational and social activities likely to further the
interests of the Union. Officers and committee are elected for
two years.

Subject to the overall authority of the Executive Council,
branches have the right to admit or expel members, in the latter
case with a right of appeal to the Executive. There are detailed
rules for the election of shop stewards by the members directly
concerned, with appointments to be ratified by branch committees.

Statistics are a cold if necessary measure of Union life and
activity but sometimes they reflect appreciation of voluntary
service and loyalty to a cause. In 1933 the Executive Council
established a system of awards for 21 or more years of continuous service as branch secretary and also for 30 years' membership of the Union. By 1978 36,960 members had received the
latter award, and a smaller though still considerable number

had qualified under the branch secretary scheme.

FEDERATIONS

Branches can form local Federations to develop and maintain contact between members and for other common purposes of the Union. As we saw in Chapter 15, these bodies were recognised as part of the Union in 1912, although not formally embodied in Union machinery until 1934. The Executive is empowered by the Rules to make grants to approved Federations.

The number has fluctuated in recent years, partly because of the reduction in the number of Co-operative branches which followed the merging of so many retail societies. But the need for contact that first led branches to seek a regular meeting ground remains, and there are signs of a revival. Apart from general topics of Union or public policy, Federations are playing a useful part in USDAW's growing educational programme, particularly in introducing young or other new members to wider aspects of Trades Unionism. At the end of 1978 there were 34 Federations.

Branches and Federations are basically local. We now move up the scale to the region or, in USDAW's case, the Division, the intermediate body between the Executive Council and the membership. The restructuring of 1969 (see Chapter 29) reduced the number of Divisions from eleven to eight. In the details of each Division which follow, the number of members at June, 1979, is also given.

THE DIVISIONS

In each Division there is a full-time Divisional Officer appointed by the Executive Council, and an elected committee of ten, plus the Divisional Officer, or Officers, one of whom acts as secretary. Members of each Council are elected for two years and are eligible for re-election.

On the key issues of wages and conditions the Councils have wide responsibilities. Their duties under the Rules include " . . . to arrange programmes in connection with wages and conditions, and to negotiate such programmes with the employers in the area covered . . .". This duty is qualified, however, by the Rule that the Executive Council, subject to any special directions of an annual or special delegate meeting, has the sole power to formulate minimum wage rates and conditions for all grades and no other body can do so without the endorsement of the Council. In practice, the feed-back between Divisions, Executive and central and national officials is so close that this provision does not appear to restrict Divisional initiative when that is the appropriate means of dealing with wages and conditions.

To secure and maintain effective contact with the branches, all Divisional Councils are required to convene not more than four conferences a year of representatives of branches in their respective territories.

Attached to each Division are Area Organisers, 120 of them; the professional field force of the Union. They are mobile within the Union, and for special campaigns or other common purposes can be directed for temporary service outside their "home" Division. At June, 1979, the Divisions, membership and officers were:

SOUTH WALES AND WESTERN 46,164. Divisional Office and Officer, Cardiff, W. John Jones. Deputy Divisional Officer, B. T. Ropke.

Area Organisers at Divisional Office, A. E. Davies, H. J. Dawkins, G. I. Gardner, Mrs. P. Phillips.

Area Offices and Organisers at—

Bristol C. E. Merrett, R. S. Purnell, R. Redden, T. E. Turvey, K. G. Walden.

Plymouth D. A. Penfold, R. G. Stock, A. G. Taylor.

Swansea Mrs. M. Rogers, A. Williams.

NORTH WESTERN 58,312. Divisional Office and Officer, Liverpool, J. W. Gardner. Deputy Divisional Officer, W. R. Snell.

Area Organisers at Divisional Office, T. A. Bennett, E. A. Booth, Mrs. M. Carey, A. K. Das, A. Duff, P. A. Gaffney, H. Pleavin, R. Snell, H. Taylor, A. Thompson.

Area Offices and Organisers at—

Belfast W. J. Hamilton, A. White, D. Wylie.

Preston Mrs. P. A. Smith, R. Williams.

EASTERN 55,513. Divisional Office and Officer, London, T. P. Callinan. Deputy Divisional Officer, T. C. Osborn.

Area Organisers at Divisional Office, D. H. Brooks, R. C. Elliott, J. Fahy, B. F. Field, E. C. Suckling, J. S. Whale,

R. White.

Area Offices and Organisers at—

Cambridge R. Kelly, B. Rowlands.

Ipswich F. Coates, R. J. Cockle.

Luton Mrs. E. Simms, J. Wright.

Norwich B. R. G. Scott, Mrs. B. E. E. Stevenson.

MANCHESTER 60,558. Divisional Office and Officer, Old Trafford, Manchester, J. C. Callahan. Deputy Divisional Officer, T. B. Feerick.

Area Organisers at Divisional Office, M. D. Johnstone, Ms. M. Leahy, D. McBride, M. G. Murray, Miss J. C. Riddiough, J. Riley, G. Roden, A. Slater, A. Storey, W. Wansell.

Area Office and Organisers at—

Hanley A. J. Dorricott, T. W. Price.

Also, Central Office, Manchester, is the headquarters of the Insurance Section.

MIDLANDS 76,415. Divisional Office and Officer, Birmingham, J. Toogood.

Area Organisers at Divisional Office, F. S. Beney, J. G. Blair, E. M. Foulkes, T. R. Hayes, G. F. Holz, W. Minns, A. E. C. Tudball.

Area Offices and Organisers at—

Leicester P. Davis, K. E. Dunn, K. B. Hazeldine, T. Savage.

Nottingham B. Porter, Deputy Divisional Officer, E. W. Bullimore, A. Collington, T. Hickingbottom, J. R. Scherer.

NORTH EASTERN 63,971. Divisional Office and Officer, Leeds, N. B. Capindale.

Area Organisers at Divisional Office, G. Brown, C. Fieldhouse, T. Jacques, G. Martin, E. Swann, S. D. Webber.

Area Offices and Organisers at—

Carlisle R. Barrett.

Hull A. Grey.

Middlesbrough W. Allison

Newcastle upon Tyne P. Morrison, Deputy Divisional Officer, J. G. Allison, A. Hamilton, R. O'Neill, W. H. Sawyer, B. Webber.

Sheffield R. Ellis, T. S. M. Paisley.

SCOTTISH 59,283. Divisional Office and Officer, Glasgow, A. Forman, Deputy Divisional Officer, A. D. Scott.

w

Area Organisers at Divisional Office, S. Crawford, C. P. Devlin, J. Glass, J. Macdermid, J. Mackie, S. Mauchline, P. McCormich, T. McLoone, P. McLoughlin, F. Murphy, J. Radigan.

Area Offices and Organisers at—

Aberdeen   F. Carroll, S. Fyfe.

Dundee   F. Feechan, A. D. Kelly.

Edinburgh   J. W. Biggar, G. Currie, R. K. Forbes, R. A. Fox.

Glasgow   W. Buller.

Area Organisers at various centres included former Scottish Bakers' Staff.

SOUTHERN 41,410. Divisional Office and Officer, London, R. A. Hammond.

Area Offices and Organisers at—

Basingstoke   M. Lunn, C. Mitchell, G. T. Morton, R. H. Woodroffe.

Faversham   B. Wakefield.

Portsmouth   A. J. Malden, B. F. New.

South East London (Woolwich)   M. B. Moore, J. F. Whitaker.

South West London (Croydon)   W. J. Clarke, Deputy Divisional Officer, J. Crawley, C. R. Farris, R. S. Shaw.

We now reach the peak of the Union's electoral and power structure—the Executive Council and the ADM.

EXECUTIVE COUNCIL

The Council consists of a President, a non-voting General Secretary and sixteen representatives, two from each Division. Voting for the Council must be at special branch meetings in the Divisions and those present are entitled by majority decision to cast a vote representing the total membership of the branch. Council members are elected for two years and are eligible for re-election.

The Council has full control of the business of the Union and its decisions are binding on members and branches, subject to appeal to the next succeeding delegate meeting, or by referendum to the membership on request of ten per cent of the branches. A member aggrieved at a decision of the Executive has the right to be heard by them at their next meeting.

The President and General Secretary are elected in a similar manner to Executive Councillors. The President must thus face re-election every two years. In the case of the General Secretary, however, he holds office "during the will and pleasure of the membership" and without subsequent re-election. The Rules prohibit him from standing as a Parliamentary candidate or for the European Assembly. Both President and General Secretary have the right to attend any meetings of Divisional Councils, Federations and branches, the TUC and the Labour Party Conference.

The elected members of the Executive Council at July, 1979, with the names of their branches, were:

President — S. Tierney (Leicester Area Co-operative), General Secretary — W. H. P. Whatley (Fallowfield).

South Wales and Western Division: D. E. Andrews (Pontypool Chemical), A. C. Waterfield (Plymouth and South Devon Co-operative).

North Western Division: R. Caton (Kraft Food, Kirkby), T. A. McLean (Port Sunlight No. 1).

Eastern Division: Christina E. Page (Cromer and District), P. Howitt (London Cooperative.)

Manchester Division: Elizabeth Wardle (Manchester General), Louisa Woolston (Stockport Co-operative).

Midlands Division: J. R. Scherer (Nottingham Area Holding), R. J. Stonehouse (Leicester Area Co-operative).

North Eastern Division: J. J. Coleby (NECS Tyneside), F. Kaye (Barnsley Co-operative).

Scottish Division: P. Hunter (Kilmarnock), J. McEwan (Edinburgh Food Trades).

Southern Division: J. L. Foweather (Oxford and Swindon Co-operative), E. T. White (Winchester).

ANNUAL DELEGATE MEETING

The Annual Delegate Meeting or Special Delegate Meeting called for a specific purpose are the supreme governing bodies of the Union. A Special Delegate Meeting may be held at the same time as the ADM whenever a three-fourths majority of the Executive Council consider it desirable; or on a requisition from not less than forty branches. A Special Meeting at some other time than the ADM may be summoned by the Executive by decision of a three-fourths majority; or on a requisition from not less than one hundred branches. But not less than three years must elapse between any two SDMs called for Rule alteration. Here again, however, the Executive can waive the provision by a three-fourths majority.

The list which follows gives the location of all Annual General Meetings since 1912. Prior to that date the annual meetings of the then AUCE were held on a Divisional basis, with votes on propositions being aggregated. The increasing membership of the Union is reflected in the concentration of the ADM on the limited number of towns with the facilities to accommodate so large a conference:

1912	Manchester	1943	London
*1913	London	1944	Blackpool
1914	London	1945	Blackpool
1915	Leicester	‡1946	Blackpool
1916	Edinburgh	1947	Blackpool
1917	Liverpool	1948	Blackpool
1918	Birmingham	1949	Blackpool
1919	Leeds	1950	Bridlington
1920	Manchester	1951	Margate
1921	Liverpool	1952	Margate
1922	London	1953	Scarborough
1923	Southport	1954	Brighton
1924	Edinburgh	1955	Blackpool
1925	Bristol	1956	Margate
1926	Scarborough	1957	Blackpool
1927	Southport	1958	Margate
1928	London	1959	Scarborough
1929	Leamington Spa	1960	Blackpool
1930	York	1961	Bournemouth
1931	Southport	1962	Blackpool
1932	Cheltenham	1963	Bournemouth
1933	London	1964	Blackpool
1934	Edinburgh	1965	Margate
1935	London	1966	Eastbourne
1936	Cheltenham	1967	Blackpool
1937	Blackpool	1968	Margate
1938	Morecambe	1969	Blackpool
1939	Southport	1970	Blackpool
1940	Blackpool	1971	Eastbourne
1941	Edinburgh	1972	Eastbourne
1942	Edinburgh	1973	Blackpool

1974	Margate	1977	Scarborough
1975	Eastbourne	1978	Blackpool
1976	Blackpool	1979	Eastbourne

* Eighteen months period, covering alteration of Union year end from June to December.
‡ 1946 Blackpool Joint Delegate Meeting with Shop Assistants' Union on merger.

Since the formation of NUDAW in 1921 and USDAW in 1947 Special Delegate Meetings not held at the time of the ADM have been: 1926, London; 1948, Blackpool; 1952, Blackpool; 1972, Manchester.

Attendance at the ADM has been fairly stable over recent year, as the following table shows.

Year	Executive & Divisional No. of Dele- gates	Councillors & Officials	Total	Number of Visitors approx. 10.30 a.m. on Sunday	at Number of Branches represented	Number of of indust- rial mem- bers rep- resented	Percentage of indust- rial mem- bers rep- resented	Percentage of political members represented
1979	781	280	1,061	548	525		79 %	79 %
1978	825	272	1,097	650	547		81 %	81 %
1977	738	245	983	648	493		79 %	80 %
1976	720	248	968	590	499		79 %	79 %
1975	660	251	911	550	462		78 %	78 %
1974	661	244	905	660	466		78 %	77 %
1973	691	260	951	610	485		81 %	81 %
1972	690	261	951	470	484		80 %	80 %
1971	652	263	915	550	471		75 %	75 %
1970	704	270	974	525	527		78 %	78 %
1969	755	267	1,022	647	565		80 %	80 %
1968	747	279	1,026	550	573		77·17 %	77·16 %
1967	830	282	1,112	930	660		80·12 %	80·06 %

CENTRAL OFFICIALS, NATIONAL OFFICERS AND HEADS OF DEPARTMENTS

USDAW has four Central Officials — the General Secretary, Deputy General Secretary, Administration Officer, and Central Treasurer and Executive Officer.

Under the Rules the General Secretary, now **W. H. P. Whatley,** must devote his whole time to the work of the Union and is not eligible to stand for Parliament. He must attend all delegate meetings and meetings of the Executive Council, keep the minutes, ensure that all documents, accounts and papers of the Union are kept in conformity with the Rules or Executive direction, and personally or through a representative he has power to inspect the documents and accounts of any branch.

He must ensure that the reports of branch secretaries are examined and that new members are recorded and the names of those who have left are erased. He must arrange for the preparation of the annual report, accounts and balance sheet, supervise notices from branch secretaries of all claims and allowances made on Union funds, and act as returning officer in Union elections. He can advise on any resolution or business brought before the Executive Council and Annual Delegate Meeting, but is not allowed to vote, can attend any meeting of Divisional Councils or Federations or any other bodies connected with the Union, and be a delegate to the Trade Union Congress, the Labour Party Conferences and such other national or international bodies as the Executive Council determines.

In his overall activities the General Secretary personalises the public face of the Union to the members and, on wider national issues, to the world outside. He leads in major recruitment campaigns against recalcitrant employers, is at the head of protest marches as well as in the negotiating room in major strikes such as the great battle against the CIS. Traditionally, he handles negotiations with the retail Co-operatives, and when necessary is involved in other trade negotiations. He is the principal speaker for the Executive at the ADM, speaks frequently for the Union at the Labour Party Conference and occasionally at the TUC, where, however, his main involvement is as a member of the General Council.

The role of the latter body in recent years has come to include a close and continuous relationship with Governments on problems of the national economy, wages policy and industrial relations generally. The relationship is usually friendly with a Labour Government, critical to hostile with a Tory Government. In either case the relationship is inevitable if the interests of USDAW and the members of other Unions are to be protected in national economic and social strategies. With equal inevitability it increases the work load of senior members of the General Council far beyond what was normal in former times.

The Deputy General Secretary, **J. Flood**, co-ordinates the nine National Officers and also the Educational, Publicity and Public Relations and Research and Economics Departments. He leads in the multiple grocery negotiations and the new

Wages Councils that were set up as this book was written. A major responsibility is the development of membership potential in multiple companies. He is also responsible for relations with other Trades Unions.

The Administration Officer, **H. L. Booth** deals with office management, personnel recruitment, relations with clerical and administrative staff and property development. He co-ordinates the Legal and Superannuation Departments and has responsibility for Divisional and Branch Office staffs and central administration relating to such matters as Rules, branch by-laws, Federations, the Parliamentary Representation Scheme, the Labour Party and its Regional Councils, Union elections, the ADM and other national conferences.

The Central Treasurer and Executive Officer, **A. W. Hilton,** is responsible for financial and investment policies, and, in direct liaison with the General Secretary, has duties and responsibilities for Executive Council meetings and business. Under him are the O and M Department (in liaison with the Administration Officer), Finance (covering accounts, benefits, records) and Audit.

The nine National Officers (referred to in connection with the Deputy General Secretary) are:

W. Connor, who services and co-ordinates the multiple food sector, including the retail side of the principal private multiples in which the Union organises. He also looks after retail furnishing, the wine trade and mail order.

T. Sullivan deals with retail multiples mainly concerned with non-food, such as menswear, footwear, department and chain stores.

G. Davies is responsible for distribution depots and warehousing operations, including the Co-operative Wholesale Society's manufacturing interests. He also covers Unigate's food division and the catering industry.

M. Gordon deals with the wholesale and retail meat trades and also services the optical, hairdressing and credit trades, together with NAAFI membership.

G. Kiely's responsibilities are the Scottish Bakers' Section, the baking/biscuit industry, soap and fats industry, food manufacturing and the Transport Section.

W. Cowan covers the Insurance Section (described earlier in this Chapter).

L. Watson is responsible for retail Co-operative Trades, Co-operative Retail Services (in which many former separate retail Co-ops are now organised nationally), the milk industry, including the Milk Marketing Board but excluding CWS milk operations, and laundry trades.

S. Williams deals with chemical industry, retail and wholesale pharmacy, surgical dressings industry and dental technicians.

S. Tierney is responsible for SATA which, as we have seen, is one of the newest of the Union's Sections, catering for white collar workers.

Only the principal responsibilities of National Officers have been specified in this list. Collectively they cover just under one hundred trades, individual firms, Joint Industrial Councils, Wages Councils and other negotiating machinery in which the Union is involved on behalf of its members.

A group of departments which come under the overall control of one or other Central Officials provide collective and individual services to members that are a back-up for recruitment and negotiation and also serve the industrial, political and other objectives of the Union. They are:

"Technical" education for shop stewards and branch officials, and also on wider political/social issues, for the membership as a whole, is carried out by the Education Department under **P. L. Rosenfeld.** Six training officers, regionally based, under Chief Training Officer, G. Walker, form part of the Department.

The Organisation and Method Department under **V. Lowe,** with one assistant, trains members in these techniques and also actively participates on their behalf when schemes are being introduced by employers.

The Legal Department under **A. C. Heywood,** with T. Isherwood as deputy, provides free legal advice and assistance on all matters arising in the course of employment — accidents, social insurance benefits, redundancy and unfair dismissal. sex discrimination, representation at Tribunals, superannuation (a special section). In 1978 £1,008,214 was recovered for members, not much short of a quarter of the sum paid in Union contributions.

The Research Department under **Diana Jeuda** maintains records and data relevant to the great number of trades covered by the Union and provides "ammunition" for negotiations over wages and conditions, or for the evidence which the Union from time to time presents to public enquiries or other bodies.

The Press and Public Relations Department under **P. H. Jones** produces *Dawn*, and special campaign supplements, a wide range of recruiting leaflets, handles advertising campaigns and maintains PR contact with the media.

Other service departments are Finance (**J. H. Wilson**) and Audit (**S. H. Hardcastle**). This Department has an important role in relation to financial and accountancy matters in the Union's many branches, and also in arrangements with employers for the check-off.

The position of Chief Organising Officer, responsible for organisation in the retail multiples and formerly included among Central Officials, was dropped early in 1979. The duties were included in the new position of Deputy General Secretary, with two of the National Officers allocated special responsibility for the retail multiple trades.

PARLIAMENTARY REPRESENTATION SCHEME
(a) The United Kingdom Parliament

This is based on two Panels — a Main and a Substitute Panel, both twelve in number. The Main Panel consists of twelve Union Parliamentary candidates who have been elected as MPs or adopted as prospective candidates. Whilst so qualified, they remain on the Panel at the "will and pleasure" of the members, who, through an annual or special meeting, have power to remove or call for resignation. The second Panel consists of twelve Substitute candidates, not more than six of whom may be MPs.

In the event of a vacancy arising in a constituency represented by a member of the Main Panel, the Executive can select a member of the Substitute Panel as a prospective successor. If at any time there are less than twelve sitting MPs or prospective candidates on the Main Panel the Executive may fill the vacancy or vacancies by appointing any member of the Substitute Panel who is a sitting MP or has been adopted as a prospective candidate. The Executive also has power to nominate a Substitute member for any constituency. Substitute members retire every two years, but are eligible for re-election to the Panel. A candidate must be, and remain, a full member of the Union,

have been a political member for not less than five years and if
elected to Parliament must accept the Labour Whip.

Chapter 29 gave the names of Union nominees elected at the
November General Election of 1974. By the end of 1978 three
other sitting MPs had been added to the Main Panel — J. C.
Cartwright (Woolwich, East), H. Lamborn (Southwark,
Peckham), and F. McElhone (Queens Park, Glasgow): making
a total of eight Members. The 1979 Election result is given on
page 363.

(b) European, Scottish and Welsh Assemblies

Following the adoption of an Executive Council resolution
by the 1979 Annual Delegate Meeting, the Parliamentary
Representation Scheme was extended to enable the Union to
sponsor candidates for the European Assembly and, when
established, the Scottish and Welsh Assemblies.

RELATIONS WITH OTHER BODIES — 1. NATIONAL

At the end of 1978 USDAW was connected with the following
national bodies in the United Kingdom:

British TUC
Scottish TUC
Irish Congress of Trade
  Unions
Wales Trades Union
  Council
Labour Party
Scottish Council of the
  Labour Party
Northern Ireland Labour
  Party
National Joint Committee
  of Working Women's
  Organisations
Workers' Educational
  Association
United Nations
  Association
Royal Institute of
  International Affairs
Scottish & other Regional
  Councils of Develop-
ment and Industry
British Institute of
  Management
Industrial Society
Industrial Law Society
Fabian Society
Industrial Participation
  Association
National Federation of
  Professional Workers
Amnesty International
National Council for
  Civil Liberties
Society for Co-operative
  Studies
Anti-Apartheid
  Movement
Trade Union, Labour,
  Co-operative Demo-
  cratic History Society
Women's National Cancer
  Control Campaign

THE SHAPE OF USDAW TODAY 347

Pre-Retirement
   Association
Haldane Society
Keynote Opera Society
Liberation
Chile Solidarity Campaign

Trade Union and
   Co-operative Esperanto
   Group
Eastern Europe Solidarity
   Campaign

RELATIONS WITH OTHER BODIES —
2. INTERNATIONAL

The Union's overseas affiliations at the end of 1978 were with the International Transport Workers' Federation, the International Union of Food and Allied Workers' Associations, the International Federation of Commercial, Clerical and Technical Employees (FIET), the International Federation of Chemical, Energy and General Workers' Unions, the Committee of Chemical and General Workers' Unions in the European Community and the similar Committees of Transport Workers Unions and Food and Allied Workers.

In addition USDAW has maintained direct relations for many years with overseas Unions organising similar groups of workers to those in USDAW and fraternal delegations are exchanged. Since the end of the war and up to 1979 delegations to the ADM have been from:

Austria

Non-manual Workers' Union, 1950.

Union of Commercial and Clerical Employees, 1956, 1963.

Food and Drink Workers' Union, 1957, 1963, 1971, 1978.

Hotel and Catering Workers' Union, 1963, 1977.

Chemical Workers' Union, 1963, 1971.

Union of Workers for Personal Services, 1964, 1977.

Union of Workers in Private Trades and Industry, 1964, 1978.

Belgium

Union of Commercial, Clerical, Bank and Insurance Employees, 1953, 1960, 1966, 1973.

Food and Hotel Workers' Union, 1960, 1969, 1978.

Denmark

Commercial and Clerical Employees' Union, 1958, 1964, 1970, 1977.

Chefs' and Kitchen Workers' Union, 1961, 1970.

Waiters' Union, 1961, 1970, 1979.

Butchery Workers' Union, 1965, 1974.

France
Commercial, Clerical and Bank Employees' Union, 1952,
1959, 1965, 1972, 1979.
Union of Workers in Agriculture, Food and Allied Trades,
1976.
Food and Restaurant Workers' Union, 1964.
Finland
Distributive and Commercial Workers' Union, 1954, 1961,
1967, 1974.
Germany
Union for Commerce, Banks and Insurance, 1955, 1962,
1968, 1975.
Food, Drink and Catering Workers, 1959, 1968, 1977.
Salaried Employees' Union, 1962, 1975.
Federation of Commercial and Technical Employees 1955,
1962, 1968.
Holland
Commercial, Banking and Clerical Employees' Union, 1953,
1960, 1966, 1973.
Hotel, Cafe and Restaurant Workers, 1957, 1965, 1972.
Factory Workers' Union, 1962, 1969.
Hungary
Commercial, Financial and Catering Workers' Union, 1972,
1979.
Ireland
Distributive Workers and Clerks, 1964, 1969, 1976.
Norway
Food and Drink Workers' Union, 1949, 1957, 1975.
Commercial and Clerical Employees' Union, 1954, 1961,
1967, 1974.
Distributive and Commercial Workers' Union, 1961.
Sweden
Commercial and Clerical Employees' Union, 1958, 1964,
1970, 1977.
Hotel and Restaurant Workers' Union, 1962, 1970.
Union of Food Workers, 1966, 1967, 1973.
Factory Workers' Union, 1957, 1974.
Switzerland
Commercial, Transport, Food Workers', 1952, 1959, 1976.
Hotel and Restaurant Workers' Union, 1967, 1976.

Commercial Workers' Union, 1976.
Trade Internationals of —
Commercial, Clerical and Technical Employees (FIET), 1950, 1956, 1968, 1974, 1979.
Food and Allied Workers, 1954, 1961, 1966, 1972.
Industrial Organisations and General Workers' Unions, 1956, 1963.
Transport Workers, 1958, 1965.
Hotel, Restaurant and Bar Workers, 1959.
Students, Guests and Overseas Visitors from —
Nigerian TUC, 1948.
Northern Rhodesian African Mineworkers' Union, 1954.
Nyasaland Shop Workers' Union, 1955.
Czechoslovakian Union of State Commercial Workers and also of the Union of Trade Union and Co-operative Workers, 1969.
Polish Union of Workers in Commerce and Co-operatives, 1970.
USSR
USDAW and the comparable Russian Union have exchanged delegations.

CONTRIBUTIONS AND BENEFITS

Throughout this history no attempt had been made to follow in detail the alterations in rates of contributions and benefits. Inevitably they have varied from time to time, according to changes in the value of money and price levels, particularly in the last few years of inflation. Also, the two amalgamations of 1947 provided that members of the Shop Assistants' Union and the Journeymen Butchers Federation could opt either for USDAW rates or those prevailing in their respective Unions before amalgamation. These, however, now represent only a minute proportion of the membership.

The pattern of benefit provision, as distinct from the contributions and benefit payments, has remained substantially the same since the adoption of the AUCE scheme in 1894. That scheme provided three scales of unemployment benefit according to contributions, three scales of sick or temporary disablement benefit, three of permanent disablement benefit and three of funeral allowance. The present USDAW scales are similar, with the addition of a distress grant in the permanent disablement section and a much higher death benefit in industrial cases than applies in non-industrial. The only new section is for dispute and victimisation benefit and this was added by AUCE when it established a strike fund in 1911.

The 1978 scales are given in the table on page 352, the weekly contribution figures in brackets being new rates to operate in 1979. The original AUCE scales are in Chapter 3. AUCE scales at 1918, 1921 (formation of NUDAW) and 1947 (formation of USDAW) are in Appendix II.

Political contributions are included in the present scales. Inflation will probably bring about subsequent increases. But for a level of contributions well below that of comparable Unions in other countries USDAW members get a first class comprehensive service.

FINANCES OF THE UNION

USDAW is financially a very strong Trade Union. At the end of 1978 the Union had total central and branch funds of:

	£	Surplus for year £
General Funds (Industrial)	3,691,859	260,971
Political Fund (No. 1 Account) ..	77,492	14,767
	3,769,351	275,738

	£	£
Branch Funds (Industrial)........	874,831	145,776
Political Fund (No. 2 Account) ..	129,059	17,000
	1,003,890	162,776

Fixed assets and Investments amounted to £3,071,715. Of the branch Industrial funds of £874,831, £559,534 had been remitted to Central Office for investment. The rates of depreciation on fixed assets were: buildings 5 per cent, fixtures and fittings 20 per cent, motor vehicles 20 per cent, land nil. The Union has properties in fifteen cities and towns, where land values have greatly appreciated since the time of purchase.

Over recent years the Union has been developing new offices in different parts of the country, amongst which was the joint development with the General & Municipal Workers' Union of a large property in Leeds, comprising an office block occupied by the two Unions, and another substantial block occupied by tenants.

Contribution and Benefit Scales operative in 1978 (1979 figures in brackets)

Scale	Weekly Contribution	Unemployment Benefit	Sickness or Temporary Disablement Benefit	Death Benefit Non Industrial	Death Benefit Industrial	Disablement through Accident or Infirmity Total	Disablement through Accident or Infirmity Partial	Total Disablement through Illness	Distress Grant	Dispute and Victimisation Benefit	Trade Protection and Legal Aid
										During Unemployment through a Strike sanctioned by the Executive Council or, through Lockout, or Victimisation due to action by or on behalf of the Union	
A	29p (32p)	£1.20 per week, maximum 13 weeks	£1.20 per week, maximum 13 weeks	£100	£500	£300	£150	£30	Up to £30	Weekly benefit at the rate of £4 to Members and associates under 18 years of age and £6 to members aged 18 and over	Members in all Scales are advised legally on matters relating to employment and Industrial Law and are protected regarding Wages, Hours, Overtime, Holidays, Unfair Dismissal, Redundancy, etc.
	23p (26p)	£2 grant after continuous period of six weeks, £2 grant after further continuous period of six weeks	£2 grant after continuous period of six weeks, £2 grant after further continuous period of six weeks	£25	£125	£150	£75	£15	Up to £15		
	17p	Applicable only to Associates under 16 years of age, part-time workers and specially admitted persons.									

Scales are subject to certain age limitations

34 ACROSS THE BORDERS— SCOTLAND, WALES, IRELAND

THE main purpose of this history has been to portray USDAW as a national Union which, under various titles, has operated throughout the United Kingdom without regard to historic national or regional boundaries.

In all Divisions and many branches there are stories of struggle and achievement that deserve a book in themselves. It is to be hoped that some will be written by local members — possibly retired — who can draw on personal experience and research. Here, however, we are concerned with the national story, and can include only a brief record of events "across the borders", beginning with Scotland.

In that country there was a period when the prevailing conditions could have led to the formation of a separate Scottish Union of Co-operative Employees. The discontents that led to the pioneering "Associations" in London and Manchester were all stirring among Scottish "Co-operative servants". Possibly influenced by developments further south, an Employees' Association was established at a Glasgow meeting in 1889, but it faded out after a brief existence. The formation of other Associations was reported from time to time in the *Co-operative News* during the nineties and early years of the present century.

There was no lack of activity. But leadership towards a national body seems to have been lacking. Moreover, the Shop Assistants' Union was already on the ground in Scotland with established branches, and this may have weakened the impulse to form an independent Union.

Meanwhile, AUCE was growing in strength across the border and, as recorded in Executive minutes, it watched with interest and sympathy the various attempts to establish Trades Unionism among Scottish Co-operative employees. From 1906 onwards the Executive moved into action. Another Scottish Employees' Association which had maintained a tenuous existence was invited to discuss amalgamation, but declined to

x

do so. Three Scottish branches of AUCE were, however, already in existence — at Paisley, Broxburn and Johnstone. A year later L. Lumley, the Union's first full-time Organiser, was despatched North of the Border on a recruiting mission. In 1907 the statistics for the year included "Scottish Branches" with 561 members. No names were given, but these branches were attached to the Union's Northern District (mainly Northumberland and Durham) and in the election of District Councillors Barrhead, Kilbirnie, Kinning Park, Paisley, Pollokshaws and Glasgow D & F (Drapery and Furnishing) branches all took part.

The next stop was the formation of a Scottish District Council on 2nd January 1908, with 54 branches and 2,000 members. District Council reports in those and later years were published with the annual reports of AUCE. The Scottish District Secretary, W. Semple, wrote of their first year "It has not all been smooth sailing here, as some folk look upon the AUCE in Scotland as a 'poacher' and as 'reaping where it has not strawed' and consequently a bitter feeling occasionally has been shown". Much of the Council's time had been taken up in preparing a wage scale, which was adopted in 1909.

The "poacher" charge would probably come from two quarters — the Shop Assistants' Union which was already in the field and some of the surviving local Associations. The Federation of Shop and Clerical Workers (see Chapter 6) attempted to mediate on the friction between AUCE and the Shop Assistants. At a special meeting in 1910 to discuss "unfriendly relations at Greenock, Aberdeen, Falkirk, etc." resolutions were adopted that AUCE should " . . . henceforth be fully recognised as a Trade Union in Scotland" that the two Unions should not oppose representation of each other's branches on Trades Councils, that joint action should be taken on wages questions in Co-operative Societies where both had branches and that " . . . nothing less than the AUCE minimum should be asked for".

Unfortunately, by then the Federation itself was hastening towards extinction (in 1913), a fate that must partly have been brought about by the continued friction between two of its principal members. That situation continued for many years, and was exacerbated before and during the first World War, when, in 1915, AUCE withdrew from the TUC and the Scottish TUC. However, there is no point in continuing the story of ancient feuds. AUCE continued to grow. Both Unions were established in Scotland and the roots of feud were plucked when the Unions amalgamated in 1947.

In the country that produced that giant of the British Labour Movement, Keir Hardie, it was inevitable that Scottish representatives of both AUCE and the Shop Assistants' Union should become actively involved in Labour politics. When the Scottish Labour Party became the Scottish Council of the (British) Labour Party in 1915 a member of the Shop Assistants' staff, Neil S. Beaton, was a Trades Union representative on the Council's first Executive. He was also Treasurer of the Scottish TUC in 1917 and Chairman of Congress in 1918. Later he became internationally known in the Co-operative Movement as Chairman of the Scottish Co-operative Wholesale Society. H. Pilkington, of NUDAW, also served on the Executive of the Scottish Council for several years up to 1931, when he moved to a position with the Union in England. He was followed by T. Scollan, who was later to become an USDAW MP.

The Scottish TUC was formed in 1897, although 25 years earlier Glasgow Trades Council had sought the establishment of a federation of Scottish Unions. Scottish Trades Unionists and Socialists accepted that they shared common problems and ideals with the rest of the British working class but many of them also sought power to deal with specifically Scottish problems within the overall ambit of the United Kingdom. The STUC was one answer to this demand. The Scottish Council of the Labour Party was formed in 1915 as the political answer.

AUCE affiliated to the former in 1910, withdrew when it left the TUC, and returned to the fold as NUDAW in 1923. It affiliated to the Scottish Council of the Labour Party in 1910.

In 1932 Agnes Gilroy, of NUDAW, was the first woman in Unions catering for shop workers to be elected to the Executive Council of the STUC. In 1940 J. Watson was the first NUDAW representative to become Chairman of Congress. The names of other members of both Unions figure prominently in the records of both the STUC and the Scottish Council. Apart from issues common to the Labour Movement as a whole, the two Unions in their day, and USDAW in more recent times, kept to the fore in Scotland problems that particularly affected distributive and allied workers.

In recent years resolutions of this order sponsored by NUDAW or, later, by USDAW, have included demands for improved hours and conditions of distributive workers, Saturday half day closing of shops, rationalisation of distribution, training of shop workers, equal pay for equal work, support for free collective bargaining and opposition to Sunday trading (which isn't illegal in Scotland).

USDAW's Scottish Division ranks third in the Union in number of members, the total at the end of December, 1978, being 60,202. It operates over the whole of Scotland, including island branches in Kirkwall (Orkney), Lerwick (Shetland). The membership is widely spread and is representative of the many trades in which the Union organises. The former Scottish Bakers' Union, which merged with USDAW in 1977, forms an important section of the Division and, under the terms of the merger, is specifically represented in the Union's delegations to the Congress of the Scottish TUC.

The Division continues to be actively involved in the STUC, which today is increasingly influential in Scottish economic affairs. In 1969 Andrew Forman, the present Scottish Divisional Officer, was elected to the General Council in succession to E. W. Craig, his predecessor as Divisional Officer. A. Forman was Chairman of the Council in 1975. Representation has also continued on the Scottish Council of the Labour Party and at the Annual STUC Summer School.

WALES — NORTH AND SOUTH

The Union story was rather different in Wales. In the Principality there does not appear to have been any widespread development of local Associations, and AUCE developed as a natural extension of its activities in England. But it was not until around the period of the First World War that it was firmly established in Wales.

Membership statistics for the Union as a whole first appeared in the annual report for 1894-5 (the Union's year then ran from June to June, but from 1913 was altered to the straight calendar year). The early statistics could be deceptive at a glance, since wherever the Union had a single member in a Co-op he was listed as a "branch". There were 18 such "branches" in the

1894-5 list, including a solitary member at Pembroke Dock. A year later three Welsh branches were named, with a total of five members — one each in Pembroke Dock and Mold and Oswestry Co-ops, three in Cross Keys.

By 1896-7 the first two had disappeared from the list, Cross Keys still had its three pioneers and a Brynmawr Branch appeared with eleven members. Brynmawr dropped to one member in 1898, and in 1899 it was marked as a "Defunct Branch". Cross Keys also disappeared without trace.

Eighteen ninety nine, however, saw the emergence of the first branch with a sizaeble and continuing membership — Newport (Mon), with 25 recruits. Newport continued as a separate branch until comparatively recent times and has the distinction of being the first branch to establish a firm and continuing foothold in Wales.

At first, all Welsh branches, North and South, were included in the Union's Manchester District. But in 1904 a Western Sub-district was created, which included branches in the west of England and seven in South Wales, four other Welsh branches remaining in the Manchester District. Western became a fully fledged District in 1907, with representation on the Executive Council, and thirteen branches in South Wales. These branches had a total of 286 members out of the 1,121 in the District. Four other branches attached to the Manchester District counted 24 members.

It was slow growth. But it must be remembered that the Union was then based entirely on Co-operative employment and most Societies in the Western District were very small. Bristol and Plymouth together represented almost exactly half the Union membership in the District.

If progress was slow, it was steady. Jumping ahead more than three quarters of a century, the present South Wales and Western Division had 45,866 members at the end of December, 1978, and half of those were in branches in South Wales. In addition, a number of North Wales branches are still in the North Western Division.

South Wales branches have reflected the militancy of the coal and iron valleys in which many of them began. As we have seen in previous chapters, in at least two cases Union campaigns for negotiating rights and improved earnings reached the turning point towards eventual national success through strike action by Welsh members — in the first case, against the International Stores Group, in the second against Woolworth. The Shop Assistants' Union, too, fought some great strike battles against the living-in system in the Principality.

The present Welsh membership has spread far beyond the Co-ops. It includes workers and branches in food and chemical processing, football pools, creameries (Co-op and Unigate), meat workers both for the home market and export slaughtering, and club stewards, who have their own Welsh Union of Club Stewards as a section of USDAW.

The Union is affiliated to the Welsh Regional Council of the Labour Party and to the Wales TUC. When the latter was formed in 1974 the Divisional Officer, W. John Jones, was a founder member of its General Council and in 1976 had the unique experience of holding office as Chairman of the Wales TUC and of the Labour Party in Wales. North Wales branches in the North Western Division join with their colleagues in Western for representation at the conferences of the two bodies.

IRELAND

When AUCE was formed Ireland was still part of the United Kingdom. Consumer Co-operative societies, which were then the Union's sole source of recruitment, were, however, very thin on the ground. In Ireland, agricultural Co-operation has been more successful than consumer societies. Only in Belfast has retail Co-operation been firmly established and the first Irish branch of AUCE was in that society, listed in the annual report for 1903-4, with 44 members. A Dublin branch was listed in 1906-7, with two members. Its peak was 40 members in 1913-14. Thereafter it steadily declined until, in 1921, it is marked as "Defunct" in the annual statistics.

Other branches were formed at Armagh, Enniskillen, Lisburn, Ballymena, Sligo, Drogheda. By 1937, when Southern Ireland became a sovereign and independent nation, all had disappeared. Belfast remained the Union's one stronghold, with five branches and 2,695 members in 1937, mainly in the Co-op.

From this base in Belfast the Union continued to grow, both in size and the variety of trades which it organised. The present membership is 7,500; mainly concentrated among distributive workers in and around Belfast. Apart from the large membership in the Co-op, the Union has achieved a high degree of organisation in department stores, chain stores, multiple grocery and multiple tailoring, and now has general distributive branches in Armagh, Ballymena and Londonderry. A new field of recruiting has been in food manufacture and processing, particularly in bacon factories. Creamery workers are also organised.

The present tragedy of Northern Ireland is common knowledge, and it was inevitable that it should affect Union members. Those employed by Belfast Co-op have been particularly involved. The Society's York Street department store, one of the major sights of the city, was totally destroyed by bomb and fire in 1972, not so very long after its opening. It has been replaced by a bigger and even more modern building. Many grocery units have been destroyed, others damaged by bomb explosions in nearby buildings. The Union's own premises have been damaged.

After each outrage Union members have rallied to ensure that supplies still reached the people, Catholics and Protestants alike. As *Dawn* described it in 1974 "If these USDAW members didn't get to work and keep things moving, despite 'the troubles', then the city and much of Antrim and Co. Down would face serious food shortages".

The human condition is rarely totally dark. Behind the mindless destruction in Ulster there are influences that forbid one to despair. Prominent among them has been the success of the Trades Union Movement in keeping widespread sectarian bitterness away from the workplace.

The Northern Ireland Committee of the Irish Congress of Trades Unions, of which USDAW is an active member, acts as a co-ordinating body and, effectively, as a Northern Ireland TUC for Unions that operate both in Britain and all-Ireland, in Britain and the North only, in all-Ireland only, and in the North only. The first full-time secretary of the Northern Ireland Committee was W. Blease (now Lord Blease), an USDAW member and one-time member of the Union's North Western Divisional Council, of which, constitutionally, Northern Ireland branches are part. The Union is also linked to the Northern Ireland Labour Party.

David Wylie, an USDAW Area Organiser, Belfast, is now

senior serving member of the Northern Ireland Committee
and was Chairman in 1964-65. It was in that period that the
then Northern Ireland Government agreed to officially recognise the N.I. Committee as the Trades Union Centre for the
movement in Northern Ireland. He also serves on the Executive
Council of the Irish Congress of Trades Unions.

Branches in the Province hold their own annual meeting,
are represented at the ADM, and take a full part in the educational activities of the Union.

One hopes that many years from the date of publication
active members of USDAW will be reading this book. Even
more fervently, one hopes that there will then be a happier
story to tell of the sorely tried people and Trades Unionists of
Northern Ireland and that they will then be free to concentrate
their qualities of skill and industry on building up the prosperity of their homeland.

Details of Divisional Officers and Area Organisers of the
three Divisions briefly covered in this chapter are included in
Chapter 33.

35 UP TO 1978 — WITH A FEW EXCURSIONS INTO 1979

THIS final chapter is less a record of history than a report of contemporary events. We begin with a theme that has continuously been present in these pages and must continuously be the central purpose of a free Trade Union — the advancement and defence of its members' wages and conditions through collective bargaining, the maintenance of industrial relations with employers, and contact with Government.

In the latter case, a former Minister of Labour, Ray Gunter, once described his job as the "bed of nails". His description was accurate but not sufficiently comprehensive. The determination of wages and the conduct of industrial relations has always been a complicated and contentious issue but since the second World War it has become a Procrustean bed not only for Ministers of Labour but for Prime Ministers and Chancellors of the Exchequer of both Parties, for Trades Union leaders and their members and for the public at large.

The Labour Government returned in the two elections of 1974 introduced a new concept — the "Social Contract". As John Phillips, USDAW's Assistant General Secretary, pointed out at one of the summer schools of 1978, this was fundamentally a new approach. Previous attempts to establish a national policy had sought to control wage increases either by exhortation to observe Government guidelines or by the arbitrary imposition of permissible rates of increase. The Social Contract in its first two stages was jointly agreed between the Labour Government and the TUC, and was based on the principle that Unions should seek to maintain real living standards but not, for the time being, increase them, with the proviso that special attention should be paid to the needs of the lower paid.

The Contract had considerable success in the first stages, and, along with other Government measures, contributed substantially to bringing down the rate of inflation. Working people also benefitted from a wide range of Labour legislation on

collective bargaining rights and job security that was part of
the agreement with the Government — the Contracts of Employ-
ment Act, Redundancy Payments Act, Trades Union and
Labour Relations Act, Equal Pay Act, Health and Safety at
Work Act, Employment Protection Act, Sex Discrimination
Act.

This was the first genuine attempt to include an *agreed* policy
on wages within a planned economy, which was the overall
object of the Wilson and Callaghan Labour Governments.
But it led to many anomalies, increasing restiveness in all
Unions and demands for a return to unfettered collective
bargaining. The TUC was not officially a party to the third
stage which should have begun from August of 1978. The
Government's new guideline figure of around 5 per cent proved
to be unacceptable to most Unions, including USDAW, and
the sequel was the great wages battles of early 1979.

If ever there is to be an economy planned for growth and
social equity, wages and other incomes must necessarily be
included. With hindsight, however, it can be seen that the Social
Contract in its first form was too blunt an instrument. One
lesson to be learnt from the experience of 1974-1979 is that any
future Contract, pact, agreement or whatever it may be called,
must be much more sophisticated and flexible in dealing with
the infinitely varying range of custom, tradition, differentials,
low pay and established negotiating practices that make up the
wages pattern.

USDAW supported the introduction of the Contract in a
lengthy resolution adopted by the ADM of 1974, which, however, reaffirmed the Union's insistent demand for " ... a
fairer share of the national wealth for the lower paid". And in a
phrase calling upon the Trades Union Movement to " ... use
every endeavour to stop the Social Contract from becoming
meaningless" it hinted at suspicions that some Unions might
not be wholehearted in their support.

The General Secretary, in moving the Executive report on
wages, economic policy and the Social Contract, also took up
this theme. "Half-hearted lip service is not enough; he said
"Nor can one or two Unions be left to carry the Social Contract
on their own. If those with power to do so ignore the guidelines ... then we in this Union have an obligation ... to ensure

that our people are not left behind".

On the wider front of the TUC the Union supported the Contract at the Congress of 1974. John Phillips, in seconding an NUM resolution in support of the contract, said "We can no longer think of wage bargaining in purely sectional monetary terms; there is a social wage also whose level is determined by the quality of life which society provides".

In the period before and during the Social Contract the Union was successful in securing, as the Executive Council reported of 1973, " . . . the best settlements possible" In that year there were three successive versions of the Heath Government's incomes policy. In the same year the Pay Code allowed increases for unsocial hours and by taking advantage of this clause extra payments for working on Saturdays were secured. Midway through the Social Contract the annual report for 1976 stated " . . . the Union has been successful in negotiating improved wage rates and conditions of labour [and] . . . progress towards the creation of a more socially just Society has continued and the mutual commitment of Trade Unionists and Government to the Social Contract has been a central feature in the struggle to sustain our social, industrial and economic advance".

It all ended unhappily in the strike-torn and weather-tormented winter of 1979, followed by the rout of the Labour Government in the Spring. As this is written, Mrs. Margaret Thatcher has become the first woman Prime Minister, not only in Britain but in Europe, leading a Government that is dedicated to bringing back the free-for-all Society that so often has been tried and so often has failed. The Social Contract was far from perfect. It was abandoned by one of its parents and perhaps the other parent expected too much of it, too soon. But its demise may yet be regretted by a great many working people.

At the General Election of April/May, 1979, the Union sponsored six candidates of whom five were returned. This was a similar number to October, 1974, but only one, T. W. Torney (Bradford, South), belonged to the group elected in that year. Others elected in 1979 who had been adopted via the Parliamentary Panel since 1974 were J. C. Cartwright (Woolwich, East), H. Lamborn (Southwark, Peckham), Frank McElhone (Glasgow, Queens Park), R. Powell (Ogmore). S. Tierney, the

Union's President, who won Yardley in 1974, lost the seat in 1979. Three Union-sponsored MPs who did not stand in 1979 were H. Boardman (Leigh), E. Fernyhough (Jarrow) and W. E. Padley (Ogmore). USDAW nominees were not selected for the first two of these seats, but, as indicated above, the third was retained by the Union, and all three were held by Labour.

£55 MINIMUM, 35 HOUR WEEK

The Union's target minimum wage had been increasing almost annually as inflation ate into earnings. A shorter working week was also a regular demand at the ADM. The two came together at the 1978 annual meeting.

An Executive Council statement on wages and economic policy called for "an orderly return to free collective bargaining", "freeing the families of low wage earners from the poverty trap", and the reduction of the working week to 35 hours, plus other improvments. This was adopted. So, too, was a proposition from Derby and Burton Co-operative, moved by W. Hall, which put a sharper edge on the wages reference in calling for "an immediate campaign for a 35 hour week, for a basic minimum wage of £55, and that differentials above this figure for additional skills and responsibility should be maintained". A proposition by NECS Teesside, moved by R. J. Smith, demanded "wage claims in line with the Retail Price Index". This, too, was adopted, on the understanding that other factors would be taken into account by those negotiating on wages.

The dual hours/wages demand was vigorously followed up in the latter months of 1978. There were advertisements in the Press, posters on buses and outdoor sites, in London's Underground. This publicity was linked with recruitment campaigns in specific firms. The Midlands Deputy Divisional Officer, Brian Porter, went "on the air" on Radio Trent daily in September in what was claimed to be the first-ever use of commercial radio for Trade Union recruitment.

This book has ended after the "winter war" over wages at the beginning of 1979, with a renewal of conflict discernible by the end of the year, and a Tory Government busily introducing policies which must lead to a dark future for industrial relations. For USDAW there is at least one encouraging fact — the continued increase in membership, reflected in a net gain of 26,639 up to December, 1978.

THE EUROPEAN ECONOMIC COMMUNITY

Under the Heath Government Britain joined the European Economic Community (the Common Market) in 1792. In one of its longest debates the Commons had discussed the issue from 21 to 28 October, 1971; and had voted for membership by 356 votes to 244. The Labour Government elected in October, 1974, was pledged to renegotiate the terms, and to submit them to a referendum. The Government decided that the new terms were satisfactory, and it recommended a "Yes" vote, which was obtained, the public voting 17,378,000 for continued membership, 8,470,000 against.

From the sixties, USDAW had been involved in the national debate over membership and, as in most other Trades Union and political organisations, the debates on the issue at the ADM and elsewhere were protracted and frequently passionate in the strength of feeling for or against.

In 1967, D. Huxstep (Booksellers and Stationers) moved a proposition which opposed and denounced the Market as being dominated by a small group of monopolists. An amendment by the Executive, moved by the General Secretary, welcomed membership provided essential British and Commonwealth interests were safeguarded, and this view was adopted by an overwhelming majority. There was another hostile proposition in 1968, this time from Leeds Co-operative, moved by J. Davies. Again it was successfully countered by an amendment, moved for East London by Mrs. E. Hanes, reaffirming the decision of the previous ADM.

Two years later the 1970 ADM voted for an Executive proposition, moved by the General Secretary, which welcomed a Government White Paper on the economic consequences of British entry and accepted that a decision could only be made when the conditions of entry were known. The meeting also rejected a hostile proposition from Birmingham Dry Goods (moved by N. Rowland), declaring that it was against the best interest of Britain to pursue application for membership.

A year later the 1971 ADM supported the principle of a national referendum before a decision to join the Market was taken, the mover being W. Hall on behalf of Derby Co-operative. The National Executive also backed the proposition. In

1972 (by which time Britain was committed to joining the
EEC) a former President, Rodney Hanes, on behalf of Royal
Arsenal Co-operative, moved that entry called for association
with Continental Unions to combat the danger which multi-
national companies could present to Trades Union rights.
Again, there was a totally hostile resolution declaring that
membership would mean higher prices and increased unemployment, moved by Mrs. D. R. Gibson for South West London.
RACS won the day. There was a lull for a year, and then in
1974 RACS and South West London both returned to the issue.
Rodney Hanes moved reaffirmation of the 1972 decision in a
resolution which called specifically for participation by the
Union in the Industrial Committee of the International Trade
Union Secretariat within the EEC. South West London
denounced the EEC and called on the Executive to campaign
for withdrawal, Mrs. C. Cowen being the mover. Once again,
however, RACS carried the day.

Up to this point the ADM had consistently supported or
kept an open mind on British membership of the Market,
against an equally consistent element of opposition.   By 1975,
however, there was a turnround. The Labour Government had
renegotiated terms of membership, which were to be submitted
to the referendum on June 5th, shortly after the Union's ADM,
and the Executive Council tabled a proposition, moved by
Lord Allen, in support of continued membership. Derby and
Burton Co-operative, in a resolution, moved by J. Dilks,
proposed that the Executive be instructed to advise the Union's
membership to vote "No". After a closely argued debate, the
Executive proposition was defeated on a card vote, the figures
being 93,504 votes in favour, 103,084 against. As we have seen,
however, the nation voted in favour of continued membership.

The referendum has not, of course, permanently settled the
question of Britain's continued membership of the EEC. It is a
subject that has continued to agitate public opinion and it has
continued to feature in USDAW's affairs. A hostile resolution
was debated at the 1978 ADM. Moved by E. W. Lamburn on
behalf of Birmingham Co-operative it affirmed that membership
had failed to improve Britain's economic performance, declared
that direct elections to the EEC would erode the sovereignty of
Parliament, and called for a campaign to withdraw. An amend-

ment by Greater Nottingham Regional Co-operative, moved by J. Peck, substituted for withdrawal a demand that the British Government should refuse to implement Common Market decisions damaging to our standard of life, and in this form the proposition was carried. In 1979 a call to seriously consider continued membership unless there were improvements in the Common Agricultural Policy was referred to the Executive. It seems probable that many future annual meetings will have this issue before them.

EXPANSION AND SERVICE

The seventies were a period of rapid advance, both in recruitment and the establishment of stronger negotiating and bargaining relationships with the great distributive and service employers. Some extracts, mainly from the columns of *Dawn*, show the impetus that was driving the Union forward.

There was a major breakthrough with Woolworth in 1977. Since the strike in South Wales (see chapter 27) the firm had recognised the Union on a store by store basis wherever it secured a substantial level of membership. The Union could make national representations on wages, but they were determined unilaterally without negotiation. Progress with recruitment was slow until 1973 when, under the direction of Chief Organising Officer Jim Hughes, a national recruitment campaign was launched. The results at first were patchy. But the momentum continued. By the end of 1976 the Midlands Division, for instance, had secured recognition in 22 Woolworth stores and had applied for it in 15 others, where at least half the staff had joined the Union.

In June of 1977, when USDAW had about 10,000 Woolworth members, the Union applied to top management for national bargaining rights. John Phillips, after a preliminary meeting, was told that the question would be considered as a matter of major Board policy. The decision was to accept the Union as the wages bargaining representative of the staff from January, 1978. The staff had been balloted on whether they wished to be represented by a Union, and 56 per cent had voted "Yes". The first national agreement was negotiated by John Phillips and National Officer John Flood, at the beginning of 1978.

From the 10,000 Woolworth members of the Union we come down to one individual. A woman member who worked as a cleaner for the firm in Cardiff was made redundant when industrial cleaners were brought in. She has a blind husband and was anxious to retain the job. Management at first refused. The case was due to go to the Industrial Tribunal. But after discussions between the Union and the firm it was agreed to re-engage her as a sales assistant, with compensation to cover dismissal. A good example of a Golden Rule — that a Trade Union is as good as the benefits it can bring to an otherwise helpless individual member.

In 1975 the Littlewoods Organisation reached an agreement with USDAW and the General and Municipal Workers' Union which *Dawn* claimed was probably the first of its kind with a major company in the United Kingdom. It provided for the indexing of wages, by replacing the annual review with a quarterly increase related to the Retail Price Index; to be maintained within the terms of the then existing Social Contract. Jack Gardner, USDAW's North Western Divisional Officer, led the Union side in the negotiations. About 13,000 workers in the firm's Liverpool headquarters and all but one of its mail order establishments were represented by USDAW; the exception being at Sunderland, where the workers were organised by the GMWU. A somewhat similar agreement for a much smaller number of abattoir workers at Fareham was negotiated by Area Organiser Derek Knapp. Later the Littlewoods agreement was extended to the firm's stores, plus an unsocial hours agreement for working on Saturdays.

Not all negotiations were concerned with improvements in wages and conditions. During the period of this chapter the great tailoring firm of Burton fell on difficult times, which drastically affected its directly owned stores and subsidiaries. Most of the staff were USDAW members. During 1977 and 1978 heavy redundancies and shop closures were planned by the company. Protracted negotiations led by John Flood resulted in agreements that considerably reduced the originally intended number of redundancies, and secured improvements in severance payments.

Lord Allen was also involved and assurances were given by the head of Burton that the company was undertaking a multi-million pounds development programme that, once reorganisation had been carried out, would improve job prospects in the firm's hundreds of shops.

It was during this period that John Flood was appointed Assistant General Secretary Designate to succeed John Phillips on the latter's retirement in October, 1978. John Flood had been a Union member since 1942, when he joined as a grocery apprentice at Greenock Co-op, became an Area Organiser for USDAW in 1959 and National Officer for the retail private trade since 1970. Before the end of this chapter we shall see that his duties have since been still further extended.

In a tribute to John Phillips *Dawn* said "His departure marks the end of the line of Central Office officials who began their full-time service in the 1930s and helped lead the Union into the 1970s". His 46 years' service had begun with the Shop Assistants' Union and his outstanding achievement had been to lead the break-through of Union membership and agreements into the great private multiples. He would probably regard as his crowning achievement the negotiation in the last few months of service of the first pay and recognition agreement with Woolworth.

On 1st August, 1977, the Union was the subject of a BBC documentary film "Divided we Stand", featuring meetings of three typical branches, the ADM in session, interviews with the General Secretary and rank and file members. The branches were Dalry Chemical (Ayrshire), Birmingham Co-operative and Manchester General. *Dawn* commented "If there was one weakness of branch democracy shown up in the film it was the relatively poor attendance at branch meetings".

The same year saw the Union's first major venture into the arts. On 22nd October, 1,800 members, their families and friends, packed the Philharmonic Hall, Liverpool, for an USDAW-sponsored concert of Viennese music by the Royal Liverpool Philharmonic Orchestra, conducted by John Georgiadis. It was doubly an USDAW event, for the Lord Mayor of Liverpool, Councillor Paul Orr, was not only the guest of honour, but as a long-standing member of the Union he was presented by Lord Allen with his 30 years' membership award. Councillor Orr had played a notable part in building up the bottling section of the Liverpool Food Manufacturing Branch.

A new problem for the Union emerged in the seventies — that of language among members of Asian origin. There was

Y

a striking case at Shire Textiles in 1978. Out of 54 Punjabi-speaking employees, all members of the Central Midlands branch, only one, Mrs. Ghataore, spoke English. Not surprisingly, she was shop steward, and played an active part with Area Organiser, P. Davis, in negotiating a recognition and procedural agreement. Translated into Punjabi, it was the first to be produced in a minority language. In the same year a "join up" appeal was printed in Punjabi for recruiting in a new food factory at Park Royal, North West London.

The issue of *Dawn* for January, 1976, reported a record of voluntary service that is unlikely to be excelled. At the end of the previous year 82 years-old Harry Wimpenny cashed up for the last time after 50 years as financial secretary of the St. Helens 'S' Branch. He had been a Trade Union member for 63 years, having joined the Shop Assistants' Union at the age of 19. He was awarded the TUC Gold Badge in 1960 and earlier had received the Tolpuddle Martyrs' Medal of Congress for recruiting and organising. And at 82 Harry was still working for the Union — he had taken on the job of corresponding secretary of the branch.

Another Union member was awarded the coveted Gold Badge in 1976. David McGibbon, a well-known Glasgow Trade Unionist and Labour man, had been a member for nearly 43 years, originally in the Shop Assistants' Union, where he served on the National Executive. From 1947 to 1975 he was on USDAW's Executive Council, and acted as chairman of the Standing Orders Committee at the annual delegate meetings.

Chapter 25 recorded the introduction in 1958 of a new educational scheme and the appointment of Peter Rosenfeld as Education Officer. In 1963 the scheme was refined into three equally important basic "needs" which the educational work of the Union should seek to meet in the closing years of this century.

The first was to provide new, and in particular, young, members with a working knowledge of USDAW's purpose and functions. The second was to provide opportunities for all members to "consider and discuss industrial, political, economic and other important Union policy issues". The third need went right down to bedrock — the provision of training opportunities for key members such as branch officers, shop stewards and collectors.

The Union's needs can be briefly described but it would take a lengthy chapter to cover the great variety of ways in which they are being met by the Department. A few examples will be given from the annual report of 1978. In that year 1,003 young members — a record total — enrolled for a six-months home study course based on six booklets *Introducing USDAW*. Special schools for young members of 25 years or less were organised by Federations. Since 1966 groups of members under 25 years of age have been invited annually to attend the ADM as visitors. A variety of scholarships to TUC and Scottish TUC summer schools had been provided. For active and committed members, Federations had organised 38 one-day or weekend schools, with an attendance of 1,100.

A priority objective of the education scheme is the training of voluntary officers. Courses of three to five days duration are held throughout the year. In 1978, for example, 85 such courses were attended by over 900 shop stewards and Union representatives from a large number of companies and Co-operative Societies. Additionally, one-week courses for recently elected branch secretaries and CIS group secretaries are held regularly at Central Office.

Much of the work of the Department is serviced by six full-time training officers based on the Union's territorial Divisions, with W. G. Walker acting as Senior Training Officer.

Apart from the educational work which it directly controls, the Union also makes grants to residential adult education colleges, to members who obtain scholarships to these colleges and to those taking degree courses through the OpenUniversity. It is also represented on the governing bodies of several educational establishments and five industrial training boards — for catering; chemical and allied trades; food, drink and tobacco; rubber and plastics; and distributive trades.

CHANGES AT THE TOP

A major change in the Union came so close to 1978, the terminal date for most of this book, that it must be included. In April, 1979, W. H. P. Whatley was elected as General Secretary to succeed Lord Allen on his retirement at the age of 65 in July. A third major change at the top was in 1977, when J. D. Hughes did not seek re-election to the Presidency and was succeeded at the ensuing election by S. Tierney, MP.

Lord Allen, who will better be remembered in the Union as "Alf" or "Alfred" Allen, held the General Secretaryship for 17 years and it can be said of him that for that period and his earlier days the Union had been his life as well as his profession.

He led USDAW during the most rapid expansion of membership in its history. He was elected 15 years after the amalgamation with the Shop Assistants' Union. At that stage the recently born USDAW had made only a modest gain of 12,901 towards the membership potential that had dazzled and to some extent deluded its founders. During his General Secretaryship there had been a further increase of 106,140 up to the end of 1978. While he is the first to allot the credit to the Union's lay activists, full-time staff and a forward-looking Executive Council, his own energy and vision have played a powerful part in that story of growth.

Lord Allen had been on the General Council of the TUC since 1962 and had held two senior positions — the Presidency of Congress in 1974, and Chairman of the Economic Committee since 1975. He undertook a full share of the heat and burden that recent years of wages controversy have imposed on the General Council and had participated in negotiations with six Prime Ministers on this contentious issue — Macmillan, Hume, Heath, Wilson, Callaghan and Mrs. Thatcher.

Throughout his term of office he held firmly to four principles, and their theme can be traced through innumerable speeches, articles, interviews and broadcasts. Firstly, that free collective bargaining is a basic element of free Trades Unionism, and, as a corollary, that any attempt to control the process by law is wrong in principle and invariably a failure in practice. Secondly, that planning the economy for growth and social benefit rather than for private profit is not irreconcilable with free collective bargaining, and in both social and economic terms is a better way of running the nation's affairs. Thirdly, that the continued existence of large groups of underpaid workers is a social sore as evil as the sweating scandal of Victorian days. Fourthly, that Trades Unionism must have an ethical as well as an economic base. Stronger Unions should not live only by their own strength. There are times when they should forebear so that the standards of weaker brothers could be raised.

And if all that sounds like old-fashioned Socialism, Alfred
Allen would probably reply "What would be wrong with giving
old-fashioned Socialist principles a real try?"

W. H. P. Whatley is another General Secretary who will be
known by his first name. "Bill" he is to those who have known
him in the many positions he has held in USDAW and Bill he
will continue to be in the highest position of all.

He brings to the role of General Secretary 31 years' experience
acquired at all four levels of the Union's recruiting and negotiating activities — branch activist, Area Organiser, National
Officer and Chief Organising Officer.

He joined the Union in 1938, and after war experience in the
Royal Air Force, he was a lay officer for some years at the
Newcastle upon Tyne CWS branch. In 1948 he was appointed
as an Area Organiser and spent the next 14 years in that role,
serving in two of the Union's Divisions. During those years
he acquired experience of almost every trade within the scope
of USDAW, both among the Co-operative membership and in
the then growing private trade sector.

As a National Officer from 1966 he was responsible for the
wholesale and retail meat trades, to which later were added the
retail Co-operative membership, the milk industry and other
trade groups. He became Chief Organising Secretary in 1976,
the position he held on his election as General Secretary.

Bill Whatley's knowledge of the Union and its problems is
wide and deep. As General Secretary he will move in the wider
world where Trades Unionism and politics interlock. In both
fields his experience and qualities fit him for the role of fifth
General Secretary in the history of USDAW. Following his
election, John Flood was redesignated as Deputy General Secretary, a role which included his assumption also of the responsibilities formerly discharged by the Chief Organising Officer.

With the new President the role of first names still applies.
He is "Syd" Tierney to the Union and in the Yardley constituency of Birmingham, which he held from the two elections of
1974 to Labour's defeat in 1979. He was the third MP to serve
as President, the others being John Jagger and Walter Padley.

Most of his adult life has been absorbed in his 36 years'
membership of the Union and in the Labour Party. In the

tradition of both, he sought to qualify for service by study;
in his case a scholarship to Plater College, Oxford, where he
gained the University Diploma in Economics and Politics.
From Oxford he returned to his milk round as a Co-operative
employee and to further involvement in local Union and political
activity, including service as a municipal councillor. Later he
became an Area Organiser for the Union, and as this is written
he has been appointed as a National Officer.

Syd Tierney is a quiet man whose unobtrusive demeanour
conceals a deep knowledge of industry, Trades Unionism and
politics acquired in the hard school of experience and sharpened
by study. He has much to give the Union, and Parliament, too,
should he seek re-election.

To successfully fill the role of Chief Officer or President at
the head of a large and complex organisation is as much an art
as it is an executive operation. Each develops his own approach
and style. The common factors required are dedication, experience, judgment and vision. USDAW has been fortunate in
these times of change and turmoil to have been served by a new
and a retiring General Secretary who fully satisfy these requirements and by a President who is in the best tradition of a long
line of predecessors.

GOODBYE!

This story of USDAW began on 18th March, 1891, when 30
representatives of Co-operative "servants" and committee
members of retail Co-operatives met on CWS premises and
decided to form the Manchester District Co-operative Employees' Association. We end this history of the Union 88 years
later, after two world wars and a triple revolution in the social,
economic and political state of Britain. Not a long time, no
greater than the life span of many men and women. In that
span the Union has grown from numerical insignificance to
become the sixth largest affiliate of the TUC, with a rate of
increase in recruitment which, if continued, foreshadows a
much larger membership in the future.

Whatever changes the future may bring it is certain that
working people will continue to need the protection of strong
Trades Unions. It may be that by the end of the century British
Trades Unionism, too, will have changed in many ways. One
cannot foresee the future but whatever form it takes it can

confidently be predicted that USDAW will continue to be in the forefront.

It is time now to say goodbye to the days of yesteryear — and may many tomorrows bring continued good fortune to a free Trade Union that for so long has done so much for so many.

APPENDIX I

FIRST NATIONAL AGREEMENT FOR RETAIL CO-OPERATIVE MOVEMENT

Top Male and Female weekly rates payable from 14 October, 1946: inclusive of War Bonuses for shop and ancillary workers only

GENERAL DISTRIBUTIVE WORKERS	METROPOLITAN		PROVINCIAL A		PROVINCIAL B		PROVISIONAL	
	Male	Female	Male	Female	Male	Female	Male	Female
Shop Workers — all depts. at age 23 except hairdressers and cafe workers. Some plussages, eg for leading and first hands, cash desk workers	99/6	75/-	96/6	73/-	93/6	71/-	89/6	68/6
Ancillary Workers — warehouse, porters, cleaners, packers etc.	93/6	70/6	90/6	69/-	89/6	67/6	88/6	65/6
Branch Managers and Manageresses, Grocery EXCLUDING War Bonuses (which totalled 28/6 at age 21 and over at the time of the agreement								
Sales under £100 weekly average	85/-	65/-	80/-	60/-	77/-	57/-	73/-	53/-
Sales up to £490 and under £510 weekly average	113/-	93/-	108/-	88/-	105/-	85/-	101/-	81/-
There were 27 sales "steps" for both managers and manageresses								

Appendix II

BASIC AUCE ORDINARY BENEFITS IN 1918

(The scales current in 1979 are in Chapter 33. See also notes on page 380)

SCALE	WEEKLY CONTRIBUTIONS		WEEKLY BENEFIT WHEN OUT OF EMPLOYMENT		WEEKLY BENEFIT DURING SICKNESS OR TEMPORARY DISABLEMENT		FUNERAL BENEFIT		LEGAL AID
	Entry Age 16 to 35 Years	Entry Age 35 to 50 Years	First Six Weeks	Second Six Weeks	First Nine Weeks	Second Nine Weeks	Member	Member's Wife or Husband dying during Member's Lifetime	
I	8d	11d	18s	9s	12s	6s	£9	£4 10s	
II	6d	8d	12s	6s	8s	4s	£6	£3	
III	5d	6½d	9s	4s 6d	6s	3s	£4 10s	£2 5s	
IV	4d	5d	6s	3s	4s	2s	£3	£1 10s	

ALL SCALES	PERMANENT DISABLEMENT AND DISTRESS BENEFITS			DISPUTE AND VICTIMISATION BENEFIT	FEMALE MEMBERS LEAVING EMPLOYMENT TO BE MARRIED AFTER THREE YEARS' MEMBERSHIP	LEGAL AID
	Disablement through Accident or Infirmity — Total / Partial	Total Disablem't through Illness	Distress Grants	During unemployment through a Strike sanctioned by the Executive Council, or through Lockout or Victimisation due to action by or on behalf of the Union.	Rebate of One-half of Union Contributions paid during Membership, *less* any Union benefits received.	Members advised legally on matters relating to employment. Legal proceedings taken to secure Members' rights, Workmen's Compensation Claims, &c.
	£100 / £50	£10 recurring yearly	Up to £20	Adults per week 20s — Juniors, per week 10s		

Appendix II — contd.

NUDAW SCALES ON AMALGAMATION OF 1921

SCALE	Weekly Contribution at 16 years of age and upwards	Weekly Benefit When Out of Employment Ten Weeks	Weekly Benefit During Sickness or Temporary Disablement Ten Weeks	Funeral Benefit on Death of Member	Permanent Disablement and Distress Benefits				Dispute and Victimisation Benefit. During Unemployment Through a Strike Sanctioned by the Executive Council, or Through Lockout or Victimisation Due to Action by or on Behalf of the Union. Per Week
					Disablement Through Accident or Infirmity		Total Disablement Through Illness	Distress Grants	
					Total	Partial			
I	1s 4d	24s	18s	£12	£100	£50	£10	Up to £10	30s
II	1s	16s	12s	£8	£100	£50	£10	Up to £10	30s
III	8d	8s	6s	£4	£100	£50	£10	Up to £10	30s
IV	6d	6s	—	—	—	—	—	—	30s.
V	Associates under 16 3d.	—	—	—	—	—	—	—	15s

Appendix II — contd.

USDAW SCALES ON AMALGAMATION OF 1947

SCALE	Weekly Contribution at 16 years of age and upwards — Industrial	Weekly Contribution — Political	Weekly Benefit when out of Employment, 12 weeks	Weekly Benefit during Sickness or Temporary Disablement, 12 weeks	Funeral Benefit on Death of Member	PERMANENT DISABLEMENT AND DISTRESS BENEFITS — Disablement through Accident or Infirmity: Total	Partial	Total Disablement through Illness	Distress Grant	DISPUTE AND VICTIMISATION BENEFIT (During Unemployment through a Strike sanctioned by the Executive Council, or through Lockout, or Victimisation due to action by or on behalf of the Union.) — 16 and 17 Years Per Week	18 Years and over Per Week	Trade Protection and Legal Aid
	s d	s d										Members in all Scales are advised legally on matters relating to Employment, such as Workmen's Compensation, Truck, etc., and are protected regarding Wages, Hours, Overtime, Holidays, etc.
I	1 4½	0 0½	18s	18s	£12	£100	£50	£10	Up to £10	15s	30s	
II	0 8½	0 0½	12s	12s	£8	£100	£50	£10	Up to £10	15s	30s	
III	0 6½	0 0½	6s	6s	£4	£100	£50	£10	Up to £10	15s	30	
IV	0 3½	0 0½	4s	...	...	...	...	...	...	15s	30s	
V	0 3½	0 0½	Specially admitted persons, 16 years of age and over							Per Week, 15s		
	0 3½	...	ASSOCIATES, i.e. persons under 16 years of age							Per Week, 15s		

Appendix II — contd.

NOTES

In 1918 AUCE had five tables of contributions and benefits, viz:

1. All ordinary Union benefits (the table on page 377).

2. All ordinary benefits except sick pay and disablement.

3. TU benefits for seasonal workers.

4. TU benefits only without sick, funeral or disablement benefits.

5. As (4) for low-paid female workers only.

INDEX

z

ERRATA

Page 98, line 22—For Charles II read Charles I.

„ 202, „ 40— „ 1961 read 1951.

„ 268, „ 19— „ experts read exports.

„ 319, „   2— „ 1980 read 1908.

ERRATA

Page 98, line 22—For Charles II read Charles I.

,, 202, ,, 40— ,, 1961 read 1951.

,, 268, ,, 19— ,, experts read exports.

,, 319, ,, 2— ,, 1980 read 1908.